The Rhineland Crisis

THE RHINELAND CRISIS

7 March 1936

A study in multilateral diplomacy

JAMES THOMAS EMMERSON

MAURICE TEMPLE SMITH

in association with the
London School of Economics
and Political Science

First published in Great Britain 1977
by Maurice Temple Smith Ltd
37 Great Russell Street, London WC1
in association with the London School of Economics
and Political Science
© Copyright 1977 JAMES THOMAS EMMERSON
ISBN 0 85117 096X
Printed in Great Britain by
Billing & Sons Ltd, London, Guildford and Worcester

Contents

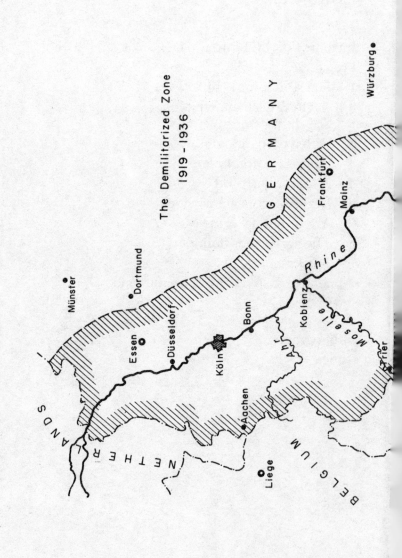

The Demilitarized Zone
1919 - 1936

GERMANY

NETHERLANDS

BELGIUM

Münster

Dortmund

Essen

Düsseldorf

Köln

Bonn

Aachen

Liège

Ahr

Koblenz

Moselle

Trier

Rhine

Frankfurt

Mainz

Würzburg

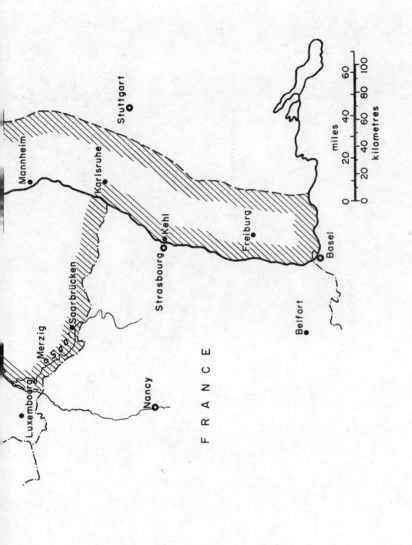

F R A N C E

Luxembourg
Merzig
Saarbrücken
Mannheim
Karlsruhe
Stuttgart
Nancy
Strasbourg
Kehl
Freiburg
Belfort
Basel

miles
0   20   40   60
kilometres
0   20   40   60   80   100

EUROPE 1919 - 1936

SWEDEN

Baltic Sea

ESTONIA

LATVIA

LITHUANIA

MEMEL

DANZIG

EAST PRUSSIA

Berlin

POLAND

U. S. S. R.

DETENLAND

CZECHOSLOVAKIA

RIA

AUSTRIA

HUNGARY

YUGOSLAVIA

RUMANIA

TRANSYLVANIA

BESSARABIA

ceded by Germany
ceded by Russia
plebiscite areas
former Hapsburg empire
the Rhineland

Introduction

by
Donald Cameron Watt

In the twenty years following the re-entry of German troops into the demilitarized zones on her western Rhineland frontier, established by Articles 42 and 43 of the Treaty of Versailles and confirmed by the Treaty of Locarno, a number of myths came to cluster around the Rhineland crisis. Most important, and most significant, was the myth that this was the last great unexploited opportunity to overthrow or 'stop' Hitler without a second world war. The myth came to play a large part in the historical writings of that school of opponents to the pre-war policies of appeasement, of whom Sir Lewis Namier was one of the most distinguished members, who regarded the outbreak of the second world war as entirely avoidable, 'evitable' rather than 'inevitable', and only rendered inevitable by the caution, if not the pusillanimity, of the governments of France and Britain.

The crisis played an equal part in the impression of this myth into the language of politics in Britain and the West generally, including the United States of America. There is a good study, still to be written, of the influence on post-1945 American policy towards the Soviet Union and the People's Republic of China, of the negative aspects of the mythology of appeasement. Such a book would no doubt follow the examples cited by Professor Ernest R. May in his 'Lessons of the Past: the Uses and Misuses of History' in *American Foreign Policy* (New York, 1973); though it would need to dwell also on the traditions of aggressive action as an index of masculinity which played so large a part in the mythology of appeasement in the United States.

This element is not entirely lacking in British indictments of appeasement. But it is usually transmuted into the generalized concept of courage (which is bisexual) rather than male aggressiveness. British mythmakers tended to depict the 'appeasers' as men ignorant of European politics, practising that generalized benevolence which is the hallmark of the

11

amateur 'interloper' in the field of professional diplomacy, men undecided, seduced by the chimera of 'justice', if not craven in the face of the need for decisive action.

Mythmakers require heroes as well as villains. Against Neville Chamberlain, Stanley Baldwin, Lord Halifax and Sir Nevile Henderson they contrasted Winston Churchill, Sir Robert Vansittart and, on the strength of his resignation in February 1938, Anthony Eden. This contrast was to make Eden the natural heir apparent to the leadership of the Conservative party after the débâcle which overtook Mr Neville Chamberlain and his supporters in the parliamentary debate of May 1940. It is of the essence of such contemporary mythmaking that while its villains become obsessed with the struggle to rehabilitate themselves, its heroes very often come to accept their own myths. Some die before history can exact its revenge on the mythmakers. The more unfortunate are those fated to discover the unreliability of the myth in attempting to re-enact it in a similar setting.

Such a one was the Earl of Avon, Anthony Eden. It was impossible for those who followed his course of action during the summer and autumn of 1956, as it is impossible for those who read his later memoirs of the period, not to realize his obsession with the mythology of the Rhineland crisis. The action of President Gamul abd el Nasir of Egypt in nationalizing the Suez Canal struck him as an obvious parallel to the remilitarization of the Rhineland. Action in 1936 would have overthrown Hitler before he became so strong that the years of war were needed for his defeat. Without action in 1956, President Nasir would similarly grow in strength, attract equally powerful and unscrupulous allies, and come to believe that aggression and unilateral action would be unopposed. Common action by the members of the United Nations, which had been so lacking in their predecessors, the members of the League of Nations, was clearly in the general interest of world peace. But a lead would be needed, a decisive lead. And force would have to be used. The natural leaders were those directly affected, the chief guarantors of the 'neutral' status of the Canal since the 1882 convention of Constantinople, Britain and France. They should act together, as they had failed to act twenty years earlier. Again and again, Lord Avon returned in his speeches to the Rhineland analogy and to equating Nasir's Egypt with Hitler's Germany. Some of the press, notably the *Guardian,* tried to challenge the analogy. No one tried to question the accuracy of the mythology evoked by the comparison.

The result, besides the personal disaster which overtook Lord Avon's career, was largely to discredit the conduct of foreign policy by the light of historical analogy in Britain, rather than to cause anyone to question the reliability of the 'received wisdom' of the authorized version of the Rhineland crisis. Unlike Munich, Abyssinia or the Spanish Civil War, it has failed to attract any detailed historical examination until now. The task has been greatly eased by the appearance since 1966 of volumes of published diplomatic correspondence from Germany, France and Belgium to add to those of the United States, and by the release to research under the Public Records Act of 1967 of British Cabinet, Foreign Office and other departmental records for the whole inter-war period. Of the principal actors only the Italian and the Soviet records remain unpublished or inaccessible to scholars. The minor actors are almost as well represented by memoirs, diaries, published collections of private papers and the like. These have made it possible for Professor Emmerson to provide as full and detailed an examination of the origins and course of the Rhineland crisis of 1936 as historians are likely to require for some time to come.

His examination of the course of the crisis is much more than a work of mere demythologization. To his clear demonstration of the military weakness of both France and Britain and the deep divisions in their publics over the rights and wrongs of the German action, he adds elements which should continue to make the Rhineland crisis an event of the deepest interest to both theorists and practitioners of international politics. He provides an object lesson in the uncertainties and impermanencies of any system of international guarantees in his examination of the way in which the Italian guarantor of Locarno was able to use that position to blackmail France into inaction on the question of the application of oil sanctions against Italy after the Italian invasion of Ethiopia. His detailed examination of the issues involved in the application of economic sanctions against Germany demonstrates the weakness of the whole concept of peace-keeping through sanctions and its inapplicability in a situation where that mutual interdependence of linked economies, praised by international economists as the best guarantee of peace, obtains.

Professor Emmerson also provides us with a fascinating case

study of skilful multilateral diplomacy in the manner in which
the German Foreign Minister, Baron von Neurath, played on
the fears and expectations of the various groups of states which
might combine against Germany: the Scandinavians, the Latin
American members of the League of Nations Council, the east
European allies of France, and Britain's affiliates, especially
Australia, also a member of the League Council. He used every
available form of pressure, but the threat of economic and
financial measures was particularly effective. He was rewarded
by a remarkable show of weakness. The Ecuadorian representative on the League Council staged a diplomatic 'illness', the
Chilean abstained from the vital vote in the Council meeting in
London. And no one of Germany's would-be adversaries
showed any idea of what von Neurath was up to or made any
effective move to match his masterly use of Germany's
international connexions.

The crisis thus provides an excellent case study of the
weaknesses of the smaller nations, so active in the League in its
balmier days. With the exception of Czechoslovakia, on whom
Germany was to take speedy revenge only thirty months later,
the record of the smaller states of Europe does little credit to
their protestations of loyalty to the principles of the League.
The Scandinavian countries made any collective pressure on
Germany impossible by their public and joint refusal to take
part in any economic sanctions against Germany at a time when
no proposal for sanctions had yet been made. The governments
of three of the Little Entente states and of the Balkan Entente
states repudiated a motion put by the Rumanian Foreign
Minister, M. Titulescu, to a meeting of their representatives at
Geneva; M. Titulescu was to lose his job very soon thereafter.
The Belgians, their security as much diminished by the German action as was that of France, retired into a stance which we
would now describe not as neutral but as 'neutralist'. Little
good it did them in May 1940.

The bulk of Professor Emmerson's narrative concerns itself
naturally with the major participants in the crisis, Britain,
France, Germany and, on the fringes of inactivity, Fascist Italy.
The general outlines of events are, of course, already familiar
to historians of the period, from the memoirs and accounts
which have already been published. The narrative here does,
however, add a great number of significant details, and fills out
the picture in a number of ways. Professor Emmerson shows

how fully the British Cabinet had compromised itself in advance of Hitler's action by its plans to offer a revision of Locarno in return for a German return to more orthodox, less unilateral, courses of diplomacy. He shows how, despite a number of clear indications of Hitler's forthcoming action, both British and French were taken by surprise by the German action. He shows how economic discontent in the Rhineland, and the activities of the Rhenish Separatists, combined with Hitler's perception of how deeply the Ethiopian imbroglio had detached Mussolini from the solidarity with France, demonstrated at Stresa the previous year, to persuade the Führer to advance his long-envisaged action against the Rhineland from 1937 to March 1936. He shows how little part Hitler took in the crisis, once the order to march had been issued, leaving the day-to-day management of the crisis to von Neurath. He shows how Mussolini was 'conned' by the German ambassador to Rome, Ulrich von Hassell, into suggesting in advance a German action whose details were unknown and one element of which, the offer to return to the League of Nations, made his own decision to withdraw untenable only a few hours before it was to have been implemented. He shows how the Soviet Union withheld any pressure for action against Germany from a conviction, to use Karl Radek's words, that preventive war against Germany would be the equivalent of committing suicide because one was scared of dying. And he traces how easily the British were gulled by Hitler's promises into playing the game of 'ideal solutions', in which each British move was answered by delays ending only in a newer and weaker 'offer', itself sufficiently ambiguous in detail to elicit a further British move until the chance of action ebbed entirely away. And he ends by arguing convincingly that for all but a handful of observers the Rhineland crisis only assumed the significance it now enjoys in retrospect, after the events of 1938 and 1939. In short, Professor Emmerson makes it clear that there are still many lessons to be learnt from the Rhineland crisis, even if they are not those which the British and French governments chose to apply at such cost to themselves and to their countries some twenty years later.

Preface

I owe a great debt of gratitude to Professor Donald C. Watt of the London School of Economics and Political Science, not only for writing the introduction, but more significantly for his suggestions and criticisms at various stages in the development of this monograph. Special thanks are also offered to Professor W. N. Medlicott for his encouragement, suggestions and generosity, particularly in connexion with his work at the Foreign Office Library. Others who were helpful include the Hon. Margaret Lambert and R. A. Wheatley at the Foreign Office Library, Dr Anne Bohm, James Joll, A. J. L. Barnes and James W. Schwartz. I would also like to acknowledge the generosity of the London School of Economics, which provided funds to publish this book.

A host of librarians also deserve recognition. In the forefront is Kenneth Hiscock of the Foreign Office Library. Thanks are also in order for a small army of persons who assisted me at the Public Records Office, British Library, Royal Institute of International Affairs, Senate House of the University of London, Beaverbrook Library, Scottish Records Office and the libraries at the University of Birmingham and the London School of Economics. I would also like to acknowledge those members of Parliament, civil servants and historians who helped to bring about the rollback of the Fifty-Year Rule, making it possible after 1 January 1967 to examine virtually all of the British documents relating to the remilitarization of the Rhineland.

Anyone who tackles a book must realize the importance of moral support, encouragement and friendship. In this connexion, my lasting gratitude is extended to Geoffrey Pridham, Regis Courtemanche, Friedrich Wilhelm Wiemann, Hans and Ruth Baumann and my friends on Randolph Crescent. My greatest debt, however, belongs to Linda, Daniel and Hilary, who ensured that sanity and good spirits prevailed. To them this book is dedicated.

J.T.E.

1 The search for security 1918-1935

The German government regards the
demilitarized zone as an exceedingly difficult
contribution to the appeasement of Europe.
                              HITLER, 21 May 1935

Europe 1918. After four years of struggle and sacrifice, Germany had been defeated. Over 2 million Germans had been killed and another 4.2 million had been wounded. But defeat was not decisive. Such a fate was inevitably forthcoming, but Berlin had surrendered before the allied armies had set foot on German soil. The adversary had been worn down by a world-wide coalition representing some 234 million people. The effort had cost the allies some 3.6 million dead and over 5.2 million wounded.

No country suffered more in victory than France. She had lost 1,393,388 men. That was 3.5 per cent of her total population of less than 39 million and 39 per cent of all allied war deaths. Another 1.5 million had been wounded, 29 per cent of the allied total. Moreover, the enemy's fighting spirit had not been broken. As a result, Paris approached the peace conference with the trepidation of a novice boxer who has floored the heavyweight champion. It was all very well to celebrate the triumph, but what would happen when the German colossus regained consciousness? With this thought in mind, the French delegation, led by Premier Georges Clemenceau and Marshal Ferdinand Foch, determined to do everything possible at Versailles to increase French security at German expense.[1]

Paris put forward three absolute demands. On two France was totally successful. Alsace-Lorraine was returned and Germany, by the terms outlined in part V of the peace treaty, was stripped of the major part of her armaments. The final and most important French demand was for the complete separation from Germany of her provinces west of the Rhine.[2] 'That river', Foch declared, 'will settle everything. Quand on n'est pas sur le Rhin, on a tout perdu.'[3] Initially, the dream was to incorporate these districts into France. Barring that, Paris would accept the creation of some sort of autonomous buffer state, so long as Germany's frontier ended east of the Rhine and so long as France was allowed total military control over the detached provinces.

But these schemes clashed with American principles and British pragmatism. President Woodrow Wilson would not budge from his conviction that 'peoples and provinces are not to be bartered about from sovereignty to sovereignty', while the British prime minister, David Lloyd George, argued that the French scheme might bring short-term security, but certainly not peace to western Europe. Any Rhenish confederation or independent state, he felt, would ultimately succumb to Paris, either as a satellite or as a fully-annexed province. Foch and Clemenceau, he feared, were attempting to create an Alsace-Lorraine in reverse.[4]

Only after two months of hard bargaining did the French fully acquiesce.[5] In exchange for dropping their demands, it was agreed that German military forces would never again be allowed west of a line drawn 50 kilometres (30 miles) east of, and parallel to, the Rhine.[6] Fortifications were also permanently prohibited in the same zone. Any violation of these articles, 43 and 42 respectively, was to be regarded, according to article 44 of the Versailles treaty, as a 'hostile act... calculated to disturb the peace of the world'. (The relevant clauses are given in the Appendix, p. 251.) Wilson and Lloyd George also agreed to a military occupation of the west Rhenish provinces and bridgeheads for 5, 10 and 15 years. It was further stipulated that the evacuation of these three zones could be delayed for as long as necessary beyond 1935, if German guarantees against unprovoked aggression were not considered sufficient by the victors.[7] But the treaty of Versailles did not oblige any country to aid France in preventing or suppressing any German attempt to remilitarize the Rhineland. Paris sought ceaselessly during the next six years to fill this gap by enlisting British and League support, especially in connexion with the ill-fated Geneva protocol of 1924, which would have treated the violation of articles 42-43 as 'equivalent to resort to war'.[8]

What really ended French demands for a buffer state, however, was the offer of an Anglo-American security guarantee.[9] This idea, proposed by the British and endorsed by Wilson, was embodied in a separate treaty signed on 28 June 1919. Its operative clause promised immediate British and American assistance if France were the victim of any unprovoked German aggression. It did not, in spite of French efforts, commit

London and Washington to upholding the demilitarized zone.[10] The agreement also stipulated that the British guarantee was contingent upon approval by the United States. But when the US Senate failed to ratify the Versailles peace pact, the Anglo-American guarantee was doomed, too. It was never reported out of the Senate's foreign affairs committee, where it died in pigeonhole. Even though both Houses of Parliament had already approved the pact, the British government activated the escape clause and the whole project collapsed — thereby becoming one of history's great might-have-beens.[11]

This 'betrayal' was deeply resented in France.[12] Not only did it make the French feel that they had 'lost the peace', but it also served for years as the classic example, the *ne plus ultra*, of Albion's perfidy.[13] It also accelerated two other trends in French foreign policy. It stimulated Paris in her efforts to create a 'système d'alliances' with European nations who felt equally threatened by treaty revision, be it from Germany or Hungary.[14] In September 1920, Paris and Brussels concluded a military arrangement.[15] This was followed five months later by a military alliance with Warsaw and by mutual-assistance pacts with Prague in January 1924, with Bucharest in June 1926, and with Belgrade in November 1927.[16] The French security network was also extended at Locarno to include British and Italian guarantees. And, in 1933, Paris signed a non-aggression pact with Moscow which eventually led in 1935-6 to a treaty of mutual assistance.[17]

The disappearance of the Anglo-American guarantee also intensified French determination to enforce the provisions of Versailles strictly.[18] When Berlin violated article 43 by despatching troops to the demilitarized zone in April 1920 to quell a communist revolt, the French responded by occupying five towns east of the Rhine for five weeks. Paris also financed and fomented separatist movements in the Rhineland. And, when promised German timber deliveries were not immediately forthcoming, premier Raymond Poincaré forced the reparations commission on 26 December 1922 to declare Berlin in default. 'L'Allemagne', he insisted, 'en tant que nation ne se résigne à tenir sa parole que sous l'empire de la nécessité.'[19] Sixteen days later French troops were sent into the Ruhr to ensure that subsequent deliveries were promptly executed. In this way, Paris proved that she was still the master and that Germany could still be brought to heel.

But the effect of these policies was disastrous.[20] In Germany, they bred hatred, violence and a desire for revenge. British opinion was infuriated by Poincaré's jackboot policy and the cabinet protested vigorously to Paris. World opinion generally sympathized with the Germans in their struggle against the French intruder. It would be difficult to over-estimate the detrimental effect which the Ruhr affair exerted on public and private opinion towards both France and the Versailles treaty for the next thirteen years. Domestically, the experience thoroughly discredited the 'politique d'isolement et de force' of the French right. No government thereafter was prepared to risk independent military action against Germany. The Ruhr affair also angered enough voters to ensure that 'Poincaré la Guerre' was thrown out of office in the elections of May 1924.

The change of government in Paris contributed greatly to a new atmosphere in Europe.[21] The Germans, now being led in foreign affairs by Gustav Stresemann, were tired of violence and seemed prepared to work for change within the system. The French, too, were tired of the old ways and were doubtless as relieved as the Germans when the Dawes plan for reparations payments provided for the evacuation of the Ruhr by the end of November 1924. And the British, after having rejected the Geneva protocol of 1924, were anxious to find some kind of regional arrangement which would guarantee peace where it counted most, namely, in western Europe. The result of this propitious political alignment was the Locarno treaty, proposed initially by Stresemann and guided to fruition by Austen Chamberlain, with the active support of French foreign minister Aristide Briand and the belated cooperation of Italy's new dictator, Benito Mussolini.

The Rhine pact of 16 October 1925 was, first and foremost, a non-aggression agreement between Brussels, Paris and Berlin.[22] This pledge to respect national frontiers was guaranteed by Rome and London, who promised to come to the assistance of any country which was the victim of unprovoked aggression by another treaty partner (see Appendix for relevant articles and clauses). Furthermore, and this was Stresemann's own suggestion, the German government voluntarily reaffirmed its obligations under articles 42 and 43 to respect the demilitarized zone. Britain and Italy also promised to guarantee the zone's continued existence, militarily if necessary. But the British rebuffed Franco-Italian efforts to

make any breach of articles 42-43 automatic justification for
military intervention.[23] Such action was promised immediately only if Germany massed troops inside the zone as an obvious
forerunner to invasion.

But, barring that, all violations were to be regarded as non-
flagrant, no matter how widespread or obvious. In the latter
case, the aggrieved power was obliged first to take his case to
Geneva, where the League council, after satisfying itself that a
violation had been committed, would notify the other Locarno
powers of its finding, or 'constatation'. Once that occurred, the
treaty's guarantors were obliged forthwith to assist the nation
filing the complaint. This procedure eliminated any immediate or independent riposte, but it had the great political
advantage of providing Paris or Brussels with the protective
cover of League sanction and Locarno support for such punitive measures as they chose to apply.

It was in the demilitarized zone that the Rhine pact was weak-
est, since, in the eyes of everyone but Paris, the prohibitions
contained in articles 42-43 were not taken as seriously as the
sections preserving the territorial integrity of France, Belgium
and Germany.[24] The French, however, insisted on treating the
demilitarization provisions as essential to their security.[25] But,
as the years passed, it became increasingly apparent that the
Rhine pact was composed of two unequal parts: one sacred to
the permanent preservation of peace in western Europe; the
other non-essential and therefore destined to be seen as
expendable.

Another soft spot in the treaty was its imprecision.[26] Pierre
Flandin described it as 'extremely confused',[27] Clemenceau
complained that it 'does not say all it means'.[28] No less a legal
expert than Britain's Sir John Simon found the Locarno treaty
'a *most* difficult topic to explain', while his cabinet and foreign
office colleagues repeatedly resisted French and Belgian
efforts to remove ambiguities on fundamental questions which
were unanswered or at least open to multiple interpretation.[29]
For example, the nature and scope of assistance had remained
undefined. Nor was it clear, then or a decade later, who decided
when and how aid should be rendered or, especially, what sort
of troop presence in the zone would constitute a prelude to
aggression or a threat to peace and security. Presumably, even
the presence of a military band could constitute a violation of
article 43; but no one knew for sure.

All this became a matter of paramount importance in 1936, but when the pact was signed in 1925 precision was less important than the general spirit and significance of the treaty, which Austen Chamberlain described as marking 'the real dividing line between the years of war and the years of peace'.[30] Besides, Germany was too weak even to contemplate the risks of violating the demilitarized zone, let alone invading anyone. France was still strong and quite capable of imposing her will on Berlin. But it was also thought that Paris would be deterred from such tactics by the knowledge that her action would immediately align London and Rome at Berlin's side. It was this prospect of the massive coalition—and not the actual provisions for execution—which was to make Locarno effective for a decade.[31]

In fact, the Rhine pact was never intended to function. Its very existence was seen as adequate to preserve peace in western Europe. The governments of both Stanley Baldwin and Ramsay MacDonald believed peace could be maintained along the Rhine so long as the other nations remained convinced of London's readiness to honour her guarantee.[32] It may even be doubted whether Baldwin's cabinet would have underwritten the treaty if it had believed in 1925 that Britain would ever be obliged to fulfil her commitments.[33] Thus, when Austen Chamberlain was asked by the chiefs of staff whether contingency plans should be prepared for executing Britain's guarantee, the foreign secretary replied that Locarno was a treaty for peace, not war. There was no need, he added, for military arrangements of any sort.[34] This philosophy, coupled with public hostility to continental connexions, explains why pre-coup staff talks aimed at implementing Locarno were never held between London and any of the three guaranteed powers, in spite of requests by Brussels and Paris.[35]

All five member powers benefited handsomely from Locarno. The French, after six years of fruitless pursuit, had finally obtained a British security guarantee and had got Italian support as a bonus.[36] An elated Briand also claimed that any German violation of the demilitarized zone would henceforth 'suffire à déclencher l'action anglaise et italienne', but this assertion was more wishful than actual.[37] Paris also received positive German recognition of existing western frontiers, which meant that Berlin acknowledged the loss of Alsace-Lorraine. Moreover, Germany had promised, of her own free will, to obey the provisions regarding the Rhineland which had been dictated to her at Versailles.

Although most Frenchmen saluted Briand for a fine piece of work, the spirit of Locarno did not erase the distrust felt in France towards Germany.[38] Thus, in 1929, when it became apparent that the occupation of the west bank was coming to a premature end, Paris authorized the erection of a network of permanent fortifications along her eastern and north-eastern frontiers.[39] The lessons of 1914-18 and the abortive Anglo-American guarantee had proved indelible. Locarno was useful and allies were valuable, but concrete and cannons were better. From 1925 onwards, the French people became increasingly introspective and pacific. To reverse the engines after Hitler arrived in 1933 proved an impossible task, as defeat in 1940 showed.

On the German side, Stresemann was obliged to make some heavy sacrifices, such as formally recognizing the territorial and political *status quo* in the west. He also failed to win any concessions on the questions of reparations or the early evacuation of the Rhenish provinces. On the other hand, he had brought back a blue-chip guarantee, underwritten by Rome and London, that France would never launch a preventive military venture against Germany — at least, not without paying a terrible price for her folly. There would be no recurrence of the Ruhr episode.[40] Also, for the first time since the war, Germany had been treated as an equal among Europe's great powers. Shortly thereafter she was invited to join the League of Nations, which she entered on 8 September 1926, simultaneously taking a permanent seat on the council. Her days of being treated as Europe's pariah were, it seemed, behind her. 'We obtained at Locarno', Stresemann wrote, 'one hundred per cent of what we desired. It preserves the Rhineland for us and allows us to recuperate the German territories in the east.'[41]

For their part, the Belgians obtained their long-coveted British guarantee, secured German recognition of their eastern frontier and generally reduced the chances of a repetition of the invasion of 1914, while Italy's Mussolini basked in the spotlight as one of Europe's peacemakers and leader of a re-emerging continental power.[42]

As for the British, they were not a little pleased at having arranged a regional security pact which encompassed only that portion of Europe in which they were vitally interested.[43]

Austen Chamberlain had achieved a détente without assuming much more than paper responsibilities and which left London free to fulfil her obligations pretty much as she saw fit.[44] 'The British government', he told the Commons in 1925, 'remains the judge, the only judge, of whether ... immediate danger has arisen.'[45] The same absolute control was apparently also true for non-flagrant violations, according to Sir John Simon, who explained to the cabinet in November 1933 that Britain could not be made to act under Locarno in any case without her own consent.[46] Having thereby stabilized the situation on the Rhine, the British felt able to turn inward, concentrating for the next eight years on their domestic, dominion and financial affairs, while pursuing their efforts to bring about an agreement for multilateral disarmament.[47]

The Locarno decade was a period of increasing, then decreasing tranquillity in the demilitarized zone. According to the treaty of Versailles, the last and largest of the three occupation zones west of the Rhine should not have been evacuated until 10 January 1935. It was even conceivable that the allied forces might exercise their right to remain longer, as had occurred in the pre-Locarno period of 1924, when the occupation of the first (Köln) sector was prolonged from 10 January 1925 until 31 January 1926, owing to Berlin's failure to fulfil certain aspects of the peace treaty regarding her armed forces.[48]

Stresemann, who had been deeply impressed by the decision to delay evacuation of the Köln zone, made it one of his cardinal aims not only to guarantee departure of the occupation forces, but to accelerate the process as well.[49] He succeeded in getting Köln cleared, but it was only in August 1929 that agreement was reached, in connexion with the Young plan, for ending the occupation of the left bank within ten months.[50] On 30 June 1930, for the first time in twelve years, Germany was free of foreign troops — a full 4 ½ years ahead of schedule.[51] Stresemann lived to see the agreement signed, but died seven months too soon to witness the withdrawal. But Germans generally, while glad to be rid of the French troops, showed little gratitude. Instead, evacuation was marked by a disturbing undertone of restlessness about Germany's other grievances, such as war guilt, eastern frontiers, the Saar and the demilitarized zone.[52]

There was, however, no change in Berlin's attitude towards articles 42-43 for the next few years. Germany was still too weak to risk complications. Even the Nazi government felt the need of the Anglo-Italian guarantee against possible French preventive measures, particularly in the early days after the seizure of power and in that same autumn when Chancellor of the Reich Adolf Hitler quit the League and the disarmament conference, and again in the summer of 1934, during the weeks following the murder of SA leader Ernst Röhm and the assassination of Austrian chancellor Engelbert Dollfuss.[53] Nor, for that matter, did Berlin feel any military need for a remilitarized Rhineland during the last years of Weimar and the first years of Hitler. Although illicit German rearmament had been organized and accelerated since May 1932 with Chancellor Heinrich Brüning's replacement by the reactionary government of Franz von Papen, the fact was that, through at least 1934 and possibly 1935, it would have been an act of folly for the Reichswehr to have attempted to thwart a French invasion west of the Rhine, even if the demilitarized zone had never existed.[54]

Throughout this period and as late as 1937, Germany's military strategists divided the demilitarized area along the Rhine into eastern and western zones.[55] The western region was subdivided into three sectors, as is shown in the map at the beginning of the book. The first and most vulnerable area, between the Rhine and Moselle, was to be sacrificed without engaging the enemy in serious combat. However, every effort was to be made to slow up the French advance through road blocks, barricades and the like. Armed resistance was to begin at the second sector, between the Moselle and the Ahr. The national police (Landespolizei), border police (Grenzschutz) and other security forces, supported by paramilitary formations, were expected to exploit the difficult terrain of the Eifelgebirge in order to harass and delay the enemy for as long as possible, but not to jeopardize their own chances of making an orderly retreat to prepared positions in the third sector, north of the Ahr, where they were to join with the Reichswehr in a total effort to keep the invader from capturing the Ruhr. Meanwhile, east of the Rhine, everything possible was to be done to keep the French from crossing the river. Bridges were to be blown up and boats sunk, by brace and bit if necessary. Nothing was to be left afloat.[56] Then, from behind their river fortress, the army was to fight to the finish—some 30-40 kilometres inside the demilitarized zone.[57]

Contrary to what was once believed, the first and only plan

for restoring military sovereignty in the Rhineland was drafted five days before the coup.[58] At the Nuremberg trials it was correctly charged that remilitarization of the Rhineland had been premeditated. But it was also claimed that positive proof of this could be found as early as 2 May 1935 in a directive issued by Blomberg for an operation carrying the code name 'Schulung', which was purported to be for a surprise reoccupation of the Rhineland at lightning speed.[59] Not only was this document nothing of the sort — it involved a pre-emptive strike against Czechoslovakia — but it also amply illustrates the rôle envisaged by Berlin for Germany's western forces in the event of a French attack, namely, 'pure defence — if necessary, delaying resistance'.[60]

An assignment of this magnitude, the army argued, required advance preparations within the demilitarized zone.[61] At the same time, the Auswärtiges Amt (foreign ministry) declared that nothing must be done which might agitate the French and perhaps give them an excuse to launch some punitive action.[62] An uneasy compromise was eventually struck, by which the Reichswehr was permitted to make only those essential defensive preparations which could either be concealed altogether or disguised with a cloak of legitimacy.[63] Into the former category fell such activities as stockpiling caches of field-grey uniforms, rifles, grenades and heavy machine guns, though artillery, tanks and planes were strictly forbidden. Obstruction and resistance zones were also constructed and preparations made for establishing as well as destroying communications and transport networks. Rifle ranges were hidden in nature preserves. What could not be concealed was disguised. Thus, observation and machine-gun posts were erected as customs and fire watch towers, while the construction of subterranean depots for *matériel* and munitions was passed off as 'exploitations minières'. Barracks were kept occupied by civilians, which gave a good excuse for keeping them maintained. Glider and air sports clubs abounded, thereby permitting the construction of 'une infrastructure aerienne', capable of development into full-fledged bases.

The army was, of course, forbidden. But war minister Werner von Blomberg kept his hand on Rhine defences through the professional police force of 31,500, which Berlin had been permitted to maintain inside the zone.[64] The German government never allowed the strength of this force to exceed the authorized limits by more than 10 or 12 per cent—a figure regarded by the Auswärtiges Amt as 'just tolerable'.[65] But no such restraint was exercised on the organization, training and discipline of the police. This was particularly true of the 13-14,000 who had been hived off in 1933 and formed into a new force called the Landespolizei.[66]

That these men were professional soldiers was apparent almost from the outset, but any lingering doubts were dispelled on 1 August 1935, when all Landespolizei (Lapo) units outside the demilitarized zone were absorbed, without difficulty, into the army.[67] The Rhineland contingents, which had to wait another seven months before they could shed their disguise, were specially trained to delay an enemy advance on the west bank and, apart from a lack of artillery, were quite capable of challenging the foe from behind the Rhine.[68]

The French were aware of these illicit activities and more than once considered filing a complaint at Geneva which would enable the Locarno powers to oblige Berlin to restore the status quo.[69] Premier Pierre Flandin even handed the British a memorandum at the Stresa conference on 13 April 1935, detailing alleged violations of articles 42-43.[70] But, whereas many of these allegations were confirmed by British intelligence as accurate, it was also admitted that few could be proved, and most could also be explained away by Berlin in perfectly plausible terms.[71] This was not untypical of the situation which existed in the demilitarized zone during the last three years of its life.[72] Berlin's breaches were never flagrant or offensive, but subtle and defensive.

Moreover, if the amount of extra-legal military activity in the Rhineland did not actually decrease during 1935, it was certainly conducted much more circumspectly after Hitler announced the reintroduction of conscription on 16 March, when the French massed troops in their eastern and north-eastern sectors and the British military attaché warned Berlin, apparently on his own initiative, that London 'would not stand for any nonsense' regarding articles 42-43.[73]

Foreign minister Konstantin von Neurath was not a little impressed by the gravity of the situation. In addition to dispensing the usual 'soothing assurances' abroad, he demanded that conscription and recruitment within the zone should be handled by civilians.[74] The foreign ministry also warned the army that 'severe damage' might ensue if it did not pay the

utmost respect to the demilitarization stipulations.[75] On 27
May 1935 Blomberg himself warned 'all authorities' that the
value of any military measures in the Rhineland was 'out of all
proportion to the great danger to the Reich in the event of their
becoming known'.[76] Six months later the war minister repeated
his admonition for 'restraint and reserve', as well as for
'patience' within the zone.[77]

Serious consideration was even given at the highest levels to
a proposal, mooted by Wehrmachtsamt chief general Walter
von Reichenau and supported by the Auswärtiges Amt, to
withdraw the Landespolizei from the Rhineland, because it was
becoming almost impossible to conceal its military nature.[78]
But Hitler sat tight, doubtless on the basis of Blomberg's
opinion that the Lapo's absence would jeopardize the Reich's
western defences.[79] By autumn, the Landespolizei was again
chafing over the limitations which had been imposed by the
March-April crisis.[80] But the Auswärtiges Amt managed to
ensure up to 7 March 1936 that the army's activities in the
Rhineland were strictly governed by the principle 'Deckung
geht vor Wirkung'.[81]

Hitler's public attitude toward Locarno and the demilitarized zone was scrupulously correct from the time he took office
until the day he sent troops into the Rhineland.[82] But, whereas
the Chancellor did not attack or impugn either of these treaty
obligations from the rostrum, it is equally true that only twice
did he actually pledge himself publicly to Locarno. The first
occasion was a straightforward promise in a Reichstag speech
on 30 January 1934 that Germany was 'ready and determined
. . . to accept both the spirit and the letter' of the Rhine pact.[83]
The other instance occurred in his peace speech of 21 May 1935,
when he declared that his government would 'painstakingly
observe any treaty . . . even if it was concluded before its acces-
sion to power'.[84] Hitler singled out Locarno and pointed to the
'exceedingly difficult contribution' which Berlin was making
toward the appeasement of Europe by accepting the demilitarized zone. But he insisted nevertheless that Germany would
'observe and fulfil all obligations arising out of the Locarno
pact so long as the other parties to the treaty for their part are
also willing to stand by this pact'.[85] This was an ominous, but
not altogether unreasonable proviso.

In diplomatic conversations, however, the Chancellor's
fervour for Locarno, after two years of fidelity, began to cool in

1935. Germany was growing too strong and Hitler was feeling too secure to evoke anything like a repeat of the series of assurances made to the French, British and Belgians between November 1933 and March 1934.[86] The first signal of a shift in attitude occurred on 3 February 1935, when the Chancellor warned the British and French ambassadors that German acceptance of articles 42-43 was not going to be eternal.[87] Sir Eric Phipps, who described Hitler's attitude as 'threatening', derived the distinct impression that the demilitarized zone would last 'not a day longer' than it took the German army to complete its expansion.[88]

What neither Phipps nor French ambassador François-Poncet realized was that at that moment the Chancellor was considering the idea of terminating the demilitarized zone at the same time as he repudiated part V of the Versailles treaty by announcing the reintroduction of conscription.[89] His decision not to do so was based on at least four considerations. First was the possibility that, whereas the French might not retaliate militarily to his repudiation of part V, the shock of Germany's denouncing articles 42 and 43 as well might be sufficient to precipitate a forceful riposte by Paris.[90] Hitler later claimed that he could have executed both moves without provoking war, but Berlin's behaviour at the time suggested far less certainty on this point.[91]

The second and most important reason was that Germany could not have rid herself of articles 42-43 without renouncing the Rhine pact. Both Neurath and state secretary Bernhard von Bülow confirmed in February 1936 that the demilitarized zone would have been done away with in March 1935 if it had not been for the existence of Locarno, whose denunciation, it was feared, could produce 'consequences of the worst possible kind'.[92] Furthermore, the Rhine pact provided strong insurance against the danger that Paris might march into Germany in reply to his conscription declaration. So long as there remained the risk of France acting violently against the Reich, Locarno was worth the sacrifice of subscribing to the demilitarized zone.[93] Although the Reichswehr was still some months away from putting up a good fight, it is probably fair to say that Locarno first became dispensable to Hitler after March 1935, when France took the Stresa, rather than the Rhine, route to Geneva.[94]

The third reason was that Rhine remilitarization was not yet essential to Hitler or his generals, either politically or militarily.[95] The National Socialist régime had just been given a vote of confidence on 13 January 1935 when 90.8 per cent of the electorate in the Saar chose to unite with the Reich. The magnitude of this victory, Phipps felt, had 'materially strengthened' the Chancellor's domestic position and had generated enough enthusiasm to carry the government forward for some time.[96]

Strategically, the zone's existence remained an irritant.[97] But, considering the state of the armed forces, any remilitarization would have been largely theoretical and generally unnecessary from a defensive standpoint, since German troops, tanks, artillery and aircraft were already as little as thirty miles away from their positions on the Rhine, which, until 1937, was to serve as the main barrier against French attack.[98] In addition, Reichswehr leaders and their staffs were completely engrossed in the problems of expanding their paper army of 100,000 into a fighting force of 550,000.[99]

Pressure from the generals through 1935 was not so much for an early solution to the Rhine problem as for the Chancellor to conduct his foreign and domestic affairs in such a way as to avoid provoking military reprisals.[100] This was accompanied by professions of respect for articles 42-43 from generals Reichenau and Blomberg, who had insisted that Germany 'did not dream of trying to wriggle out of Locarno', even though the general staff considered the demilitarized zone a 'grave disadvantage' for a sovereign state.[101] Only in January 1936, when it became apparent that the Franco-Soviet pact would be ratified, did there develop anything like a military lobby for early abolition of articles 42-43—and even then the emphasis was entirely on a diplomatic, or at least a non-violent solution.[102]

Last, but not least, in deciding Hitler against Rhine remilitarization in the spring of 1935 was the probability that repudiation of the treaty of Locarno would have had a negative effect on Anglo-German relations. To have renounced the Rhine pact might have destroyed Hitler's hopes for a naval agreement with London.[103] By holding back over articles 42 and 43, Berlin was able to sign on 18 June a pact which not only permitted Germany to build a fleet of up to 35 per cent of the British total tonnage, but which also earned for Germany recognition of her right to possess an ocean-going navy, hitherto forbidden by Versailles.

After springing his March surprise for 1935, Hitler appear-

ently decided that he could, after all, tolerate the Rhine régime
for another couple of years if necessary, until the army's expansion became cramped by the restrictions which had demilitarized 18.5 per cent (33,655 square miles) of the Reich's total
land mass and 24 per cent (15.4 million) of its population. But
Berlin never ceased thinking about the problem. And whereas
the Rhine statutes were adhered to in principle for the rest of
their existence, much time was spent rehearsing arguments
and preparing a case for eventual repudiation.[104] This was
largely a matter of keeping all options open by challenging
every conceivable breach of Locarno, or its spirit, in order to
protect Berlin from the later charge that she was reviving
grievances which had been passed over in silence when they
originally occurred.

The classic case involved the Franco-Soviet pact, which was
signed in Paris on 2 May 1935 and according to which immediate assistance was pledged if the other partner were the victim of unprovoked aggression.[105] This pact was violently
attacked in Germany as a military alliance exclusively directed
against the Reich.[106] This, in turn, was portrayed as a blatant act
of bad faith on the part of Paris, since Berlin had promised in
Locarno not to attack her western neighbours and Hitler had
frequently declared his peaceful intentions.[107]

The Auswärtiges Amt also argued that Moscow and Paris
had set themselves up as judge and jury on the critical questions of whether unprovoked aggression had been committed
and by whom.[108] This, it was argued, even applied to a situation
where the League council might fail to agree in unanimity that
action should be taken. If so, then, according to the terms of the
protocol, 'effect shall nevertheless be given to the obligation to
render assistance'. Such action, Berlin insisted, would be incompatible with article 16 of the Covenant and would therefore
constitute a flagrant violation of the Rhine pact (see Appendix
for relevant clauses). On 21 May Hitler warned the Reichstag
and the world that the Franco-Soviet pact had introduced 'an
element of juridical uncertainty' into Locarno.[109]

These oral reservations were followed on 25 May with a
memorandum to the other Locarno capitals, recapitulating the
German case against the compatibility of the two pacts.[110] This
document was accompanied by an oral declaration to the effect
that denunciation of the Rhine pact and articles 42-43 was 'far
from our thoughts'.[111] The French categorically refuted these

contentions on 25 June and, during the next four weeks, Brussels, Rome and London all advised Berlin that they, too, could see nothing in the Russian pact which conflicted with Locarno.[112] On 27 July the Auswärtiges Amt instructed its Locarno embassies to reject verbally the French argumentation.[113] It was also explained, however, that Germany saw no advantage in further exchanges of juridical memoranda. By raising these calculated doubts and expressing only conditional fidelity to the Rhine pact, Hitler and Neurath laid the foundation on which to build a case for justifying subsequent action on the grounds that the French themselves acted unilaterally by composing with Moscow without consulting their Locarno allies. No one could claim in 1935 that Berlin had tacitly accepted the Franco-Soviet pact and for the next seven months the German press ensured that the compatibility question was not forgotten.[114]

Hitler's state secretary, Otto Meissner, claimed that the Chancellor was ready to repudiate Locarno immediately after the Russian pact was signed, but had been dissuaded by Neurath, who feared a military riposte.[115] Although his contention is not supported by any documentary evidence, it is possible that Hitler had already decided as early as May 1935 to use the Franco-Soviet agreement as his pretext for repudiating articles 42-43. But it is not absolutely certain, in view of Hitler's remark to ambassador Ulrich von Hassell in February 1936 that he had hitherto 'always envisaged' the spring of 1937 as the date for disposing of the zone.[116] In this connexion, it is worth observing that if Hitler had a master-plan during this period, he was not tied to any timetable, as can be seen from the fact that he jumped from 1937 to 1935 and back again. That he was also a first-class political opportunist is equally obvious from his ultimate decision to march in 1936.[117]

The same desire to keep options open involved Berlin in disputes with her Locarno partners in connexion with the Abyssinian crisis in the autumn. The first occurred in October, when Paris tried to capitalize on Britain's Mediterranean anxieties to secure undertakings from His Majesty's Government aimed at ensuring speedy application of Locarno against Berlin.[118] The German press, under the direction of Joseph Goebbels's propaganda ministry, immediately argued that arrangements of this nature over the heads of the other Rhine pact partners were 'hardly admissible'. 'It would occasion no surprise', the *Deutsche diplomatisch-politische Korrespondenz* (DDPK) warned, 'if those against whom this policy is directed . . . felt obliged to make all reserves on its side.'[119]

The other Abyssinian dispute was precipitated by Anglo-French staff talks, which took place on 30 October and 8-10 December. These conversations were strictly confined to the possibility of a mad-dog act by Italy in the Mediterranean.[120] But the Germans charged that some kind of bargain was being struck which also involved the presence of British air forces in north-eastern France. This, it was added, or any other attempt to prolong or extend the Anglo-French agreement to spheres outside the immediate Mediterranean imbroglio, would contradict both the letter and the spirit of Locarno. In German eyes, the Rhine pact did not admit of such one-sided agreements between two of the parties to it.[121]

A similar stance was taken in connexion with French and British efforts throughout 1935 to negotiate a pact which would guarantee more automatic and immediate assistance to any Locarno power attacked from the air.[122] In this case, Berlin objected to the French demand that bilateral arrangements should be permitted to ensure effective and timely intervention. The German government insisted that arrangements of this nature were not compatible with the Rhine pact in spirit because of the opportunities created for powers to plot against each other.[123] Not only did the Chancellor object to discussions *à deux,* but Neurath also warned Phipps on 13 December that persistence on this point might necessitate abolition of the demilitarized zone, since Germany could hardly be expected to keep her aircraft any farther from the frontier than the French.[124]

These references to Locarno and the demilitarized zone served a variety of purposes.[125] Sometimes they were meant solely to annoy Poncet. More frequently they aimed to illustrate publicly the burden which Berlin was bearing, sometimes for the sake of European tranquillity, but more often to satisfy French *amour propre.* They also sought to test reactions on the part of London and Paris toward articles 42 and 43. The results were not unpromising, if only because the British guarantor had not once responded negatively or threateningly to any German hint about ending the Rhine régime. Nevertheless, there is nothing on record for 1935 or the first five weeks of 1936 to suggest that the demilitarized zone was the object, rather than still a pawn, in German diplomatic manoeuvrings.

Elsewhere, however, 1935 had wrought a striking improvement in German fortunes.[126] The government's internal grip
was stronger. The SA had been purged, the press muzzled and
the Reichswehr pledged to unconditional obedience to Adolf
Hitler. Pockets of nationalist, socialist and communist resistance had been beaten down. So, too, had the trade unions, Jews
and Masons. Protestants were still struggling against 'coordi-
nation', but the Catholics were bound to a concordat. Hitler was
not only the Chancellor, but also President and people's
Führer—already a legend in his time.

The economy, while still shaky, continued to confound the
prophets of orthodoxy by its resilience under the resourceful
direction of economics minister Hjalmar Schacht and his 'New
Plan'.[127] Economic disaffection existed, but, as Phipps reported, 'everything is subordinated to the needs of the defence
forces' and the people seemed prepared to make 'considerable
sacrifices' to rebuild the army.[128] Unemployment was rising,
but only seasonably, and more Germans than ever had jobs.[129]
Thanks to an unusually mild December, the butter ration had
been quadrupled—from ¼ lb to 1 lb—and there was even pork
for Christmas.[130]

The Reich was also much safer. The Wehrmacht's expansion had made such notable headway since March that Phipps
described Germany on 6 January 1936 as 'fast becoming the
most powerful military nation in Europe' and his military
attaché pronounced the army 'a serious deterrent' to any
potential aggressor.[131] Furthermore, the British embassy in
Berlin believed the majority of young Germans was so deeply
imbued with the national socialist faith and so possessed by
enthusiasm that 'they could be led into any form of aggression,
whilst still believing profoundly that they themselves were
being attacked and were fighting for the existence of their
Fatherland'.[132]

Nor had the high command proved immune to the Chancellor's respectful approach, his willingness to spend freely on
rearmament and his political successes, both foreign and
domestic.[133] In fact, at no time during the twelve-year existence
of the Third Reich did Hitler enjoy more amicable relations
with his generals than in 1935 and 1936.[134] During these years,
there was nothing like an organized military resistance to party
politics.[135] As general Ludwig Beck, chief of army general staff,

put it, 'Mutiny and revolution are not words in the dictionary of a German soldier.'[136]

Externally, the Saar had been restored and the conscription crisis weathered. Important British ministers had journeyed to see the Chancellor and a naval pact had been concluded with London. Pierre Laval was still clinging to power in France, which meant that Paris was hardly bellicose.[137] Indeed, between 18 October and 18 December, the French premier or his emissaries made no fewer than six attempts to elicit from Berlin a favourable reaction to a Franco-German understanding.[138] But the Chancellor was content to do nothing for the duration, doubtless enjoying the pleasure of having Europe's wrath directed away from the Reich—for the first time since the Machtergreifung—and towards Mussolini's invasion of Abyssinia.[139] Besides, no policy was also wise policy as long as Germany's potential opponents were at loggerheads. Not only had the Stresa front been severely strained by the war in Abyssinia, but Mussolini had revealed its fragility as early as May by initiating the first of several attempts to secure a *rapprochement* with Berlin.[140] In addition, the uproar over the Hoare-Laval proposals in December had exacerbated Anglo-French relations and effectively eliminated hopes of early peace. It also seemed at year's end that Rome was headed for disaster, if not defeat, on the battlefields of East Africa.[141]

In these circumstances, one of Berlin's major concerns was that the League might yet emerge from the troubles of December determined to recoup lost prestige by imposing its authority on Italy.[142] Such a success could have serious repercussions on Germany. As a result, Hitler told Hassell, Berlin must do everything to prevent the manifold opponents of the authoritarian system from concentrating upon Germany as their sole object.[143] This was one important reason why Berlin maintained an attitude of benevolent neutrality toward Rome.[144] The Führer was also concerned that the defeat of fascism in Italy would benefit only the communists.[145] Nevertheless, there still existed in Berlin a deep reservoir of mistrust and suspicion towards Mussolini, who had not so very long ago rushed troops to the Brenner and chaired the conference at Stresa, where he had pressed for stern measures against the Reich.[146]

Thus, when the Duce suddenly proposed on 6 January 1936 to eliminate the 'only dispute' separating Rome and Berlin by

allowing Vienna to become a German satellite, his overture
was treated as a sign of weakness, deriving both from Italy's
military failures in Abyssinia and from her difficult economic
and financial position at home.[147] However, the Chancellor
decided to give cautious encouragement to Rome. The time
was now politically correct to treat the events of 1934 as a closed
chapter. In doing so, Hitler hoped to ensure the permanent
destruction of the Anglo-Franco-Italian front and to open a
breach in what he described as Germany's position of almost
complete isolation.[148] This surprisingly pessimistic assessment, made to Hassell on 17 January 1936, was given to justify
the Chancellor's decision to swallow his own personal feelings
about Mussolini. But, if Berlin felt isolated, her potential anta-
gonists all believed that their political and military position
vis-à-vis Germany had deteriorated during 1935.[149] Phipps
described Berlin's year-end position as 'more favourable' and
her prospects as 'brighter' than at any time since 1918.[150]

2 Anglo-French anticipation
1935-1936

*Le gouvernement français compte que l'Angleterre
est prête à appuyer la France, même seule, pour le
maintien de la zone démilitarisée.*   3 March 1936

*The view of the cabinet, however, was that
demilitarization of the Rhineland was not a vital
British interest.*   14 January 1935

That the government of the Third Reich would seek to
remilitarize the Rhineland was an unarguable factor in
European diplomatic equations by 1936.[1] Moreover, the
Abyssinian crisis had caused such havoc with Italy and with
Franco-British relations that the new French government of
Albert Sarraut, formed on 24 January with Flandin as foreign
minister, had every reason to suspect that Hitler might seek to
put an early end to articles 42 and 43.[2] This prospect was increased in January by German press assaults on the Anglo-
French Mediterranean military consultations, which Berlin
claimed were contrary to Locarno.[3] So persistent were these
charges that Poncet had twice rebuked state secretary Bülow,
accusing Berlin on 13 January of behaving as if she wished for
a pretext to justify 'une action ultérieure dont le projet serait
déjà dans votre tête et qui consisterait, par exemple, à occuper
un beau jour, la zone démilitarisée'.[4]

French anxieties were further increased in mid-January
when the German press resumed its attack on the alleged
incompatibility of the Franco-Soviet and Rhine pacts.[5] These
criticisms had coincided with more than the usual number
of reports concerning active preparations inside the
demilitarized zone.[6] They were also accompanied by predictions that Hitler would celebrate the anniversary of his
seizure of power on 30 January by marching troops into the
Rhineland.[7]

All this activity confirmed to Flandin that a German move
against articles 42-43 was inevitable.[8] But there were at least
seven reasons why Paris did not regard it as imminent. First,

the Abyssinia affair looked like lasting a long time, which meant that Hitler was unlikely to be hurried by external events into precipitous action.[9] Furthermore, the Chancellor had given informal assurances to Poncet on 1 January about Germany's fidelity to Locarno.[10] These had been followed by Bülow's protestations on the 13th that 'il n'y a aucune urgence à soulever ce problème'.[11] And on 27 January, Neurath had officially declared to the British foreign secretary, Anthony Eden, in London that Berlin had no intention of tampering with the Rhine restrictions.[12] Even the press outbursts were regarded as being inspired by the traditional German desire to work up grievances in order to be able to lay before the world one day a dossier of excuses and justifications for her actions.[13] Flandin also came to accept the attacks on the Franco-Soviet pact as more perverse than menacing, since, as he told Eden in January and the Belgian premier, Paul van Zeeland, in February, Berlin already seemed resigned to its ratification.[14] As for the reports of illicit activity in the Rhineland, they had been coming into the Quai d'Orsay for years and turned out to be largely unprovable, inconclusive or insufficiently important to justify filing a complaint at Geneva.[15] Nor did anyone take the prognosticators too seriously — an attitude whose wisdom was amply proved by the peaceful passing of 30 January.[16]

Furthermore, there existed throughout pre-coup 1936 an influential body of expert opinion which believed that Germany would not take action against the zone in the near future.[17] The holders of this view included Eden, Zeeland, the Soviet foreign minister, Maxim Litvinov, and practically the entire diplomatic corps in Berlin.[18] Their reasons varied widely. For example, Zeeland argued that the Rhineland was already so well defended that Hitler would probably take no action at all against articles 42-43.[19] Poncet, on the other hand, felt confident that his sharp words to Bülow about 'des conséquences redoutables' of such action, coupled with other indicators of French and British determination, had worked their effect on Berlin, at least for 'l'avenir prochain'.[20] The ambassador also argued that Hitler would hesitate for some time before divesting himself of the benefits of Locarno.[21] Nor did Poncet believe that Berlin would be in any hurry to commit an act which would contribute to her political quarantine, while at the same time leaving Brussels and Paris as the sole recipients of the British and Italian guarantees.[22] In addition, he argued that the German general staff would be able to convince the Führer of the folly of risking his embryonic army when, in a few more months, it would be strong enough to march unchallenged into the Rhineland.[23]

Although a few observers predicted action as early as spring and others gave the zone another 10-12 months, the best and most widely held guess was that Hitler would not move until autumn 1936, when the new class of conscripts would increase the army's need for territorial expansion.[24] This argument coincided with the view that the Chancellor would do nothing to compromise the success of the Olympic games, scheduled for 1-16 August at Berlin. Not only was the Führer supposed to be anxious to preserve the proper atmosphere and to use the opportunity as a showcase for his achievements, but he and his economic advisers were also said to be counting on the games to bring into Germany a great deal of desperately needed foreign currency.[25]

These arguments did nothing to ease the feeling that a German move would eventually be forthcoming. They only served to show that there was still time to formulate policy.[26] It was in this context that Flandin asked Eden in London on 27 January what he thought Paris should do about the demilitarized zone.[27] But the foreign secretary refused to be drawn, arguing that it was for France to decide how much importance she attached to articles 42-43. Flandin, who was only in his third day as foreign minister, agreed and set out to produce a policy.

He could hardly have been impressed by the state of the military and diplomatic thinking which had gone into the topic. Although Laval had answered every German allegation against Locarno, little fresh thinking had occurred since 1932 when Herriot's ministry had decided that it would call upon the League of Nations if Germany remilitarized the Rhineland.[28] Since then, and especially in the past eighteen months, French policy towards articles 42-43 had been almost exclusively preventive. Instead of developing counter-measures and contingency plans, governments had concentrated on impressing Berlin with the idea that Paris and her partners would tolerate no nonsense over the demilitarized zone.[29]

The main effort followed Hitler's declaration of conscription and was manifested in two ways. First, the Flandin

ministry poured troops into France's north-eastern frontier
regions in an attempt to notify Berlin that her next treaty
breach would be met with an even more energetic response.[30]
The absence of any sign of determination, he believed, might
tempt Hitler to violate the demilitarized zone as early as April
or May 1935. Flandin was equally anxious that London and
Rome should demonstrate their concern to Berlin.[31] Such a
joint effort, he hoped, would not only ensure that Hitler fulfilled his Locarno obligations, but also stop all surreptitious
military activity within the Rhineland.[32] In spite of resistance
to the idea in London, the French succeeded in organizing a
conference at Stresa, chaired by Mussolini and attended by
the British prime minister, Ramsay MacDonald, to discuss
ways of resisting aggression.[33]

The result was a communiqué in which Rome and London
reaffirmed their Locarno obligations and a draft resolution,
approved by the League council on 17 April 1935, which
created a committee to examine measures to be applied
against any power which endangered peace 'by the unilateral
repudiation of its international obligations' (see Appendix for
the text of the resolution). France's success at Stresa was
followed a few weeks later by an equally fruitful effort to
ensure that London, Rome and Brussels joined Paris in rejecting Hitler's arguments of 21 May about the incompatibility of the Franco-Soviet and Locarno pacts.[34] Poncet's
rebukes of Bülow in January were in keeping with this preventive policy.[35] So was Flandin's declaration to the foreign
affairs committee of the Chamber of Deputies on 12 February
that the remilitarization of the Rhineland 'ne peut être admis
sous aucun prétexte'.[36]

In addition to keeping a close watch on Germany, Paris had
laboured to elicit from London some additional assurances in
defence of the demilitarized zone. Although British ministers
had suspected that Flandin and Laval would try this in
February 1935 and again at Stresa, the French did not act until
autumn, when the British naval build-up in the Mediterranean raised, in the government's eyes, the possibility of an
Anglo-Italian clash even before the League council could
declare Rome in violation of article 16 of the Covenant.[37] On
24 September, London asked if Paris could be relied upon in
such a contingency.[38] But, instead of returning an un-
equivocal affirmative, Laval replied that the contemplated

assistance must not only be reciprocal, but also go into effect only after joint investigation into the circumstances and after agreement had been reached on the measures which were justified.[39] The French also insisted that similar pre-cautionary measures and consultations would be in order between Locarno powers if it seemed likely that the Rhine pact's assistance obligations would be invoked.

These prerequisites stung the British foreign office into bitter, albeit private, recriminations against Paris for trifling with their security.[40] But that did not prevent the government from recognizing that Laval was seeking to trade on what London regarded as France's duty in order to extract from Britain what could become an Anglo-French military agree-ment against a German violation of the demilitarized zone.[41] However, the French did not possess sufficient leverage to succeed. The British foreign office simply delayed action on the offensive request for as long as possible and then notified Paris that events had rendered the original question un-necessary.[42]

This attempt to elicit added guarantees from London was only subsidiary to Laval's paramount aim, which was to save the Stresa front. Unfortunately for Paris, his efforts not only failed to rescue Rome, but also angered London, including such friends as permanent under-secretary Sir Robert Vansittart.[43] 'If there were a better hole,' he wrote, 'I would go to it.'[44] Doubts were expressed within the cabinet as to whether Laval could ever be trusted, while the chancellor of the ex-chequer, Neville Chamberlain, complained that the French had been 'as disloyal as they could'.[45] Baldwin even found it necessary to warn ministers against being drawn into a quarrel with Paris as well as Rome.[46]

Not only did the French fail in every attempt to commit Britain more closely to defending the demilitarized zone, but they actually lost ground as a result of their efforts. This occurred as a result of a brief exchange in September when Paris asked to what extent Britain could be relied upon in the event of an Anschluss.[47] Although the British reply did not mention Locarno, it was unmistakably clear that London's answer was formulated with an eye on a possible Rhineland violation.[48] Whilst affirming her fidelity to the Covenant, Britain declared that there were 'degrees of culpability' which, in turn, meant that 'procedure which might be appropriate as regards the positive act of unprovoked aggression would not necessarily be appropriate as regards the negative act of the failure to fulfil the terms of a treaty'.[49]

The French already realized from London's refusal to be drawn into discussions of the demilitarized zone that the British did not regard a German violation of articles 42-43 in the same light as an attack on France or Belgium. But they could hardly have taken any comfort from the fact that London's reply, which was published, was accepted as an accurate indication of her attitude towards the demilitarized zone and her unwillingness to be bound to any strict defence of the *status quo*.[50] This was especially true in Berlin, where Neurath described Britain's declaration as a 'noteworthy departure from the theory, presented at Stresa, that the League of Nations must also institute a fixed sanctions procedure for cases of mere non-fulfilment of international treaties'.[51]

In considering policy alternatives in February 1936, Flandin started from the assumption that any coup must be treated as a *casus foederis*.[52] This was agreed upon by the council of ministers on the 8th and publicly announced by the foreign minister, who declared on the 12th that the demilitarized zone 'ne peut être subordonnée à aucune condition'. The government, he added, was 'décidée à assumer la responsabilité des décisions qu'elle prendrait'.[53] The reasons for this decision were based on both politics and principle. No French government, it was felt, could simply do nothing in face of a *fait accompli* in the Rhineland. Nor, on the eve of elections, could any government, especially one of the left, risk the repercussions of a passive surrender to the hereditary foe at a moment when France was engaged in imposing sanctions against her new Italian friend.[54] Public opinion had too long been told that the demilitarized zone was essential to France's security; that it was the lifeline to France's eastern allies and Europe's guarantee against German aggression.

Although the cabinet's 8 February decision ruled out acquiescence, it did not eliminate the possibility of negotiations. This idea had been raised by Poncet in November 1935 and was thoroughly discussed again during February.[55] At least five proposals were mooted, but only two approached even the edge of reality. The other three came from the military. One of these involved offering to exchange official

French recognition of Germany's right to possess arms in excess of Versailles treaty restrictions in return for a fresh undertaking by Berlin to respect articles 42-43. Another would have allowed a limited troop presence in the Rhineland provided London agreed to station small contingents permanently on the French side of the frontier. A third suggested that Paris offer to agree now to the termination of fortifications restrictions in the Rhineland—but only in 1940 or 1942. By that time, the *classes creuses* contingents, weakened as a result of the 1914-18 war, would have passed through the army and France's eastern allies would have been able to complete their own defence preparations.

The remaining ideas came from Poncet and the Quai d'Orsay.[56] The ambassador's proposal was simply to trade a limited troop presence for a renewed German pledge to abstain from fortifications. The foreign ministry stopped short of remilitarization, but was prepared to consider permitting Berlin to establish anti-aircraft defences within the zone in exchange for fresh pledges otherwise to fulfil articles 42-43 'tout au moins pour quelques années'. In every case, it was agreed that talks could not conceivably occur before the May elections and that no initiative could come from Paris, since it would be regarded as a sign of weakness.[57]

Even so, and in spite of the fact that such a conciliatory move would have done a great deal to restore Anglo-French harmony, the Laval and Sarraut governments discarded the idea of negotiating over the Rhineland for five reasons. First was the feeling that to make any concessions to Germany would inevitably lead to additional revisionist demands.[58] Moreover, successive French governments, which had refused to 'legitimize' any of Germany's previous violations, saw some advantage in allowing Hitler to repudiate his treaty obligations.[59] Thirdly, if Hitler acted unilaterally against the demilitarized zone, which Berlin had voluntarily pledged to uphold, this could only convince world and, especially, British opinion of the lawless nature of the Nazi régime.[60] This distrust of the Third Reich also gave rise to the suspicion that Hitler would not keep any fresh promises any longer than it suited him.[61] Finally, France also feared that once the Rhine régime became negotiable, the British and possibly also the Italians would support the inevitable German demands for eradication of all restrictions. What Paris might get in return could well prove insufficient to satisfy either her security requirements or French public opinion.[62]

These were objections of long standing. But in the midst of the Abyssinian imbroglio, two other factors played even more decisive rôles. First was the belief that negotiations over the demilitarized zone would re-open the whole Locarno question.[63] This, Paris feared, could have disastrous results in view of Rome's estrangement and her hints, not to say threats, to quit Locarno if sanctions were increased or even maintained.[64] Such a development would have been politically crippling for any French government after all the efforts expended during the autumn of 1935 to bring Mussolini back to the Stresa front against Germany. It made no sense to submit the Rhine pact to such a risk when there was good reason to believe that once the Duce had achieved his aims in Abyssinia, he would rejoin the Stresa front, if only to protect his Austrian interests and reassert his influence in south-eastern Europe.[65]

Worse still, there was reason in 1935-6 to think that if Rome independently repudiated the Locarno treaty, Britain might insist that her obligations be renegotiated. Nor was it considered inconceivable that London, especially after the Hoare-Laval affair, might respond to the pressure of public opinion and pull out altogether.[66] On the other hand, if Germany acted unilaterally against the Rhine statutes, Britain's honour would come into full play, making it morally impossible for her to shirk her responsibilities. Moreover, and this was a critical point, especially in French military thinking, Germany could not repudiate articles 42-43 without also terminating her Locarno membership. If Paris managed such a crisis properly, one positive outcome, irrespective of any punitive action against Hitler, would be a contraction and not the collapse of the Rhine pact.[67] Thus, the effect of any German coup in the demilitarized zone could lead to nothing less than an Anglo-Franco-Belgian alliance. Such an arrangement, in the view of France's military leaders, would constitute an eminently advantageous trade for the no-man's-land in Germany's western provinces.[68]

Paris would have found this exchange infinitely preferable to a negotiated settlement which would probably only have removed all reference to articles 42-43 from Locarno. This solution, which the British were known to favour, would have given Germany full military sovereignty while still allowing

her to retain the Anglo-Italian guarantee.[69] It would also have
enabled her to continue effectively to thwart all Anglo-French
military consultations on the grounds that they contravened
'the spirit of Locarno'. To be rid of that particular millstone
would be a relief to France's security planners, whose efforts
to organize an effective front against German aggression had
been consistently hampered by Britain's susceptibility to
Berlin's assertions that the essence of the Rhine pact was its
mutuality and equilibrium.[70]

Two axioms dominated all French pre-coup Rhineland
thinking. First was the desire to avoid any action which made
France alone appear to be an aggressor. This appears time and
again in both Quai d'Orsay and military records.[71] The
second was the desire to coordinate her policies and actions
with Britain.[72] Not since the Ruhr had Paris violated her first
rule. The same was not altogether true of her determination to
foster *entente* relations, but Flandin was personally dedicated
to repairing the damage done by Laval; hence his promise on
27 January always to endeavour to consult Eden before taking
any action.[73]

Within this framework, Flandin's task was to identify all
practical means of resisting, to determine when and under
what circumstances to apply them and then to see what could
be done to prevent a *fait accompli*.[74] This he hoped to achieve
by settling beforehand with Britain on a course of action, complete with proposals for possible military reprisals, and then
apprising Berlin jointly of the consequences of any violation
of the Rhine statutes. If all worked well, the effect of this
'avertissement' might prolong the zone's life for several years,
thus rendering unnecessary any resort to punitive measures.[75]
Meanwhile, every effort was made in Paris to emphasize
Flandin's 12 February declaration of French determination to
preserve articles 42-43 and, especially, Eden's statement to the
Commons on the same day that Great Britain intended to fulfil all her Locarno obligations.[76]

In examining ways of resisting a coup, almost no thought
was given to the possibility that Hitler might commit the sort
of massive violation which would justify immediate military
retaliation. Germany was not regarded as powerful enough or
foolish enough to commit such a blatant act when less dangerous methods were available.[77] Although some consideration
was given to piecemeal remilitarization, the main thrust of

Flandin's efforts was towards determining French reaction to a clear-cut, but non-aggressive reoccupation, such as actually did occur.[78]

Against this sort of action, Paris could reply politically, economically or militarily at any of three moments.[79] She could ignore the Locarno pact and march into all or part of the Rhineland on the grounds that this was permitted by article 44 of the Versailles treaty, which stated that any violation of articles 42-43 was to be regarded as 'a hostile act . . . calculated to disturb the peace of the world'. Otherwise, she could act after a League finding in France's favour. Paris could then either impose military or economic sanctions of her own choosing against Berlin and call upon her Locarno guarantors for assistance, or forgo her right to determine the punishment independently and submit the question to her Rhine pact partners for a joint decision.

Independent and immediate action in response to a non-flagrant German violation was dismissed by most ministers as too dangerous.[80] Since there would probably be no solid justification for military measures, France risked being branded as an aggressor.[81] The impact of any such riposte on Britain might also be disastrous.[82] For these reasons, the council of ministers decided, apparently as early as 29 January 1936, to reaffirm the decision taken in 1932 by the government of Edouard Herriot to act only after securing a 'constatation' of the treaty violation from Geneva.[83]

The second alternative was also flawed by the likelihood that Paris would be constraining London into forceful action against the will of her people.[84] The stress which even this would place on the *entente* might be too great, especially since, according to Flandin's estimate, the Baldwin cabinet was still so badly shaken by Hoare's 'lâchage' that it did not dare adopt any policy 'sans s'être assuré, au préalable, de l'appui de l'opinion publique'.[85] Nor did the Quai d'Orsay believe at this time that the British people were prepared to prevent their government from 'beating a retreat' in the face of German action against Locarno.[86] The Belgians also shared these views.[87]

The third possibility, on the other hand, provided League cover and guaranteed willing partners. But it also carried the risk that any agreed reaction against Germany would be too feeble to make the desired impression on Berlin.[88] And, as far as the Quai d'Orsay was concerned, this was the main reason for resisting.[89] They recognized the futility of trying to over-throw Hitler or defeat Germany — both were too strong — but they felt that it was imperative that the Chancellor should not be allowed to get away with any Rhine coup. The effect of such a success, they feared, would demoralize a dozen European states who depended upon London and Paris for their security.[90] Moreover, after all her military and political activity following the conscription declaration in March 1935, France could not comfortably consider doing any less in reply to a direct challenge in the Rhineland.

All these possibilities involved action against Germany directly. Another alternative — and one which was visible on the fringe of pre-coup planning — was to accept the fact that Britain would oppose punitive action, but to use the leverage provided in Locarno to obtain from London the tripartite military alliance which was implicit in a Rhine pact without Germany and Italy. This aim was paramount among the French general staff.[91] But, whereas the Quai d'Orsay was also resolute against allowing Locarno to collapse as a result of any action by Hitler or Mussolini, it was equally convinced that Paris could not permit a German treaty breach to pass un-challenged.[92]

In this respect, however, Flandin's efforts to prepare puni-tive measures against Germany were seriously hampered by the military's refusal to contemplate offensive action.[93] Al-though he had cabinet authorization to prepare means of effecting military reprisals, the foreign minister's request for specific counter-measures were brushed aside by the army high command.[94] On each occasion war minister Louis Maurin and the general staff restricted their replies to detailing defensive precautions aimed solely at safeguarding France from attack.[95] They only involved manning the Maginot fortifications and moving active field forces to the proximity of the frontier. But Maurin cautioned on 12 February that even these measures should be minimized to deprive Berlin of any possible pretext for invading France.[96]

Flandin was no more successful when he pressed the war minister to furnish specific measures which could be employ-ed 'non seulement de répondre à une initiative éventuelle de l'Allemagne, mais, si possible, de décourager le Reich de s'engager dans cette entreprise'.[97] In reply, Maurin simply outlined the four stages of pre-mobilization preparedness: *alerte, alerte renforcée, sûreté* and, finally, *couverture*, which involved the recall of 600,000 *disponibles* and reservists and would put a million men *sur pied*.[98] But, instead of detailing what could be done with these forces at each stage, he merely observed that these dispositions would enable Paris to move to the offensive with her Locarno allies 'if this measure came to be envisaged as a consequence of political negotiations'.[99]

The war minister also expressed the view on 17 February that it would be 'contrary to the French interest to use our right to occupy the demilitarized zone'. Paris risked appearing as the aggressor, Maurin warned, and she risked finding herself alone against Germany. Any such operation, he added, should not be considered without the full accord of the British government.[100] Two days later, Maurice Gamelin, the chief of army general staff, underlined these points to his colleagues, saying 'qu'il n'y a pas lieu d'envisager que la France seule pourrait occuper la zone démilitarisée'.[101]

Maurin's response provoked another irritable note from the Quai d'Orsay on 24 February, complaining that the war ministry had evaded the issue and reiterating the need for some 'positive ripostes' which France could take 'to intimidate the adversary or cause him to recoil'.[102] Flandin, who described the quality of military response as 'impromptu and superficial', was in the end obliged to get the council of ministers to direct the army general staff on 27 February to produce plans and prepare for some rapid, but limited, moves into the frontier regions of Germany.[103] But, contrary to Gamelin's subsequent assertions, the only plans for immediate action at hand on 7 March were for the defence of France and mainly involved manning the Maginot fortifications.[104]

The absence of any mini-max contingency plans was primarily the result of two inter-related factors. First, the army had written off the demilitarized zone as a sphere of military operations as early as 1930, when the final occupation forces evacuated the Rhineland.[105] From then on, and perhaps even earlier, the high command had concentrated on organizing a fighting force capable of defending France—but nothing else. This explains why a plan submitted by General Vaulgrenant in 1931 for an immediate and localized riposte in the Rhineland had been shunted aside by Gamelin and his staff as a personal initiative.[106] The only existing offensive idea the army had was to occupy part of Belgium, and this was primarily aimed at preventing the enemy from penetrating France's unfortified northern frontier.[107]

Otherwise, the concept was to mobilize the nation behind the Maginot line and await the attack. As chief of army general staff, Gamelin did not intend to allow the enemy to select the battle site. If Hitler wanted to conquer France, he would have to fight on French terms.[108] This refusal on the army high command's part to think offensively, in spite of France's many assistance obligations, was summarized by war minister Maurin in March 1935, when he asked the Chamber of Deputies how anyone could believe that France should again think of an offensive after having spent milliards fortifying her frontiers. 'Serions-nous assez fous aller, en avant de cette barrière', he added, 'à je ne sais quelle aventure?'[109]

This attitude only partly explained why the French military establishment proved so evasive. Gamelin was also convinced that the moment German troops entered the demilitarized zone, Hitler would have 'passait le Rubicon à ses risques et périls'.[110] And, although the army chief still talked about the strategic importance of the demilitarized zone, he was not basically opposed to its disappearance, partly because it no longer possessed any significant defensive value to French military leaders, but primarily because its demise would remove from the army a heavy obligation, namely, to respond to any German aggression—even because of a Soviet-provoked incident—by marching into the Rhineland.[111] Once German military sovereignty were reestablished, Paris could hardly be expected to act differently from any other power. This doubtless explains why the French high command did little to counteract the post-coup impression that the west German frontier had been effectively sealed on 7 March, even though it was still 2½-3 years before permanent fortifications were erected in any strength.

As a result, Gamelin and Maurin urged the government to concentrate its efforts in the face of any *fait accompli* entirely in the political sphere.[112] It was here, they insisted, that the greatest good could be achieved, especially if Paris could extract from London a mutual assistance pact, complete with military accords.[113] The only other constructive idea they advanced was that the Sarraut ministry should be prepared to capitalize on public anxieties created by any coup to secure additional credits for France's rearmament effort.[114] But, in spite of the army's opposition to military retaliation, the general staff was, as Flandin observed, nothing if not obedient. There was, therefore, every reason to expect that it would in due course produce operations which would enable France to 'résister par les armes', if she so chose.[115]

Meanwhile, the foreign minister was in no position to approach the British government about issuing a joint warning to Berlin.[116] Nor did Flandin intend to inform Germany without at least London's support. The reason may be entirely because he was still uncertain about France's own position, but there is equal ground to believe that Flandin was influenced by the argument that a *démarche* made without London and, obviously, Rome, would be taken by Hitler as an indicator, not of French determination, but of Anglo-Italian disinterest. This was one reason why Paris had not pressed the idea of explicitly warning Berlin about the demilitarized zone in the spring of 1935 when London refused to be drawn in.[117] Conceivably, such a threat, delivered only by Paris and possibly Brussels, might now encourage the Chancellor to attempt an early repudiation of articles 42-43, or even to demand the very kind of negotiations for abolition of the zone which the French government wished to avoid, at least until after the elections.[118]

There is also ample evidence to show that the Quai d'Orsay still felt confident that Hitler would make no early move against the demilitarized zone unless provoked—or unless Mussolini provided an opportunity by repudiating his Locarno obligations. Barring that, the foreign ministry foresaw no immediate danger.[119] Nor was the government disturbed by Gamelin's warning at the end of February that Berlin would strike against articles 42-43 if the Franco-Soviet pact were ratified.[120] His opposition to the Russian agreement was too well known for such statements to be taken seriously, especially when viewed against all the indicators from British, Belgian and American sources, as well as Poncet, that the Chancellor was planning to reply to ratification by lodging a stern diplomatic protest which would keep the question open until he was prepared to act against the Rhine régime.[121]

These signs were encouraging to Flandin, not only because they suggested that his military advisers still had time to prepare, but also because his chances of persuading Britain

to support a 'politique de coercition' over the Rhineland
increased fractionally with every passing day. As matters
stood, however, the Baldwin government was still regarded as
too shaken from the criticism it received from the Hoare-
Laval affair during December to take any definitive stand,
preferring instead to adapt its policies 'aux nécessités du
moment'.[122] In fact, Flandin's main concern at this moment
vis-à-vis London was apparently that Berlin should not learn
the extent of Britain's 'mollesse'.[123] But there was little he
could do other than to ensure that allusions to British determination to uphold Locarno appeared regularly in Le Temps
during the last half of February.[124]

These two problems — the military's reticence and Britain's
weakness — stood as monumental obstacles in the path of
resistance. They did not, however, alter the Quai d'Orsay's
determination, voiced publicly by Flandin on 12 February
and again on the 22nd in a despatch to seven French missions,
that Paris 'n'acceptera pas qu'il soit porté atteinte par une
répudiation unilatérale aux stipulations des traités'.[125] At the
same time, even the strongest partisans of the preservation of
the Rhine régime could not have avoided the conclusion that
the chances of success were not bright.

Thus, on 27 February, the council of ministers adopted a
policy which encompassed the foreign minister's hopes as
well as his fears and suspicions.[126] In response to any 'flagrant
and incontestable' violation of article 42 or 43, the French
government would take no isolated action. Instead, she would
act only in agreement with her Locarno allies, presumably
after a League 'finding' in their favour. This suggested that
Paris might allow herself to be dissuaded by London. On the
other hand, the council had by no means indicated that France
would not furnish the leadership and employ whatever leverage might be required to persuade or pressure the British and
Belgians into following her lead in imposing sanctions against
Berlin.

This possibility was underlined by the council's declaration that Paris reserved the right to take all preparatory
measures, including military, 'en vue de l'action collective'
which might be decided upon by the League council and the
Locarno guarantors.[127] And, although mobilization was orally
ruled out as being too immediately aggressive in nature, the
government's decision kept alive the possibility of military

action, say, with the *armée de couverture*, which was precisely
what Gamelin had been asked to prepare for by the council of
ministers on the 27th.

It was a stance which looked firm, but which provided sufficient leeway to prevent Paris from later having to fight alone
or to take full blame if her friends and allies refused to accept
their responsibilities. It was certainly not a decision not to
act.[128] And, although based on several weeks' consideration of
the domestic and diplomatic possibilities, there was nothing
about this procedure which could not be reversed or ignored
whenever Hitler entered the Rhineland, especially if the
French people insisted that the challenge be accepted.

These decisions, which were communicated the same day
to the Belgians, were taken in Brussels as a sign of French
determination.[129] At the same time. Flandin impressed the
Belgian ambassador, Count Kerchove de Denterghem, as
being not particularly concerned by the current crop of
rumours which 'n'ajoutaient rien de neuf à ce qu'il savait déjà
ou à ce qui existait en Rhénanie depuis 1931'.[130] The absence
of immediate French anxieties over the demilitarized zone
was also clear from the fact that Flandin delayed telling the
British of the ministers' conclusions until he could see Eden
personally in Geneva.[131] This conversation might have
occurred only on 9 March had it not been for Britain's insistence that the committee of eighteen's scheduled meeting to
discuss Abyssinia should be advanced by one week.[132]

The reason for this became clear on 2 March when Eden
surprised Flandin by declaring Britain's determination to
support the imposition of an oil embargo against Rome.[133]
This decision came in the face of a report on 12 February by
the committee of experts that an embargo universally applied
could not be effective inside 3-3½ months, while one
supported only by League members would merely render
Italian petroleum purchases more difficult.[134] As a result of
the experts' pessimistic analysis, Paris and most of Europe
had written off petroleum sanctions, particularly after the
decisive defeat of Emperor Haile Selassie's forces in the
Tembien on 15-16 February had been followed within a fortnight by the destruction of four Abyssinian armies at Amba
Alaji.[135] This success by Marshal Pietro Badoglio had opened
the northern route to Addis Ababa and raised Mussolini's
hopes of total victory 'within six weeks'.[136]

It was precisely this danger of a débâcle which had caused Eden to reverse his position and support the oil embargo.[137] As long as it had looked as though Mussolini would be forced to the conference table, either by mud and dust or by the strain on Italy's economic, financial and spiritual resources, the foreign secretary had seen little sense in further exacerbating relations with Rome by extending sanctions.[138] But Eden did not see how the League council could now sit idly by while Abyssinian forces were being routed.[139] The foreign secretary also argued that tougher measures would help to restore the prestige of Geneva, as well as that of the Baldwin government, both in the United States and, especially, with the British people.[140] As a result, the cabinet had decided on 26 February to support, but not champion, an oil embargo. French opposition at Geneva, however, was to thrust Eden to the forefront of the sanctionist movement.

The news of Britain's determination not only caught Paris by surprise, but irritated and embarrassed Flandin, who had the day before sent assurances to Rome that France would pursue a policy of moderation at Geneva.[141] Now Eden had put Paris in an acute dilemma at a moment when Mussolini had renewed or intensified his warnings to France of the disastrous consequences which might accompany the extension of sanctions. Since January, the Duce or his agents had been warning Paris that such action might oblige Rome to disengage herself from the Stresa front and nullify the Gamelin-Badoglio military arrangements of June 1935.[142] Mussolini had threatened, according to Flandin, to refuse to subscribe to any limitation agreements reached at the London naval conference and to quit the League if an oil embargo were imposed.[143] The French foreign minister also reported that Rome had alluded to the spectre of Locarno without Italy, as well as a *rapprochement* with Berlin—a possibility described by Gamelin as 'l'hypothèse la plus défavorable'.[144]

As a result of this development, Flandin produced on 3 March an *aide-mémoire* asking the British government for an undertaking that London would fulfil her Locarno commitments alone, if Rome walked out.[145] The note also requested fresh assurances of British support in maintaining the Rhine régime. The French foreign minister added orally that Paris could not agree to an oil embargo against Italy until France had received satisfactory replies from London on both points.[146]

It may be that Flandin, whom Eden described as having argued the Italian case with 'blatant confidence', was primarily interested in getting London to relax her attitude toward sanctions.[147] If so, he failed. Nor was success in this sphere likely once Britain had made her position public. Flandin may also have been looking for an excuse for not supporting the oil embargo or at least for a consolation prize with which to appease domestic critics of sanctions. It was, however, more probable, as Eden suggested, that Flandin simply recognized an opportunity to wring from the British that specific commitment to uphold the demilitarized zone which London had studiously avoided making for nearly a decade.[148]

Reaffirmation of British fidelity to Locarno without Italy presented Britain with the lesser of two major problems. Even though the treaty promised assistance collectively and severally, ministers were disturbed by the prospect of Britain's becoming the pact's sole buttress where two had stood since 1925.[149] But, as ministers recognized, Britain could hardly withdraw without the other remaining powers' acquiescence, especially since the original Locarno treaty had been conceived as a four-power pact; Italian cooperation had only been introduced at the last moment. Instead, they believed that the whole situation would have to be reconsidered and presumably renegotiated if Mussolini abandoned his obligations. Although events overtook a final decision, it appears from the cabinet minutes that Britain would not willingly have accepted that she should remain as the pact's only guarantor. Nor, to judge by the same and subsequent discussions, would London have tolerated continued membership in the Rhine pact without Germany after 7 March if Paris had not pressured London by threat of war to remain committed to Belgium and France.[150]

The request for a fresh pledge to uphold the demilitarized zone presented Britain with a more serious, though not necessarily more immediate, problem. The origins of the difficulty went back to 1934, when His Majesty's Government began considering ways in which it could persuade Paris to accept an arrangement that would permit Germany to possess an army of 300,000. In searching for contributions it could make to supplement French security, and thereby win her cooperation, the cabinet had been asked, *inter alia,* to consider a formal declaration that the government regarded the demilitarized zone as 'a vital British interest'.[151] But the MacDonald cabinet came to precisely the opposite conclusion, namely, that whereas London was willing to preserve Belgian and French security—and to keep any aggressor away from the Channel—she did not consider the Rhineland régime as a vital British interest.[152]

This decision of 14 January 1935 only formalized sentiments which were being expressed within the foreign office some ten months earlier and which had found public expression in Baldwin's declaration that Britain's frontier was on the Rhine—by which he meant that part of the river which separated France and Germany.[153] The position regarding articles 42-43 was summarized a few weeks later by Ralph Wigram, head of the central department of the foreign office. 'Nothing is less certain', he wrote, 'than that we would be ready to resist . . . an open violation of the zone.'[154]

From January 1935 through pre-coup 1936 and beyond, British policy towards the Rhineland was conducted on the basis of these conclusions. This meant that London steadfastly resisted all French efforts to get her to make pledges or other statements on the zone's behalf. The British government would only reaffirm its fidelity to Locarno generally. This was the attitude with which Britain had approached consultations with Flandin and Laval in London during February and again at Stresa.[155] On both occasions, the cabinet and foreign office fully expected to be pressed for some specific guarantees of articles 42-43. But, to their surprise and relief, the matter was not raised in London, and at Stresa the French settled for a joint Anglo-Italian statement of loyalty to the Rhine pact.[156] Eden went no further in a reply to a Commons question in February 1936.[157] And in every other instance, such as during the Mediterranean crisis and again just before Laval's resignation, the British refused to give Paris even private assurances about articles 42-43.[158]

During these same fourteen pre-coup months, Britain practised a double policy toward Berlin. On the one hand, the government avoided anything resembling a direct warning to Germany to respect the demilitarized zone. Not that this was new; in March 1934, the foreign office had recommended that Hitler be told of the 'most serious view' that Britain would take towards any violation of the Rhine statutes.[159] But the proposal was never acted upon, apparently a victim of the diplomatic turmoil created by the French rejection on 17 April of a scheme to permit limited German rearmament.[160] A year later, Vansittart and Wigram proposed again that Simon, during his forthcoming Berlin visit, should give Hitler 'a little timely truth' about the 'really gratuitous' effect on Anglo-German relations of any open breach of articles 42-43.[161] 'We may not be going to *do* anything about it,' Vansittart wrote, 'but surely we cannot contemplate *saying* nothing about it either.'[162] Such silence, Wigram argued, 'will almost mean that we are encouraging Germany to regard part of the Locarno treaty as a dead letter'.[163]

But the cabinet rejected this recommendation as 'most unwise' for two reasons.[164] By 1935, Hitler's strength and potential for mischief-making were daily becoming more apparent.[165] In these circumstances, the government did not wish to get itself in a position of one day having to decide whether to carry out any threats or climb down in face of a *fait accompli*— especially since the cabinet had just written off the Rhineland as a vital interest.[166] But probably more important in March 1935 was London's desire to open a dialogue with Berlin which, it was hoped, would lead to an eventual *détente* in western Europe.[167] The Chancellor, it was felt, would be more cooperative if his relations with London were cordial and flourishing.[168] Besides, Hitler had pledged himself publicly only a year earlier to fulfil the spirit and letter of Locarno. To send two British ministers to Berlin in order to warn him to keep his word was hardly conducive to friendly relations.

At the same time, however, the foreign office and probably most cabinet members firmly believed that the interests of peace and security were better served by the presence, rather than the absence, of the Rhine restrictions.[169] Their existence reduced the chances of German expansion in any direction, whereas a remilitarized and fortified Rhineland would deprive Europe of its best deterrent to pan-Germanism. In terms of foreign policy, this meant that the British, while unwilling to make any specific commitment or give any warnings about the zone, were equally anxious to keep Hitler thinking that articles 42-43 were regarded by London as inviolable and that she expected all five Locarno powers 'scrupulously to carry out their obligations'.[170]

That was one reason why the British never bothered to correct the impression created in some German circles that Baldwin's frontier on the Rhine included the demilitarized zone. It also explains why, if the Rhineland issue had been raised by Hitler during the Simon-Eden visit, British ministers were prepared to declare that Britain considered the question to be 'not a matter for discussion'.[171] The same desire to foster this impression among Germans was behind British participation in the Stresa declaration. Admittedly, His Majesty's Government's declaration in the autumn about 'degrees of culpability' had eroded some of its efforts, but this 'clarification' was made necessary by the enthusiastic response to Sir Samuel Hoare's speech at Geneva on 11 September in which the foreign secretary had sought to emphasize Britain's willingness to fulfil her League commitments, but which had been taken as a ringing endorsement of the collective security system and, along with it, the *status quo*.[172] That was why Hoare had subsequently also emphasized that 'elasticity is a part of security'.[173]

This phrase was indicative of growing British interest by this time in trying to produce a general settlement with Paris and Berlin which would secure peace in Europe.[174] Not everyone, especially in the foreign office, believed it was a good idea or that it would succeed.[175] Laurence Collier, head of the northern department, adamantly opposed any agreement with Berlin. Vansittart, while willing to try, was at the same time convinced that Germany was already seeking, not the removal of grievances, but 'the satisfaction of ambitions'.[176] Others were more optimistic about the chances of achieving a reasonable agreement. Eden and most of his cabinet colleagues believed they could achieve at least a *modus vivendi*, and possibly something more permanent. To them it seemed worth trying, if only because the policy alternatives were either continued drift or encirclement, which carried what was regarded as a high risk of early explosion. The prospects for maintaining peace, it was argued, were greater if the western powers could come to honourable terms with Berlin as equals.

It was further felt, especially by Eden and Vansittart, that such an effort was essential if Britain were ever going to win the full support of public opinion for her rearmament policy.[177] So long as the opposition could argue that Baldwin

was rearming without first having tried to negotiate a political
settlement, the government felt vulnerable. On the other
hand, a genuine attempt to come 'by friendly arrangement' to
fair terms with Berlin would finally clear the air. Either
Hitler would subscribe to a reasonable plan, thereby rendering massive military expenditures unnecessary, or he would
refuse, in which case the British people would have a better
view of the danger posed by the man who had only recently
warned the world that there was nothing pleasant about being
compelled 'to wander unarmed through such a dragon's
den'.[178] Even if Hitler agreed, but later repudiated his signature, it was argued, Britain would have gained valuable time
for her rearmament efforts, which in 1936 were judged to be a
full three years from bearing fruit.[179]

The general settlement was aimed at deflecting Germany,
either into south-eastern Europe or overseas.[180] Some
members of the foreign office were willing to hand over some
or all of Germany's former colonies if that would suffice to
bring Hitler into the ranks of the satisfied powers. Vansittart,
in particular, preferred this to condoning what he described
as 'political cannibalism' in Europe.[181] On balance, however,
ministers and officials were more reluctant to part with any
British possession than to try to channel German energies east
or south-east.[182] It was anticipated that His Majesty's Government would recognize the Balkans or Danubian countries as a
German sphere of influence. Britain would even reduce her
economic connexions in that region, provided Germany
undertook to effect her penetration peacefully and in accordance with League principles.[183]

This idea harmonized with the views of men like Simon,
who wanted, as early as the Stresa conference, to ensure that
any German 'breakout' went eastwards or south.[184] Phipps
had graphically expressed the idea in April 1935 when he
stressed the necessity of carefully regulating the heights of the
various fences in order to make certain that the German beast
would not be tempted first to jump the Locarno obstruction.[185]
To achieve this, the foreign office initially planned to demand
as part of any settlement a fresh German undertaking to respect the demilitarized zone.[186] This would also have helped
ensure that Berlin acted honourably towards the countries in
eastern and south-eastern Europe. As far as Wigram and a few
others were concerned, the preservation of the Rhine régime

was perhaps the strongest argument 'for getting on terms with Germany with as little delay as possible'.[187]

But only a few weeks after arguing for its continued existence, the head of the central department made a volte-face, urging instead that the demilitarized zone should be transferred into the column of concessions which could be made in exchange for a western air pact and other German commitments, including her return to the League of Nations.[188] This reversal was inspired by a combination of factors which led Wigram to conclude that the demilitarized zone would be 'stolen' unless it were put up for 'sale' at a reasonable price.[189]

This decision was not based so much on what Hitler had been saying, though his 21 May promise of only conditional adherence to Locarno was regarded as ominous.[190] Nor did Britain possess any evidence of activity within the zone which pointed towards early remilitarization.[191] But by autumn of 1935 it had become clear, not only that German action against articles 42-43 was the obvious next move, but also that the Abyssinian imbroglio and the Wehrmacht's progress had brought much closer to hand the fulfilment of Phipps's warning of February 1935 that Hitler would not hesitate to remilitarize the Rhineland the day he felt strong enough to do so.[192]

At the same time, the foreign office was coming to the conclusion, as Eden later wrote, that the French would not attack Germany 'merely in order to maintain the demilitarization of the Rhineland'.[193] This feeling had been reinforced during the Abyssinian crisis by Flandin, who was regarded as having a better understanding of 'le français moyen' than any other French politician.[194] He twice told the British embassy that his countrymen would fight for their homelands, for Belgium and 'probably' also for Britain. But otherwise they wanted 'peace at any price' and would 'never fight outside France', even to fulfil their League obligations.[195]

It was equally believed, as early as July 1935, that no French government would do more than make paper protests in response to the remilitarization of the Rhineland.[196] Even Vansittart, who had some reservations about whether Paris would do nothing in the face of a direct German threat, had pronounced France in the autumn of 1935 'too rotten to honour her bond.'[197] It was also accepted in Whitehall that Paris lacked the military and moral strength to venture into the 'German hornets' nest' without British support.[198] These assessments were fully endorsed by the foreign secretary and subsequently adopted by the cabinet on 9 March 1936.[199]

At the same time, however, the foreign office suspected that the French might seek 'to excuse themselves for not fighting on the ground that we would not join them.'[200] It also seemed in character that Paris might attempt to capitalize on any Rhineland crisis solely to wring additional security guarantees from London.[201] Nor could the possibility be entirely ruled out that the Sarraut ministry might react precipitously to a coup, perhaps even by mobilizing, as Flandin had asserted at Stresa.[202] If that occurred, Paris would almost certainly be compelled to follow through, thereby binding Britain morally, if not also legally, to support punitive measures against Berlin. This possibility, coupled with the increasing likelihood of a *fait accompli*, prompted Eden to advise the cabinet formally on 14 February against adopting any attitude which might oblige the government to 'either have to fight for the zone or abandon it in the face of a German reoccupation.'[203]

Since Britain was in no position to resist an open violation of articles 42-43 and was equally unwilling to accept the blame for inaction, the foreign office felt that the most promising solution was to eliminate the Rhineland problem 'in due season' within the framework of the general settlement.[204] Of all the proposed concessions put forward in connexion with this 'coming to terms', the abolition of the demilitarized zone was the most widely endorsed.[205] But there was equally no groundswell in favour of treating it as a special case. The reasons were fourfold.

First, the demilitarized zone was not Britain's to give away; nor was it considered likely that Paris would agree to the idea, for reasons already mentioned.[206] On the other hand, the foreign office felt that the chances of striking a bargain would be improved after the May elections, especially if the zone's abolition were accompanied by proposals providing greater protection for France's eastern allies, thus enabling Paris to justify acquiescence as being in the interests of European security. Until then, however, London did not feel she could initiate negotiations over the demilitarized zone, at least not without compromising her relations with Belgium and France. Nor would this be any different so long as Paris and Brussels insisted that articles 42-43 were essential to their national security.

Finally, British foreign policy advisers regarded the Rhine statutes as their best bargaining counter.[207] If articles 42-43 were abolished in a separate arrangement, London would have little of value to offer Berlin in any general settlement. Germany might not be satisfied with a colony or even two.[208] Britain's economic activities in south-eastern Europe were minimal, so renunciation of her most-favoured-nation status would have little impact in an area where peaceful German penetration was already well advanced.[209]

But none of these reasons would have prevented Britain from taking action over articles 42-43 if the government had thought that the Rhine régime was in immediate danger of being repudiated. Most members of the foreign office and cabinet agreed with Eden, Flandin and Zeeland, as well as their diplomats in Berlin, that the zone's demise was inevitable, but not imminent.[210] The Rhineland, Vansittart wrote, was 'a nettle which we should be wise to grasp before it stings us'.[211] But the permanent under-secretary saw no cause for urgency and even less reason to hurry into negotiations. He was willing to wait as long as necessary to prepare thoroughly and even longer if possible, partly because Britain's rearmament efforts would then be more perceptible, but primarily because he believed that any premature breakdown would heighten tensions, reduce alternatives and polarize attitudes — all of which could result in war before London had remedied even the worst of her arms deficiencies.[212]

Wigram, on the other hand, had come by mid-January to the conclusion that the Rhine régime was 'one of the questions of the hour' and would probably not survive until the end of the Abyssinian crisis, which was when Eden envisaged opening general negotiations with Berlin and Paris.[213] Wigram's anxiety dated back to 13 December 1935 when Hitler had expressed what Phipps described as a 'cynical note of regret' at having failed to reoccupy the zone on 16 March in connexion with his conscription declaration.[214] As a result of the Chancellor's 'patronizing' attitude, itself a reflection of Germany's improved military position, Phipps had warned London that the Rhineland would be remilitarized 'whenever a favourable opportunity presents itself'.[215] Subsequent German press attacks on the Anglo-French staff talks, encirclement and the Franco-Soviet pact all pointed, in Wigram's opinion, to the possibility that Hitler was preparing to take 'some foolish initiative' against the demilitarized zone.[216]

The head of the central department feared that Berlin might soon act violently and that Paris herself might 'go off the deep end' unless London dispensed 'a great deal of calming medicine' in both directions.[217] He spurred Vansittart into seeking, as a matter of urgency, assessments from British chiefs of staff as to the zone's strategic value.[218] These showed that the disappearance of articles 42-43 could have far-reaching political repercussions in eastern Europe and Danubia, but that the zone was dispensable as far as British security was concerned.[219] In addition, Wigram compiled German references to, and Phipps's warnings about, the demilitarized zone in order to demonstrate just how uncertain was the future of the Rhineland régime.[220] He and assistant under-secretary of state Orme Sargent also circulated a collection of documents and despatches under the title 'The German Danger', both to underline the Rhineland's vulnerability and to spotlight Phipps's warning of 13 November 1935 that the Abyssinian imbroglio was 'mere child's play' compared with the storm brewing in Germany.[221]

Wigram urged that the demilitarized zone should immediately be traded for an air pact, whose one great merit would be the absence of any reference to articles 42-43.[222] This, he added, would allow Britain to 'escape' a grave crisis.[223] He even sought to forestall any precipitous German action by hinting to ambassador Leopold von Hoesch on 4 February and confiding to counsellor Prince Otto von Bismarck on the 12th that Britain was preparing a 'working agreement' which would include Berlin, Paris and London, but which would omit certain 'things' contained in Locarno.[224] But Wigram did not succeed in convincing his colleagues or cabinet ministers of the early threat to articles 42-43.

The major reason for this failure was summarized by Phipps, who declared in December that Berlin would probably not raise the Rhine question 'so long as friendship with the United Kingdom remains their ideal'.[225] Thus, according to the ambassador and his supporters, Hitler would not act against the demilitarized zone until he had made one final effort to 'square' Britain.[226] Not only did this seem plausible in view of Hitler's many pro-British utterances, but it also proved a highly seductive thesis and one which appeared in foreign office minutes as late as 4 March 1936, when the southern department dismissed as 'inconceivable' the suggestion that Berlin would 'throw away' any chance of alliance with Britain by making a fresh *fait accompli*.[227]

British confidence was in many respects sustained by the feeling that Hitler would be reluctant to commit any act which might alter the conciliatory attitude which London had adopted towards Germany during the preceding twelve months.[228] British ministers had visited Berlin only a fortnight after the Chancellor had repudiated part V of the Versailles treaty. And, although British ministers had joined in censuring Hitler at Stresa, they succeeded there in keeping alive the proposition of negotiations for a general settlement with Berlin.[229] This had been followed by the Anglo-German naval agreement and a sustained British effort to bring Hitler into negotiations on an air pact.[230] Moreover, in 1936 naval relations seemed more cordial than ever and one of Eden's first acts as foreign secretary had been to send Berlin some positive indications of his desire to work in harmony with Germany as well as France.[231]

This had been accompanied in January and February by British efforts to prepare the ground for eventual presentation of the general settlement proposals. Thus, not only was Berlin given categorical assurances about the limited nature of the Anglo-French Mediterranean staff talks, but London also quietly abandoned any idea of continuing air and naval conversations with France.[232] Energetic efforts were made to allay anxieties, expressed in the German press, that Britain was composing with Moscow.[233] Hoesch was assured that London was 'fully conscious' of the disastrous effect which any *rapprochement* with Russia was bound to have on Berlin.[234] Eden had the same idea in mind when he declared to the House of Commons on 24 February that the British government would have 'neither lot nor part in encirclement'.[235]

Everything possible was done to demonstrate to Hitler that the United Kingdom had no connexion or direct interest in the Franco-Soviet pact. Wigram twice assured the German embassy that London had not been consulted beforehand, was aware of the 'unfavourable repercussions' which the pact would have on the Reich and, therefore, regretted its existence.[236] Lord Cranborne, the parliamentary under-secretary of state for foreign affairs, insisted to Bismarck that no British issues were involved, while Eden left Hoesch on 27 February

with the impression that 'he himself would be, very glad' if
ratification by the Senate did not take place.[237] The Baldwin
cabinet even shelved a proposal to grant Russia a guaranteed
loan on the grounds that it would irritate Berlin, while the
foreign office sought to prevent any fresh restrictions on
German trade with Britain.[238] The foreign office also declared
on 15 February that criticism of Nazi internal policies 'must be
avoided so far as possible' and succeeded in getting Fleet
Street to reduce what Bismarck had described as 'tendentious
anti-German reporting' on Austrian affairs and rearmament.[239] In addition, Hoesch's embassy was promised that 'in
no circumstances' would the defence white paper in March
1936 repeat last year's 'mistake' of blaming Berlin for the
rearmament spiral.[240] London also did all it could to promote
the Reich's collaboration in shaping the outcome of the
London naval conference.[241]

Nothing which could improve the atmosphere was left
undone. Even Eden's reply to a parliamentary question about
Britain's Locarno obligations was given in the most per-
functory manner.[242] And, although Wigram insisted that he
was speaking privately to Bismarck about the 'working agreement', its effect was precisely in line with British efforts to put
Hitler in a cooperative mood for a peace effort which the
cabinet had been contemplating since 1934 and for which in
February 1936 a special ministerial committee, headed by
Baldwin and including Eden, MacDonald, Simon, and
Neville Chamberlain, had been created to formulate specific
proposals.[243] Three days before its first meeting on 17 February, Eden had formally recommended that Paris and
London should 'enter betimes into negotiations . . . for the
surrender on conditions of our rights in the zone while such
surrender still has got a bargaining value'.[244] This, the foreign
secretary advised, should occur as part of the comprehensive
settlement which was about to be examined.[245] On these points
there was no ministerial disagreement. Nor was there any
recorded discussion of the Rhineland, *per se,* even though
Eden had observed that its reoccupation 'in the immediate
future' could not be entirely discounted.[246]

Instead, the debate focused on whether to open negotiations by proposing an air pact or to accept the foreign secretary's recommendation to begin with an offer aimed at
improving Germany's access to colonial raw materials.[247]

Although no decision was reached, Eden's impression was that the cabinet would ultimately settle on the air pact, partly because of Berlin's public restiveness over Locarno, but perhaps primarily because ministers feared the question of access to raw materials was bound to provoke a German demand for full restoration of her colonies.[248] It was also felt that the foreign secretary's original proposal, which involved a Geneva enquiry into raw materials questions ran too great a danger of becoming bogged down, when what was needed was an initial success.[249] And, although the demise of the demilitarized zone was not regarded as 'necessarily imminent', the foreign secretary and his subordinates feared that it might not survive the length of time that might be required to settle colonial questions first.[250]

The other problems confronting the ministerial committee and its foreign office advisers were when to move and whether to bring Paris into the planning stage. Since the committee did not meet again before the coup, its precise timetable is not known. But on 24 February Eden wrote to Phipps that it might be difficult to wait even until after the French elections before making a 'supreme effort' to reach an understanding with Germany.[251] The only reason given for abandoning Vansittart's 'waiting game' was the desire of ministers to use the negotiations to ease the way for the defence white paper.[252] Some ministers were equally anxious to capitalize on the impression created by the new rearmament programme to strengthen Britain's bargaining position.[253] It was also argued, especially within the foreign office, that the chances of success were better at that time than they would be when Germany was stronger and Hitler's desiderata correspondingly larger.[254]

There is no evidence to suggest that this desire to open talks 'before long' was prompted by any pressing fear for the demilitarized zone.[255] On the contrary, Sargent told the Belgians on 24 February that London had no reason to believe that any reoccupation of the Rhineland was imminent.[256] This view was shared by Phipps, who continued to predict that the question would be raised whenever it seemed opportune to Berlin, but who also believed that Hitler was still not prepared to denounce Locarno.[257] Although the projected early opening of negotiations may have been solely due to domestic considerations, it doubtless pleased Wigram that the fate of the demilitarized zone was going to be determined in the near, rather than the distant, future. Eden, too, was prepared to view favourably any German attempt to open talks about the Rhine statutes.[258]

It can also be surmised from foreign office documents that London intended to open private and secret conversations with Berlin before telling Paris about what Eden described as 'an isolated feeler'.[259] Only after a basic outline for negotiations had been agreed would France be brought into the deliberations—probably, but not necessarily, after her elections. This proposed initial exclusion of the French ally was criticized by Ramsay MacDonald. But it was deemed necessary, not only because of the danger of leakage, but also in view of the fact, as Vansittart wrote, that France had missed 'one opportunity after another' of coming to terms with Germany in 'far more favourable conditions'.[260]

Meanwhile, the foreign office pursued almost a non-policy towards Paris. The less France did, the better.[261] In this respect, Laval's resignation was regarded as no gain and the possibility of a Herriot ministry was seen as a positive liability.[262] Sarraut's succession was accepted without much comment, but the foreign office was not at all disturbed by Flandin's declaration that his foreign policies would deviate from Laval's only in some details.[263] Nor was the British government unaware of the advantages offered by France's desire to consult Britain on the Rhine question.[264] Not only did this suggest that Paris was uncertain as to what attitude to adopt and was, therefore, more susceptible to suasion, but it also indicated that London was becoming increasingly well-placed to administer the sedatives which Wigram thought were essential to the peaceful passing of the demilitarized zone.[265]

Eden's refusal to be drawn by either Laval or Flandin during January into making any statement about the Rhine régime was entirely in keeping with Britain's determination to do or say nothing to encourage France to think she could expect active British support against Germany.[266] The foreign secretary's terse answer to a question in the House of Commons about Locarno also served this purpose — though it was to some extent misinterpreted in Paris.[267] But the most specific example of London's attitude toward France at this time was contained in a despatch from Eden to Sir George Clerk in

Paris on 13 February, mildly rebuking the ambassador for having become engaged with Flandin in a conversation about the demilitarized zone and deprecating any further discussion with the French of such 'hypothetical questions'.[268]

This, the ambassador had managed. But at Geneva on 3 March Flandin's request for specific British assurances to uphold the Rhine statutes had created for Eden an extremely awkward dilemma.[269] He could hardly promise to support articles 42-43 so long after the cabinet had dismissed them as non-vital and so soon after he personally had recommended their abolition through negotiations.[270] Any such statement, it was felt, would have remained a secret only as long as it took the Quai d'Orsay to find a friendly journalist.[271] If the Hoare-Laval affair had shown anything, it was that Paris distinguished between secrets that were worth keeping and those that it served French interests to have known.[272] A fresh British pledge to maintain the demilitarized zone would only have encouraged the French to resist compromise over the Rhineland, while at the same time alienating Hitler and endangering the prospects for negotiations.

On the other hand, in view of Flandin's demand, the foreign secretary could hardly admit that London was already preparing to negotiate articles 42-43 out of existence.[273] Nor could Britain refuse to reaffirm her existing commitments towards the demilitarized zone without expecting to be censured in France for taking a selective attitude towards her treaty obligations.[274] This, in turn, would almost certainly have provoked Paris into retaliating by refusing to impose the oil embargo against Mussolini on the grounds that French security required a strong and friendly Italian ally.

This situation confronted the Baldwin cabinet on 5 March with its first Rhineland crisis. It was not created by Berlin or by any particular concern about 'the growing threat of occupation', but by the French requests and by Eden's own desire to reply to Flandin within a week in order to get the oil embargo going against Italy.[275] No British minister wanted to assume a fresh commitment which would oblige the United Kingdom to take up non-existent arms, in opposition to public opinion, in order to restore a unilateral discrimination whose abolition was seen as indispensable to any negotiated settlement of European problems.[276]

After a long and unrewarding search for solutions, Eden

suggested that the way out was via Berlin. If Britain could persuade Hitler to agree to open immediate negotiations on an air pact, it might be possible to provide fresh multilateral guarantees covering only the Franco-Belgian frontier with Germany. The demilitarized zone, Eden felt, was bound to come up early in the discussions, since Neurath had already mentioned to Phipps in December that Germany could hardly subscribe to an air pact unless she could keep her planes and anti-aircraft artillery at the frontier.[277] Once the question was raised, Eden hoped, some arrangement could be made which would permit Paris and Brussels to relinquish the zone. If this first move proved successful, then the foreign secretary thought there would be an opportunity for Britain to open wider talks on the general settlement.[278]

This was, in fact, the course which Eden had anticipated on 24 February—only it was to be implemented before the cabinet committee had had a chance to examine all the departmental reports it had requested on possible concessions and demands.[279] Rushing into negotiations was hardly conducive to success, but apart from straight acceptance or rejection of the French request, either of which could produce drastic consequences, the quality of alternative proposals did not extend beyond Ramsay MacDonald's suggestion that Eden should speak man-to-man with Flandin, emphasizing that he did not believe French public opinion would support action over the demilitarized zone and getting him to withdraw the question.[280] The only other possibility was a declaration warning Hitler against violating articles 42-43. But this was not even mooted, doubtless because, as Eden later explained, 'neither the British government nor people would have been willing to carry it through'.[281] In these circumstances, it was not difficult for the foreign secretary to convince his cabinet colleagues.

On the afternoon of 6 March, the air pact proposal was presented to the German ambassador, along with a pressing request that negotiations should open quickly.[282] It was a desperation move which might just possibly have succeeded had it occurred a month or possibly even a fortnight earlier. It would at least have provided Neurath with a strong argument in favour of seeking a negotiated solution and it might even have given the Chancellor reason to suspect that London and Paris were aware of his plan or had anticipated it to perfection.[283] But once Hitler had settled on his course of action, nothing short of a direct warning, accompanied by military preparations, could have deterred him from a step which he never ceased to describe as the most daring of all his undertakings.[284]

3 Hitler prepares another surprise

*Sometimes there are moments when one has to
take the sword and cut the knot.*
                    GOEBBELS, 17 January 1936

It was in early February, barely four weeks before the event,
that Hitler apparently first told anyone outside his most
intimate circle that he was thinking of putting an immediate
end to the Rhineland régime.[1] The idea had been on his mind
for at least a year, but it seems likely that he first began to
brood seriously again about advancing his 1937 target date
just after mid-January, when Laval announced that the long-
delayed ratification debate over the Franco-Soviet pact would
finally occur.[2] This announcement may have provided the
stimulus, but there would still have been no change in time-
tables had it not been for internal and external factors which
favoured an early solution.[3]

Domestically, the arguments for acting were economic,
strategic and political. Not that the people generally were
suffering unduly; the winter had been mild and food ration-
ing was working reasonably well.[4] But inside the demilitarized zone, economic conditions had deteriorated to the point
where press criticism was becoming heated and strong
representations were being made to Schacht for immediate
relief.[5] Unemployment, housing shortages and rising costs
were once again encouraging the communists and Rhenish
separatists, whose activities in January had brought Goebbels
to Köln, where he scolded dissidents and attempted to raise
local morale by alluding to the possibility of the army's return
to the western frontiers.[6] These problems of the Rhenish
provinces were not new. But as long as the government was
obliged to adhere to a *Versackungspolitik* in the face of enemy
aggression, the zone was regarded as vulnerable by indus-
trialists, who either refused to build new plants there or,
where possible, had transferred existing operations to the
hinterland.[7] Nor were there any prospects of Rhinelanders
sharing the prosperity associated with arms contracts or a
military presence. This grievance had intensified throughout
1935 with the quintupling of the army's paper strength and

the corresponding increase in its material and supply requirements.[8]

Strategically, too, the situation had deteriorated with Laval's decision to submit the Franco-Soviet pact for ratification. German military leaders, who were already chafing over the difficulties posed by the demilitarized zone to their efforts to organize a twelve-corps army, now became concerned over the security threat posed by the possibility that Moscow might provoke some clash with Germany, say, in the Sudetenland, which would oblige Paris to attack the Reich.[9] Furthermore, according to Neurath's testimony at Nuremberg, German military intelligence learned in the winter of 1935 of the existence of French plans, apparently also connected with the new Czech-Soviet agreements, to attack and divide the Reich by driving along the river Main until a link-up was made with the Czech and Russian forces advancing from the east.[10]

On the other hand, the likelihood of this occurring had been considerably reduced in the previous ten months. Thanks to the advancements made by the army and air force, Berlin could claim without contradiction that Germany was secure from invasion — at least everywhere east of the Rhine.[11] Improvement since conscription had been remarkable and was so acknowledged by foreign experts, including the British and French attachés in Berlin.[12] But it was not nearly as great as alleged (vide Hitler's assertion in March 1935 that Germany had already achieved air parity with Britain) and it was certainly not as astonishing as portrayed by a small army of emigrés and other outside 'experts' who claimed during 1935-6 that billions of Reichsmarks (RM) had been pumped into a war machine which was producing or capable of producing unlimited quantities of men, munitions and material.[13] Such stories had the effect of persuading many non-Germans that the Third Reich was already an armed camp and that General Hermann Göring's Luftwaffe was not only capable of inflicting great damage, but was also led by a man who would not hesitate to unleash his bombers if Germany were driven into a corner.[14] These over-estimates of Berlin's land and air power were to pay substantial dividends for the Chancellor in March 1936.

Furthermore, and this was of vital importance in Hitler's calculations, Germany's relative military position, which had improved so dramatically, was likely to be less favourable in

1937, since most of her potential foes had also begun to put right their own military deficiencies.[15] Paris had started allocating defence credits to artillery and tanks instead of concrete, while the British were already beginning to make good Baldwin's pledge to match Germany, plane for plane. In another year, they would be better prepared; Russia might be a threat and the Italians, who had betrayed Berlin in 1915, could be back at the Brenner under the Stresa banner. By contrast, apart possibly from the French, none of these powers could be said to be *aktionsfähig* as regards the Reich at the moment.[16]

Hitler also had personal and political reasons for wanting some action now. Surprises were part of his nature; he liked spectacles, too. If the two could be combined, so much the better. It had been almost a year since he had last startled the world — longer than any previous lapse since the Machtergreifung — and his desire for activity had returned. But, contrary to what has been argued, Hitler's Rhine coup was not a desperate bid to retain his grip on the country.[17] His position was by no means insecure. On the contrary, as Phipps observed in April 1935 and confirmed in January 1936, 'There are few Germans who deny that Herr Hitler has "delivered the goods".'[18] Here, then, was an opportunity for the Chancellor to consolidate his personal position, perhaps permanently, as leader of the German people, while at the same time increasing the prestige of the National Socialist party, which had not enjoyed the popularity of its Führer and whose officials were frequently blamed for excesses and blunders which, according to the man-in-the-street, would never have occurred 'if only Hitler knew'.[19]

The restoration of military sovereignty in the Rhineland was certain to dwarf the enthusiasm generated by the Saar plebiscite. For nearly a year — since the reintroduction of conscription — the demilitarized zone had stood as the sole remaining major domestic symbol of Germany's second-class status.[20] Few were the citizens of the Reich, young or old, who would not hail its disappearance, by fair means or foul, either as a step towards peace and understanding, or as a triumph over the architects of the Versailles treaty.[21] Nor was the repudiation of Locarno likely to be regretted, not only because of Berlin's increasing conviction that Britain would not and Italy could not come to her aid, but also because, as

Phipps observed, most Germans regarded the Rhine pact as having been signed under duress as a means of getting rid of the hated occupation forces.[22]

These political factors were obviously an important aspect in Hitler's decision to act when he did. But in assessing relative weights, there is little evidence beyond the fact that Neurath and Hassell were deeply disturbed by the *massgebend* internal motives underlying the Chancellor's decision and the persistence of post-coup stories that domestic considerations carried the day against military, economic and diplomatic objections to a *fait accompli.*[23]

In spite of the importance to Hitler of creating the proper atmosphere for fresh elections, it was the favourable juxtaposition of external events, coupled with the domestic difficulties and disunity of Germany's major opponents, which gave the Chancellor his opportunity in the spring of 1936 and which convinced him and Neurath that the operation would not provoke military retaliation or other serious consequences.[24]

Most important was the Abyssinian conflict. As a result of Italy's invasion and Rome's subsequent political isolation, the Stresa front had been broken and it now seemed possible that Mussolini might not feel disposed to fulfil his Locarno obligations against Germany over the demilitarized zone.[25] This was all the more likely in view of the fact that Berlin, by not imposing economic sanctions against Italy, had become Rome's most important trading partner. This benevolence towards the Duce was not something Hitler expected to provide gratis.[26] Nor was its importance likely to be reduced as long as the possibility of an oil embargo was held over Italian heads.[27]

Mussolini's adventure in East Africa had also benefited Hitler by disrupting Anglo-French relations. Although relations between Paris and London had been strained in the autumn, the most profitable result, as far as the Chancellor was concerned, was the ill-feeling generated between the two peoples, most recently as a result of the Hoare-Laval affair. But tempers had been frayed for several weeks beforehand over the belief in Britain that the French were dragging their feet in defence of the aggressor, and the conviction in France that the British were destroying the front against Germany by driving Mussolini into the wilderness.[28] Bitterness on either side of the Channel during the six months from October 1935 to March 1936 reached such heights, at least in the press, that comparisons were being made with the state of Anglo-French relations during the Fashoda, Chanak and Ruhr crises.[29] This public animosity could not fail to have an effect on Britain's attitude in response to any French request for support over the demilitarized zone.[30]

The Abyssinian crisis also proved helpful to the German cause in four other ways. As Hitler observed, sanctions against Italy had not only become a 'thoroughly unpopular' burden on most nations, but had reduced both the ability and willingness of 'the followers' to undertake a second such obligation.[31] This, in turn, helped expose the physical and moral weakness of the Geneva security system. The war also diverted attention from Germany, while at the same time providing a contrasting backdrop for Hitler's proposed bloodless occupation of German soil. Moreover, it enabled German leaders and many others to argue that it was absurd for France to support only economic sanctions against an aggressor and then demand heavier penalties for an internal action that posed no threat to anyone's security.[32]

The other external event which aided Hitler was the French government's decision to lay the Franco-Soviet pact before parliament for ratification. The Auswärtiges Amt's legal experts and even Neurath may have believed that the Russian pact was incompatible with Locarno.[33] Whether or not Hitler agreed is immaterial. For him it was an ideal pretext, and one he was not prepared to lose by warning Paris of the consequences of ratification.[34] He was more than willing to trade passage of the Soviet treaty for a remilitarized Rhineland, especially since it provided a far more plausible and emotive excuse for action than the argument that Anglo-French staff talks over the Mediterranean crisis had violated the spirit of Locarno.[35] And it was far more certain than the Russo-Japanese war which the Chancellor had originally hoped would provide the required diversion for executing his plan to repudiate articles 42-43 in 1937.[36]

Moreover, since May 1935, Berlin had succeeded in stigmatizing the Franco-Soviet pact in the eyes of most Germans as a threat to the Reich. Having been constantly exposed to anti-Bolshevik arguments for more than three years, they could reasonably be expected to regard the Chancellor's coup as a justifiable, if not altogether juridical, reply to ratification. Hitler also felt confident that these anti-communist arguments would find a sympathetic echo throughout significant segments of British and French opinion, as well as in almost every other European and American country.[37]

In spite of the opportunities offered by the Abyssinian conflict and the existence of a handy pretext, Hitler would probably not have risked his coup in March 1936 had it not been for the weakness and disunity of the opposition.[38] In gauging probable French reaction to the remilitarization of the Rhineland, Hitler had to take into account three essential factors which compounded the hazards of a coup. First, Locarno was the cornerstone of her security. In theory, at least, no French government could normally be expected to acquiesce in its repudiation.[39] Second was the legal and moral grip that the Rhine pact gave France over Britain. Even though the extent and nature of a guarantor's commitment might normally be open to wide interpretation, Paris could impose her own rules by taking decisive action and then demanding that London fulfil her obligations.[40]

Finally, there was the fact, according to German chargé d'affaires Dirk Forster, that 'for months on end' French public opinion and various officials had been 'haughtily admonishing Germany before the eyes of the world' not to take precipitate action against articles 42-43.[41] Poncet had warned Berlin to this effect in January and Flandin had promised the Chamber's foreign affairs committee on 12 February that Paris would not allow herself to be confronted by *faits accomplis*.[42] This kind of commitment raised the possibility that the Sarraut government might find itself compelled by its own words to act.

Nevertheless, neither Hitler nor Neurath nor Forster believed the French would react violently to a coup, so long as it was not and could not be seen as a preparation for an attack on France.[43] Their confidence stemmed from their knowledge of French domestic weakness and from the conviction that Paris would not march without Britain, whose desire for a military solution was deemed non-existent.[44]

The French had reacted volubly during the conscription crisis in March and April of 1935. But France had not marched. Now, some eleven months later, the Reich was considerably stronger, while internal developments in France

had caused a general deterioration in her ability and willingness to take action.[45] Admittedly, Flandin, who was prime
minister during the March 1935 affair, was back in office and
in a key position. But as Hitler and the rest of the world knew,
the Sarraut ministry was strictly a caretaker government,
whose avowed aims during its 100 days in power were to
maintain the *status quo* and, above all, to do nothing that would
endanger the franc, which, along with the country generally,
was still feeling the effects of Laval's deflationary economic
and financial policies.[46] Moreover, the alliance of the communists with the socialists and radical socialists and the
emergence of this *front populaire* as a political force had led to
a series of ugly leftist-rightist confrontations in Paris, culminating in mid-February with a brutal assault on Léon Blum,
the 64-year-old socialist leader.[47] The Sarraut government
had shown surprising decisiveness in ordering the immediate
dissolution of the neo-fascist Ligue d'Action Française and
Camelots du Roi.[48] But these actions served only to exacerbate
the bitter internecine struggle which had consumed France
since the street riots of February 1934.[49]

All these problems were thoroughly discussed in mid-
February during a meeting which Hitler held in Berlin with
Forster, who, as acting head of mission, had been specially
summoned from Paris.[50] Although Forster refused to
'guarantee' French inaction, and even suggested that Paris
might reply by calling up the *armée de couverture* and
demanding a withdrawal, he likewise expressed doubt that
the Sarraut cabinet could keep up its determination in the face
of a coup in the Rhineland. Equally useful during the
pre-coup period were the assurances reaching Berlin that
the French people were so deeply pacific — possibly even
defeatist — that they would only fight again if France were
invaded.[51] A 'very influential' member of the French government had said this to the late German ambassador, Roland
Köster, on 13 December.[52] Five days later, premier Laval had
confirmed to Köster that French public opinion was in all
circumstances opposed to military action beyond the frontiers
of France.[53]

The Chancellor's confidence *vis-à-vis* France's infirmity was
in no way lessened by the debate in the Chamber of Deputies
over ratification of the treaty with Moscow.[54] The formal
proceedings, which opened on the 11th and closed on the 27th,

lasted only six sittings, but each day's debate brought fresh confirmation of the political and ideological divisions in the republic. On 18 February, for example, rightist deputies Pierre Taittinger and Phillipe Henriot predicted that ratification would be met by remilitarization of the Rhineland.[55] Neither deputy doubted that Berlin would succeed—a point which editor Charles Maurras had already made in his *Action Française* on the 17th when he predicted that France 'would find herself in the tragic dilemma between the acceptance of the *fait accompli* and the immense risk of defeat'.[56]

This inclination by the foes of the Franco-Soviet pact to embroider on the justification for retaliation which its ratification by the Chamber would provide for Germany was strong enough to provoke a reproach from Flandin on 25 February for 'the dangerous thoughtlessness of their words'.[57] This, of course, could only have drawn Berlin's attention to the willingness of the extreme right to accept in advance the abolition of articles 42-43.[58] Hitler and his advisers must also have been aware during the ratification debate of the absence of any significant strength from the benches of the traditional nationalists, like Georges Mandel and Paul Reynaud, to whom resistance against pan-Germanism represented an unshakeable tenet in their political creed.[59]

It was also believed, at least within the Auswärtiges Amt, that France's military superiority had vanished and that, if Paris had wanted to attack the Reich, she would have done so before Germany had rearmed.[60] This opinion was in every way reinforced by right-wing journals, such as *Action Française* and *Candide,* which paraded French military weakness before the public during February.[61] 'We could give no strong answer' to remilitarization of the Rhineland, Maurras declared on 17 February. Four days earlier *Action Française* had announced that 'the time for preventive war has decidely passed'. Everything, it continued, militated against the government taking the position of aggressor, including 'alas! the state of our military forces'.

Hitler also believed, in spite of Berlin's public warnings of the Soviet menace, that Moscow was at the moment 'only intent on having peace in the west'.[62] This absence of belligerent spirit was attributed by Neurath primarily to the Red Army's inability to fight beyond Russia's frontiers.[63] It was further felt that Moscow was too preoccupied with internal

problems to desire any European catastrophe, particularly
since the Japanese were thought to be awaiting an opportunity
to attack the Soviet Union.[64] No other European power was
apparently even considered by Hitler or Neurath as a potential source of military support for France if she chose to react
forcefully to the remilitarization of the Rhineland.[65]

Although internal weakness and the absence of European
support strongly suggested that France would not react
violently, much depended on how her British ally responded
to the proposed coup.[66] If London took an active, aggressive
part, then the worst consequences could occur. But Hitler
believed, and Neurath agreed, that the British would not only
provide no support, but would actively seek to prevent Paris
from taking any action, apart, perhaps, from economic
sanctions, which was the worst penalty either the Chancellor
or his foreign minister anticipated as a result of the coup.[67]
This confidence was based on British military weakness, the
preoccupation of the Baldwin government with domestic and
Abyssinian affairs and the presence in Britain of a reservoir of
sympathy for Germany and respect for Hitler's achievements.[68]

The Chancellor was well aware that Britain's military
services were not only seriously deficient, but had also been
heavily strained by the Mediterranean crisis.[69] As early as
March 1935, prime minister Ramsay MacDonald had warned
in the defence white paper that Britain's contribution in any
Locarno crisis could have 'little decisive effect'.[70] Hitler himself had been told by Phipps in December that British aircraft
could not operate effectively against Germany from home
bases.[71] Moreover, British participation in the Hoare-Laval
fiasco and Baldwin's famous 'sealed lips' had been openly
attributed to the nation's 'utter unpreparedness'.[72] And,
although the *Morning Post* had created a small sensation in
mid-January with a three-part series which detailed Britain's
armaments deficiencies, these stories contained little which
was not already known to Berlin or readily available through
His Majesty's Stationery Office.[73] Nor was the German
government ignorant of London's desire at this time to avoid
any conflict in Europe or the Mediterranean which might
give Japan an opportunity to attack British interests in the Far
East.[74]

The impact on British public opinion of the Hoare-Laval

affair was also well known to Berlin, as was its effect on the government, whose prestige had been further diminished in mid-February when Sir Austen Chamberlain, now the *éminence grise* of the Conservative back benches, had attacked Baldwin's leadership.[75] At the same time, Berlin had been receiving some positive indications of British friendliness toward Germany. Not only was the new king a known admirer of the Chancellor, but the Third Reich also had influential friends around the palace and even in Whitehall.[76] At least that was the main conclusion of an extensive report to ambassador extraordinary Joachim von Ribbentrop, which was submitted to Hitler, from the Duke of Coburg after a week of conversations in London with four cabinet ministers and several other influential personages on the occasion of King George V's funeral in January.[77]

Neurath, too, had brought back a favourable impression of Eden's desire for cordial relations with Berlin.[78] Tangible evidence of this could be seen in London's efforts to reassure the Chancellor in January about the insignificance of the Anglo-French staff talks and in London's desire to be divorced completely from the Franco-Soviet pact.[79] Cranborne and Eden both sought during February to dispel German anxieties about Britain's relations with Russia, while Wigram's hint on 12 February about a working agreement reinforced the feeling that the United Kingdom was pursuing a conciliatory policy.[80]

More specifically, Eden's parliamentary adherence to Locarno on the twelfth was described to Berlin as 'strictly juridical', when it could have been much firmer, particularly since the Rhine question was, as ambassador Hassell put it, 'clearly in the air'.[81] Further encouraging signs appeared in the British press, notably in the *Manchester Guardian* and *News Chronicle* of 1 and 20 February.[82] The former urged early negotiation of a western pact which preserved only the bilateral aspects of Locarno. If this did not occur quickly, the *Guardian* warned, Hitler would act unilaterally, daring the West to do their worst, 'which, whatever it may be, will not be war'. Even more decisive was journalist Vernon Bartlett, who wrote in the *News Chronicle* that the British people would not accept the indefinite maintenance of a régime which had no counterpart in France. In view of the French attitude, he concluded, the best idea would be to accept a *fait accompli* in the

Rhineland.

The effect of these press commentaries, which were widely circulated in Berlin, coupled with Ribbentrop's advice and friendly remarks by such influential persons as former air minister Lord Londonderry and historian Arnold Toynbee, gave rise to a feeling, as one Auswärtiges Amt official put it, that the British people would never act against Germany so long as she stayed within her frontiers.[83] It was equally believed that the Baldwin cabinet was unlikely to deviate much from that attitude.[84]

By the time Hitler opened the Winter Olympic Games at Garmisch on 6 February, he was preoccupied with the possibilities and prospects of abolishing articles 42-43 within weeks, rather than months.[85] He may have confided in no one during this period, but if he did discuss his thoughts, it was probably with Ribbentrop, Göring and Goebbels. Ribbentrop served his Führer as an enthusiastic echo-chamber, alter ego and adviser on things British.[86] He may also have contributed some original ideas, but this was not one of his strengths. As for the two so-called 'wild men' of the régime, Goebbels and Göring were both known as hot-heads, who had incited Hitler to violence whenever possible in the past. There is no reason to doubt that this was the case with the Rhineland, as was widely believed in Europe at the time.[87]

During the next week, the Chancellor moved a stage further by bringing in his top military and diplomatic advisers for consultations. Each was invited to express his objections to, or reservations about, the idea.[88] Hassell later questioned privately whether Hitler was sincere in seeking these opinions.[89] His suspicions were partly confirmed by Ribbentrop, who said that the *modus procedendi* was unalterably determined from the outset.[90] Nevertheless, and contrary to his later contempt for second opinions, Hitler proved an eager interrogator and a good listener, though how selectively is an open question.[91]

Fritsch, who was interviewed in Berlin on 12 February, agreed with the Führer that restoration of full military sovereignty was 'an absolute necessity'.[92] But, while welcoming the plan in principle, the army chief agreed to it only after receiving Hitler's assurance that the operation would on no account involve hostilities or apparently even the risk thereof.[93] Even less resistance was encountered from

Blomberg, who, according to Hitler's adjutant Friedrich Hossbach, accepted his Führer's ideas without protest—and, indeed, at a dinner given on 15 February at Garmisch by Poncet, the Wehrmacht chief made a strong case to French guests for remilitarizing the Rhineland.[94]

By mid-February, it appeared that Hitler was determined on action and would change his mind only if presented with convincing evidence that his coup would produce a military reply from Paris, London or possibly even Rome.[95] None of his diplomatic counsellors could produce this sort of proof; least of all Neurath, who felt confident that the opposition would not march.[96] But, whereas the foreign minister approved of the aim and even agreed that the Franco-Soviet pact was incompatible with the Locarno treaty, he was disturbed by the Chancellor's choice of method.[97] Admittedly, the French had shown themselves implacable foes of any negotiated revision of the *status quo*.[98] Neurath, as well as many other Germans, later argued that a coup was the only way in which Germany could 'obtenir son du' from France.[99] But the foreign minister was equally convinced that even Paris could not prevent the zone's peaceful disappearance, say, within a year or two. In Neurath's view, this acceleration of events was not worth the consequences, which he feared would be an 'automatic and general concentration' against a Germany which in his opinion was already 'isolated enough as it was'.[100]

The foreign minister probably expressed his personal reservations to Hitler. But Neurath did not openly challenge his chief.[101] Moreover, although he continued to voice his strongest doubts privately, the foreign minister did not contest the issue with Hitler in the two meetings for which there are records.[102] Indeed, as Hassell observed on 19 February, Neurath 'appeared to have resigned himself to the decision'.[103] This compliance in the presence of the Führer distressed the ambassador, who shared the foreign minister's misgivings about the wisdom of risking political isolation and even economic sanctions for the sake of an earlier, but no more satisfactory solution to the Rhineland problem.[104]

In this respect, Fritsch was probably right when he surmised that, once Neurath realized the futility of trying to change the Chancellor's mind, he fell in with the plan and did his best to ensure a favourable outcome for Germany.[105] He had, after all, witnessed the sarcasm which Hitler had heaped on Forster when the chargé d'affaires had argued against unilateral action.[106] Had Neurath done the same, he very likely would have found himself isolated.[107] Further conduct of foreign affairs might then have been entrusted to Ribbentrop, who was already being touted as the next foreign minister. Neurath was too loyal a civil servant and too good a German to want that.[108]

Most of the final three weeks before the coup were devoted to preparations. Generally, these activities fell into three categories. It was first essential to create the best possible diplomatic conditions. The second task involved presenting the operation in such a way as to appeal to domestic and world opinion. And, finally, there were military details to attend to. All these areas involved critical decisions and careful planning.

Diplomatically, attention was paid only to Rome, London and Warsaw. Initially, Blomberg and Göring had favoured sending the Luftwaffe chief to Rome as a personal representative of the Führer to help ensure that Mussolini would not betray Hitler's plans to the other side.[109] But that idea was abandoned because it would have been impossible to keep the trip secret and, as Hassell warned, would give the *démarche* 'a ten-fold importance in the eyes of the world'.[110] Instead, this most delicate task was assigned to Hassell, who had been ambassador in Rome since 1932 and whose embassy was enjoying a wave of popularity, thanks largely to Berlin's refusal to impose sanctions against Italy.[111]

Originally, Hitler hoped to capitalize on Mussolini's recent friendly overtures and his desperate military and political situation over Abyssinia in order to get Rome to take the lead in denouncing Locarno on the grounds that it had been rendered invalid by the Franco-Soviet pact.[112] Berlin would then follow suit, thereby creating for Italy a much-needed diversion of Anglo-French energies from the Mediterranean to the Rhine.[113] By acting first, Hitler thought, Mussolini would also avoid finding himself, in 'an extremely difficult' position *vis-à-vis* both his treaty obligations and his relations with Berlin.[114]

The Chancellor had summoned the ambassador from Rome to Munich on 14 February to discuss this possibility with him.[115] Hassell did not believe that Italy would actively oppose a German repudiation of Locarno. Anglo-French opposition to Rome, he explained, had recently rendered Mussolini 'less opposed to clear, far-reaching decisions'. On the other hand, the ambassador felt far from certain that the Duce, in his current 'terrible mess', would want to risk getting completely into the western powers' 'bad books' by taking the initiative on Germany's behalf or even by acting simultaneously with Berlin in repudiating Locarno.[116] But Hassell did not think this would prevent Mussolini from standing aside, partly to spite Paris and London for their rôle in promoting sanctions against Rome and partly to compensate Germany for having kept open his economic supply line.[117]

Hassell's views on Mussolini's likely response were apparently a decisive factor in persuading Hitler to continue planning his *fait accompli*.[118] Moreover, by the time the Chancellor and the ambassador met again in Berlin a week later, Hassell's contacts in Rome had supplied ample unofficial and quasi-official evidence that the Duce would merely 'stand at the window and watch with interest' if Berlin should undertake some action against Locarno.[119] Even so, no one could be certain until Mussolini himself had been asked. This was especially true in view of the existence in Rome at this time of opposing factions, each struggling to win the Duce to its concept of foreign policy.[120] One was led by under-secretary for foreign affairs Fulvio Suvich and supported by Count Dino Grandi and Vitorio Cerruti, ambassadors at London and Paris. It was said to favour Italy's continued membership of the League of Nations and her eventual return to the Stresa front.[121] The other was headed by Mussolini's son-in-law, Count Galeazzo Ciano, under-secretary for press and propaganda, and was supported by Dino Alfieri, also an under-secretary in the same ministry, and Bernardo Attolico, ambassador to Berlin. This group was determined to create what later became known as the Rome-Berlin axis.[122]

These cross-currents of policy were still thought to affect Mussolini, who sometimes supported the Palazzo Chigi and on other occasions endorsed his son-in-law's ideas.[123] The contradictions which this situation produced had been demonstrated by two semi-official statements issued during the previous four weeks; one argued that the Franco-Soviet pact had compromised Locarno and the other reaffirmed Rome's fidelity to Stresa and her Rhine pact obligations.[124] Moreover, Hitler did not trust Mussolini sufficiently to rule out the possibility that the Duce might give the German game away to Paris or London—perhaps as a means of escaping an oil embargo or even as part of a bargain to secure relaxation of existing sanctions.[125]

Hassell, on the other hand, agreed that the Italian picture was imprecise regarding Locarno, but he did not believe there was any chance of a betrayal.[126] Nevertheless, Hitler, Neurath and the ambassador contrived an interview procedure in which Mussolini's opinions would be elicited step by step.[127] In this way, it would be possible to stop at any point if the Duce's answers proved unsatisfactory. At the same time, the ambassador's approach was devised to extract favourable responses and then to employ the previous reply in such a way that Mussolini could not retreat without also reneging on his earlier statements. The aim, however, was not to get Rome to take the lead or even play an active supporting rôle. Hitler had come by 20 February to accept Hassell's judgement that it was neither possible nor necessary as long as the Duce agreed to remain quiescent.[128]

The interview, which occurred on 22 February, was conducted precisely as planned and yielded all the desired results.[129] Hassell cleverly exploited the conflicting statements about Italy's attitude toward the Franco-Soviet pact in order to get from the Duce an agreement that an element of juridical uncertainty had been created. He then got Mussolini to reaffirm his conviction, expressed in *Popolo d'Italia* on 26 January, that the Anglo-French staff talks had endangered the Locarno equilibrium and then pointed out that the Duce's view coincided, *mutatis mutandis,* with Hitler's attitude toward the Franco-Soviet pact. Having established this identity of views, the ambassador asked if Italy planned to do anything about its ratification and, when Mussolini said no, Hassell replied that he presumed Rome would also remain aloof if Berlin reacted. The Duce twice confirmed that Italy would not cooperate with Paris and London against Germany over any violation of Locarno.[130]

This was exactly what Hassell wanted. Mussolini's statement guaranteed that, barring a major reversal in the Mediterranean, Italy would refuse to honour her obligations as a guarantor. The Duce had also pronounced the Stresa front dead and described the Locarno pact as an appendage of Geneva that would disappear the moment Italy left the

League. So smoothly had the interview gone that the ambassador at no time admitted that Berlin would actually repudiate Locarno.[131] Nor had he mentioned the demilitarized zone—though the Duce had surmised that repudiation of articles 42-43 and the Rhine pact would be Germany's reply to French ratification of the treaty with Russia.[132]

Hassell's efforts brought immediate rewards the next day when *La Stampa* reversed its earlier position by adopting the German position on the question of the compatibility of the Franco-Soviet and Locarno treaties.[133] But a few days later, the ambassador was presented by Suvich with an *aide-mémoire* of the conversation with the Duce which quoted Mussolini as saying only that he would not oppose any German move which was 'within legitimate bounds'.[134] Hassell feared that the forces at the Palazzo Chigi had persuaded Mussolini that he had made altogether too sweeping a commitment.[135] But these anxieties were partially allayed when Suvich readily agreed to every emendation which the ambassador made.[136] And, six days later, on 3 March, Hassell was handed a revised copy of the note which Mussolini had endorsed as accurate and which contained the promise that Italy 'would not participate in any counter-reaction which might be called forth by a German reaction to the ratification of the Russian pact'.[137]

Berlin's diplomatic efforts toward Warsaw, on the other hand, were not aimed at securing any commitment or even learning her likely reactions, but at ensuring that Polish-German relations were in good enough condition to keep the Poles happily pursuing their 'politique d'équilibre' between Paris and the Reich.[138] Hitler neither needed nor wanted Poland as a silent partner; nor did he believe any real trust could be placed in Polish policy.[139] But he could ill afford to do anything which might encourage Warsaw to lean too far towards France.

The chances of this occurring were not great, bearing in mind Poland's long-standing dislike of the Locarno treaty and the restiveness which the Franco-Soviet pact had created among Poles who feared Moscow might one day demand transit rights for the Red Army through Poland in order to assist their mutual French ally.[140] These factors worked in favour of Warsaw maintaining an indifferent, if not sympathetic, attitude towards Hitler's repudiation of the Rhine pact. So, too, did the fact that Danzig had momentarily ceased to be a bone of contention.[141] But relations between Warsaw and local national socialists had been exacerbated right up to mid-January, when Berlin had ordered Gauleiter Albert Forster to do everything possible to ensure that the Danzig question did not appear on the League council's May agenda.[142]

Far more serious at the moment was the friction caused by Germany's failure to pay charges for railroad transit across the Polish corridor.[143] By the end of February, the outstanding debt had reached 80 million zloty (over £3 million) and was rising at a rate of 8 or 9 million zloty per month. The situation had become so bad that Warsaw actually threatened on 21 January to curtail rail traffic to and from East Prussia by more than 50 per cent unless Berlin started paying current charges immediately and produced a plan for settling her arrears. To complicate matters further, Dr Schacht had incensed the Polish on 28 January when he declared in a speech at Beuthen that it had been 'an act of sheer madness' by the framers of the Versailles treaty to hand over parts of Upper Silesia to Poland.[144]

To repair the damage, General Göring was despatched on a hunting expedition. But the Luftwaffe chief did not just hunt lynx. He stressed to his Polish hosts his determination to find a swift and satisfactory solution to the corridor debts question.[145] These assurances of 19 February were followed up a few days later by the despatch of a Polish economics expert to Berlin for talks. Although a breakdown occurred on the eve of the Rhineland coup, it was at least possible to say that the Poles had reason by March 1936 to be more optimistic than they had been for some time that this vexing problem would soon be amicably settled.[146]

Göring also did his best to mitigate the effect of Schacht's Silesian speech and to remove the accompanying impression that Berlin's policy toward Warsaw was two-faced.[147] Precise details are not known, but it seems likely that he tackled the problem by employing language similar to that used a week earlier by German Justice Minister Hans Frank when he declared to Polish officials that 'dumme Reden' could not possibly deflect the Führer from a policy as fundamental as rapprochement with Warsaw.[148] Göring also denounced rumours that Berlin intended to seek a détente with Moscow. Such left-handed assurances also served to remind Poland of what might occur if she alienated Berlin.[149] Although the Luftwaffe chief was accompanied wherever possible by foreign minister Józef Beck and his wife, the Poles generally maintained more reserve towards him than they had shown during his previous visits.[150] But, if subsequent Polish performance is any measure of pre-coup German efforts, then Göring certainly succeeded in his mission.[151]

In their dealings with the British from mid-February to the coup, the Auswärtiges Amt concentrated on appearing as cooperative and constructive as possible.[152] They were assisted in this by the contrast provided by the French, who were currently irritating Britain with their attempts to introduce what His Majesty's Government regarded as 'extraneous' political questions into the London naval conference negotiations.[153] In this sphere, therefore, it was not difficult for the German government to outshine Paris. This was accomplished on 29 February — one week before the coup — by notifying London that Berlin had accepted Britain's invitation to conclude a bilateral pact which would link Germany to the results of the naval conference.[154] Whether Hitler would have been quite so amenable in other circumstances is questionable. But the documents clearly demonstrate that German naval policy in February and March 1936 was conducted with the Rhineland firmly in mind.[155] The success of this policy was evidenced by Britain's unwillingness after 7 March to suspend negotiations and, more immediately, by Eden's eve-of-coup expression of 'profound satisfaction' to Hoesch that the Chancellor had made such a 'hopeful contribution towards a *détente*' by agreeing to cooperate.[156] Berlin also learned on 5 March that the foreign secretary had told the British journalist, Vernon Bartlett, at Geneva that he was now 'less concerned than he had been' about the German attitude.[157]

The Auswärtiges Amt was also in a position to ensure that German press attacks on the Franco-Soviet pact were silenced almost immediately after Eden complained to Hoesch on 27 February that Berlin was over-reacting to its ratification and that her fears of British participation in an encirclement front against the Third Reich were groundless.[158] The same desire to foster a good impression was probably behind Neurath's instructions to Hoesch on 25 February to enquire unobtrusively of Eden whether Britain had yet formed a more concrete idea of her 'working agreement'.[159] It is, however, at least possible that the foreign minister was attempting to encourage London to make some formal statement or proposal which could be used to dissuade the Chancellor from his *fait accompli*.[160] Any such hopes were effectively ended by Eden's admission on the 27th that nothing could be done until he had discussed the situation with Flandin at Geneva during the first week of March. The foreign secretary was not prepared to discuss 'ways and means' until after he had satisfied himself that the French were also prepared for an understanding with Berlin.[161]

Nothing came of Britain's 'working agreement'. In fact, Neurath and Hassell suspected the possibility that the British feelers might be a diversionary manoeuvre.[162] But Hoesch's enquiry succeeded in giving the impression that Germany was both prepared for talks and anxious to cooperate with London.[163] Certainly these were assumptions on which British policy was formulated in the days immediately following the German *fait accompli*.[164] Hoesch's conclusion that Eden was 'devoting himself most actively' to finding a basis for Anglo-Franco-German collaboration must also have confirmed Hitler's conviction that London would rather negotiate than fight.[165] The same conclusion could only have been drawn from the foreign secretary's urgent efforts on 6 March to get air pact negotiations started and by his express willingness to omit both the limitation of air arms and Germany's return to the League as appropriate topics for these negotiations.[166]

Simultaneously, and no less skilfully, the German government devoted itself to creating the best possible climate of public opinion, both at home and abroad, but especially in Italy, Britain and France. Italy was, of course, given a more favourable press—a reversal rendered less difficult by her military victories of mid-February.[167] The main effort, however, involved preparations or decisions in four areas. The first aimed at providing justification for the German action. Here the problem was not one of finding a pretext. The Franco-Soviet pact had been the obvious choice for some time.[168] Nor was there any need to send the Auswärtiges Amt's legal experts on a fresh search for arguments about its incompatibility with the Rhine pact. This had been done in the previous May by the staff of Friedrich Gaus, who had helped draft the Locarno treaty a decade earlier.[169] Even the German press attack on the French connexion with Moscow was already under way, thanks partly to Laval's decision to proceed with ratification and, more lately, to the week-long visit to France in early February of Russia's top military leader, Marshal Mikhail Tukhachevsky.[170]

All this made Berlin's task easier, since there could be no doubt anywhere about German objections to the Franco-Soviet treaty. The primary problem was to handle the situation in such a way as to make certain that nothing occurred which might either arouse French suspicions about a retaliatory act or cause Paris to postpone final ratification, pending a judgement from the Hague court on the validity of Germany's argument about the pact's compatibility with Locarno. In fact, Flandin offered to do just that in a Chamber speech on 25 February. But he did not follow through, partly because it meant capitulating to German carping and partly because it was bound to irritate Moscow, which was already showing signs of having had her patience over-taxed by French procrastination.[171] Nor did Berlin give the foreign minister sufficient reason to believe that Germany would reply to ratification with anything stronger than paper protests.[172]

It is not certain that Hitler or the foreign ministry gave precise instructions to the German press, but two points were remarkable about the newspaper attacks on the Franco-Soviet pact in February. First, the French government, as distinct from the French people, was consistently blamed, not only for embracing communism, but also for practically every other European problem since the war. The French peasant, on the other hand, was pictured as a peace-loving person who deserved pity for having been burdened with a succession of narrow-visioned governments.[173] The other point was that the press carefully avoided drawing any conclusions about the consequences of ratifying the Franco-Soviet pact.[174] Here journalists and editors were responding to instructions issued by Goebbels on 13 February two days after the debate in the Chamber had opened, forbidding them to give the impression that Berlin wished to prevent or even warn against, ratification of the Franco-Soviet treaty.[175] The Locarno rampart, according to this directive, had been seriously breached, but not destroyed. The Rhine pact was not to be portrayed as having lapsed. 'Contrary to the letter and spirit' was as far as editors were permitted to venture in what was expected to be a calm and moderate examination of the question of the compatibility of the two treaties. There were frequent references in the press to the 'regrettable consequences' of ratification, but these were allusions to the dangers inherent in any alliance with Russia, not just to Germany, but to the whole of Europe.[176]

After 17 February, however, the German press shifted its attention to the compatibility question and for ten days the advantages of Locarno were discussed in a concerted attempt to demonstrate that the French were jeopardizing the spirit which had preserved peace on the Rhine for over a decade.[177] But the press remained reticent on the key questions for how, when and where Hitler might translate his objections into practical policies.[178] After the pact was ratified by the Chamber of Deputies on 27 February by a vote of 353 to 164, there was no burst of outrage. Instead, Goebbels ordered journalists to cease comment until further notice.[179] This unexpected silence gave rise to reports that Berlin had decided, on the principle that it was no use crying over spilt milk, to abandon efforts to stop the pact's ratification by the Senate.[180] It was a shrewd tactic, for it not only preserved the pretext, but also created a feeling in France and elsewhere that German opposition to the Russian treaty had been both artificial and exaggerated.[181]

In view of German determination to use the Franco-Soviet pact as the excuse for action, it becomes clear that Hitler's interview with French journalist Bertrand de Jouvenel on 21 February was not intended to stop its ratification, as was originally believed, but to create an even greater contrast in the eyes of the French and German peoples between a Reich government anxious to be friends with France and a French ministry determined to compose instead with communist Russia.[182] In the interview, Hitler directed a strong appeal to the French people to join him in burying the hatchet and opening a new chapter in Franco-German relations. He also offered France an opportunity to put 'an end forever to the "German Peril" ' and pledged that the anti-French portions of *Mein Kampf* would be amended in 'the great book of history' if he could bring about the desired *détente*.[183]

The Chancellor's gesture was widely discussed in France, where the press reaction was generally cool and cautious, but more hesitant than unfriendly.[184] It did not fail, however, to make an impression on the man-in-the-street, as well as with some political leaders.[185] And, even though publication of the interview in Paris *Midi* was deliberately delayed until after the Chamber's vote of ratification, it provided Hitler with the opportunity to declare, as he did on 7 March, that he had acted unilaterally only after the French government had snubbed the extended hand of German friendship.[186]

The second major decision focused on the Chancellor's desire to convince Europe that his *fait accompli* was not only defensive, but also purely pacific, and that his ultimate aim was to reach an understanding, especially with Germany's western neighbours. To accomplish this, he constructed an attractive set of peace proposals.[187] It does not appear from the documents, however, that Hitler intended at the outset to accompany his coup with any such offerings. They were not mentioned during either his conversation with Forster or his first talk with Hassell.[188]

This decision to submit peace proposals was made before 19 February. It may well have been inspired by Wigram's hints of a 'working agreement' or Flandin's assertion that Paris had already agreed on counter-measures against treaty violators, or even by Forster's refusal to guarantee a non-violent French reaction.[189] This question may never be resolved. Nor is it yet possible to determine whether the idea was Hitler's, Neurath's or even Ribbentrop's. However, there is no doubt that the Chancellor's predominant motive in putting forward the proposals was 'to deprive the other side of the possibility of declaring our action to be aggressive' and to divert as much attention as possible to the peace offerings.[190] The opposition was to be given the choice on 7 March of either accepting the *fait accompli* or forfeiting an opportunity, which the British had been seeking for well over a year, of stabilizing the situation in western Europe.[191]

No other decision was as critical in determining the success for Hitler of his operation in the Rhineland.[192] The proposals were neither new nor particularly novel, with the exception of his offer to re-demilitarize the Rhineland, provided France and Belgium created similar zones on their sides of the frontier.[193] This suggestion, which had been made to Göring by Lord Londonderry some three weeks earlier, would have meant abandoning and probably destroying the Maginot line and was therefore put forward mainly to highlight the inequality which had existed for eighteen years.[194]

Of the remaining six proposals, three amounted to nothing more than the resurrection of the old Rhine pact 'adjusted to the present situation', which meant eliminating articles 42 and 43.[195] This new Locarno would take the form of 25-year non-aggression pacts between Brussels, Paris and Berlin, guaranteed by London and Rome, and including the Netherlands if she desired. Germany was additionally prepared to conclude a western air pact 'calculated to prevent automatically and effectively the danger of sudden air attack'. This was presumably a concession to the French demand for bilateral arrangements which had thwarted, in the German view at least, any progress in this direction since February 1935. But, like much of the plan, the phrasing was more cunning than candid.[196] The fifth proposal repeated an offer to conclude long-term non-aggression treaties with the Reich's eastern neighbours, including even Lithuania, which had hitherto been excluded owing to her 'barbarous' treatment of the Memel Germans.[197]

Finally, Hitler declared his readiness to return to the League of Nations. This fundamental reversal of policy he explained on the grounds that the restoration of full sovereignty to Germany had removed the chief reason for Berlin's departure from Geneva on 14 October 1933.[198] But the real reason, as Ribbentrop later admitted, was to ensure a peaceful outcome to the coup.[199] The Geneva offer was all the more remarkable, Berlin pointed out, because the Chancellor was not demanding that the League covenant should be separated from the Versailles treaty or that her river and colonial claims should first be settled.[200] It was made clear, however, that the German government expected that these issues would be 'clarified through friendly negotiations in the course of a reasonable period of time'.[201] This was shrewd phrasing, since it meant not only that Berlin would be guaranteed favourable decisions on three important questions as the price of her return, but that if Hitler was in any way dissatisfied with the final terms, he could justify his rejection on the grounds that the other side had broken faith. It was also stressed, especially to Rome, that Germany's return to Geneva could only occur after agreement had been reached on the other points in the peace proposals.[202]

Very little is known about the background of the League

offer, which was not part of the proposals outlined by Hitler on 19 February.[203] Ribbentrop claimed that he and the Chancellor were simultaneously and independently responsible for the idea.[204] If so, then it almost certainly occurred to them during the weekend of 29 February and 1 March, while the Führer and his ambassador extraordinary were together in Bavaria.[205] It also seems probable that the Geneva proposal only came under consideration after 22 February, when Hassell secured Mussolini's assurance that Italy would not intervene in any Locarno crisis. Nor is it impossible that the final decision occurred only after rumours reached Berlin around 2-4 March that Flandin was attempting to commit Britain more firmly to upholding the Rhineland régime.[206]

The offer to return to Geneva prompted Hassell to stigmatize the proposals of 7 March as an indication of weakness, if not fear, on the part of the Chancellor and his immediate advisers.[207] Perhaps he was right, but, notwithstanding, the peace plan proved to be a brilliant success, especially in Britain, where Hoesch emphasized that the difficult decision to return to Geneva was inspired largely by the Chancellor's desire to cooperate as fully as possible with London.[208] The ambassador was also instructed to declare that Berlin's offers had given London 'an opportunity effectually to counteract a possible tendency in France to react rashly'.[209]

Hitler's third decision involving public opinion was to link remilitarization of the Rhineland with what amounted to a plebiscite in which the German people would be asked to reaffirm their faith in him as their leader.[210] By setting the election date on 29 March, only three weeks after Z-day, the Nazis created an ideal platform from which to proclaim that the Chancellor had not only restored honour, sovereignty and equality to the country, but had also presented the world with the most comprehensive and generous peace plan since the war. In this way, flag, fatherland and Führer would be inextricably entwined with the abolition of what had come to be widely regarded as an intolerable burden on a great nation.[211]

The Chancellor's main aim in holding elections was obviously to aggrandize himself and help the party, as well as his régime.[212] But the proximity of the election to the coup rendered compromise virtually impossible during the campaign. At least, Berlin claimed that this was and would be the case until after polling day. This argument was accepted, at least in London, as an unfortunate, but not altogether invalid, excuse for Hitler's intransigence during the weeks following the coup.[213]

The only other pre-coup decision of importance was to determine the precise method for remilitarizing the Rhineland. Seven alternatives existed. The first three involved a simple announcement, repudiating the Locarno treaty, article 42 and article 43, or any combination thereof.[214] But these were apparently not considered, presumably because they were only half-measures. Another alternative would have involved piecemeal occupation, executed through a series of minor infringements, until *de facto* remilitarization had been achieved. But this would have taken time and carried a high risk of detection by French intelligence or the consul in Köln, Jean Dobler, who kept a vigilant watch for military activity within the zone.[215]

It would, however, have been possible to declare that the 14,000 men of the Landespolizei within the zone had been incorporated into the army, thus creating a *fait accompli* without having moved a single soldier.[216] One can only speculate, but it seems in keeping with Hitler's character that this was precisely the reason why this alternative was not followed. He wanted the people to see fighters over Köln cathedral and to hear the Rhine bridges reverberate with the sound of marching columns. He also wanted to savour the Reichstag's tumultuous reaction when he announced that 'at this historic moment, when German troops are marching into their future peacetime garrisons in the western provinces of the Reich. . . .'[217]

The army's presence would be tangible proof to the world of the Chancellor's action.[218] It would also effectively eliminate all possibility that Paris could score an easy victory by forcing Berlin to rescind a paper proclamation. Instead, the French would have to apply enough pressure to force Hitler to order a military withdrawal. It also seems probable that the Chancellor wanted the army to be involved from the outset since that would mean that France could not claim to be only taking political action against the Nazi régime. Soldiers would make any forceful French reaction a matter for the entire German nation, including, especially, the generals, whose professional honour would be involved in defending the country.

The remaining alternatives were either to march in with sufficient strength to put up a determined defence or to employ only a token force in the operation. Even though Hitler professed to believe that the opposition would not react forcefully, he obviously did not wish to risk frightening the French people, who might conceivably then demand that Paris reply in kind. Nor did he wish to give Flandin an obvious legal right to immediate retaliation.[219]

According to the treaty of Locarno, the only breach of article 43 which could justify an immediate military riposte was one which involved an imminent threat of hostilities.[220] The presence of troops within the demilitarized zone without aggressive intent was to be regarded, according to article 4 (2) of the Rhine pact, as a non-flagrant violation.[221] All such infractions were a matter in the first instance for the League council. France could still act, but only after a decision by the council in her favour. Since the council was not currently in session, this procedure was bound to be delayed by five or seven days, since it would take that long for members to assemble and hear the arguments, presumably from both sides.[222] Meanwhile, passions would have time to subside. French and world opinion could grow accustomed to the new situation, and the Auswärtiges Amt could argue its case individually with League members, who, Hitler believed, had grown tired of being the 'whipping boys' of the great powers.[223]

To capitalize on these procedures and deprive Paris of any opportunity to claim that a 'flagrant' violation had been committed, Hitler and his advisers decided to send only 19 infantry battalions and 13 artillery units, or a total of 22,000 regulars, into the zone.[224] The Landespolizei was to be immediately incorporated into the army as 21 infantry battalions, making a total of 36,500 men, including some 500 Luftwaffe personnel. These forces were to be supported by 156 artillery pieces and 54 fighters, but there were to be no offensive weapons, such as tanks and bombers.[225] Only 3 infantry battalions, or less than 3,000 men, were to be sent to frontier posts at Aachen, Trier and Saarbrücken.[226] Of the remaining forces, 28 battalions were to be stationed behind the Rhine and 7 within a few kilometres of the river's western bank.[227]

The Chancellor's decision to employ moderation may also

have been partially based on the idea that a French riposte, if it did occur, would probably also be minimized, say, in the shape of a *prise de gages*. If, on the other hand, Paris mounted a major offensive to throw a few thousand troops out of the Rhineland, she risked committing a major psychological error on the same proportion as the Ruhr incursion by giving the world 'the hateful spectacle of war-mongering'.[228] It would be wrong, however, to suggest that these military dispositions were dictated solely by the desire to appease Paris and public opinion. Hitler might have caused an open rift with the entire army high command if he had insisted on a massive remilitarization.[229] As it was, some generals were deeply enough disturbed to protest to their superiors about the risk of retaliation which they thought the Chancellor was running with even a token occupation. Beck was said to have argued against sending any troops across the Rhine, while commander-in-chief Werner von Fritsch apparently protested to Blomberg or Hitler — possibly for the same reason — after receiving his orders on 2 March.[230]

Important strategic considerations were also involved, since the main line of defence against French invasion was still the Rhine.[231] Moreover, the bulk of the Rhine forces were clustered around Düsseldorf in the north and inside the Koblenz-Karlsruhe-Frankfurt triangle, which was also in keeping with German determination to shield the Ruhr and stop any French drive along the Main to link up with Czech forces.[232] This grouping also offered the possibility of counter-attacking from both flanks if the French tried to push through the Köln-Wiesbaden gap.

These preparations strongly suggest that Hitler and his generals were prepared to fight if invaded. The evidence is heavily in favour of this possibility, as opposed to the earlier belief that the troops occupying the Rhineland would have fled as soon as the first French soldier set foot on German soil.[233] Withdrawal orders did exist. All the entering units had been instructed to remain ready to *ausrücken* at only one hour's notice.[234] Moreover, the three advanced battalions were told to retreat if they discovered on their way west that the French had launched a pre-emptive action.[235] However, the Aachen, Trier and Saarbrücken battalions were under orders, not to flee, but to fall back to previously prepared positions, where their job was to 'halt the enemy advance' for as long as possible before pulling back again to designated defensive areas.[236] This was entirely in harmony with Blomberg's insistence that counter-measures should be taken in accordance with Aufmarsch Rot, dated 10 July 1935, which was defined as a 'general order for concentration and battle'.[237] It envisaged a fighting retreat to the Roer-Rhine-Black Forest line, where the army was expected to hold the enemy advance (*den feindlichen Vormarsch aufzuhalten*) and, according to 1934 instructions, compel the enemy to abandon its war aims (*zum Aufgeben seines Kriegszieles*).[238]

For this particular contingency, 4 army corps and 13 infantry divisions were alerted, giving the forces inside the Rhine zone a back-up support of at least 61 infantry battalions, as well as tank and artillery units.[239] In addition, there were some 24,000 other police within the zone, trained in small arms and capable of demolition and destruction.[240] And, although neither Blomberg nor Fritsch mentioned utilizing the para- and pre-military formations, such as the SA, SS, NSKK (motorized corps of the SA) and Arbeitsdienst (labour service), it was certain that they would have been employed in the defence effort in accordance with the war minister's decree of 25 October 1933 that any invasion was to be met 'by local armed resistance without regard to the chances of military success'.[241] The determination to resist was also reflected in commander-in-chief Erich Raeder's orders to the navy to bring the fleet to readiness and to congregate ships in deployment harbours. And, if the situation deteriorated, the pocket battleship *Deutschland*—Europe's most feared warship—was to be prepared for action.[242] Presumably, similar preparations were made by the air force, but Göring's orders have not been found.

It is well known that Hitler subsequently asserted to interpreter Paul Schmidt, Hans Frank and Austrian premier Kurt von Schuschnigg, as well as to his wartime table partners, that the Reich's military weakness would have obliged him to withdraw 'mit Schimpf und Schande' if France had replied forcefully.[243] In every instance, however, the Führer was seeking to impress his listeners, either with his nerves of steel or his generals' apostasy or, in the case of Schuschnigg, with the futility of resisting the Reich.[244] Moreover, in the case of the Austrian premier, the Chancellor's statement when quoted in full throws an entirely different light on the portion most frequently cited. What Hitler said during his Berchtesgaden harangue on 12 February 1938 was: 'If France had marched then, we would have had to withdraw, perhaps about 60 kilometres; even then we would have held them.'[245]

It is still possible, however, to contend that Hitler would have ordered a withdrawal in the face of a French march into Germany, but such a command would have been in sharp contrast to all military planning of the period and a contravention, not only of the orders issued on 2 and 3 March, but also of the Chancellor's own vow on the day of the coup 'to yield to no force . . . in the restoration of the honour of our people and to succumb to the direst distresses rather than ever capitulate'.[246]

Throughout the entire period of decisions and preparations, the Chancellor and his consultants managed to preserve the element of surprise. This was a vital factor and perhaps even the key to success. If Paris or London had discovered what was pending, they could easily have ruined everything for Hitler, either by publicly warning Germany of the consequences of her action or even by threatening to reply in kind as soon as the violation took place. If either had occurred, it would be difficult to imagine that Hitler would have risked the confrontation which would then have been inevitable.

This was undoubtedly a major reason why the Chancellor selected 7 March for his action. That the *fait accompli* should occur on a Saturday had by now become an axiom of German foreign policy, since the British and French cabinets would have dispersed for the weekend.[247] But most observers were expecting some German initiative only after the French Senate had followed the Chamber in ratifying the Franco-Soviet pact in mid-March.[248] Thus, the Chancellor's best choices were to strike between acts or to delay until anticipations had subsided.[249] The latter idea, however, was risky, not only because Eden might complicate matters with his 'working agreement', but also because of the danger that the demilitarized zone would become a sort of inviolable institution which would make it increasingly difficult to touch.[250] That left Saturday the 7th, which Hitler may have preferred anyway, since it enabled him to frame his action against the next day's sacred ceremony honouring Germany's war dead.[251]

One of the most remarkable aspects of the coup was the fact that no one outside the inner circle appears to have correctly guessed the Chancellor's intentions.[252] The Berlin diplomatic corps and the great majority of foreign correspondents were taken by surprise, if not by the fact of the zone's disappearance, at least by the timing and method of an action which must rank as one of the most heavily telegraphed moves in Europe since 1918. One reason for this was undoubtedly the fact that the abolition of articles 42-43 had been so frequently predicted that journalists and diplomats had come to treat such reports almost as part of their daily routine.[253] Moreover, in the diplomatic world, ambassadors and ministers tended to trust one another. Hitler and his entourage were suspected, but the assurances of Germany's fidelity to Locarno had emanated from Neurath and the Auswärtiges Amt right up to the end.[254] And, although practically every outside observer in Berlin realized that something was afoot, most suspected that Hitler was preparing only to lodge a stern public protest against ratification of the Franco-Soviet pact.[255]

This secrecy was maintained by involving a minimum of persons in planning the operation. Although the records are by no means complete, it is probable that Hitler confided in only nine persons during February and the first few days of March.[256] Those who were consulted or charged with preparing the coup's execution were either trusted colleagues or, as in the case of Forster, threatened with their heads if they did not keep silent.[257] Others whose advice might have been helpful, but who were not trusted, were excluded altogether. They included Schacht and Hoesch, who may well have been questioned, but not confided in, while on a fortnight's leave in Garmisch and Berlin during the Winter Olympics.[258]

How far knowledge of the coup extended down the ranks of the Büro Ribbentrop and Auswärtiges Amt is debatable. Most diplomats, with the exception of Forster and Hassell, were informed less than twelve hours before the coup.[259] Hitler himself may only have settled on 7 March just a week beforehand.[260] Military preparations were also delayed as long as possible. Blomberg's orders were not issued until 2 March and the operations divisions of the three services had less than a day to produce plans and orders.[261] These were despatched to all affected departments and units on the 3rd, but no date was given for the operation until 5 March.[262]

Most of the soldiers involved in *Winterübung* knew nothing of their mission until they reached the edge of the demilitarized zone on the morning of 7 March.[263] The same sort of secrecy was maintained with the German press. Goebbels had selected journalists sequestered overnight before having them flown to Frankfurt and Köln, where they first learned where they were and why.[264] Most members of Hitler's own cabinet were informed on the night of 6 March, when the Chancellor presented his coup decision as a *fait accompli* and urged ministers to keep their nerve in the face of foreign reactions.[265]

This admonition came just a day after Hitler's own nerve had buckled.[266] On 5 March, only hours after Blomberg's order to commence preparations was issued, the Chancellor apparently succumbed to reports reaching Berlin that London and Paris had come to terms and were about to warn the Reich against precipitate action in the Rhineland.[267] It was also rumoured that the French were marshalling a motorized army of 250,000 just behind the Maginot line.[268] Hitler reacted by summoning Hossbach, explaining that a western *démarche* seemed imminent and asking him to find out at what moment it would become impossible to stop the military operation. But he had recovered his confidence before the adjutant could report back with the answer.

By the time the Saturday morning mist had risen, German soldiers had entered the demilitarized zone. Just before 1 p.m. the troops destined for positions west of the Rhine crossed the Hohenzollern bridge at Köln — almost at the precise moment when Hitler was reaching the climax of his speech to the Reichstag. The other Locarno ambassadors had already been notified by Neurath of the coup and of the Chancellor's peace proposals.[269] Apart from Attolico, they stayed away from the Kroll Opera, where Hitler delivered one of his best speeches — a ninety-minute oration in which he dwelt on the achievements of his régime, attacked the Franco-Soviet pact and defended his decision to repudiate the Rhine pact.[270] Göring then announced the dissolution of the Reichstag for fresh elections and Hitler stepped down from the podium amid thunderous applause and cheers.

Everything had gone as planned. It had been, as Eden rightly observed, 'the most carefully prepared example of Hitler's brazen but skilful methods. The illegal deed was abundantly wrapped up with assurances for the present and promises for the future. . . . The appeal was nicely judged. . . . The timing was perfect, including the usual choice of a week-end.'[271]

Although Hitler and Neurath had done everything possible to present the *fait accompli* in the best possible light, it was still true, as Hassell had noted, that 'ninety-five per cent of the French, and probably most of the British, too, would, in spite of everything, be conscious of the threat involved in the occupation'.[272] To this observation the Führer had made no reply.[273] Events in Paris would determine now whether the French were prepared to translate this awareness into action.

4 'Aucune action isolée'

*Négociations ne seront possibles que lorsque, de
bon gré ou de mauvais gré, la loi internationale
aura été rétablie dans toute sa valeur.*

FLANDIN, 10 March

News of the Chancellor's thunderbolt set loose in Paris a series
of ministerial and military consultations which resulted in
tentative agreement to implement the cabinet's decision of 27
February, namely, to react via the League of Nations and to
consult France's Locarno guarantors 'with a view to organizing joint opposition' to the unilateral repudiation of article
43.[1] This was reported to the press on the evening of the 7th,
along with the announcement that Paris was taking the first
steps towards defending herself militarily.[2] These measures
were kept to a minimum and only involved troops on active
duty within the affected frontier regions.[3]

On Sunday morning, however, when the full cabinet had
gathered, ministers were confronted by Mandel, who
demanded an immediate, independent French military
riposte.[4] The absence of any formal records makes it difficult
to know precisely what occurred.[5] But it appears that Mandel
insisted that the chiefs of army and air staffs, generals
Gamelin and Pujo, should be instructed to assemble all the
military means needed to march forthwith into, and re-
demilitarize, the Rhineland.[6] France, he argued, must reply
directly and forcefully to restore the *status quo*, otherwise
Hitler would believe he could try anything. Mandel was
supported by Sarraut and one or two other ministers, including Joseph Paul-Boncour, who later argued that 'to go to
the League of Nations before taking action was to invert the
order of operations'.[7] But these demands for 'action isolée'
encountered stiff diplomatic, military, financial and political
objections. Not that Flandin opposed Mandel's aims, but he
felt constrained to point out that Britain would follow
France's lead with a bad grace and that the United States
would accuse Paris of imperialism. The foreign minister also
warned that German hatred of France would be intensified,
whereas joint action would at least diffuse it.[8]

In the presence of a strong cabinet and united country, Flandin's considerations might have been waived. Paris might have been willing to launch another Ruhr-type operation in the conviction that the world would later praise her for having dealt a crippling blow to Hitler personally, as well as to his ambitions for German hegemony in central Europe. But economic and financial crises, as well as political scandals and street warfare between ideological extremists, had sapped France of her strength.[9] Even so, the proponents of immediate action might have carried the cabinet and the country into a forceful riposte if the military establishment had possessed the proper instrument and if its leaders had shown any enthusiasm for the task proposed by Mandel.[10]

The French army of 1936 had no strike force capable of marching as far as Mainz, to say nothing of occupying the whole of the demilitarized zone.[11] Nor did it possess a single unit which could be made instantly combat-ready.[12] Gamelin could not act at all on German soil without *couverture*, which required eight days and involved the call-up of enough reservists to put 1.2 million men *sur pied*.[13] 'The idea of rapidly sending a French expeditionary corps into the Rhineland', Gamelin explained, was 'chimérique'.[14] When politicians speak of entering enemy country without mobilization, he added, 'ils oublient que nous n'avons pas d'armée de cette politique'.[15] There was, therefore, no way in which Mandel's demand for immediate action could be executed without using the air force, which, it was agreed, would constitute an act of war.[16]

The absence of any highly mobilized, independent strike force which could be employed at a moment's notice was not caused by any oversight.[17] French military planners had considered and rejected the idea more than once. Although fear of producing a professional élite was one factor, the major reason was that a *troupe de choc* did not fit their strategic and tactical concepts. War, as envisaged by Gamelin, would be largely a repetition of 1914-18. Armies would mobilize and then march to the battlefield, which would quickly be saturated. It would then become a matter of attrition. There would be no lightning strikes or massive breakthroughs, since, with machine guns, barbed wire and fortifications, defence would always remain superior to offence. The army's job was to defend the nation and not to conduct aggressive warfare. The gravest mistake France could make, the high command believed, was to allow its armies to be drawn out from their prepared positions behind the Maginot fortifications.

Strategic and philosophical considerations only partly explain why the military chiefs did everything within their power to discourage the government from implementing *couverture.* The other and more critical reason was that all three service ministers and chiefs of staff believed that any incursion on to German soil would be resisted.[18] 'Si nous nous opposons par la force à cette occupation,' Gamelin declared, 'c'est la guerre.'[19] On this point the military leaders were as consistent as they were adamant. 'Nous mettions le doigt dans l'engrenage', Maurin warned, and France must be prepared for the worst.[20]

Under *couverture,* he explained, the army could seize some German territory near the frontier.[21] For this he recommended immediate industrial, as well as air and naval mobilization in order to be prepared against any German reply by bomb or submarine attacks on French targets.[22] But, since the Wehrmacht was bound to resist, the war minister insisted, as did Gamelin, that the government must be prepared, preferably beforehand, but certainly at the first shot, to issue 'l'affiche blanche' decreeing general mobilization.[23] Otherwise, Maurin argued, Paris would be risking 'un échec ou recul' capable of producing the gravest consequences, since France would then be forced to attempt hastily to re-establish 'une situation qui aurait été compromisé.'[24]

The army's anxiety about the possibility that it might immediately 'casser le nez' was not caused by the arrival of 30,000 Wehrmacht troops into the zone, but from the conviction that the Rhineland had been militarized for a long time.[25] At the time of the coup, French military intelligence estimated German strength inside the zone at 295,000 men, including 90,000 'regulars'. This was achieved by counting 30,000 members of the labour service, along with 30,000 members of the Landespolizei and other police organizations as combat forces. Lists were then apparently tallied of all Germans in the Rhineland who belonged to such organizations as the SA, SS and NSKK.[26] These 'auxiliaries', some 205,000 in total, were considered capable of putting up a determined defence in familiar and difficult terrain, certainly for as long as would be required to bring up the reinforcements which, it was expected, Blomberg would have marshalled during the eight days required to place *sur pied* the *armée de couverture.*

Gamelin and Maurin also stipulated, as a *sine qua non* of action, that France be supported actively by her three Locarno allies and at least indirectly by Prague and Warsaw, who would be asked to take military steps designed to force Berlin to maintain a significant presence of troops on her eastern and Prussian frontiers.[27] 'It would be without doubt illusory', Gamelin warned, 'to anticipate decisive results *vis-à-vis* Germany *outside the cadre of a coalition.*'[28] These demands for what amounted to a six-power coalition revealed a significant lack of self-confidence in the ability of the French fighting forces to achieve a favourable result in a straight fight against a foe whom Maurin described as being 'a great deal better prepared than we think'.[29] By 1936, the French high command believed that the military balance had swung perceptibly in Hitler's favour.[30]

In manpower, it was argued, even the *couverture* decree would not produce any advantage for France, since Germany already had at least a million men under arms.[31] And behind them were millions of members of pre- and para-military formations, all disciplined, partially trained and capable of being incorporated into fighting units with reasonable speed. They would perhaps be useful only as cannon fodder in the short run, but in the kind of protracted warfare foreseen by Gamelin the weight of their presence would soon tell, particularly since France had no equivalent pool of semi-skilled manpower.[32] Thus, although the army chief was confident that he could establish a foothold on German soil, he also anticipated that his advance would be halted rapidly, both by the enemy and by supply difficulties. Once the front were established, Gamelin believed Germany's numerical superiority would begin to make itself felt, especially since French forces would be operating in unfriendly terrain and without fortifications.[33]

Moreover, the *classes creuses* were now passing through the French army, which meant that her metropolitan strength in 1935 had dropped to 350,000 and was expected to decrease by another 13,000 in 1936—a trend which would continue until 1940.[34] As a result, Gamelin stressed, his active elements 'did not even represent by a long chalk half of those which the

Germans had at their disposal'.[35] On the basis of early 1936
calculations, France had one soldier in barracks for every 2.4
Germans.[36] And, if the army's 11 March estimate of nearly 1.2
million men under arms is accepted as accurate, then
Blomberg, thanks to the presence of the para-military
'auxiliaries', enjoyed an immediate advantage over Gamelin
of nearly 300 per cent.[37]

Furthermore, the generals warned, the Reich had been
massively rearming for at least three years and possessed a
war potential which could not be rivalled by France.[38] In
contrast, Paris had done almost nothing during this period to
improve her moderate capabilities, preferring instead to
spend her military credits mainly on fortifications.[39] Not only
had French rearmament 'hardly begun' by 1936, but, according to former war minister Jean Fabry, 'la machine à fabriquer
grincait de partout'.[40] As a result, Gamelin feared that industrial mobilization would not produce 'les résultats réels
qu'on devrait pouvoir en attendre'.[41] The army, too, had
suffered for the sake of the Maginot line, which Fabry described as the only accomplishment in French rearmament
between 1918 and 1935.[42] Maurin warned the cabinet, according to under-secretary Jean Zay, that even the fully-mobilized
army was in no condition to wage war successfully by itself.[43]

Maurin and Gamelin both blamed the politicians for
having deprived the fighting forces of 'les moyens nécessaires
pour vivre et combattre au-delà de la frontière'.[44] After
having slashed military funds, the war minister asserted,
parliament could hardly expect to find at hand an army
strong enough to fight victoriously 'du jour au lendemain'.[45]
France, he added, was now paying for 'l'anesthésie des traités
de Locarno'.[46] This was certainly not untrue. But the high
command itself was responsible for the army's deficiencies.
Between 1919 and 1935, the war ministry had budgeted only
4.3 per cent of its 92-milliard-franc allotment for new and
modern material.[47] Moreover, some 30 per cent of the 1934
credits and 59 per cent of the 1935 allocation were not even
spent by Gamelin.[48] Rearmament on a serious scale was begun
only in 1936 and even then the amount budgeted—2
milliards—was, according to Maurin, 'infinitesimal' compared with Germany's 'fabulous expenditures', which he
accepted as being 100 milliards.[49]

Consequently, the French war machine, for all its paper

strength, had hardly changed its character or equipment since 1918.[50] The army was still dependent on the 75 mm cannon which had been developed in 1897.[51] It possessed no modern anti-tank weapons and only thirty-eight modern anti-aircraft guns, which meant that Paris and every other French city was virtually helpless against aerial attack.[52] Numerically, the tank force looked formidable. But most of the machines were wartime Renaults, poorly protected and lightly armed.[53] Of the forty-two modern D-type light tanks put on alert, not one was judged fully fit for combat.[54] Nor was the D-type considered a match for Germany's tanks.[55] Only with the new 24-ton B-1 tank did the position look encouraging. But even in June 1936 France had only seventeen of these *chars de bataille*.[56] By contrast, the French believed that Blomberg already possessed a modern force of 1,500 to 1,800 tanks.[57] Furthermore, German industry was considered capable of producing tanks on a large scale at a moment when French manufacturers were producing five B-1s per month.[58]

The discrepancy between air forces was seen in 1935-6 to be even greater. Not only were Luftwaffe machines all modern, but some 60 per cent were thought to be bombers, which would have given Göring a first-line strike force in March 1936 of 400 or 480 or even 828 aeroplanes, depending upon whose estimate was accepted.[59] Furthermore, the German aircraft industry, already on a war footing, was believed to be capable of manufacturing from 750 to 1,000 machines within ninety days of mobilization.[60] According to British estimates, that was 2.3 or even 3.4 planes for every French machine.[61]

The French air force, on the other hand, had deteriorated steadily.[62] By the spring of 1936 the first line of 1,000 planes, while quantitatively competitive, was 60 per cent composed of out-dated or 'transitional' machines. Worse still, the French aircraft industry was in a state of chaos. A crash programme had been launched in 1934 to make up in eighteen months the effects of sixteen years of neglect. But, by attempting too much too quickly, the confusion was only compounded, so that by autumn 1935 the potential for expansion was reduced to less than half that of the estimated German capability. And, as late as June 1936, French production arrangements were described as 'non-existent'.[63]

Although the records have subsequently shown that German strength was not nearly as great as was widely presumed, it remains no less true that the French general staff consistently overrated Hitler's military strength.[64] As early as 1934, fears were being expressed in Paris that the illegal Reich forces had surpassed the French army numerically and that Germany's war industry would shortly be able to sustain a military venture.[65] During the last half of 1935, the question most exercising French military experts was not whether Berlin could successfully defend herself, but how soon Hitler could launch an offensive.[66] These alarums may have been voiced initially to arouse the French public to the need for greater rearmament, but there can be no doubt that by 1936 the army high command had become convinced that Germany was an armed camp and that the Rhineland had already been effectively remilitarized.[67]

Another factor which contributed to French military anxieties was the conviction that the Nazis were gamblers who might plunge into war while still only partly prepared.[68] This possibility was based on the assumption that radicals like Goebbels and Göring might persuade the Chancellor that the chances of victory were better now than they would be in a year or two, when British, French and Russian rearmament efforts would have narrowed the advantage which Berlin presently enjoyed as a result of her military efforts since 1933.[69] From the general staff's point of view, therefore, France had everything to gain by postponing any confrontation until her rearmament programme had produced results.

In addition, Sarraut, for one, came to suspect his chiefs of staff, if not of cowardice, at least of lacking 'cet élan, ce raidissement de muscles, ce sens combatif . . . qui porte à faire front et à aller de l'avant'.[70] This opinion was formed after a series of consultations, culminating on 11 March in a meeting at Sarraut's private apartment, when the prime minister invited his generals and admirals to explain how France could execute a *prise de gages*.[71] This they did, but without any visible enthusiasm. Instead, they elaborated on the dangers and inflated their demands to such levels that all options were effectively eliminated except inaction and war.[72]

All the doubts and reservations of the chiefs of staff were mirrored within the cabinet by the three service ministers.[73] Maurin made a persuasive and pessimistic presentation.[74] He was supported by the naval and air ministers, who demanded mobilization and declared their opposition, even hostility, to any kind of military riposte. Piétri stressed the impossibility of justifying war without having been invaded, while naval minister Marcel Déat warned that France would not only be abandoned by her allies if she acted independently, but would also be courting 'the worst moral and material disasters'.[75]

These arguments only deepened the existing anxieties felt within the Sarraut cabinet about the domestic repercussions of any isolated action.[76] Many, perhaps most, ministers would probably have opposed Mandel's demands for an immediate riposte even if the service chiefs had shown themselves confident of executing a *prise de gages* under *couverture* with only a 50 per cent risk of German retaliation. But the twin spectres of mobilization and war caused an outburst of protests which were both heightened and summarized by Déat, who declared that the government would be 'swept out of parliament tomorrow' and possibly even faced with a popular revolt, if it issued 'l'affiche blanche' within six weeks of the elections.[77] Even ministers who understood the long-range strategic and diplomatic implications of acquiescence agreed that the French people would not make such a sacrifice without first being shown that all peaceful possibilities had been exhausted.[78]

Economic and financial considerations also contributed to the government's unwillingness to act forcefully alone.[79] The nation, it was feared, had not recovered sufficiently from Laval's deflationary policies and decree laws to sustain such an effort.[80] If French industry proved incapable of supplying the material and arms required, the resulting confusion would not only disrupt the rearmament effort, but also encourage German expansionists.[81] Ministers were also afraid that the cost of mobilization, estimated at 100 million francs daily, or even *couverture* at 30 million, would overtax the franc, whose vulnerability throughout 1935 had been an important reason why Laval had been allowed to remain in office after the Hoare-Laval explosion.[82]

No politician had wanted to risk being held responsible for devaluation, since such a step was still regarded as political suicide. That was primarily why five men before Sarraut had refused invitations to form ministries.[83] Sarraut himself had dedicated his 100-day government to defending the currency and staving off the threatened financial crisis.[84] It was conceivable that independent military action against Germany might cause outside financiers and governments to register their disapproval of such measures by withholding support for the franc or by starting a wave of selling, either of which could force Paris to devalue.[85]

Faced with what the service ministers believed would be certain war as soon as French troops entered Germany, some cabinet members proposed that Hitler might be induced to retreat if Paris mobilized and metaphorically rushed troops to the Brenner.[86] But Maurin rejected both the idea and the analogy, pointing out that Mussolini's had been a preventive measure against a much weaker Reichswehr, whereas France was confronted with a *fait accompli* and a militarily superior Wehrmacht. Moreover, Hitler had staked his head on the Rhineland operation, whereas it was no disgrace for him to stay out of Austria.[87] To mobilize without being prepared to act, Maurin argued, would oblige the government to climb down in ignominy, because Hitler could not be bluffed. Mobilization in these circumstances, the war minister added, would 'strike at the morale of the army, because you know very well you will do nothing'.[88] Maurin also warned that the government risked public ridicule if it even decreed *couverture* since, after mustering a million men, it would be obliged, on the eve of the elections, to march them all home again.[89]

For all these reasons, the council of ministers came down 'by a large majority' against Mandel, but not necessarily for inaction.[90] Only 'action isolée' had been once again discarded—unless, of course, Hitler perpetrated some dramatic escalation of tension. The government reaffirmed its decision to treat the coup as a *casus foederis*, but to act only after a League finding and in concert with its Locarno allies.[91] Meanwhile, the chiefs of staff were instructed to prepare such supplementary land, sea and air measures as were required for the nation's security.

Within the context of the League-Locarno approach, however, one major question remains unanswered. How far was the French government prepared to push its Rhine pact partners to secure the evacuation of the Rhineland or otherwise punish Hitler for his *fait accompli*? It is by no means inconceivable, in view of ministerial apprehensions about pursuing any policy of force and their knowledge of Britain's passive reaction to the coup, that a majority of the cabinet had

decided as early as 8 March to eschew direct measures against
Germany and instead use France's juridical right to a riposte
in order to achieve the very political aims which Maurin and
Gamelin so strongly favoured.[92] That meant, at least in the
opinion of the army chief and presumably also his colleagues,
that Paris should prevent all negotiations which could lead to
the conclusion of a new Locarno, with its cumbersome equilibrium, while at the same time pressing London until she
compensated France by promising to give firm and automatic
assistance guarantees, complete with military consultations in
order to ensure immediate and effective support.[93]

On the other hand, there remained within the cabinet a
small, but powerful element which favoured pursuing an
aggressive policy directed at securing the full restoration of
the demilitarized zone.[94] They did not disapprove of the
aforementioned aims, but were unwilling to abandon further
efforts to strike a blow against Hitler which could severely
weaken his position and curtail his ambitions.[95] Within this
group, Mandel and Sarraut seemed prepared to compel
Britain to join them in punitive measures on the grounds that
the worst possible outcome would be for Germany and the rest
of Europe to conclude that Paris and London were weak and
unwilling to meet the Chancellor's challenges.

Flandin, however, was not prepared to go this far.[96] Nor was
the Quai d'Orsay or its secretary general, Alexis Léger, who
was a strong opponent of the Third Reich.[97] They agreed with
Mandel about the importance of teaching Hitler a formidable
lesson and reasserting French authority.[98] They were also
aware that Paris could bring London into any action which
France chose to execute.[99] She could even act first and oblige
Britain to follow.[100] She could threaten to pillory London
publicly if Britain failed to fulfil her Locarno obligations,
which were ironclad once the League had declared that
Germany had committed a treaty violation.[101] Flandin could
also threaten to raise sanctions against Italy unless London
fulfilled all her obligations uniformly and without exception.

The foreign minister possessed the means, but not the will,
to coerce London.[102] To force Britain against her will to
march, Flandin felt, would have a grave effect on *entente*
relations, probably between governments and most certainly
between peoples.[103] Having fulfilled their obligations and
secured re-demilitarization of the Rhineland, he feared the

British would repudiate all other commitments to France and
either retire into isolation or negotiate directly with Berlin.
Nothing, he believed, would be worse for France or Europe
than the collapse or even weakening of Anglo-French unity in
the face of the German menace. This anxiety over the impact
on London of a 'politique de coercition' undoubtedly
explains why, when ministers began to object to Mandel's
demands of 8 March, Flandin reportedly closed his portfolio
and said to Sarraut, 'I see, M. le président, that one must not
insist.'[104]

From the foreign minister's point of view, therefore, the
cabinet was right to reject immediate and independent action,
even if he did not necessarily agree with their reasons. His job
was to persuade Britain to endorse, and preferably support, a
punitive expedition into Germany.[105] If he could at least
secure London's approval, then he could almost certainly
persuade the entire council of ministers to endorse forceful
measures, since no French politician would want to risk being
stigmatized as having opposed action against the hereditary
foe once the traditionally aloof British had agreed to support
Paris.[106] If Flandin could have managed that, he might have
become the next French premier; he would almost certainly
have become a permanent alternative possibility for both left
and right.[107]

There could be no illusions at the Quai d'Orsay about the
magnitude of the task which it had undertaken.[108] Only hours
after the coup, Eden had sent a pressing request to Paris to
keep calm and do nothing to 'engager irrémédiablement
l'avenir', pending careful consideration of the Chancellor's
proposals.[109] The foreign secretary's attitude, according to
ambassador Charles Corbin, was not outrage or even resistance, but that of a man 'who asks what advantages can be
drawn from a new situation'.[110] The British press, too, had
insisted from the outset that Paris would be foolish to risk a
conflict at a moment when an important peace initiative had
been made.[111] This apparent willingness in Britain to accept
the coup prompted Flandin to complain that London had
failed to understand the gravity of the situation and to instruct
Corbin to stress that only by firm resistance could negotiations produce any agreement which would not be illusory.[112]
But before the ambassador could act effectively to alter these
attitudes, Eden delivered another blow by declaring to the

House of Commons on 9 March that Britain was dedicating herself to the process of rebuilding.[113]

Paris was not surprised by Britain's attraction to Hitler's proposals, but the Quai d'Orsay was stung by the foreign secretary's failure to refer to the need to punish the German treaty-breaker.[114] His entire speech had contained no reference to Britain's obligations under Locarno to ensure respect for articles 42 and 43.[115] Eden had only declared His Majesty's Government's determination to fulfil her commitments if France or Belgium were invaded. Even this assistance had been promised only for the period of negotiations. This, to the French, meant that Hitler had it within his power to rob Paris and Brussels of their British guarantees by refusing to conclude a new Locarno or by otherwise causing the talks to break down.[116] On the other hand, if Berlin cooperated, Paris would lose the demilitarized zone and have the Rhine pact reconstituted as a five-power arrangement in which Germany would once again be able to prevent Anglo-French consultations as being contrary to the spirit of the agreement. This meant that Flandin was faced, not just with securing British support for punitive measures, but also with ensuring that France's position did not deteriorate as a result of Hitler's coup. On the basis of Eden's declaration of 9 March, a passive attitude could leave Paris in a worse position, since Britain was prepared to accept a remilitarized Rhineland and negotiate with Germany as if nothing had happened.

Flandin's first task, therefore, was to make sure that Paris retained the British guarantee, regardless of Hitler's subsequent attitude.[117] To achieve this, the foreign minister was prepared to make heavy demands on Britain so that she would be willing to grant concessions in order to escape having to fulfil her obligations regarding the Rhine zone. But that is not to suggest that this was the only reason for Flandin's attitude. He still wanted to punish Hitler and, if possible, force evacuation of the German troops.[118] He therefore set out immediately to prepare to confront the British from the strongest possible position.

Internally, Flandin and Sarraut were faced with the task of trying to give some sense of direction to the people, not only to make them understand the reason for resisting the German coup, but also to combat the impression abroad that the French cared nothing about the demilitarized zone and would only fight in defence of their frontiers.[119] The magnitude of this task was fully revealed during the first forty-eight hours after the coup when the French press overwhelmingly reject-ed coercion in reply to what was described as a diplomatic conflict.[120]

'Non, non, mille fois non!' exclaimed *Petit Journal* to the idea of a forceful reply.[121] *Populaire* and *Journal* warned against delivering any ultimatum, while *Jour* argued that sanctions would only land France in a war which she would be obliged to fight alone—and for the sole pleasure of Moscow.[122] Even papers like *Echo de Paris* and *Petit Journal,* which saw the events of 7 March as part of a grand German scheme for aggression, urged nothing more energetic than application of economic sanctions, while *L'Humanité* and *Journal des Débats* agreed with journalist André Geraud (Pertinax) that the only hope for peace was the immediate creation of 'un réseau d'accords militaires' among all France's allies in order to contain Nazism.[123] Anger was expressed over Germany's intransigence and concern voiced over the consequences if Hitler were allowed to escape unpunished.[124] Many news-papers drew perceptive conclusions about the effect of a refortified Rhineland, but few were prepared to prevent it and many appeared to be at least as worried about Britain's attitude towards her Locarno obligations as they were about making Berlin suffer for her treaty violation.[125] There was also a widespread feeling that Paris could best counter the coup by redoubling her military preparations, thereby demonstrating that France was determined to resist any external German aggression.[126]

Nowhere in France was there any indication that the press was not providing an accurate reflection of the calmness, even resignation, of the French people.[127] Anxiety and shock, there was; but there was no panic, not even on the Bourse or in the savings banks of Alsace-Lorraine.[128] No meetings of protest were held against the coup. No condemnatory resolutions reached Paris; nor did any demands for vigorous action.[129] On the contrary, socialist deputies in parliament unanimously adopted a declaration urging that fascist and militarist states should now be confronted with concrete proposals for universal disarmament.[130]

Comfort was everywhere taken in the existence of Maginot's fortifications and, behind them, the presence of a

French army which was still believed to be the best in Europe.[131] Most people could see no reason to become alarmed because Hitler had accelerated by a few years what was regarded widely as part of the inevitable abolition of those clauses in the treaty of Versailles which restricted Germany's sovereignty. The method employed may have been distasteful, but to the great majority, that alone was not worth a fight.[132]

In an effort to galvanize opinion behind the government, the Quai d'Orsay drafted a speech, read by Sarraut over French radio on the evening of 8 March, in which he harshly rejected all negotiations with Hitler so long as German troops remained in the Rhineland in contempt of international law.[133] 'Nous ne sommes pas disposées', he declared, 'à laisser Strasbourg sous le feu des canons allemands.' To rectify this situation, the prime minister explained, the League and Locarno powers were being asked to fulfil their assistance obligations. But, he added, the effort required national unity and a political truce.

These pleas for unity, however, were submerged in an outburst of anxiety over the government's intransigence.[134] The wisdom of refusing to negotiate opened a breach in the press and parliament.[135] But the prime minister was taken most heavily to task for talking as if he wanted to throw the Germans out of the Rhineland.[136] The statement about Strasbourg, according to *Paris Soir* editor Pierre Lazareff, was 'more criticized in the French press than Hitler's initiative'.[137] It also earned for the prime minister the label 'Sarraut la Guerre' — the same term which had been applied to Poincaré during the Ruhr incursion.[138]

The sentiments of many Frenchmen were summed up by *République,* which declared that there must be other alternatives than Eden's surrender or Sarraut's war.[139] But, if forced to choose, there could be little doubt as to which policy was preferred. The communists published a manifesto demanding united resistance to those Frenchmen who wanted to conduct war and massacre, while the socialists warned the government against 'narrow formulas' capable of reducing the dispute to a mere question of *amour propre.*[140] From the right came demands for creation of a national government — something which the left dismissed as an attempt to postpone the elections or otherwise deprive the popular front of victory in six weeks' time.[141]

No one was prepared to risk having his candidate branded at the outset of the electoral campaign as having wanted war.[142] Although the extent of opposition to the government's conduct (as opposed to Sarraut's words) may have been subsequently overstated, it is equally true that Hitler's action was widely regarded in France as a 'complication of internal politics', with each end of the political spectrum seeking to inflict the opposition with blame or responsibility for what had or had not occurred.[143] The left charged that Germany would never have acted but for the chaos caused by the Abyssinian policies of Laval and his supporters. The right retaliated by arguing that the Franco-Soviet pact was the real villain. The coup itself, and the interests of France, were made subservient to the search for scapegoats. In the wake of the social, economic, financial and political problems which had beset France since the street riots of February 1934, Flandin was not unjustified in writing that the French people by 1936 had 'décidément . . . perdu le sens national'.[144]

The government's inability to stop the drift towards acquiescence represented a serious handicap to the advocates of resistance.[145] Flandin could not point to any general, or even particular pocket of support for this policy. But that did not prevent him and Léger from insisting that the French people, as distinct from the politicians and the press, were united and would respond to any call to arms.[146] The fact that they never succeeded in convincing the British would not have been so damaging to their cause if they had been prepared to force the issue. But, in the circumstances, Britain's resistance to Flandin's requests was increased by her belief that Paris was considerably more intransigent than the French people, who, according to former premier Joseph Caillaux and Sir George Clerk, were quietly applauding London's efforts to avert war.[147]

Concurrently, Flandin and the Quai d'Orsay did their utmost to put indirect pressure on Great Britain in an effort to show London that other powers besides France were concerned about the consequences of the coup.[148] Initial reactions, however, were not encouraging. Europe's press had generally condemned Hitler's action, but also ruled out any recourse to force and, to a lesser extent, urged examination of the Chancellor's proposals. And Eden's statement to the

Commons on the 9th had precipitated a diplomatic swing towards the British position, or at least away from the apparent collision course which Sarraut had outlined the night before.[149]

Only the Czech government had voiced its emphatic and repeated determination to 'conformerait exactement son attitude à celle de France' in every contingency.[150] The Rumanians, Yugoslavs and Poles had promised, à la Eden, to come to France's aid if she were the victim of unprovoked aggression.[151] But Belgrade was equally determined to fight in no other circumstances and to avoid any involvement capable of jeopardizing either her own economy or her flourishing trade with Germany.[152] The Rumanians, too, were reluctant to force a confrontation over Hitler's action, which apparently disturbed King Carol only by 'sa forme' rather than 'son fond'.[153] Bucharest intially expressed her willingness to support economic sanctions, which foreign minister Nicholas Titulescu believed would 'toucherait le Reich dans son oeuvre vive' if applied by the League as a whole.[154] But, as early as 8 March, Rumanian cabinet ministers concluded, in the presence of the French minister, that the best possible reply to Hitler was the creation of a solid bloc, 'non pas pour partir en guerre, mais au contraire pour empêcher la guerre'.[155]

In Poland, Colonel Beck allegedly declared to friends that he would resume his old army command if France were invaded.[156] But at the same time he made no secret of the fact that Warsaw did not regard the reoccupation of the Rhineland as a *casus foederis*. This position had been adopted after a close examination prior to 7 March revealed no obligation other than to assist each other in the event of unprovoked aggression.[157] In spite of Flandin's subsequent assertion that Beck promised Polish support if France 'entrait en guerre avec l'Allemagne', neither Paris nor London believed at this time that Warsaw would commit herself to any act which might upset Polish relations with Berlin.[158]

This conclusion was confirmed on 7 and 8 March in a semi-official communiqué published by the Iskra news agency which declared that Poland would be guided in the current crisis by her well-known desire for 'clear and practical' solutions and not by 'intricate formulas of procedure which have obscured political life in recent years'.[159] Nothing in

Beck's subsequent behaviour contradicted this initial judgement by Paris, especially after 14 March when the Polish foreign minister declared to both Flandin and Eden that Warsaw 'would feel no enthusiasm whatever for economic sanctions on behalf of an unpopular treaty which did not directly affect Poland'.[160]

The Russian position was equally ambiguous. The French ambassador in Moscow, Charles Alphand, reported on 8 March that 'diverse Soviet personalities' were urging Paris to react vigorously, starting with immediate Senate ratification of the Franco-Soviet pact.[161] Alphand also assured Flandin that France could count entirely on the support of the Soviet delegation at Geneva. But the documents do not indicate any direct French contact with the Kremlin or Litvinov before his departure for the League meeting on 11 March. This may have been a calculated omission, since Litvinov was apparently anxious to avoid any action that might encourage France to march into the Rhineland. Such a riposte, he told US ambassador William Bullitt on 7 March, would mean immediate war. Instead, the Soviet foreign minister favoured lifting economic sanctions against Italy and imposing them on Germany.[162]

It is still not inconceivable that Moscow gave some specific early assurances to Paris; Russia may even have offered immediate and unqualified military support for any action by her French ally.[163] If so, these promises were undoubtedly given in the belief, as Litvinov had explained to Bullitt on the 7th, that there was 'no chance whatsoever' that France would send troops into Germany.[164] Nor does it appear that Paris believed totally in the sincerity of any Russian assurances. Gamelin said that the government was uncertain of Moscow's attitude on 8 March.[165] Sarraut later testified that 'only Czechoslovakia' had been loyal during the Rhineland crisis.[166] Cabinet colleague Georges Bonnet also omitted Russia from his list of French supporters, as did Czech president Edouard Beneš, ambassador Léon Noël and a chief of the French air staff.[167] Nevertheless, Flandin was persuaded, or at least told Eden he was, that Moscow would fully support progressive sanctions against Germany.[168]

Mussolini, on the other hand, had remained noncommittal, leaving it to Suvich to emphasize to the French ambassador on 9 March that Rome could hardly turn against her German trading partner so long as Italy remained herself under sanctions.[169] Cerruti adopted a correspondingly reserved attitude, while Attolico in Berlin warned Poncet that Rome would never forgive Paris if she succumbed to any attempts by London to trade a tough British stand in the Rhineland for a redoubled French effort against Italy.[170] Cerruti and Rome apparently also gave the Quai d'Orsay sufficient signals to convince Flandin and Léger that Mussolini's assistance could, and therefore should, be obtained by dropping all sanctions against Italy.[171]

Even without the support of Rome and Warsaw, however, Flandin felt certain that most European powers would respond to an Anglo-French lead and that London and Paris could count upon enough outside support to guarantee the success of both economic and military measures.[172] To reinforce both the opportunity and the need for action, the foreign minister sought to persuade as many governments as he could to stress to His Majesty's Government the importance of British leadership in upholding collective security, the sanctity of treaties, and the impact on both the League and the international treaty system of acquiescence in the face of a *fait accompli*.[173] The immediate implications of the coup on French security were deliberately played down. The Quai d'Orsay was more anxious that London should be warned of the long-range strategic and political consequences for eastern and central Europe if the Rhineland were sealed and of the demoralizing effect on non-aligned nations if the western powers did not react with firmness when they were challenged directly. These points were included in five despatches sent between 8 and 11 March to League council countries, as well as other European capitals. *Démarches* were not in every case ordered, but Flandin expected the French thesis to be forcefully argued in order to secure a unanimous vote and to encourage non-Locarno powers both to understand what was at stake for Geneva and to relay these concerns to Britain.

Three specific efforts were made by the Quai d'Orsay. Flandin first tried to get president Franklin Roosevelt to condemn unilateral treaty violations on moral grounds.[174] Firmness from across the Atlantic, he believed, would have an important effect on London, since even as early as 1935 the British government had been conducting its foreign policy with an eye to the United States—it being already an axiom in Whitehall that victory in any war against Germany or Japan would depend to a large extent on American resources.[175] But, in spite of Roosevelt's public criticism a few weeks earlier about dictators and their methods, Washington refused to become involved in what was described by secretary of state Cordell Hull as 'a European development in which we were not involved'.[176] This isolationist attitude, coupled with a certain sympathy for Hitler's arguments in some American newspapers, not only did Flandin no good, but enabled Eden to wage his campaign of crisis deflation in the knowledge that London, not Paris, was acting more in harmony with the sentiments of the United States.[177]

No sooner had his American bid foundered than Flandin despatched telegrams to the Little and Balkan Entente powers, which, he argued, were well-placed to exert pressure on Britain as a result of their having made heavy sacrifices to support London's drive to impose sanctions on Rome.[178] These five powers, the foreign minister hoped, would emphasize to His Majesty's Government that her attitude toward her obligations would in large measure determine whether the League and collective security system survived the crisis.

However, Flandin was only 40 per cent successful. The Czechs complied willingly.[179] So, too, did Titulescu, who organized an informal meeting of Entente representatives at Geneva on 11 March and afterwards told journalists that all five powers had pledged to support Paris 'absolutely and without reservation . . . with all the means at their disposal'.[180] But the impact of this declaration was undermined by strongly-worded denials from Belgrade, Athens and Ankara, all of which publicly repudiated Titulescu's communiqué and privately reaffirmed to London and Berlin their desire for a peaceful solution to the Rhineland problem.[181] Nevertheless, French officials did not hesitate to give the impression that Paris was being pressed by her eastern allies to take resolute action.[182] The Quai d'Orsay also used the ambivalent reactions to the coup of non-Locarno powers to argue that the outcome of the current crisis would largely determine the future orientation of countries like Poland, Yugoslavia, Austria, Rumania, Turkey and even Czechoslovakia.[183] 'La question', it was argued, 'est celle de savoir si l'Europe sera ou non allemande.'[184]

Most important and most successful of Flandin's diplomatic efforts was his enlistment of Belgian support in dealing with both the League council and London. This was no small achievement in view of the fact that even the pro-French Walloon press had responded to the coup without displaying any desire for direct retaliation, while the Flemings generally called for a calm examination of Hitler's proposals.[185] From both communities had come almost universal condemnation of Sarraut's radio speech. The prevailing sentiment, summarized by *Nation Belge,* was 'above all, let us not imitate the French'.[186] Instead, Eden's statement on the 9th was broadly considered as a model for Brussels's own attitude.[187]

The chances of securing wholehearted Belgian support were further reduced by the fact that Hitler struck at a time when relations with Paris had cooled, primarily because of Belgium's desire to terminate the Franco-Belgian military agreement of 1920 in order to secure parliamentary approval for rearmament.[188] The existence in 1936 of this pact, whose contents had remained secret, gave rise to fears that Brussels might be committed to allowing Gamelin's armies to cross Belgian soil to attack Germany as a result of France's fresh agreement with Moscow.[189] Brussels had just been given an example of the hazards posed by the Franco-Soviet pact, since Hitler had used it as the pretext for repudiating his Rhine and Locarno obligations to Belgium, thereby making her an innocent victim.[190]

This evolution of the French ally into a potential liability to Brussels and the re-emergence of Germany as a military power had stimulated two other trends in Belgian opinion. First was the desire to substitute Britain for France as Belgium's major benefactor.[191] Even more significant was the emergence of a feeling that Brussels should stop acting like a great power and revert to a position of guaranteed neutrality in which she maintained her own defences and retained her Locarno guarantees, but abandoned her role as a guarantor.[192]

These currents of Belgian opinion ultimately benefited Britain. But initially premier Zeeland was persuaded by Paris to support a hard line in resisting *faits accomplis,* rather than the acquiescent British approach to the coup.[193] Brussels joined France in pressing London for an early meeting of Locarno powers, in Paris on 10 March, instead of the 12th or 13th at Geneva, as Eden had preferred.[194] Most important,

Zeeland agreed with Flandin that a German refusal to comply voluntarily should be regarded as grounds for forcing Berlin by all necessary means to meet a reasonable request.[195] This Franco-Belgian identity of views proved extremely effective during the early meetings of the Locarno powers.[196]

But Belgian support was not total or sustained.[197] Zeeland did not subscribe to Flandin's demands for the full restoration of the *status quo*.[198] Instead, he believed that Hitler should be obliged to make a partial withdrawal or perform some other gesture which would re-establish confidence in Germany's respect for international law.[199] The prime minister was also more willing than Paris to seek compromise in the face of British objections in order to preserve Anglo-French unity.[200] Moreover, Belgium was prepared to accept a new Locarno, with Germany, so long as she retained Britain's guarantee, whereas France was determined to deprive Berlin of these benefits.[201]

Flandin's third task in preparing to face the British was to produce a plan of action capable of persuading London that Germany could be forced into withdrawing from the demilitarized zone without the Locarno powers having to resort to arms.[202] This was probably the foreign minister's most important job, since, without a workable scheme, there was no chance of inducing London to cooperate. Above all, that meant devising a course of sanctions which moved progressively towards military measures, rather than starting, say, with a request that His Majesty's Government subscribe to a *prise de gages*. Such an approach would also give London every opportunity at each stage to exert her influence with Hitler in order to secure a peaceful withdrawal, on the understanding that negotiations could begin thereafter to allow a limited troop presence, but not fortifications, west of the Rhine. At that time, the other points in the Chancellor's proposals of 7 March would be considered.

Thus, according to Flandin's plan, after the League council had declared Germany to be in violation of her Locarno obligations, Hitler would be expected to restore the *status quo* in the Rhineland.[203] If he refused, the League council would be asked to invoke economic or financial sanctions in accordance with the Stresa resolution of 17 April 1935, which authorized such measures in response to a treaty violation. In spite of widespread reluctance on the part of League members

to undertake a second such burden, the foreign minister felt it
would not be difficult to win support so long as London and
Paris supplied the leadership—and especially if sanctions
against Rome could be simultaneously wound down or even
terminated.[204]

If an embargo against Berlin did not produce the desired
withdrawal, then, as a last resort, Flandin anticipated that the
Locarno powers should take some military action, such as a
prise de gages, which would be held until Hitler climbed
down.[205] Flandin did not believe that such measures would
ever have to be implemented, but he realized that the British
would insist on knowing precisely what Paris had in mind.[206]
To meet this inevitable request, the naval and military staffs
were requested to produce some specific plans for limited
land and sea measures to be effected without mobilization.[207]

Hopes for any joint naval action, such as a *coup de filet* or
blockade of a German port, were dashed by naval chief of staff
G. E. J. Durand-Viel and Piétri, who insisted that there was no
such thing as a peaceful *prise de gages,* unless executed by a
strong power against a weak and helpless victim.[208] Such
action was possible against Germany in 1920 and 1923, Piétri
explained, but in 1936 'n'est plus en question'.[209] What would
happen, the admirals asked, if a German vessel refused to
heed a challenge? If the French navy allowed it to escape, they
risked humiliation. If they opened fire, it would be 'guerre
totale'.[210]

Gamelin responded with two specific ideas.[211] The first
involved the military occupation of Luxembourg, both as a
show of strength and to protect the Grand Duchy from
possible German invasion. But the army chief acknowledged
that this would probably not secure the zone's evacuation. The
other plan was to employ the *armée de couverture* to seize a strip
of the German frontier from Saarbrücken to Merzig—an area
about 25 miles long and ranging in depth from 1 to 8 miles.
The advantages of this scheme were that French forces could
execute it without straining supply lines and German troops
would have the river Saar at their backs. If this occupation of
Saar meadowland passed off peacefully, then Gamelin was
prepared to take Saarbrücken, Kehl and whatever else the
government wished. But he still insisted that Hitler would not
rest until the French had been thrown out of the Rhineland.
Thus, Gamelin warned, France risked not only losing her best

active soldiers at the outset of hostilities, but also having her forces concentrated in one area, thereby leaving the rest of the frontier vulnerable to counter-attack. For France, this meant mobilization and war and required that Paris be assured in advance of sufficient allied support to defeat the German armies.[212]

The military's inability to produce a low-risk plan did not deter the Quai d'Orsay, for two reasons. First was the suspicion that the chiefs of staff were intent on avoiding any confrontation with Germany.[213] Moreover, Gamelin was drawing political conclusions about Hitler's reactions which the foreign ministry and Poncet were in a much better position to make.[214] But even those who agreed that any French move across the frontier would be resisted were not discouraged, since there existed within the Quai d'Orsay a strong conviction that it would never come to military measures, provided London and Paris showed themselves at the outset determined to take whatever action was necessary to achieve results.[215]

In the first place, it was believed that the German economy was so vulnerable that Hitler could not risk having sanctions imposed, especially if they cut off Berlin's access to foreign exchange.[216] The corollary to this was that imposition of such restrictions would quickly bring the Chancellor to reason. Even if a deadlock then developed, the Quai d'Orsay felt confident that the mere threat of military action would suffice, especially if the Locarno powers were supported by Prague, Moscow and possibly Bucharest.[217]

In the face of such a powerful coalition, the French foreign ministry believed that Hitler would voluntarily withdraw his troops from the Rhineland.[218] Paris did not altogether discount the possibility that the Chancellor, once driven into a corner, might fight to avoid humiliation.[219] But Léger believed the army would disobey orders rather than embark on what he described as a policy of suicide.[220] Flandin went even further in a conversation with the Belgian ambassador on 9 March. He argued that the general staff would refuse to commit 'la folie' of engaging the country in a 'hopeless escapade' against the allies, and that if Hitler refused to order a withdrawal, his reign would collapse and the Reichswehr would establish a military dictatorship in Berlin.[221] This was all the more likely, the foreign minister explained, in view of reports reaching Paris that the coup had been instigated by Göring and Goebbels over the objections of the army, Auswärtiges Amt and business community—all of whom were thought to be hoping that the Nazi radicals would receive a crushing setback.[222]

On 10 March, the French scheme for successive economic, financial and military sanctions was laid before Eden and lord privy seal Lord Halifax at a meeting of the remaining Rhine pact powers in Paris.[223] Flandin's presentation was fully endorsed by Zeeland, who agreed that respect for international law must be restored 'de bon gré ou de mauvais gré'.[224] The key to this operation, they argued, was that the Locarno powers must make clear to Germany both their intentions and their determination to face war if necessary. If Berlin were convinced that Britain, Belgium and France were resolved on this course of action, Zeeland added, then the chances of Hitler allowing it to come to war were only one in ten.[225]

Even if the Chancellor did precipitate a conflict, Flandin stressed, it was better to accept the challenge now and put an end to German pretensions while Berlin was still without allies and not yet so strong.[226] On the other hand, the Belgian prime minister warned, acquiescence over the Rhineland would guarantee a terrible conflict in two or three years when Germany was much more formidable. It was this inevitability, Zeeland added, which would ensure the full support of the Belgian peoples. Flandin, too, insisted that even the most pacific Frenchmen realized what was at stake and would willingly support such a policy, even to the extent of taking up arms, once the Locarno governments had set the tone and provided the leadership.

Equally, Flandin and Zeeland emphasized that it was no good embarking on this course if all those concerned were not prepared to go all the way.[227] One could not rely on a 'politique de bluff' to succeed against Hitler. The worst possible result of the Rhine coup, they argued, would be for Britain and France to begin and then back down.[228] If that occurred, they felt, Berlin would have scored a moral and psychological victory over her two most immediate and strongest potential opponents.[229] Such a capitulation, it was feared, would not only encourage Hitler to move quickly in every direction, but would also convince several European powers, including even the Czechs, that they had better compose with Germany before the Wehrmacht arrived in their capitals, as Hitler later described it to Schuschnigg, 'just like a spring storm'.[230]

In the face of this surprising show of Franco-Belgian solidarity, Eden probed for weaknesses or divergencies.[231] But the only point of any consequence was Zeeland's willingness to accept a partial withdrawal of German troops, so long as Hitler took some positive action to demonstrate his respect for treaties, and provided that Britain gave some security guarantees to compensate Paris and Brussels for the loss of their Rhine *glacis*. The Belgian prime minister also maintained that if the affair were handled in such a way that Hitler performed his act of contrition without withdrawing his proposals, then it might be possible, under Britain's leadership, to reach a settlement which would bring a generation of peace. Nevertheless, while Zeeland believed that the Chancellor should not be asked to take any step involving total loss of face, the prime minister remained convinced that the Locarno powers were duty-bound to ensure that a German gesture was forthcoming.[232]

As a result of these conversations, Eden cabled the foreign office, pronouncing the situation 'so complex and so critical' that he could not proceed as planned to Geneva without further consultations with the cabinet.[233] He therefore proposed that, in order to keep events 'as closely as possible under British influence', the League council's special session and all subsequent Locarno power consultations should be moved to London. This was agreed to, not least by Flandin, who, far from being misled or somehow tricked into acceptance, realized that his best chance of succeeding was if he could work directly on the British public and, especially, on the opinion leaders and foreign policy makers in Whitehall and Westminster, as well as in the clubs and on Fleet street, where 'the voice of France . . . had ceased to be heard or understood'.[234]

The decision to cross the Channel has been described as the beginning of the end for the French intransigents.[235] Others have charged that Flandin went to London determined only to place the responsibility for inaction on Britain. Neither assertion is entirely accurate. Far from feeling beaten, the French delegation arrived determined to press home the arguments which had driven Eden back to London.[236] But the limits of French diplomacy had been circumscribed in three important ways. First was the refusal to act alone—a decision which was imposed upon the Sarraut government on 27 February and 8 March by the attitude of its military establishment.[237] It was reconfirmed on the 11th, when the council of ministers authorized Flandin to act in London 'au mieux des intérêts de la France'.[238] The second limitation was the foreign minister's refusal to jeopardize the Anglo-French *entente*, either by forcing Britain to fulfil her obligations against the will of her people, or by applying so much pressure that London felt compelled to declare publicly her inability to keep her pledged word.[239] Short of that, however, Flandin was prepared to use every argument and lever at his disposal.

Thirdly, the foreign minister did not intend to place Britain and France in any position from which they might later be forced to retreat in the face of German intransigence.[240] To capitulate after having challenged the Chancellor, he felt, would have the worst possible effect. Rather than risk isolated action or a rupture with London or a diplomatic and moral defeat at Hitler's hands, Flandin was prepared to abandon his hopes of punishing Berlin directly.[241] Instead, he would agree to indirect measures, so long as they clearly demonstrated that the Chancellor had suffered for his action. But the French government was not prepared for at least a week to acknowledge that it would accept anything less than total withdrawal of all the regular German soldiers who had marched into the Rhineland on 7 and 8 March.[242]

Perhaps it was possible to have realized from the outset that French policy militated against any breach with Britain and that Sarraut, Mandel and Flandin were acting in advance of the rest of the cabinet and country.[243] Indeed, Eden later described Flandin's attitude as resembling that of a man who, having declared his intention to leap off a cliff, casts longing looks over his shoulder at his coat-tails.[244] But it was a far more worried foreign secretary who confronted his cabinet colleagues on 11 March with the news that Paris and Brussels were prepared 'to see it through to a successful end'.[245]

5 Britain rejects force

*Everyone agreed that we could not contemplate
war, but we must make every effort to avoid
repudiation of Locarno.*
                    Neville Chamberlain, 11 March

Events at Paris had revealed a fundamental British misinter-
pretation of French intentions. The foreign secretary and his
subordinates had surmised from the weekend's activities that
the French were not planning to cause difficulties.[1] This
conclusion was based on several pieces of evidence. First was
the absence of any panic in Paris or Strasbourg.[2] The French
press, while condemning the coup root and branch, had
shown no disposition to treat the matter as a *casus belli*.[3] Both
Corbin in London and Flandin in Paris had reacted calmly,
with the foreign minister pledging that the French government would do nothing to render the situation more difficult.[4]
At the same time, the decision to appeal to the League of
Nations looked promising.[5] So did the suggestion by Flandin
to Clerk that Paris envisaged asking the League council to
condemn the German action in terms analogous to those used
in the resolution of 17 April 1935 in connexion with Germany's reintroduction of conscription.[6]

Eden had also been pleased by the ease with which he had
avoided having the United Kingdom associated with the
French and Belgian appeals to Geneva on 8 March. This, he
felt, had preserved London's full freedom of action and had
thereby put Britain in an optimum position to ensure that the
League council did some 'constructive work'.[7] Moreover, the
French government had implemented only defensive
military preparations. No steps had been taken which could
be described as threatening or provocative.[8] Finally, Flandin
had shown the utmost interest in concerting with the remaining Rhine pact powers before taking any position at
Geneva.[9] The French foreign minister had insisted on an
early meeting, but he had also agreed to Eden's demand that
no decisions of any sort should be made during the Locarno
deliberations in Paris.[10] That meant that Britain would have a
chance to present her arguments before France committed

herself to any irrevocable position. It also improved Eden's
and his colleagues' chances of managing the crisis.[11]

In this connexion, the foreign secretary was also assisted by
the sudden manner in which the coup had been executed. The
situation was thus stabilized almost from the outset. And, by
employing a relatively small force without tanks or other
offensive weapons, Hitler had minimized the danger of the
French being panicked into retaliation or treating the coup as
a flagrant violation of Locarno.[12] This conspicuous absence of
aggressive intent meant that Flandin would face an exception-
ally difficult task if Paris wanted to reply forcefully without
being denounced by British and world opinion.[13]

The only cloud on the French horizon in the first seventy-
two hours had been Sarraut's refusal to negotiate with Berlin
as long as the Rhineland remained remilitarized. This speech
had 'most unfavourably impressed' the cabinet, which had
thought it 'ominous'.[14] But, instead of rallying support for the
French position, the prime minister's speech had intensified
European support for Eden's policy of quick condemnation
and early negotiations.[15] It may have been because of
nervousness precipitated by the prime minister's speech that
Eden had asked to be accompanied to Paris by Halifax. But it
seems more probable that the foreign secretary and the
cabinet were anxious to reassure British public opinion and
protect themselves from any repetition of Sir Samuel Hoare's
fateful visit to Laval in Paris three months earlier to discuss
Abyssinia.[16]

The contrast between British hopes and French expectations was at no point greater than during the first three or four
days of the crisis. For example, in a cabinet paper prepared on
8 March, Eden had all but dismissed a military riposte because
France was 'not in a mood for military adventure'.[17] This
seemed a reasonable assumption in view of Flandin's declaration to Clerk only a month earlier that French public
opinion utterly excluded any idea of marching into
Germany.[18] As a result, Eden had envisaged that the French
government would probably adopt an attitude of 'sulking and
passive obstruction' towards negotiations. Unfortunately, he
added, Britain was in no position 'to browbeat her with what
we think reasonableness', because of the absolute juridical
grip which the Locarno pact gave to France.[19]

To 'induce or cajole' her to come to the conference table,

the foreign secretary had thought it would be necessary for His Majesty's Government to make some concessions.[20] But, in considering alternatives, he had rejected any suggestion of economic or financial sanctions by the League. Nor did he like the idea of referring to The Hague the German complaint about the incompatibility of the Franco-Soviet and Locarno pacts. Both of these demands, he argued, were 'impracticable' and 'inconsistent' with any idea of negotiations, which he described as being 'inevitable'.[21] Instead, the foreign secretary and his cabinet colleagues had hoped to trade simple condemnation of the coup by the League council for French participation in talks on the proposals in Hitler's memorandum, which Eden regarded as 'one of the most important documents . . . since the war'.[22] No one took the mutual demilitarized zone as anything but a propaganda trick.[23] But the other six proposals were judged by the foreign secretary as constituting a *contre-partie* capable of producing a 'very considerable effect on public opinion'.[24]

This was especially true of the Chancellor's willingness to return to Geneva.[25] After all, the British government had been urging Berlin to rejoin the League almost from the moment of her withdrawal.[26] Now, after nearly thirty months, Hitler had apparently yielded, ostensibly out of deference to Britain's attachment to the Geneva principle and the collective security system.[27] Such a move, while intrinsically good, had the added advantage of being incapable of impeding Britain's freedom of action, especially regarding rearmament. There was nothing in the proposals involving mutual restrictions or serious concessions, such as the limitation of air arms, which could put London and Paris at a disadvantage if Hitler surreptitiously violated his undertakings. This held true equally for the new Locarno and air pacts, which Eden described as coinciding generally with Britain's own desiderata.[28]

Nor were Hitler's proposed non-aggression pacts with his eastern neighbours out of harmony with the feelings of such foreign office officials as Wigram, Sargent, William Strang and the two parliamentary under-secretaries, Lords Cranborne and Stanhope, all of whom were prepared to assist Germany's peaceful penetration into Danubia and the Balkans.[29] Some reservations were felt towards Hitler's raising the colonial question, but this did not come as a surprise and the Chancellor's proposal was moderate compared with recent demands by Nazi extremists for the immediate restoration of all Germany's former possessions.[30] As far as Eden was concerned, the main flaws were not with the six serious proposals, but with the method employed and with the fact that the Chancellor's *fait accompli* had deprived London of her best bargaining counter, which meant entering negotiations at a disadvantage'.[31]

Parliament, press and public had cheered the foreign secretary's promise to the House of Commons on 9 March that the government would 'clear-sightedly and objectively' examine the Chancellor's proposals with a view to rebuilding the foundations of peace in western Europe.[32] The prime minister had also been well received when he had said that Britain's aim in Europe was 'to bring France and Germany together in a friendship with ourselves'.[33] Now, barely two days later, cabinet members were told that, instead of endorsing a policy of quick condemnation and early negotiations, the French government was determined to enforce the Locarno treaty to the letter.[34] Eden expressed some reservations about whether French and Belgian public opinion was as determined as Flandin and Zeeland had indicated.[35] But neither the foreign secretary nor Halifax could or would gainsay the argument that acquiescence would inevitably lead to a 'very dangerous' conflict within two or three years.[36]

For the first time since 7 March, the British cabinet faced major decisions capable of leading the United Kingdom and Europe into war.[37] At least that was how Phipps, the foreign office and most cabinet members viewed the consequences of the Franco-Belgian demand for successive sanctions to achieve a full or even partial restoration of the demilitarized zone. The assumption that Hitler would climb down in the face of external pressure was seen as untenable. So was the suggestion that the Führer would be brought down from within, especially by the same generals who, nineteen months earlier, had sworn an oath of loyalty to him as their supreme commander. This clash of views over the impact, effectiveness and consequences of sanctions was one of the most fundamental of all differences separating London and Paris. As long as it existed, there could be no meeting of minds on the question of punishing Germany directly for her action. And, no matter how hard they tried, the French failed to convince

Eden and his colleagues that coercion could be peaceful or
that Hitler could be brought to heel if only he were confronted by a firm Anglo-French front. In this respect, Neville
Chamberlain spoke for most of Britain's foreign policy
makers when he declared to Flandin that His Majesty's
Government could 'not accept this as a reliable estimate of a
mad dictator's reactions'.[38]

Almost to a man, the cabinet believed that effective
economic sanctions could, and military measures would, precipitate a 'mad dog' act.[39] This was no less true of the foreign
office, where it was held that 'the whole atmosphere in
present-day Germany is such that war would in almost any
case be preferred to the dishonour of surrender in the face of
foreign pressure'.[40] Even the mildest embargo frightened
London, since it was felt that if, as expected, Berlin did not
capitulate quickly, there would be great pressure on the
Locarno powers to apply a blockade and then even harsher
measures in order to avoid being humiliated.[41] It might then
prove impossible to reverse the process and Britain could find
herself slipping, willy-nilly, into military action—and on the
side of the 'aggressor' in the eyes of world opinion.[42]

Nor was there much doubt in London that the German
people would support their Chancellor in order to repel any
invader.[43] The prime, but by no means only, exponent of
these ideas was Eric Phipps.[44] 'It must not be imagined', he
warned, 'that Herr Hitler and his friends are building up the
most formidable military machine in the world today merely
to relegate it to the scrap-heap when threatened with sanctions.' On the contrary, Phipps believed Germany was ruled
by 'bold and determined adventurers', who would plunge
into war with 'fanatical and formidable courage' rather than
submit to being drowned by sanctions. The ambassador was
also convinced that the German people would 'rally like one
man to the clarion call' of their Führer in such a contingency,
particularly since the public had never regarded Locarno as
anything other than a device to induce the French to remove
the occupation forces from the Rhineland. The world would
be 'astonished', Phipps predicted, by the fortitude and
resolution of this resistance.[45]

As early as 1935, the British war and foreign offices had
concluded that Germany was already capable of defending
herself successfully.[46] Indeed, their primary concern during

this period was to predict when the Wehrmacht would be able to launch an attack.[47] Thus, the military attaché in Berlin, Colonel F. Elliott Hotblack, was only preaching to the converted when he reported on 11 March 1936 that the German armed forces, while still unprepared for offensive action, were capable of putting up 'very determined' resistance, especially if Germany were attacked on only one front.[48] This held true even for an invasion via the Rhineland, Hotblack explained, since non-regular forces in the demilitarized zone had long been trained to make demolitions and resist any attack.[49] To this Phipps added his own conviction that the German army and its chiefs would not only refuse to quit the Rhineland, but 'fight to the finish' in any defensive war.[50]

As far as the cabinet was concerned, the question was not whether Flandin's sanctions policy could be implemented short of war, but whether Britain should, could, or would fight Germany at this time. Even though most ministers and military leaders had no quarrel with the conclusions drawn by Phipps about the increasing threat to the United Kingdom and Europe posed by the Third Reich, no member of the government, foreign office or chiefs of staff wanted to run the risk of war which they believed was implicit in Flandin's demands to restore the *status quo* in the Rhineland. The reasons fell into four categories: military-strategic, domestic, personal-political and ideological.

The spectre of a conflagration was abhorrent to a government which had just begun to remedy the worst of the arms deficiencies which had accumulated during the initial postwar decade.[51] These were due at first to a natural decrease in spending and the presence of vast quantities of surplus war material, which had become largely obsolescent by July 1929. That was when Chancellor of the Exchequer Winston Churchill persuaded the government to instruct the service chiefs, not only to plan henceforth for no major war for ten years, but also to advance this date annually, so that war was never closer than a decade away.[52]

Events in Manchuria and Europe soon revealed the folly of such an assumption. But when the rule was abandoned after thirty-two months Britain's military leaders had been reckoning on no war before March 1942! Nor was it immediately possible to attack the re-equipment problem, since Europe generally and Britain in particular were by then deeply in-

volved in the effort to bring about universal disarmament.
Finally, in the autumn of 1934, with Hitler's withdrawal from
the League, the disarmament conference on the rocks, and
Germany's clandestine rearmament an open secret, British
officials were able to begin repairing the damage. But most of
the preparatory work had to be done behind closed doors,
since ministers feared, as late as the elections of November
1935, that the British electorate was easy prey to opposition
charges that Baldwin had abandoned the principle of 'pooled
security' and was extensively rearming for some unspecified
purpose.[53]

This parlous state of affairs, Baldwin pointed out, was
perfectly well known to the French.[54] And yet Paris seemed
intent on pursuing a policy which would ultimately force
Britain to admit that she was militarily incapable of fulfilling
her treaty obligations. At no time in the pre-war period was
the situation worse than in March 1936. With the bulk of her
ships and planes concentrated in the Mediterranean and
Egypt, Great Britain was, in the opinion of the chiefs of staff,
'perilously exposed in the air and completely open to attack by
sea'.[55] Mobilization was deemed imperative if home defence
forces were to have any value whatever. But even this could
not compensate for the fact that Britain had been denuded of
naval and air forces 'to an extent almost unparalleled in the
past'. To go to war over the Rhineland, they concluded, would
be 'a disaster for which the Services with their existing commitments in the Mediterranean are totally unprepared'.[56]

Even the mobilized navy, it was reported, would still lack
sufficient strength to deal with the Germans, or to secure the
British Isles, or her trade routes. It would not even be capable
of providing adequate escorts for any expeditionary forces.
Coastal air defences south of a line from Milford Haven to
Harwich consisted of 16 antiquated guns and 25 searchlights.
There were no defences at all at Scapa Flow. Only two ports
(Rosyth and Portsmouth) had even limited anti-submarine
defences. The rest were unprotected.[57]

Nor could much be expected of the mobilized air force of
218 first-line and 218 reserve craft, especially since many of
these machines had been stripped of oxygen apparatus, bomb
carriers and electrical gear to provide reserves for the forces
in Egypt. To make matters worse, Britain's 72 light bombers
did not have the range to attack German targets from home

bases. Her 30 heavy bombers could only reach the Ruhr and were capable of a total retaliatory effort of about 25 tons of explosives daily 'for a short period'. Of the 84 fighters available on mobilization, 36 were of 'very doubtful operational value'. Only 24 fighters were capable of night flights. In short, the air chiefs warned, both Britain and her shipping would be exposed to Luftwaffe attack. It would be difficult, Swinton added, 'to imagine a worse situation. . . . if an emergency should arise'.[58]

The position of the army, already 10,000 men below strength, would also be 'thoroughly unsatisfactory' after mobilization, and little help could be expected from the territorials, who were 40,000 men short.[59] It would be possible after three weeks to send only two divisions abroad—largely on a horsed basis and without any anti-aircraft personnel. In addition, this field force would have no tanks, anti-tank guns or mortars and only four months' supply of artillery ammunition.[60] Nor would mobilization improve the home air defences, which were non-existent outside greater London and which consisted of 68 anti-aircraft guns and only enough searchlights to cover a fighting zone some 40 miles wide and 12 miles deep. Not only was there 'very little' anti-aircraft ammunition still in Britain, but unavoidable circumstances had caused production to drop from 8,000 to 4,000 rounds per week between December 1935 and March 1936. Although manufacturers were working to capacity, the fact was, as Baldwin admitted, 'we have hardly got any armaments firms left'.[61]

It was therefore essential, the chiefs of staff concluded, that all war material should be immediately withdrawn from the Mediterranean if there was 'the smallest danger' of hostilities with Germany. But, even if peace could be secured at once in that region, Britain's military posture would not be improved for some time, since the 'excessive strain' of seven months of 'instant readiness' without mobilization had 'exhausted practically the whole of our meagre forces'.[62]

The major beneficiary of a restoration of normal relations with Rome would be the navy. Almost the entire fleet could be back in home waters within ten days. Most important, however, the battle-cruisers *Hood* and *Renown* would then be available. This was essential, it was felt, since they were the only ships in European waters capable of dealing effectively

with Germany's three new pocket battleships, which, along
with her seventeen sea-ready submarines, were regarded by
the admiralty as a 'serious threat' to British shipping.[63] For
the army, the removal of contingents from Egypt and Malta
could only mean that the missing anti-aircraft and tank units
could be supplied to the expeditionary force. But the total
strength of that force would remain at two divisions 'for some
months', owing to the impossibility of equipping and maintaining a larger force from the outset. The air force stood to
gain 144 first-line planes—but no heavy bombers—from such
a withdrawal. However, the chiefs of staff reported that it
would require three or four months before these machines
would be operational again. At that time, the home air
strength would be 362 first-line and 362 immediate reserve
aircraft. This force, the air chiefs warned, would be 'quite
incapable' of securing Britain against Luftwaffe attack and
effectively prosecuting an air offensive against Germany.

The impact of this military weakness on Britain's leaders
cannot be assessed fully unless it is viewed together with four
other convictions: that the bomber was unstoppable; that a
European conflagration would almost certainly produce two
other explosions; that anything less than Germany's total
defeat could have worse consequences for London than for
Berlin; and that allies in a war over the Rhineland would be
scarce.

The Germans, it was believed, were building an air force of
unparalleled strength, consisting primarily of bombers, and
capable in 1936 of delivering the greatly-feared knock-out
blow.[64] This prospect weighed heavily on the government,
particularly in view of Britain's utter defencelessness against
aerial attack.[65] Baldwin himself had more than once declared
that the survival of civilization might depend, barring all-
round aerial disarmament, on possession of a strike force
capable of bomb-for-bomb retaliation—it being almost
universally assumed in this pre-radar era that 'the bomber
will always get through'.[66]

In this respect, it had been feared for some months by both
the air ministry and foreign office that the position *vis-à-vis* the
Luftwaffe would be 'extremely dangerous' during 1936
because British aircraft production could not be accelerated,
whereas German industry was already capable of expanding
its output to war levels.[67] And, since it was also felt that all

existing first-line and reserve aircraft would either be in pieces or worn out after the first one or two months of combat, control of the air would go to the belligerent who could produce planes fastest.[68] Thus, even if the knock-out blow proved illusory, German industrial superiority would enable the Luftwaffe to gain mastery, perhaps permanently, if Göring's bombers were then to concentrate on destroying enemy aircraft plants.[69]

The spectre of a war with Germany was itself abhorrent, but, as the Chief of Imperial General Staff, Sir Archibald Montgomery-Massingberd, warned on 8 March, such a conflict would be 'impossible to limit'.[70] Baldwin and his colleagues also had to face the danger of war on two or even three fronts.[71] Only a few months before the coup, the committee on defence requirements had implored the cabinet to conduct its foreign policy so as to avoid the simultaneous and 'suicidal' hostility of Japan, Germany and any power on the main line of communication between the two.[72] In March 1936, it seemed possible that a clash with Hitler might inspire Mussolini to attack Egypt.

Any conflict in Europe or the Mediterranean, it was felt, would almost certainly prompt Tokyo to attack British interests north of Singapore, which were regarded in London as being 'at the mercy of the Japanese'.[73] This threat was sufficiently serious for the first lord of the admiralty Sir Bolton Eyres-Monsell, to have warned the French in January 1936 that Japanese aggression would be of 'greater concern' to Britain than German action in eastern Europe.[74] Furthermore, the chiefs of staff had consistently maintained that 1936 would be a critical year in the Pacific, since Tokyo would have modernized most of her capital ships and expanded her air forces.[75] In contrast, Eyres-Monsell reported on 3 March that the British fleet was in no condition to undertake a war with Japan.[76] The entire eastern half of the empire might be doomed, it was feared, if the Japanese attacked while the United Kingdom was fighting Hitler.[77]

The chiefs of staff also warned regularly of the disastrous effect which even mild losses in any clash would have on Britain's ability to fulfil her worldwide responsibilities.[78] They also stressed the disruption which such a conflict could cause to her rearmament efforts and, especially, her pursuit of air parity with the Germans.[79] Unless the ultimate enemy,

Germany, were destroyed, it was considered possible that the
United Kingdom might incur the heavier blow in the long
run, since German industrial organization and capacity
would make it possible for Hitler, or his successor, to replace
war materials much more quickly than the victors.[80] No one
emphasized this point better than Winston Churchill when he
declared to the House of Commons on 10 March that the Nazi
government had pumped £1,500 million into warlike preparations since 1933, including £800 million in 1935 alone.[81]
By contrast, he doubted if Britain in 1936 could spend even
£187 million, owing to the unpreparedness of her armaments
industries. This, he lamented, was an 'unprecedented and
unparalleled fact to face'.[82]

The chances of dealing a crippling blow to Nazi ambitions
at this time were further decreased by a belief in Whitehall
that there would be little outside support for a forceful policy
over the demilitarized zone. The Italian guarantor had
declared that she would fulfil none of her Locarno obligations
as long as Rome remained under sanctions.[83] Nor would
Britain under any circumstances have acquiesced in the
French desire to secure Mussolini's support by raising the
embargo against Italy.[84] Indeed, it is more likely that the
British people would have abandoned France before agreeing
to such a bargain at this time.[85]

Every country not directly allied to France had made it
clear that Hitler's action was not something that they were
prepared to fight over.[86] Nor had anything resembling enthusiasm been expressed for imposing an economic or financial
embargo against Germany, especially since most nations had
already discovered from their Italian experience that the
sanctions sword was double-edged.[87] Of France's five non-
Locarno allies, the Yugoslavs were immediately eliminated as
a source of support for any punitive measures.[88] So were the
Rumanians, in spite of Titulescu's efforts on behalf of the
French position.[89] The Poles, too, were considered as adamant
opponents of any action against Berlin.[90]

This meant that any coalition against Germany would
probably be limited to Britain, France, Belgium, Czechoslovakia and, perhaps, Russia. But the British could contribute nothing of any military significance for several
months.[91] The Belgians, with their small forces and pitiful
defences, might prove more of a liability than an asset, since

their belligerency would open the unprotected northern French frontier to German invasion.[92] The Czech government, it was argued, would certainly fight, if only because it realized that Hitler's next move might be against Prague.[93] But the Czech army was considered capable of only delaying the Wehrmacht for a week at best.[94] The head of the southern department in the foreign office even predicted that a clash with Germany would trigger a 'pretty savage' civil war by the Sudeten Germans, Magyars and Ruthenes, who composed 32 per cent of the military and civilian populations of Czechoslovakia.[95]

The Russians remained an enigma, both politically and militarily. Moscow had delayed making any formal policy statement, or apparently even communicating with ambassador Ivan Maisky, until 10 March.[96] Not until after Eden had set Europe on a course of compliance did Russia promise London her full support in any action which might be decided upon by the League council.[97] At the same time, the Soviet press had confined itself largely to heaping verbal abuse on Hitler, denouncing his proposals and calling for the creation of an Anglo-Franco-Russian bloc to resist German expansion.[98] These factors gave rise to a feeling in British quarters that Moscow did not want a confrontation with Germany at this time.[99] Nevertheless, it could not be said in Whitehall that the Soviet Union would not join in economic or even military sanctions against Berlin.[100]

Even if Russia did join forces against Germany the British foreign and war offices doubted whether Soviet military assistance would be of much value. In the first place, it was widely accepted that the Japanese would react to any European clash by attacking Russia in the east, thus involving her in a two-front struggle.[101] This, in turn, would dangerously jeopardize her vital agricultural and industrial programmes. The Soviet air force was regarded as useful, at least for provoking trouble, but the Red Army was thought to be only capable of self-defence. It was also believed that the Russian transport network would collapse under the first strain of war.[102] Moreover, it seemed virtually inconceivable that Tukhachevsky's armies could get to the western front, since neither Bucharest nor, especially, Warsaw was likely to risk either Germany's wrath or their own eastern provinces by granting transit rights to Russian forces.[103] The accuracy of this assessment was underlined by Tukhachevsky himself, when he confided to ambassador Bullitt on 7 March that the Soviet Union would be unable to bring any military aid to Czechoslovakia in case of German attack.[104]

Worse still, suspicions were harboured in London over both the will and the efficacy of the French fighting forces.[105] Some eight months before the coup, the British war office had predicted that France would be 'very unlikely' to go to war without military and economic assistance from the United Kingdom.[106] The committee of imperial defence's strategic report for 1936 concluded that Paris was 'not in a position to embark on a war of national effort for any purpose save resistance to direct invasion'.[107] As late as February 1937, the British chiefs of staff anticipated that, whereas France had the manpower to mobilize fifty-three divisions, her industry could support no more than forty for any length of time.[108] Concern was also expressed throughout this period over how Gamelin's armies, with their 'dangerously' low stocks of mobilization material, their twenty-year-old tanks and ancient artillery pieces, would fare against the modern weapons and armour of the mechanized Wehrmacht.

Even greater anxiety was felt over the deplorable state of the French aircraft industry, which, it was feared, rendered it impossible in 1936 for Paris to sustain an aerial war effort.[109] The conclusion was inescapable: in any conflict, the Luftwaffe, supported by Germany's vast industrial capability, would soon gain command over western Europe. From there it would be a short flight to London, whose vulnerability was compared by Churchill to a 'tremendous, fat, valuable cow tied up to attract the beast of prey'.[110]

All these factors pressed heavily on the cabinet. But, even if the arsenal had been moderately full, allies more readily available, and Germany a less formidable opponent, it is by no means certain that London would have agreed to a policy which would have been in complete contradiction with the desires of the British people, including King Edward VIII, for peace and negotiations.[111] Virtually everyone in Britain was saying that he or she saw no reason why Hitler should not be allowed to do whatever he liked in his own back garden.[112] These assertions were frequently accompanied by expressions of guilt over the 'dictat' of Versailles and remorse for the 'grossly unfair' way the Germans had been treated by the same Frenchmen who had refused to disarm, had seized the Ruhr and had played such a large part in producing what author A. A. Milne sarcastically described as the 'security, happiness, and good faith of 1918-1936'.[113]

Whether these were sentiments of convenience or conviction was not always clear. But, for the moment, Germany enjoyed a degree of sympathetic understanding in Britain which was nearly matched in intensity by the outburst of francophobia, especially among ex-servicemen, who had not forgotten the horrors of the Somme or the mutinies of 1917, and who vowed that the next war would find them either at home or on another side.[114] Some of this irritation stemmed from what was widely regarded as French attempts to weaken the sanctions effort against Mussolini. Some of the pro-German feeling could also be attributed to a desire to avoid conflict. In any case, the pendulum of public opinion had swung decisively in Berlin's favour.[115] Even those who were strictly pro-British, and generally enlightened, argued that Hitler, while 'utterly wrong' in method, was 'right in fact'.[116]

Others, who held no particular brief for Nazism, but who hated communism and disliked France's eastern commitments, believed the Franco-Soviet pact had given Hitler a 'not altogether unwarranted' excuse for making a *fait accompli*. Some British conservatives even saw the coup as a blessing in disguise, since a remilitarized Rhineland drastically reduced the danger of Britain's being dragged into a conflict as a result of some Austrian, Czech or Polish problem. In this respect, France's alliance with Russia was regarded by the political right in the United Kingdom as little short of 'a betrayal of our western civilization'. This fear of communism did as much as anything in 1936 to strengthen British tolerance, if not support, for Hitler's régime as Europe's bulwark against bolshevism.[117]

Nowhere in the press was there any cry for action. There was no call for sanctions or even a demand that Berlin should be diplomatically ostracized.[118] On the contrary, the *News Chronicle, Daily Express* and *Daily Herald* led the British press in declaring that the British people would not raise a finger to prevent the occupation of Köln by German forces. Even normally sceptical papers like the *Morning Post, Star* and *Scotsman* avoided taking a position that might complicate the situation. The only course of action they could support was

negotiations. Here they echoed *The Times* and the *Observer*
and their editors, Geoffrey Dawson and J. L. Garvin, as well as
Lord Lothian, the Astors and the rest of the so-called Cliveden
set, whose call to rebuild a new and lasting peace reflected
with remarkable accuracy the sentiments of foreign secretary
Eden.[119]

For the next three weeks editors and letter writers, as well as
clergymen, politicians and other opinion leaders, kept up a
steady flow of statements in support of the government's
policy of reconciliation and reconstruction.[120] Not a single
rally or public meeting was held to protest against Hitler's
deed. At the same time, the foreign office was being inundated
by resolutions pledging full support for the foreign secretary
and by private pleas for peace which also revealed wholehearted opposition to, and misunderstanding of, the French
position. From all quarters, the government was urged to seize
this opportunity to negotiate a fresh settlement on terms of
full equality.[121] As Lloyd George put it, the door of opportunity had been blasted open by a bomb, but that was no
reason for refusing to go through it.[122] The bedazzled British
people, according to one contemporary historian, were so
busy admiring the plumage that they forgot the dying bird.[123]

The same held true for the dominion high commissioners,
who expressed themselves as being 'entirely in favour' of the
policy outlined by Eden on 9 March. Some proved almost
embarrassingly eager for negotiations and revealed such
insensitivity towards the French that government spokesmen
felt it necessary to emphasize four times in a week that His
Majesty's Government could not escape the consequences of
its Locarno signature.[124] This was especially true of Vincent
Massey and te Water, the high commissioners for Canada and
South Africa, respectively. Massey, who severely criticized
France's vindictiveness and pedantry, urged Britain to act as
an 'honest broker and nothing else'.[125] Even more outspoken
was te Water, whose alarming reports inspired prime minister
James Hertzog to cable London on 14 March, expressing his
government's 'very strongest disapproval' of France's
attitude and warning that Capetown 'would feel compelled to
withhold its support' if Britain allowed Paris to provoke a war
over the Rhineland.[126]

Among the other dominion governments, Ottawa, with its
large French minority, adopted a low profile, acting only to

inform London that Canada felt no obligation to join in any
coercive measures against Berlin.[127] Dublin declared itself in
favour of 'peace on a basis of equality', while both Canberra
and Wellington concurred completely with London's handling of the crisis.[128] Only New Zealand showed a flicker of
interest in economic or financial sanctions, whereas the press
in South Africa, especially, but also in Canada, Ireland and
Australia, voiced hostility to any action which could jeopardize peace or the prospects for fruitful negotiations.[129]

Whatever the reasons, however good or real, the overwhelming mass of press and public opinion, both at home and
in the dominions, was strongly opposed to any forceful
restoration of the *status quo* in the Rhineland.[130] Eden was only
guessing when he said that 99.9 per cent of the people felt this
way, but as things stood and without a strong governmental
lead, this estimate of one in a thousand could not have been far
from the truth.[131] Nor, as far as the foreign secretary and his
colleagues were concerned, was this desire for acquiescence a
bad thing in view of Britain's armaments situation. At the
same time, Valentine Lawford, then a junior official in the
foreign office, detected in Whitehall 'a feeling of profound
relief . . . that there could be no question of endorsing any
foreign policy at all since arms were so palpably lacking'.[132]

This unfortunate set of circumstances was accepted by most
persons who later came to be identified with anti-
appeasement.[133] Vansittart, the arch enemy of Nazism, could
see no other alternative than acquiescence.[134] Nor, to judge
from foreign office records, did any of his subordinates argue
in support of Flandin's scheme for progressive sanctions.
Even Churchill supported the government, acknowledging
that Britain possessed neither the solidarity of conviction nor
adequate defences to take 'a line of undue prominence over
the Rhineland'.[135] For his part, National Labour MP Harold
Nicolson believed that military measures against Germany
would cause a general strike, while Conservative MP Robert
Boothby, who was willing to risk war to call Hitler's bluff,
admitted that British public opinion would not support
sanctions unless Germany attacked someone.[136]

Anxieties over the government's handling of the crisis were
largely focused on the possibility that London might bypass
France and Belgium for the sake of immediate negotiations
with Berlin. Such a scramble, Vansittart believed, was bound

to strengthen the position of the Nazi radicals, whereas moral condemnation of the coup might assist moderates such as Neurath and Schacht to regain the Chancellor's ear.[137] It was also argued by Austen Chamberlain and a few others that the best way to avoid both action and dishonour would be to refuse to treat with the unrepentant lawbreaker and to conclude some sort of mutual-assistance pact with Brussels and Paris and possibly other interested powers.[138] But that was the extent of the objections.

Although military weakness and domestic opposition were doubtless each sufficient grounds for rejecting the Franco-Belgian demand, cabinet members also had ideological, practical or personal reasons for eschewing sanctions.[139] Many, including Eden and Neville Chamberlain, saw no particular reason why Hitler's latest act of faithlessness should deter them from implementing their plan to seek a general settlement. If anything, the Rhine coup appears to have convinced them that this might be the 'last bus'. Not that they liked or trusted the Nazi régime. On the contrary, they detested its internal violence and resented its strong-arm tactics. They also agreed that Hitler would probably repudiate any agreement whenever it became a burden or unnecessary in view of growing German strength.

But it was still felt that a peace effort was imperative, if only to assuage a public which was still far from convinced that war was inevitable.[140] Most people in Britain, including cabinet members, wanted to try for a fresh settlement in western Europe which would stand outside the shadow of the Versailles treaty. They believed a policy of cooperation offered more hope of delaying, if not averting, an explosion than did ostracism. Ministers also generally accepted the foreign office's argument that Hitler's sincerity should now be publicly tested on a footing of equality in such a way that any failure could be clearly seen to be Germany's responsibility.[141]

In this connexion, it was felt that even limited or token economic sanctions would ruin prospects for fruitful talks, whereas military measures were regarded as being out of all proportion to the 'crime', which Conservative MP Leo Amery described as 'almost venial' in the eyes of the British people in comparison with Mussolini's rape of Abyssinia.[142] How could armed force be justified against Germany, when only limited economic measures were being imposed on an aggressor who was using mustard gas against shoeless natives and bombing open cities and Red Cross tents? At no time during the crisis would Eden, his colleagues, or the British public concede that Hitler's 'invasion' of the Rhineland was remotely as culpable as the unprovoked attack by one nation on another.[143]

Some cabinet ministers, including Baldwin, were also anxious about the possibility that an allied victory in another great war at this time might very easily cause Germany to succumb to bolshevism.[144] No British conservative could regard that as worth fighting for.[145] Hitler, it was argued, might one day attack Britain; but even Eden believed that the Russian 'bear' had only 'hatred in his heart' for the British empire.[146] Within the cabinet and foreign office, as well as the military, there existed a substantial conviction that, whereas Hitler was the more immediate menace, Josef Stalin posed a greater long-term threat to British interests.[147] Baldwin also reminded ministers of his personal pledge during the November election campaign never again to take the country into sanctions until Britain's rearmament deficiencies had been remedied.[148] Besides, only two days earlier the prime minister had publicly committed His Majesty's Government to bringing France and Germany together, not driving them apart.[149]

Taking all things together, it was 'generally accepted' that 'almost any risk' was worth taking 'in order to escape' from this dilemma.[150] 'Everyone agreed', Chamberlain noted, 'that we could not contemplate war, but we must make every effort to avoid repudiation of Locarno.'[151] This meant, according to education minister Oliver Stanley, that the cabinet would pursue a policy which combined 'peace with as little dishonour as possible'.[152] In these circumstances, the cabinet agreed wholeheartedly with Eden and Halifax in rejecting Flandin's plan to forcefully restore the *status quo* on the grounds that it was incapable of producing a 'satisfactory settlement'.[153] Ministers also endorsed the foreign secretary's opinion that the only hope of securing a peaceful and permanent solution—and the best chance of breaking the deadlock with Paris—was to continue trying for negotiations, but in a more realistic framework, based on three elements which Zeeland had outlined privately to Eden in Paris and which aimed at combining pressure on Germany with saving

Hitler's face.[154]

First, for the sake of French and Belgian susceptibilities, international morality would somehow have to be vindicated. Equally, 'reasonable regard' would have to be shown for the position into which Hitler had got himself. This meant that His Majesty's Government would not support demands for a complete withdrawal or any other 'unreasonable' request. Finally, France and Belgium would require fresh and perhaps additional assurances of British support to compensate for security lost by the disappearance of the demilitarized zone. Initially, the foreign secretary adopted the Belgian suggestion that London's assistance in the event of unprovoked aggression should be made more automatic by eliminating the League of Nations from the Locarno procedure. But Baldwin thought it 'dangerous', in view of the possibilities of air action, to sacrifice the breathing-space provided by the need for a Geneva pronouncement.[155]

The next week was spent in seeking solutions which encompassed these three considerations. But, in view of the looming confrontation with Flandin and Zeeland in London on the morrow, the foreign secretary concentrated his attention on the immediate problem of producing some fresh factor capable of preventing France from taking military measures and asking Britain to follow suit. If that occurred, Eden warned the cabinet, 'we should have to decide whether we intended to fulfil our treaty obligations — and we should be in an impossible position if we refused'.[156] For his part, Baldwin thought it was 'very unfriendly' of the French to expose London to such embarrassments. 'People', he added, 'would take a long time to forget it.'

The best avenue around this 'very grave' impasse, Eden believed, was via Berlin.[157] The foreign secretary proposed to ask the Chancellor to extricate His Majesty's Government from its predicament by spontaneously withdrawing all troops above a truly symbolic level and promising not to erect fortifications in the zone pending a fresh settlement. If Hitler would vindicate international law in this way, then Eden felt confident he could win Zeeland's support and together they could persuade Flandin to abandon his intransigent position.

It was a gamble which could easily misfire if Berlin refused and Paris discovered that London had acted behind her back, especially since, as Ramsay MacDonald pointed out, Sarraut and Flandin had apparently burnt their boats over negotiations while troops remained in the Rhineland.[158] But the cabinet could think of no alternatives other than war or repudiating their treaty obligations. Besides, no one knew yet whether Hitler was prepared to act as reasonably as he had talked in expressing his desire for peace with France. Eden was also encouraged by the Chancellor's willingness, voiced via Ward Price in the *Daily Mail* on 11 March, to have Britain serve as an 'honest broker' and by the journalist's private impression that Hitler was genuinely anxious at the moment to come to a definite settlement.[159]

That same evening the foreign secretary impressed on the German ambassador the 'acute anxiety' with which the cabinet viewed a situation whose 'extreme gravity' he could 'scarcely exaggerate'.[160] Not only were the French determined to hold London to her assistance obligations, he explained, but, considering Germany's 'inexcusable' behaviour towards Belgium and Britain's traditional respect for treaties, the cabinet had been forced into a position of 'near compulsion'. Nevertheless, Eden added, the British government was anxious to play the rôle of an honest broker. But this would only be possible if the Chancellor quickly made a conciliatory contribution in the shape of the foreign secretary's suggestion. If Berlin responded 'generously and well', say, by reducing the occupation force to 10,000, then His Majesty's Government would do its utmost to get negotiations started.[161] But urgency was paramount, Eden emphasized, if he was to be in any position to deal with the anticipated French demand for a forcible solution when the Locarno powers reconvened on 12 March.

6 German crisis management

*Nothing, absolutely nothing, will induce us to
renounce this regained sovereignty.*
HITLER, 12 March 1936

Eden's request for a gesture confronted Berlin with her first
important decision of the post-coup period. For the first five
days everything had passed almost exactly as Hitler and
Neurath had anticipated. Domestically, the reaction to the
events of 7 March had probably exceeded expectations.[1] Not
only had the Rhinelanders showered prayers and flowers on
the soldiers, but Germans throughout the Reich seemed
genuinely pleased by the news. Whatever opposition there
may have been was inundated by support for the Chancellor's
action. The people had too long been told that the Franco-
Soviet pact had violated Locarno and threatened the Reich;
that the demilitarized zone was an insult to German honour;
and that there were higher laws than those which were written
in ink.[2] A few extremists, especially in Bavaria, complained
that the peace proposals were a sign of weakness. They would
have preferred a *fait accompli* without any counterpart.[3]
Others dreaded the consequences, either for Germany if
France reacted, or for the world if Hitler's action went unpunished.

But the massive majority—estimated by American ambassador William Dodd at 90 per cent—believed the Chancellor
was entirely justified in his unilateral restoration of sovereignty to the western provinces.[4] Some may have regretted his
choice of method, but they also endorsed the government's
contention that a nation's sovereignty could not be bartered.
Besides, and this should not be undervalued, the Chancellor
had put up the most comprehensive and constructive peace
plan yet offered. If the French now refused to negotiate for the
benefit of all Europe, that would prove yet again how unreasonable they would have been at the conference table over
the old demilitarized zone. This was particularly true in the
Rhineland where the British consul at Frankfurt reported on
30 March that he had not yet met a German who believed that
the remilitarization could have been achieved through

negotiations.[5]

These themes were driven home by Goebbels's press, where it was repeatedly emphasized that the new residents of the Rhineland were 'representatives of peace'.[6] It was inconceivable, according to the *Deutsche diplomatisch-politische Korrespondenz*, that France could consider herself menaced by these guardians of the frontier.[7] At the same time, however, German journalists stressed that Europe was faced with only two choices: peace with negotiations or war. Newspapers and radio stations not only emphasized the opportunities created by the coup for appeasement and understanding, but also warned that the German people would stop at nothing to free themselves from any economic or financial sanctions. Even the respected and rational *Frankfurter Zeitung* cautioned that 'the only person who can change things is the man who is willing to make war', since it was 'inconceivable' that Hitler would yield to anyone after swearing to the Reichstag on the 7th that he would never capitulate where German honour or sovereignty was at stake.[8] But, in spite of the defiant tone, there was no deviation in the media from the ebullient confidence which the Chancellor and his colleagues manifested, at least in public, throughout the crisis.[9]

Nevertheless, the forty-eight hours after the coup were almost surely as filled with tension as Hitler later claimed, for every fresh report to the Auswärtiges Amt was capable of bringing news of serious complications.[10] There is even some evidence to suggest that Blomberg almost immediately lost his nerve and urged Hitler to withdraw the three exposed battalions.[11] This request was apparently precipitated by erroneous reports of French military intentions, coupled with the knowledge that the overall capacity of the Wehrmacht left so much to be desired that, as General Alfred Jodl later acknowledged, Gamelin's covering army alone 'could have blown us to pieces'.[12] Hitler may well have shared these anxieties.[13] But nothing occurred in the first five days to cause him or Neurath to take, or apparently even consider, such a step. On the contrary, from no quarter did Berlin receive any indication of serious trouble during this period.[14] Reactions abroad, both initial and sustained, were either favourable, neutral or reserved.[15] Hostility over the treaty breach was largely confined to the means, rather than the end, and was muted by the German peace offers.[16]

The proposals proved a success everywhere but in Rome, where the German counsellor of embassy reported that Mussolini could not have taken the memorandum in a worse manner.[17] The Duce declared that Hitler had gone 'viel zu weit' by offering both to rejoin the League of Nations and to conclude a non-aggression pact with the Czechs. He also voiced fears that London and Paris would wring further concessions from Germany over Austria, Danubia and disarmament. Mussolini even questioned the Führer's wisdom in committing himself to the *status quo* for a quarter of a century.

These complaints were immediately answered by Neurath, who assured Rome that Berlin would under no circumstances expand her offers now that she was in possession of the Rhenish bone of contention.[18] Nor, he explained, had the Czech offer added anything to earlier German propositions which Prague had hitherto been unable to accept.[19] The League offer, on the other hand, required more attention, since Mussolini apparently had not only decided to reject the committee of thirteen's latest peace bid and stalk out of the League, but was within half an hour of announcing his decision to the fascist grand council when Hassell reached him with Hitler's message of 7 March.[20] Had the connexion been missed, the result might have been as 'catastrophic' as Hassell had feared.[21] As it was, there could be no escaping the fact that, by proposing to return to Geneva, the Chancellor had deprived the Duce of his chief weapon in the struggle against the intensification of sanctions.[22] Before Z-day, it seemed conceivable that Italy's withdrawal might have dealt a crippling blow to the League. That possibility had been extremely useful to Rome in dampening France's enthusiasm for sanctions.[23] But now, with Hitler's offers, the Geneva threat had been suddenly and unexpectedly kicked from Mussolini's hands.[24]

Rome's feelings of betrayal on this point were deepened by reports that Hitler had acted only after having reached some understanding with London. These, in turn, gave rise to Italian concern over the possibility that Berlin might even join the sanctions front in a bid to cement Anglo-German friendship at Italy's expense.[25] After all, Mussolini had repeatedly told Berlin during January and February that he would quit Geneva in reply to any intensification of

sanctions.[26] During Hassell's crucial conversation of 22
February, Mussolini had declared this intention no fewer
than three times.[27] And, in the weeks before the coup, not just
Hassell, but also the Führer personally had assured Italian
personages that Berlin had no intention of returning to the
League.[28] On one occasion, Hitler reportedly had even
pounded a table and shouted 'niemals, niemals, niemals'.[29]

To judge by the anxieties initially aroused within the
German embassy in Rome, it seemed at least possible that
Mussolini might regard this 'stab in the back' as grounds for
repudiating or at least not honouring his pledge to Hassell of
22 February. Nor was it inconceivable that the Duce might
seek to profit from the crisis by offering Paris his support
against Berlin in exchange for an even more benevolent
attitude towards his Abyssinian adventure.[30]

But Neurath unquestionably realized that London would
not tolerate such an arrangement, which meant that acceptance by Paris of any bargain with Italy would be at the expense
of Britain's friendship and support. Moreover, in spite of
recent Italian military successes, the Auswärtiges Amt knew
that Rome still needed Germany's commercial assistance to
survive against sanctions.[31] In these circumstances, the
foreign minister could afford to take a more detached view
than his ambassador. This undoubtedly explains why Berlin
responded to Mussolini's complaints by requesting that Rome
should return Germany's past favours not only by refusing to
support Paris, but also by actively working against any
attempt to punish Berlin for her remilitarization of the
Rhineland.[32]

Nevertheless, on the principle that it was imprudent to
alienate prospective friends unnecessarily, Mussolini was
assured that Berlin's return to Geneva would not occur overnight and certainly not until agreement had been reached on
the other points in the German offer.[33] The Abyssinian
campaign might well be over by the time Germany took her
seat, but if not, then the Duce could count on his fascist
comrade to exercise a salutary counter-pressure against
Litvinov and his followers.[34] Neurath also promised Rome
that Berlin would definitely not support any sanctions
currently being imposed on Italy or alter her Abyssinian
policy in any way.[35] At the same time, however, he refused to
grant Hassell's request for permission to assure Mussolini

that Berlin would accede to his 'heart-felt hope' that Germany
would not return to the League so long as it seemed possible
that Italy might be obliged by Abyssinian affairs to
withdraw.[36]

These assurances satisfied Mussolini, who also acknowledged the accuracy of Berlin's contention that the German
diversionary 'offensive' had already eased his position, even
if it had not, in his opinion, eliminated the danger of sanctions
being intensified.[37] Whilst still insisting that Hitler had
offered too much, the Duce promised on 9 March that Rome
would remain faithful to the principle that states under sanctions did not impose sanctions on others.[38] That was the least
he could do both to retain Hitler's friendship and to keep
open the economic lifeline from Germany. Mussolini also
confirmed that he had already made it 'quite clear' to Paris
and London that any Italian action against Berlin was out of
the question.[39] And, although Italy did not champion the
German cause, as the Auswärtiges Amt had desired, neither
Hassell nor Neurath had reason over the next and most critical ten-day period to fault Mussolini's behaviour.[40] Whether
by choice or through lack of opportunity, Rome took no active
part in the Locarno powers' deliberations, thereby playing
Hitler's game.[41]

The only other problem concerning the German peace
proposals developed because the Chancellor had not included Vienna or Prague by name in his offers of non-
aggression pacts.[42] The omission of Austria not only distressed Vienna, but aroused anxieties in Italy and Britain,
where fears were expressed that an Anschluss might be
imminent.[43] Berlin moved swiftly to silence the alarmists.
Neurath gave diplomatic assurances, while Hitler declared
through Ward Price and the Daily Mail on 9 March that his
offer extended to all of Germany's neighbours.[44] But the
Auswärtiges Amt avoided giving any specific assurances to
Prague, partly to punish her for supporting Paris, partly out
of deference to Nazi extremists, and partly to appease the
Hungarians, Italians and Poles, all of whom had little respect
for Czechoslovakia as a national state.[45]

The German peace proposals received no better reception
than in Britain, where Hitler had most wanted to make the
best impression.[46] Eden had indicated both to Hoesch and to
the House of Commons that he appreciated the importance of

the German offers, especially Hitler's willingness to accommodate London by returning to the League.[47] The foreign secretary had also lectured Hoesch about the sanctity of treaties and deplored the unilateral repudiation of Locarno. But it was a finger-wagging, rather than a fist-pounding performance and had been followed by 108 hours of calm, interrupted primarily by admonitions to Berlin not to aggravate the situation further or otherwise hamper London's efforts to get negotiations started.[48] Eden had incorporated this advice into his Commons statement, which, by making no mention of punishment, gave a clear impression that Britain had accepted the *fait accompli,* as well as the German contention that transferring the basis of Locarno from the artificial demilitarized zone to the permanent frontiers would contribute to western stability.[49]

The foreign secretary's declaration of British aims on 9 March was widely endorsed by the press and public.[50] Hoesch's embassy was showered with friendly messages and offers of assistance.[51] Indirect contact with the court of Edward VIII also revealed sympathy for the German point of view and approval of the Chancellor's proposals.[52] Even war minister Duff Cooper, who was no friend of appeasement, had admitted to the ambassador that the British people did not give 'two hoots' about the demilitarized zone.[53] Only Sir Austen Chamberlain had objected strenuously, insisting to Hoesch on 9 March not only that Hitler's action justified immediate military counter-action, but that Britain would be honour-bound to support any French riposte.[54] However, Sir Austen did not push this conviction publicly, much to the relief of the German embassy.[55] So favourable was the overall public response, in fact, that Hoesch felt obliged to remind Berlin that certain elements in Whitehall and Westminster took a far less kindly view of her actions.[56] But the warning in this message was against over-confidence, rather than danger.

Even from Paris and Brussels, the two most affected capitals, the initial reports contained nothing to suggest danger. The Belgian press had condemned the treaty breach, but calls for any kind of sanctions against Berlin had quickly subsided, especially after Sarraut's radio speech, which was received as if he, not Hitler, had threatened the peace.[57] By Sunday night, Brussels appeared to have dissociated herself from French intransigence in favour of the British line and to be concentrating, not on the demilitarized zone, but on preserving the frontier guarantees provided by Locarno.[58] Zeeland's statement to the Belgian parliament on 11 March had confirmed his government's desire to pursue a policy of calm conciliation and reconstruction.[59]

Military preparations in both countries had been restricted to those measures that were essential to secure their frontiers.[60] The French could hardly have done less. The prime minister's refusal to tolerate German cannons within range of Strasbourg could have provoked some anxiety.[61] But this sabre-rattling was not sustained by the pace of Gamelin's preparations or supported by the French press or public.[62] Sarraut himself was reported by the German chargé d'affaires to have realized by Tuesday the impracticability of his 'absurd' demand that Hitler should evacuate the Rhine zone before negotiations could begin.[63] The impact of the prime minister's speech was reduced further by the ministerial decisions of 7 and 8 March to eschew independent action in favour of the Geneva approach to the Locarno problem.[64] This announcement, which eliminated any immediate riposte, must rank as one of the most important of all the early indicators reaching Berlin.[65] It almost certainly allowed Hitler the luxury of departing by train on Sunday night 'for a rest' in Bavaria—barely forty hours after the first troops had returned to the Rhineland.[66]

The Chancellor later confessed to being uncertain when he left Berlin whether the next day would bring war or peace.[67] But this statement, like many he was subsequently to make, was either delivered in a belligerent tone in the presence of someone like Schuschnigg, whom he was bent on intimidating, or in conversations with cronies whom he delighted in impressing with stories of how he alone had carried the Reich from success to success in these, his salad days.[68]

Apart from the obvious psychological effect of such a show of sang-froid on Germans generally, Hitler's absence proved relatively unimportant since nothing occurred which could not be competently handled by Neurath and the Auswärtiges Amt, which, for the most part, managed the German side throughout the crisis, even when the Chancellor was in town.[69] The Führer's reliance on the diplomats is evidenced from the documents and his war-time praise of Neurath as 'sturdy and obstinate' in the face of adversity.[70] Throughout the entire pre- and post-coup period, no one wavered less than the foreign minister, who had maintained from the outset that remilitarization of the Rhineland was an inevitable development which could be hastened, even by a *fait accompli*, without serious opposition.[71]

A few hours before Hitler's departure on Sunday night, Neurath took the diplomatic offensive, despatching instructions to German missions in all fourteen League council countries which underlined his confidence that France could be stopped short of sanctions or condemnation.[72] In fact, the foreign minister was determined to prevent 'even the mere determination of a violation', such as had occurred in connexion with the reintroduction of conscription. Any repetition of the events of 17 April 1935, he wrote, would 'ruin the political situation for the future'. This could be avoided, he thought, by stressing the 'historical importance' of the Chancellor's offers, by warning that 'precipitate resolutions' would postpone Germany's return to the League, and by arguing that Paris had committed the original violation by presenting her Franco-Soviet pact to the world as a *fait accompli*.

Nor did Neurath seem to feel that this assignment would be especially difficult in view of reports reaching Berlin from the dozen or so non-Locarno powers whose opinions were most important.[73] Only three states, Czechoslovakia, Russia and Rumania, displayed the sort of reserve which indicated they might follow a French lead. Although the Czechs maintained correct relations with Berlin and did nothing publicly to incur Hitler's wrath, the Auswärtiges Amt learned from its secret sources by 11 March that Prague would follow Paris 'unreservedly' and that Beneš was advocating economic sanctions 'in order to bring about the collapse of the German régime'.[74] Throughout the crisis, the Czechs enjoyed the dubious distinction in Berlin of being regarded, next to France, as Germany's most implacable opponent.[75]

Next ranked the Russians, who had immediately, but only temporarily, suspended negotiations on a 500 million RM credit agreement with Berlin.[76] But no military preparations were discernible; nor did the Soviet press try to arouse public enthusiasm for any such adventure.[77] On the contrary, Moscow's chief propagandist and spokesman on foreign affairs, Karl Radek, declared in *Izvestia* that preventive war against the Reich was the equivalent of 'suicide for fear of death'.[78] The only effective counter to the Rhine coup, he argued on 8 and 10 March, was 'swiftly evolving defensive counter-measures', in the shape of an Anglo-Franco-Soviet bloc to resist future Nazi expansion.[79] Neither Count Friedrich von Schulenburg's embassy nor, apparently, German military intelligence uncovered any indications to contradict the Radek line, which, in fact, reflected Litvinov's feeling that any military reprisals would mean immediate war — and one for which neither he nor Marshal Tukhachevsky displayed any enthusiasm.[80] Nevertheless, the Auswärtiges Amt took it for granted that Moscow would actively support any punitive measure against Germany so long as it did not actually lead to hostilities.[81]

Bucharest's attitude during this period was more difficult to assess, partly because Titulescu was inclined to act more as a League collectivist than as a Rumanian foreign minister. In addition, the German mission there displayed a marked tendency to see what Bulow called 'ghosts' emanating from 'overheated' imaginations about Czech and Soviet machinations against Berlin.[82] But in spite of Titulescu's efforts on behalf of Paris and his apparent desire for a 'decisive' solution, Berlin recognized that many, if not most Rumanians had no desire to risk war, while great segments of the army and political right were known to be opposed to punitive measures.[83] It was believed, however, that Bucharest would participate in economic sanctions against Germany, if only because Rumania would not be able to resist the dual pressure of France and Russia.[84]

The only other potentially troublesome power, Poland, had made it clear from the outset that she wanted nothing to do with problems arising from the Locarno treaty.[85] Beck had immediately assured Berlin that Warsaw remained faithful to the principles of non-aggression and friendship embodied in the Polish-German pact of 1934.[86] Press and public opinion had responded favourably to the peace proposals and especially to Hitler's recognition in the Reichstag of Poland's right to an outlet to the sea.[87] Many of these same ideas had been incorporated into the semi-official Iskra communiqué which apparently had been drafted in the Polish foreign ministry, possibly even by Beck, and which had incorporated in large measure the German arguments against the Franco-

Soviet pact.[88]

These pro-German sentiments were followed on 9 and 10 March by reports from Reuters and Havas, undoubtedly leaked by the French, revealing that, within hours of the coup, Beck had pledged full support to Paris.[89] The possibility of a double-deal by Poland instantly brought back memories in Berlin of Warsaw's vote for the Stresa resolution of 17 April 1935 after she had given the clear impression that she would support Germany.[90] Beck, too, was aware of these suspicions and speedily assured German ambassador Hans-Adolf von Moltke on 9 March that Poland's pledge to Paris was 'in practice, without effect', since, like Eden's, it had guaranteed assistance only if France were the victim of unprovoked aggression.[91] The foreign minister also emphasized that no *casus foederis* existed for Poland. Nor could he see any juridical basis for sanctions by the League of Nations.[92] Moltke was also assured that Berlin's anxieties in this respect were mild compared to the nervousness which the Polish attitude had aroused in Paris.[93]

This sequence of events served primarily to confirm Berlin's conviction that the Poles, while too slippery to be trusted, could be relied upon to practice the same duplicity with Paris, especially on matters relating to the despised Locarno pact.[94] On balance, however, Germany profited more than France from Poland's attitude, not only because Warsaw was anxious to avoid any *coups d'épingle* against the Reich, but also because Beck personally afforded Berlin useful public and private support in London, where he consistently opposed French efforts to enlist League support against Hitler.[95] He also volunteered to explain the Chancellor's position to the League council and even offered to deliver a testimonial on behalf of Germany as a reliable treaty partner.[96]

In view of the satisfactory reactions abroad and the absence everywhere of offensive military preparations, Berlin saw no compelling reason for gestures.[97] Hitler and Neurath almost certainly believed that Eden was over-reacting to Flandin's demands, which were not only exaggerated, but which they did not think would be supported by either British or French public opinion.[98] To concede anything, they felt, would be seen as a sign of weakness.[99] Nothing would be better calculated to whet French appetites for even greater gestures or to damage domestic confidence in the Führer.[100] Furthermore, as long as no tangible preparations for action existed, any kind of withdrawal would expose Hitler to subsequent charges, especially in France, that he had been bluffed into submission. It is hardly conceivable that a man who employed this weapon so successfully against his opponents would fail to realize its possible effect on his own position.

Any concession would also imply doubts on the part of the German government towards both the righteousness of her cause and the legal basis for her actions.[101] A climb-down would also constitute a betrayal by Hitler of his pledge to the people not to sacrifice a particle of German sovereignty.[102] Having staked his political and electoral fortunes on the success of this venture, he was not prepared to expose himself to charges that he had allowed outsiders to dictate the strength and position of German troops on German soil.[103] There is no reason to doubt that Hitler's refusal to compromise was based almost as much on domestic considerations as on Neurath's assessment of the possible external repercussions of such a step. Even in the absence of direct evidence, Neurath's anxieties, recorded by Hassell, about the intrusion of politics into foreign affairs is ample proof.[104] The same conclusion may be drawn from the tone and content of Hitler's eleven campaign speeches between 12 and 28 March.[105]

Berlin's unwillingness to accommodate Eden was relayed by Hoesch on 12 March and underlined by Hitler in his speeches of 12, 14, 16 and 20 March.[106] The Chancellor categorically rejected any unilateral limitation of German sovereignty, even temporarily. He was willing, however, for the period of the negotiations, not to strengthen existing contingents nor to move troops closer to the frontier, provided France and Belgium adopted the same attitude. This proviso was certain to irritate the French, since it meant bringing Paris down to the same level as the law-breaker. The German reply was also accompanied by four warnings—two privately to London and two publicly by Hitler—that the peace proposals would be revoked if either they or Germany were mistreated.[107] This threat irritated Whitehall, but Eden and the cabinet were still determined not to let slip the opportunity to negotiate a fresh western settlement.[108]

The British were bitterly disappointed by the German response, which Eden insisted 'would hardly contribute to a solution of the crisis'.[109] Indeed, the foreign secretary, Halifax and Vansittart each told Hoesch that Hitler's reply would probably do more harm than good if the French found out. All three British representatives insisted that the ambassador should seek something better, especially in the nature of a temporary renunciation of fortifications construction. Hoesch was also urged to leave Berlin in no doubt about the thoroughly bad impression created by the German refusal. But British hopes to keep secret both their *démarche* and Berlin's response were shattered almost immediately when the Deutsches Nachrichtenbüro issued a long statement which included all the points in the Chancellor's reply.[110]

The news of Berlin's unhelpful attitude precipitated the first real crisis for Germany over the Rhineland. At least, that was how German diplomats and service attachés in Paris and London viewed the situation created by their government's intransigence.[111] From France, the military and air attaché warned on 12 March that, barring some conciliatory move 'to make up for the nature of our previous action', the 'gravest consequences' were to be expected.[112] This was followed by reports of increasing press and public restiveness and a warning of growing support for economic and financial sanctions, which were said to be under serious study.[113] On 13 March, Forster quoted a 'very reliable source' as saying that the majority of French politicians were becoming 'increasingly vehement' in their demands that Paris should 'go the limit', including the use of armed force, if necessary, to resist the Reich's challenge.[114] The chargé acknowledged the existence of more moderate voices, but emphasized that they were being submerged by the intransigents, some of whom were even talking of going it alone against Germany as a last resort.

The situation in Britain was even more disturbing, according to embassy reports. Not only had Hitler's refusal caused a marked stiffening in the press, but a meeting of conservative members of Parliament, addressed by Sir Austen Chamberlain and Winston Churchill, had apparently come down heavily in support of demands for a German gesture.[115] Soundings by military attaché Geyr von Schweppenburg convinced him that the 'nerve centre' in Berlin did not sufficiently appreciate the gravity of the situation.[116] He believed it 'altogether difficult to conceive' that pacification could be achieved on the basis of the *status quo* and warned against placing too much faith in the ability of Edward VIII to preserve peace unconditionally.

Geyr's nervousness was shared by the ambassador, who had become alarmed by the emergence of parliamentary intransigence and, especially, by London's feeling of commitment to her pledged word.[117] France, Hoesch wrote, had got Britain 'grasped by the throat', thanks primarily to Locarno, but also to the fact that Flandin could point to the pressure which London had put on Paris during the sanctions campaign against Italy. The government's sensitivity to accusations of unreliability and inconsistency, he feared, seemed capable of impelling His Majesty's Government to support punitive action in spite of the sentiments of the British people.

To counter 'the threat of war', Hoesch urged his superiors to reconsider the evacuation of a 'substantial proportion' of the occupation forces in order to give Britain 'the means for controlling the course of events', which he described as being 'in so many respects. . . reminiscent of 1914'.[118] This despatch was followed on the evening of 13 March by a most urgent telegram, signed by the three service attachés, describing the political situation as 'ausserordentlich ernst' and warning that 'an extremely unfavourable' development was possible in the next few days.[119]

The arrival of this warning was the last straw for Blomberg, whose resolve had been shaken by the attachés' earlier reports and, especially, by Hoesch's warning of the danger of war.[120] Apparently fearing the outbreak of hostilities on the French side, Blomberg had already summoned Hossbach twice during the day of 13 March in his efforts to get the Chancellor to agree to evacuate the garrisons at Aachen, Trier and Saarbrücken. Now, for a third time, the war minister despatched the adjutant, telegram in hand, to request a personal interview so that Blomberg could press his case for a gesture which would obviate either war or the risk of a massacre of unprotected and unsupported German soldiers. But Hitler stuffed the despatch, unread, into his jacket pocket and continued his conversation with Göring, thus leaving Blomberg with the humiliating task of later having to ask the Führer for its return.

The Chancellor's casual action was made possible by the fact that he already knew the contents of the despatch, thanks

either to Göring's Abhördienst, which was said to have inter-
cepted the message, or, more probably, to the Auswärtiges
Amt, whose copy had arrived a full hour before Blomberg's.[121]
Hitler's nonchalance also reflected the influence of Neurath,
who took a 'wesentlich ruhiger' view of the situation.[122] 'Jetzt
sind mer drinne und bleibet drinne', he is said to have
declared.[123] Apocryphal or otherwise, this quotation captured
the feeling which prevailed, not only in the foreign ministry
and the Reich Chancellery, but also even among the army
leadership, where Beck anticipated that France would calm
down and Fritsch was quoted to Paris as having declared that
war would be inevitable if French troops entered Germany.[124]

This confidence was expressed in several ways. Not only
did the Auswärtiges Amt reject Eden's second plea for a
gesture, but the counsellor of embassy was sent instead of the
ambassador to deliver the news.[125] Ambassador Hoesch and
chargé d'affaires Wilhelm Pochhammer in Bucharest were
each reassured that matters were well in hand, while
American ambassador Dodd was told that Berlin expected
nothing worse than an impasse to develop.[126] At the same
time, the German government took steps to avoid any unnecessary provocation. The press was instructed to publish
nothing alarming, and military parades scheduled for Frankfurt, Köln and Koblenz on 16 March were cancelled.[127] The
foreign ministry also persuaded Hitler to break a week's
silence and release official figures putting German strength in
the Rhineland at 36,500, including the Landespolizei.[128] This
was done primarily to counteract French newspaper assertions that the occupation forces had been increased since 7
March to 60,000 or even 90,000 regulars, plus 200,000 to
400,000 auxiliaries.[129]

These were measures born of prudence rather than anxiety. As matters stood at the weekend, Berlin had every reason
to believe she was going to succeed.[130] Certainly that was the
impression conveyed by Hitler in Munich on 14 March when
he declared publicly that Germany was in no mood to yield on
any issue involving her honour or tolerate 'being hauled
before international courts', especially when she was in the
right.[131] During the same speech, the Führer asserted that he
went 'with the assurance of a sleepwalker' on a path dictated
by Providence.

In addition to divine guidance, Hitler's route was marked

by concrete indicators that Germany could expect nothing worse than League condemnation and mild economic or financial sanctions imposed by a half-dozen states.[132] This represented a deterioration from Neurath's professed expectations of 8 March, but it was nothing more than Hitler and his foreign minister had anticipated before the coup.[133] The reasons for Berlin's confidence are only partially recorded, but one vital consideration must have been the fact that the Locarno powers had withstood the shock of her refusal to make a gesture and were still talking. Flandin had not forced a showdown, despite being handed a perfect reason for doing so.[134] This failure persuaded Hoesch by the weekend that the French foreign minister's real objective was to blackmail Britain into a military alliance against Germany.[135] Nor, during this critical period, had there been any intensification of French military activity — a fact which Berlin regarded as paramount.[136] Nowhere during the week of 7-14 March did the Auswärtiges Amt or army detect 'any serious talk of military sanctions or preparations for war'.[137]

Less obvious, but equally assuring, was the continued lack in France and, especially, Britain of any public support for drastic solutions.[138] The press generally scolded Hitler for his unreasonableness, but also warned against allowing the French government to bring matters to a crisis.[139] Members of Parliament touring their constituencies discovered as early as Friday afternoon that the electorate was far less concerned with honouring obligations than with avoiding conflict and preventing Paris from jeopardizing peace talks.[140] Even the opponents of Germany did not support Flandin's punitive demands. As one British politician told Hoesch on 15 March, 'A pro-French policy hasn't a hope.'[141] Berlin was also aware that His Majesty's Government did not want to force the issue, but were pressing for gestures as a means of escape from France. This, in turn, suggested that Eden's resistance to Flandin's demands would be sustained so long as Paris did not mobilize or Germany did not provoke Paris, say, by sending reinforcements into the Rhineland. Nor was there any indication that London's patience had been exhausted or that she was struggling any less strenuously to avoid having to fulfil her punitive obligations.[142]

The German government's refusal to panic, or even to accept that grounds existed for alarm, was almost exclusively based on its assessment of the principal Locarno powers' reactions. Equally encouraging were reports from elsewhere which indicated that support for the French position was not only small, but shrinking. There was no accompanying increase in the ranks of German sympathizers, but by the time the League council convened in London, it was clear that the retreat from collective action against Berlin was already well under way.[143]

Most members of the League council asserted that a breach of treaty did not oblige them to impose economic, financial or military sanctions, since there had been no 'resort to war', as stipulated by article 16 of the Covenant.[144]

The Scandinavian states made this point *en bloc* to London and Berlin after meetings on 11 and 13 March.[145] Norwegian foreign minister Dr H. Koht even suggested to the British that he would face the break-up of the League rather than see his country embroiled with the Reich.[146] Swedish sources had told the German legation in Stockholm that the government hoped any action against Berlin could be avoided, while foreign ministry officials plied Eden with suggestions for counteracting French intransigence, particularly on the sanctions question.[147] The Danish government, visibly nervous about antagonizing its powerful neighbour, displayed the same desire to 'ménager' Germany which had led Copenhagen to abstain on the Stresa resolution some eleven months earlier. Foreign minister Dr Peter Munch made it clear to both London and Berlin that he was not only strongly opposed to sanctions, but would also resist even a resolution of censure against Germany.[148]

Meanwhile, Europe's two traditional neutrals, the Swiss and Dutch, had claimed their ancient right to stand aside and assured Hitler of their disinterest.[149] As for Germany's former allies, both the Hungarians and Bulgarians applauded the coup.[150] The Austrians, on the other hand, reacted according to their feelings about an Anschluss. But since that meant taking their diplomatic cues from either Hitler or Mussolini, no one considered Vienna as a potential sanctioner.[151]

Farther south, the Turks, Greeks and Yugoslavs, still trembling after Titulescu's mid-week attempt to align them with the French position, were repeatedly promising Berlin that they would do nothing to jeopardize their good political and growing commercial relations with the Reich. Ankara had already reaffirmed her desire for a peaceful solution,[152] while Athens was insisting that she was in no way obliged to become involved in non-Balkan affairs.[153] The Yugoslavs missed no opportunity to assure Berlin that they would reject economic sanctions as both harmful and a threat to peace.[154] Minister President Milan Stoyadinovitch even went so far as to solicit German support in the event that Paris, angered by Belgrade's refusal to impose sanctions on Berlin, should seek a *rapprochement* with Rome at the expense of Yugoslavia.[155]

Both of the two remaining non-aligned European states, Spain and Portugal, sat on the League council. Lisbon remained mute during the crisis, but in view of her traditional British friendship and her growing anxieties over left-wing successes in Spain, Berlin had reason to think Lisbon would, at worst, follow London's lead.[156] The same held true for Madrid, which on 9 March had signed a new trade agreement with Germany.[157] The Spanish representative had been instructed initially to work to prevent future treaty violations, but his orders had been changed, apparently as early as 11 March, to concentrate instead on preserving peace.[158] This suggested that Spain and Portugal would condemn the coup, but not support sanctions against the Reich.[159]

Four council places were held by non-European states. One of these belonged to Australia, which, like the other four British dominions, wholeheartedly supported Britain's conciliatory and mediatory efforts.[160] The other three seats were occupied by Latin American nations. Argentina had reacted with reserve towards Berlin, promising only to support a 'peaceful development'.[161] At the same time, Paris was informed that Buenos Aires, while agreeing that a treaty violation had occurred, would abstain on any vote to impose sanctions, because the government could not risk damaging congressional criticism after having had its majority slashed in recent elections.[162]

Ecuador, whose friendship with the Reich had been confirmed in December by a substantial trade agreement, revealed more fervent aversion to sanctions.[163] President Federico Páez described the idea as both 'nonsensical' and incapable of furthering the cause of world peace.[164] He also hinted to the German chargé d'affaires that Quito would drop Geneva before she would become embroiled in a dispute which he regarded as having 'no importance' to South

America. This attitude, coupled with Ecuador's behaviour at the League council, was gratefully acknowledged by Berlin.[165]

Chile proved no more courageous than her neighbours, in spite of the fact that she was involved at the time in an irredentist struggle with Bolivia and was relying on the League and the rule of law in her case against La Paz.[166] Santiago did promise Paris that her representative, Don Agustin Edwards, would pronounce himself frankly against unilateral repudiation of treaties. But Edwards, on the other hand, assured the Auswärtiges Amt of his country's sympathies, while the British were told that Chile would quit the League before agreeing to an embargo against one of her best customers.[167]

Of the remaining League council powers, there could be little doubt as to Mussolini's position, in spite of certain reservations about Rome's desire to keep open all possibilities as regards the Abyssinian conflict.[168] Warsaw's attitude was also judged 'not altogether predictable', in spite of Beck's promise to Berlin to vote against sanctions and his declarations to London and Paris of Polish aversion to an embargo 'on behalf of an unpopular treaty which did not directly affect Poland'.[169] But the Auswärtiges Amt believed that Warsaw would 'hardly constitute a serious threat' in the sanctions question, unless she received 'very far-reaching promises' from the other side.[170] Good grounds also existed for suspecting that Britain's leaders and a substantial portion of the British public would oppose any proposal which went beyond moral condemnation of the German treaty violation.[171]

That left only Rumania and Russia to endorse Flandin's demands for condemnation and punishment when the League council convened at St James's Palace on Saturday afternoon.[172] The French foreign minister's speech, however, was coolly received by most members, who did not relish having to acknowledge even the treaty violation.[173] They were much more interested in asking Berlin to send a representative to their subsequent sessions. This drive was led by Munch and Beck, but in all probability the British instigated the proposal, which coincided with Eden's desire to keep control over developments through direct contact with both sides.[174] In any case, the foreign secretary was instrumental, in spite of French opposition, in securing for Berlin a full-fledged invitation to return, albeit temporarily, to the seat which she had vacated nearly 2½ years earlier.[175]

This decision must have been a source of satisfaction to Berlin, if only because it showed how isolated Flandin was. Better still, the invitation's arrival was followed a few hours later by a 'pressing personal appeal' from London for Berlin, not only to accept, but also to send a representative who really knew the Chancellor's mind.[176] The Auswärtiges Amt received similar suits on Saturday and Sunday from the Chileans and Spanish, as well as from Munch and Beck.[177] All four representatives predicted that nothing would happen to Germany beyond 'constatation' of a treaty breach, since there existed neither a legal basis for sanctions nor the support for any condemnation. They also emphasized that ·a refusal to send a representative would cause general displeasure and strengthen the French position, whereas acceptance would create an entirely different atmosphere and improve the chances of negotiations.

But Hitler, whom Phipps described on Sunday noon as still heavily intoxicated from his fantastic reception by 200-300,000 Bavarians in Munich the night before, was in no mood to send anyone to London 'merely to have his head washed'.[178] It was only after the ambassador promised that Germany's honour would not be impugned that the Chancellor agreed. The tone of the acceptance note, however, revealed that Phipps had not succeeded in shaking the Führer's conviction, pronounced at Munich, that only God Almighty and the German people had the right to judge his actions.[179] As a prerequisite to acceptance, League secretary Joseph Avenol was asked to confirm that the German representative would be granted equality in the council's discussions and decisions. Hitler also declared that Berlin would participate only if she were assured that the powers concerned were 'prepared to enter into negotiations forthwith *alsbald* on the German proposals'.[180]

Although the Chancellor's note was generally repugnant to France, it was the *alsbald* stipulation which provoked Flandin into declaring that he had not come to London to negotiate with the Reich.[181] 'S'il devait en être autrement,' he warned, 'je préférerais rentrer à Paris et s'il le faillait même, cesser de représenter la France a la Société des Nations.'[182] The foreign minister, whose firmness was widely approved in Paris, was even quoted in some French newspapers as having threatened to mobilize.[183]

For the first and only time in the Rhine controversy, the

German government backed down in the face of widespread feeling that she was trying to dictate terms to the League council.[184] This apparent miscalculation was probably caused by Neurath's desire to divert the discussion from punishment to peace, but it may also have occurred as a result of over-confidence or Hitler's desire to impress his German audience.[185] The problem was resolved on 16 March by blaming a faulty translation of the word *alsbald*. Thus, it was explained, Berlin had asked only for an assurance of negotiations 'in due course' or 'as soon as possible'.[186] This 'correction' eased tension sufficiently to allow the League council to grant Berlin equality with the other two guaranteed powers, France and Belgium, which meant that, as parties to the dispute, their votes would not be counted.[187] However, the chances for early negotiations were eliminated by Flandin, who categorically rejected all talks until reparation had been received for the German treaty breach. He also stifled a proposal by Munch to permit Berlin to submit all the proposals it desired to make to the League council. In the face of such stiff French opposition, members decided to say only that it was not for the council to give desired assurances respecting the Chancellor's peace offer.[188]

By now, however, Berlin had warmed to the idea of sending a representative, not only to promote the German cause, but also to capitalize on the aversion of council members towards what Hoesch described as 'the aggressive behaviour of Flandin, the poison brew prepared by Litvinov and the intrigues of Titulescu'.[189] And, in spite of failing to secure from His Majesty's Government anything more than a demi-assurance that Hitler's proposals would be discussed 'at the proper moment', the Auswärtiges Amt declared on Tuesday 17 March that Ribbentrop would be available in London from Thursday morning.[190]

The absence of haste in the ambassador extraordinary's travel arrangements showed that Berlin no longer expected to stop the League proceedings short of any formal acknowledgement of a German treaty breach.[191] It was virtually impossible that Ribbentrop could have done anything to affect the council's decision between his late afternoon arrival on Wednesday and the vote less than twenty-four hours later. Although the German delegation could have come earlier, it was almost certainly held back, partly because Hitler did not want to risk having his representative put in the dock and cross-examined, and partly because Berlin did not wish to give the impression of having to canvass publicly for support.[192] Nor, obviously, did she wish to appear to be intimidated by the League council. Moreover, the chances of preventing a unanimous vote of 'constatation' of the treaty breach had been reduced almost to nil after the fracas over *alsbald,* which had been followed by two days of forthright speeches, the tone and quality of which surprised and pleased Paris after the temporizing of the first sessions of the council.[193]

For all practical purposes, Ribbentrop's speech, delivered in German on the morning of 19 March, was a formality, since council members had already decided that there was no way in which the League of Nations could retain any respect if they refused to acknowledge such an obvious breach of the Locarno treaty.[194] The writers of Ribbentrop's speech appear to have recognized this. And, although the ambassador extraordinary harped back over the old German grievances, he stressed that his government's latest action had closed a sad chapter of discrimination, misunderstanding and hatred. It was now the moment to lay fresh foundations for European tranquillity. To this end, he declared, the Chancellor had put forward his 'historical and unique' proposals for a quarter-century of peace. It was these rather than the 'susceptibilities of the moment', he insisted, which would 'pave the way for a better future in our peaceless Europe'.

Most council members listened attentively to both the speech and the translation—except for Litvinov who read a newspaper and Ecuador's Gonzalo Zaldumbide, who, on his government's instructions, had contracted an 'illness' which kept him from his seat until after the vote.[195] Members then adjourned for a few hours, ostensibly to reflect on Ribbentrop's remarks, but primarily to avoid giving the impression that their decision was a foregone conclusion. The result was almost unanimous: thirteen nations agreed that Germany had violated the treaties of Versailles and Locarno. Chile abstained on the grounds that the vote should be delayed until The Hague could give an opinion on whether Paris or Berlin had committed the first violation.[196] Ribbentrop voted against the resolution, but in calculating the result, no account was taken of the German, French or Belgian ballots. Ribbentrop immediately lodged a formal protest, declaring that the council's decision would 'not be ratified by history'.[197]

Ribbentrop may have failed to convince council members that they 'would have done exactly the same under similar circumstances', but his main mission was almost certainly to prevent anything worse from happening to Germany.[198] And, although he pressed Berlin's case for early negotiations, his message was unmistakably that any support by council members for punitive resolutions would not only obstruct the cause of peace, but also be regarded by Berlin as an unfriendly act. The ambassador extraordinary also warned, albeit indirectly, that any further anti-German measures might cause the Führer to revoke his proposals and retire into isolation.

In this effort to thwart economic sanctions or even a condemnation by the the League, Ribbentrop and the Auswärtiges Amt were able to draw on political and ideological considerations and, above all, the economic and financial web which Dr Schacht had spun around more than two dozen countries in Europe and Latin America.[199] So powerful were these factors and so obvious the consequences of antagonizing Germany at this time that both Berlin and London believed only Russia, Rumania and Czechoslovakia would be willing to join France, Belgium and Britain in imposing economic or financial sanctions against Germany.[200]

Such limited measures would have deprived Germany of an estimated 23.5 per cent of her total trade and half (£30 million) of her free foreign exchange, based on 1935 figures.[201] But these losses, according to the British treasury, would only prove vexatious, since Schacht would have no major difficulty in finding countries eager for a larger share of Germany's business.[202] Nor did the Reich's political advisers seem especially perturbed by the effect of sanctions on this scale.[203] After all, Hitler claimed, if the entire League of Nations could not thwart 42 million Italians, what chance did sanctions imposed by a handful of countries have against 66 million Germans?[204]

Barely four months earlier, fifty nations had agreed to impose an embargo against Mussolini. The subtraction in March 1936 of forty-four states from any prospective sanctions front cannot be explained entirely by the absence of Anglo-French accord or the argument that the Rhine violation did not merit such stiff punishment. The fact was that, compared with Italy, Germany was an economic octopus. She was, for example, Italy's main supplier and the principal customer of all six Danubian states, as well as Greece and Turkey, which conducted 40.5 per cent of all its trade with Germany in 1935.[205] Bulgaria's commitment was even deeper. Nearly 52 per cent of her entire import-export market belonged to the Reich.[206] Yugoslavia's position was no better. Germany, which had replaced Italy as Yugoslavia's number one trading partner, accounted for 17.5 per cent of her import-export totals in 1935 and there were already strong indications of the upswing which would raise that figure to 25.2 per cent in 1936.[207] Moreover, Belgrade had sacrificed all her trade with Italy—some billion dinars worth—and was determined to take no action without receiving full compensation.[208] Elsewhere in this area, Germany's trade in 1935 with Austria, Czechoslovakia, Rumania and Greece averaged just under one-fifth of their totals.[209]

Germany was also the second most important trading partner of eight other nations: all four Scandinavian states, Chile, Estonia, Portugal and Spain. Of these, the Swedes did 359 million RM and the Danes 260 million RM worth of business with Germany during 1935 and each country increased its trade with the Reich in 1936, by 18 and 33.5 per cent respectively.[210] Moreover, Copenhagen had to take into account the domestic repercussions if she caused Berlin to repudiate the month-old agreement with Germany which was widely acknowledged as being the 'best thing' that had happened for Danish agriculture for a long time.[211] Three other limitrophe states, Poland, Switzerland and the Netherlands, accounted for 1,079 million RM, or 12.8 per cent of Germany's total trade in 1935.[212] They, along with the other seventeen states mentioned, stood to suffer as much as, if not more than, the Reich. To many of these governments, economic sanctions were regarded as suicide by self-strangulation. This sentiment was so widely held that that United States consul at Geneva was prompted to describe the chances of such measures being imposed by the League council as 'almost fantastic'.[213]

The prospects were even further dimmed when one considered the millions which Berlin owed, not just on loans and interest, but also in unpaid rail transit charges to Poland and, especially, to her trading partners, many of whom had entered into clearing or barter agreements with the Reich.[214] Schacht was alleged to have warned, and the possibility could not be doubted, that his first move would be to write off some 1,000 million RM in debts with a stroke of the pen, on the grounds that sanctions had rendered their repayment impossible.[215] For Poland, Greece and the Danubian states, the cost would have been over 231 million RM, or the equivalent of 42.9 per cent of their total exports to the Reich in 1935.[216] Similar losses would have been experienced by Turkey, the Netherlands, Denmark and Chile.[217]

Britain, too, would have felt the cutting edge of sanctions.[218] Not only would her coal industry be hard hit, but so would the British firms which were then handling about 30 per cent of Germany's oil trade. It was also within Schacht's power to repudiate some £40 million (488 million RM) owed to the city, as well as the standstill agreement, under which interest on these debts was paid regularly. Such a move, according to foreign office economic advisers, could bring some financial houses to insolvency. This, in turn, would impair confidence and might even lead to a withdrawal of capital from London and a drain on sterling. At the same time, it was predicted that some Swiss banks would fail and Dutch financial establishments would suffer gravely. It also seemed possible that Berlin might seize on sanctions as an excuse to devalue the mark, thereby dealing a heavy blow to all her creditors.[219]

It was also suspected that, after any sanctions against Hitler were lifted, a revengeful Reich would be reluctant to restore commercial relations, preferring where possible to maintain economic relations with those countries which had remained loyal.[220] Nor were the prospects especially good for finding alternative markets for foodstuffs and raw materials or substitutes for German machinery, instruments and other manufactured goods.[221] Another concern was that an embargo would spur Hitler into seeking autarky as quickly as possible, which, on completion, might make the Nazi leadership precipitously bold.[222] Thus, it seemed entirely plausible, for example, that the Reich's capacity to produce synthetic nitrates would be so greatly expanded that saltpetre—Chile's most profitable export—would no longer be required by a customer which took 45 per cent of her exports in 1935.[223]

From an economic standpoint, Hitler could not have

chosen a better moment to strike than at a time when German trade was expanding and League members were themselves feeling the bite of economic sanctions. Several states claimed immediately that they had been 'sanctioned out' by their efforts on behalf of Abyssinia, while others warned that they could not sustain the simultaneous loss of two markets, especially when the second was of such immediate and long-term importance. Nowhere was this more true than the Balkans, where, thanks to Italy's commercial eclipse, Germany's share of the total trade—and influence—was greater in 1936 than at any time between 1929 and the Anschluss. Even Latin American countries, which had hardly been affected by the Italian embargo, were reluctant to do anything which might jeopardize their chances of signing a lucrative trade agreement with Berlin.[224] In many cases, the prospects proved more alluring than the reality, but few countries wanted to take themselves out of contention by antagonizing the world's third largest import-export market.[225]

Many of these same states also had political or ideological reasons for not wanting to alienate Berlin. Sofia and Budapest, for example, were not only old friends of Germany, but ardent supporters of revisionism. Rome and Tokyo identified closely with her expansionist ambitions, particularly in the colonial sphere. Belgrade depended heavily on Hitler's influence, not only to resist the Hapsburgs, but also to keep Mussolini out of Austria and the eastern Adriatic.[226] Nor could the Poles, owing to their problems with the corridor and Danzig, afford to antagonize the Reich. In addition, Warsaw ran the perpetual risk that a wrathful Hitler might come to terms with Russia at Poland's ultimate expense.[227] Every other state which had gained territory at Germany's expense since 1918 felt some fear that Hitler might retaliate to an unfriendly attitude by stirring up their particular problem. Lithuania had already incurred Berlin's anger for her treatment of the Germans in Memel.[228] The Belgians felt vulnerable over Eupen-Malmédy and the Danes over Schleswig.[229] Nor was it inconceivable that sanctions might cause the Chancellor to rescind his public renunciation in January 1935 of Alsace-Lorraine as German provinces.

Nations which possessed sizeable German minorities were also worried by the Nazi potential for organizing fifth-column activities. Czechoslovakia was troubled by the Sudeten

German problem and Belgium by the Rexists, while Vienna lived in the memory of Dolfuss and the shadow of the Anschluss.[230] Chile, too, had its potential problem with a large and powerful colony of 150,000 Germans, who composed 10 per cent of her total white intelligentsia and who were bound to view with disfavour any act by Santiago against the fatherland.[231] Bucharest also had its vociferously pro-German element, whose ranks extended well beyond Rumania's 750,000 Germans.[232] Berlin also seemed capable of arousing revisionist grievances in Hungary and Bulgaria which could directly threaten all five members of the Little and Balkan Ententes.

For many of these states, nothing good would be gained by supporting punitive measures against Hitler. This was particularly true of Germany's neighbours. Indeed, within a week of the coup Göring was reported to have threatened the Lithuanians and Czechs with extinction and warned that Denmark and the Netherlands would be occupied immediately if they attempted to join any trade boycott.[233] Such threats illustrated the risks of alienating a government already noted for its ruthlessness and run by men like Hitler, Goebbels and Göring, who talked about 'higher laws', 'the powerful voice of guns' and 'explosions' if Germany were not allowed to recover 'her place in the sun'.[234]

Berlin's position was also strengthened by the fear and hatred of communism which permeated Latin America, Kings Boris of Bulgaria and Carol of Rumania, Prince Paul of Yugoslavia and Mussolini, as well as the people of Poland, Portugal, Bulgaria, Finland and significant segments of society in France, Belgium, Britain, Austria, Sweden, Spain, Holland and Rumania.[235] Although no country actually refused to consider punishing Germany simply because of the Reich's resistance to bolshevism, Chile's Edwards assured Hoesch on 14 March that all three South American council members supported Berlin's stand against the third international 'to the full'.[236] Such was the pervasive dread of communism at this time that Litvinov's strong call on 17 March for a collective League effort to avert future treaty infringements was, as A.J.P. Taylor has written, 'in itself enough to damn the proposal'.[237] It was also true and perhaps even more important that persons who held no brief for Hitler or Nazism were frequently less sympathetic than they might otherwise have been to Paris for having allied France with Moscow.

All these factors combined with Germany's military resurgence and the unpredictability of her leadership to cut a swath through the ranks of those non-aligned members of the League whose support was essential if France were to succeed in getting the council to initiate economic sanctions or even to approve a resolution of condemnation against Berlin.[238] But, for all their success with League members, the Germans achieved little in their attempts to influence the outcome of the week-long Locarno discussions which had been resumed in London on 12 March. Informally, German diplomats concentrated on encouraging friends like Lloyd George and Lords Lothian and Londonderry, as well as a handful of MPs and other opinion-leaders whose voices could be used to espouse the German case and undermine the French position.[239] But neither Berlin nor her agents managed to influence her former partners' deliberations.

Had he withdrawn some troops from the Rhineland, Hitler would have been offered a place in the discussions. The Chancellor had proposed, via Ward Price on 13 March, that Germany should be invited to London or that Eden and Lord Halifax should come immediately to Berlin to hear the German case at first hand.[240] Both ideas appealed to British ministers, but the despatch of the foreign secretary to Germany was dropped as too provocative to Paris.[241] Nevertheless, the British would almost certainly have forced the French to allow Germany's participation in the Locarno talks as a quid pro quo for a gesture of substance. But the Chancellor's only concession, not to reinforce his Rhineland contingents, fell far short of providing Eden with sufficient leverage to overcome Flandin's resistance.[242]

As a result of her intransigence, Germany forfeited her chance to influence the course of events from within, since the Italians gave Berlin no active assistance. Instead, Hitler was limited to alternating frequent threats to withdraw his peace package with predictions of the millennium which could be achieved if only France would agree to join the other western powers at the conference table on a basis of equality and mutual respect. But the German government did nothing to help Britain escape from her French predicament. That was a job for Eden and his colleagues. The task proved more strenuous than almost anyone in Berlin expected.

7 A solution nevertheless

*Negotiations dragged on until March 19, when
that abortion, the proposals of the four Locarno
powers, was brought to birth.*

HOESCH, 21 March

It required a week and nine difficult meetings between the
remaining Locarno powers before Flandin pronounced himself satisfied. The negotiations passed through two phases.
During the first period, from 12 through 14 March, the French
maintained their demands for a German withdrawal from the
former demilitarized zone. The scale of this withdrawal
request varied somewhat, but not the insistence that progressive sanctions must be invoked if Hitler refused to make such
a gesture.[1] During the second phase, from 16 through 18
March, the nature and extent of French demands were approx-
imately the same, but the aim had changed. Flandin abandoned hope of inducing London to support a policy of force.
Having accepted that international law would have to be
vindicated in less direct ways, the foreign minister devoted
his efforts to extracting as much compensation from Great
Britain as he could. When that point was reached, he dropped
his demands for sanctions and cashed the blank cheque which
Paris held against her Locarno guarantor.[2] These periods
were separated by a weekend in which Flandin, after extensive conversations with Baldwin and Neville Chamberlain,
privately acknowledged the hopelessness of securing British
support for forcing a full or partial withdrawal of German
forces from the Rhineland.[3]

Throughout these Locarno talks in London, Zeeland
played a leading rôle as a mediator and peacemaker between
Britain and France.[4] This did not prevent him from shifting
his support from Flandin to Eden and then back to Flandin.
His foremost aim was to preserve Anglo-French unity in the
face of the German threat, but he was also anxious to ensure
that Belgium retained, or even improved upon, the guarantees provided by the Locarno pact.[5] When he concluded
during the first few days of talks that France's demands for
punishing Berlin seemed capable of causing a breach between

London and Paris, the Belgian prime minister joined Eden in overcoming French resistance to alternative solutions. For the next few days Zeeland assisted Eden by undertaking to persuade Flandin to concede on fundamental differences.[6] But, towards the end of the negotiations, the Belgians declared that the French had given enough ground and that it was Britain's turn to make concessions.[7]

At the outset of the Locarno talks, London's vulnerability appeared manifest. Flandin possessed the power to say 'we march' and oblige Britain to follow.[8] Moreover, Hitler's refusal to remove any soldiers from the Rhineland had cut away a great deal of middle ground and minimized Eden's room for manoeuvre with the French.[9] It also tended to underline the correctness of Flandin's assumption that Hitler would only respond if requests were backed by bayonets.[10] But the British government remained determined to keep the talks alive and to gain time to allow passions to subside.[11] Eden was also counting on the atmosphere of acquiescence in Britain and the absence of any support for sanctions among League council members to help persuade the French to drop their demands for punitive measures. In this respect, the British were encouraged by the fact that Flandin had not demanded immediate action when he was told of Hitler's unwillingness to reduce his occupation force to a truly symbolic level.[12] Moreover, Zeeland's support still seemed obtainable, even though the Belgian prime minister had declared in Paris on 10 March that a German refusal of a reasonable proposition should be regarded by the other Locarno powers as a *casus foederis*.[13]

But Zeeland was not yet prepared either to initiate sanctions or to support Eden's desire to accept the coup as an accomplished fact.[14] He still hoped to secure a German gesture, but only if the request were accompanied by a clear warning from all the remaining Locarno powers of the consequences of rejection. It was this omission, he felt, which had enabled Hitler to refuse Eden's request. That was why the Belgian prime minister supported Flandin on 12 March when the French foreign minister proposed that Berlin should be asked only to withdraw the units which had marched into the Rhineland on or after 7 March.[15] All other forces, including the Landespolizei, would be allowed to remain. According to Flandin's estimates, that would still leave an occupation force of 20,000 regulars in the Rhineland.

This request was to be accompanied by what Flandin described as a 'quasi promise' that negotiations would begin immediately if Hitler accepted and that one result would be recognition of Germany's right to station troops in the Rhineland. The foreign minister also stressed, however, that French acquiescence depended upon the fulfilment of two conditions. First, the Locarno guarantors would be expected to compensate France and Belgium for the resulting diminution of their security by agreeing to hold regular staff consultations in order to make their assistance more immediate and effective. Second, Germany must not be allowed to erect fortifications in the old demilitarized zone. Flandin thought it was 'hardly conceivable' that Berlin would refuse to withdraw temporarily a few thousand troops in order to secure such a satisfactory settlement. But, if she did, then he expected the Locarno powers to join Paris in taking all appropriate measures, including even the seizure of one or two key positions to be held until Hitler accepted the French plan.

Nothing in these demands on Germany during this period commended itself to Eden, Lord Halifax, Neville Chamberlain or the other British ministers who sat in on these discussions.[16] The Chancellor, they argued, would concede nothing. Moreover, after Berlin's first refusal, this request would amount to an ultimatum, which was practically an invitation to hostilities. Even if Hitler were subsequently defeated, the foreign secretary argued, what would the world have gained? 'Was it to be thought that Germany could be taught a lesson by such means?' Besides, British public opinion would never agree to spill blood driving the Germans out of the Rhineland, only to allow them to return legally the following week, as Flandin had suggested. This observation, Eden believed, had made some impression on the French.[17]

The Belgian prime minister acknowledged that it might be possible to push Hitler too far, but remained convinced with Flandin of the need for a German gesture.[18] In the face of this deadlock and possible breakdown of talks, Eden suggested that France and Belgium should consider instead what additional security might be required to compensate them for the loss of the demilitarized zone.[19] Zeeland, who was fearful of an Anglo-French rupture, agreed to draft proposals, while

Flandin, though making all reserves, also consented to pursue this line. But the Belgian prime minister, too, stumbled over the problem of the German troop presence, since Flandin chose to regard additional security guarantees as a reward for tolerating token forces in the Rhineland, rather than as a substitute for obliging Hitler to vindicate international law.[20] Nor did Zeeland's proposals alter the foreign minister's insistence that fortifications could in no circumstances be permitted in the Rhineland.[21]

Even though the Zeeland plan contained several features which were unpalatable to both sides, neither was anxious to reject it out of hand.[22] Moreover, Flandin's reaction to those sections offering compensation gave rise to the belief that his demands for punishing Germany could be overcome if Britain offered additional security guarantees which would remain in force regardless of the outcome of any negotiations with Berlin. But further probes in this direction were interrupted by the arrival from Paris on 13 March of minister of state Paul-Boncour, who had favoured an energetic French riposte on the 8th and who now professed to be 'staggered' by how far the conversations had drifted from what he described as true French feeling.[23] France, he declared, would accept nothing less than the full restoration of the *status quo*.

Paul-Boncour's statement not only disappointed Eden, but caught Flandin by surprise. Only a few hours earlier he had instructed military leaders in Paris to examine urgently what supplementary guarantees or concessions would be required from London, Rome and Berlin before France could agree to negotiations while troops remained in the Rhine zone.[24] Flandin was clearly well ahead of his government in his appreciation of the difficulties of persuading—and the consequences of forcing—Britain to support French demands for even a 'reasonable' German gesture.[25]

The apparent discrepancy between Paris and Flandin was due to several other factors. French resolve generally had been hardened by Hitler's refusal to make a gesture and by alarming newspaper reports that reinforcements and other illicit forces had swollen German strength in the Rhineland to 460,000 men.[26] Even more important, at least to Sarraut, Mandel and Léger, were fresh reports of Germany's extreme economic vulnerability. These came from both the consulate in Köln and the embassy in Berlin. Dobler described

Germany's situation as 'truly strained to the point of rupture', adding that economic or financial sanctions would, in his opinion, be even more effective than any military reprisals.[27] Meanwhile, Poncet and his financial attaché had despatched six telegrams in three days, stressing Schacht's opposition to the coup and his fear that Germany's economic and financial crisis was too serious to endure the consequences of such sanctions without danger.[28] Above all, however, it was the appearance at mid-week in Paris of Dr Hermann Straus, the director of the Deutsche Bank, and one of several such *démarcheurs* in search of monetary assistance for Germany, which convinced the Quai d'Orsay that Berlin's fear of economic sanction was 'infiniment plus grande qu'on ne le croyait'. The mere threat of such action, it was argued, could thwart Hitler's 'triomphe de bluff' and deal 'un coup sensible au prestige et à la force allemands'.[29] And, even if that did not work, it was argued, economic sanctions by the Locarno powers alone ought to bring the desired results, especially if Germany were denied access to the London free exchange markets.[30]

The intransigents in Paris also had taken heart over what they saw as a swing by the British towards greater understanding of the French thesis.[31] Corbin reported on Thursday, 12 March, that both the cabinet and foreign office now realized the full gravity of the situation.[32] This was followed by newspaper reports of increased parliamentary support for France's demand that Germany should give evidence that future treaties would be honoured fully.[33] Even *The Times,* which anxiously desired to capitalize on Hitler's offers, agreed that negotiations depended on the Chancellor's making a 'constructive contribution to re-establish confidence'.[34] And Sir Austen Chamberlain, the elder statesman of the conservative party, had broken four days of silence with a strong public demand that Hitler accompany his reassuring words with some peaceful deeds.[35]

Finally, there was the domestic political aspect of the problem. With polling day only six weeks away, no French government could afford to expose itself to charges of having imposed sanctions on her Italian friends and then having fled from the traditional foe.[36] And if, during the campaign, the parties in power risked negotiations with the chronic German treaty-breaker based on the *status quo,* they would create a

spectacle suggestive of *opera bouffe*.[37] With rightist opponents
like former premiers Laval and André Tardieu ready to
capitalize on any sign of weakness, the government needed
some sort of success in London to preserve the prospects of
electoral victory for the popular front.[38]

The next afternoon, Flandin confirmed privately to Eden
that the French government was adhering to its original
demands for a full withdrawal.[39] The foreign minister also
regretted that he would be obliged to repudiate Zeeland's
proposals and the entire compensation approach, which, he
thought, had offered some interesting possibilities. At the
same time, Flandin, who seemed to Eden 'more than usually
depressed', urged London not to take this news too tragically.
The foreign minister explained that he would subsequently
produce his own personal proposals, which, he believed,
would come much closer to the British position than his
government's current attitude. If London accepted this plan,
then Flandin would return to France and persuade the
council of ministers to abandon its demands in favour of his
compromise scheme.

Eden agreed to this procedure which, if nothing else, would
allow more time for French emotions to subside.[40] But the
foreign secretary also expressed doubts to ministerial colleagues as to whether, in fact, Flandin's private project would
be an improvement over France's previous position.[41] The
reasons for this pessimism are not recorded, but Eden was
certainly aware that Flandin and Paris were at odds primarily
over the scale of, rather than the need for, a withdrawal.[42] Nor
had the French foreign minister yet wavered from his government's insistence that fortifications must be prevented and
progressive sanctions invoked if Germany did not restore all
or part of the *status quo*.[43]

But Eden and his colleagues were unaware of the change of
attitude which Flandin had undergone since his arrival in
London on the evening of 11 March.[44] The foreign minister
had quickly and accurately assessed the depth of public
opposition in Britain to his position. He could also see that
there was no chance of persuading His Majesty's Government
that Hitler would succumb to threats or, in fact, to any
measure short of invasion. To insist on British support in
securing even a token withdrawal, he reasoned, would
involve a heavy sacrifice of friendship and goodwill. Flandin

was doubtless also aware that London's participation in any punitive action would have grave consequences on a British public which was as much in favour of negotiations as it was opposed to French demands for coercion.

By the weekend, Flandin had found himself confronted by a backlash of francophobia which had been caused by the same press reports that Paris had found so encouraging a day or two before.[45] The foreign minister could also see more clearly than his cabinet colleagues at home that the supporters of punitive measures in Britain were not only small in number, but did not even accept the French demand for a withdrawal of troops from the Rhineland. They had only endorsed the view that Hitler ought to give some evidence of his good faith before negotiations or that His Majesty's Government had an obligation to give Paris and Brussels some 'genuine guarantees' against future German aggression.[46] In either case, their aim was to avoid betrayal as well as action, whereas the bulk of the British people wanted His Majesty's Government to act solely as a mediator, if that were required to bring both a peaceful solution and negotiations.[47] So intense was this hostility towards the French for their 'continual coercion and everlasting complaining' that when Sir Austen Chamberlain readdressed his parliamentary colleagues on 17 March, he received no support from MPs, who themselves had been given a difficult time by their constituents at the weekend whenever they spoke about the importance of a German gesture.[48]

If Flandin required any additional evidence of the futility of further attempts to persuade London to join in punitive measures, it was provided during what he described as an 'extremely important' private talk with Baldwin on the night of 14 March.[49] There is good reason to doubt the foreign minister's recollections of his own side of the conversation, especially when he writes that all he asked of Baldwin was an assurance that His Majesty's Government would not disapprove of a quick march into the Rhineland by Gamelin's armies—without any British assistance.[50] Nor do the documents confirm his contention that French military intelligence had discovered already that German troops in the zone had orders to withdraw if they encountered French resistance.[51]

But Baldwin's recorded remarks are in harmony with both

British policy and the prime minister's personal position. His
Majesty's Government, he is said to have replied, could not
endorse, let alone pursue, any policy involving even a one per
cent risk of war. The prime minister then gave such a vivid
description of Britain's military weakness that Flandin could
only concur with Baldwin's conclusion that 'l'Angleterre n'est
pas en état de faire la guerre'. This was apparently the first
admission that London could not honour her Locarno commitments, although the French had known for months of
Britain's armaments deficiencies.[52] Nevertheless, the prime
minister's declaration, which was repeated privately to
Flandin by Neville Chamberlain the next day, had put
matters in a far graver light.[53] Paris had been anticipating that
London would cooperate in order to avoid the dishonour of
non-fulfilment, but it now seemed possible that she might
plead impotence. A public confession of this nature would
almost certainly have produced more serious consequences
than failure to punish Germany for her treaty violation.[54] It
could easily have been taken by Hitler and the Japanese as an
invitation to early expansion. It also seemed likely that a
dozen European states would feel less willing or capable of
resisting covert pressures from Berlin.[55]

Flandin must also have been aware of the implications of
this situation for British policy.[56] Until London was reasonably well re-equipped she could not consider any step which
might provoke a premature clash. If, for example, Britain
agreed to impose economic sanctions over the Rhineland, she
would be under pressure to take stronger measures in response to any act of German aggression, including an
Anschluss. If Austria fell too soon, it seemed entirely possible
that Berlin's next step could precipitate war before Britain
was adequately prepared. Thus, any action which brought
conflict closer or even encouraged Hitler to accelerate his own
armaments programme would have the effect of depriving
Britain of time at a period when, as Vansittart stressed, time
meant as much as weapons.

Baldwin's disclosure, taken together with London's
imperative need for three years of peace and the uninformed
state of the nation, convinced Flandin of the impossibility of
enlisting British support for any coercive policy.[57] These
factors also underlined the wisdom of not forcing His
Majesty's Government into sanctions. And they confirmed to

the foreign minister that London would make important concessions to Paris and Brussels in order to avoid the dishonour of having to repudiate her treaty obligations. This meant that the threat of economic, financial or military sanctions could still be employed effectively to extract some unprecedented security guarantees as the price of letting Britain escape the full consequences of her Rhine commitments.[58]

Several other factors also played a part in Flandin's decision to abandon his hope of imposing progressive sanctions against Germany. First was the tepid response of League members, whose private aversions to punitive measures had culminated in the council's overwhelming decision on Saturday to delay the task of confirming the German treaty breach in favour of issuing an invitation to Berlin.[59] Most non-aligned powers had refused to acknowledge any obligation to impose sanctions on Germany, while Munich, Beck, Edwards and others were openly expressing their opposition to a simple resolution of condemnation.[60] Even France's friends had retreated from their earlier positions. Although the Czechs and Russians remained loyal, both powers were now talking less of sanctions and more of forming a solid bloc of alliances against future German aggression.[61] Titulescu, too, had turned his efforts to blocking examination of Hitler's offers until France and Belgium had received satisfaction of some sort.[62]

Nor could Flandin have remained unimpressed by Poncet's reports of German determination to maintain the *status quo* and, especially, by the ambassador's warning on 14 March that any serious aggravation of the Reich's economic and financial position would push Hitler 'presque automatiquement à des solutions extérieures violentes'.[63] The foreign minister's resolve was doubtless also weakened by the fact that French military leaders had done nothing during this period to strengthen his position. Gamelin continued to insist on a million men and industrial mobilization before he would willingly cross the frontier. He also gave the British military attaché the distinct impression on 12 and 14 March that Paris was not going to take forceful action to eject any German troops from the Rhineland.[64] And Flandin's attempts to arm himself with plans for a coercive naval measure had evoked only amazement from Piétri and Durand-Viel that the foreign minister could think that 'mesures de coercition' could be divorced from 'guerre navale'.[65]

Flandin also doubted whether the French people would loyally follow their government into any solo adventure against Germany.[66] To judge by despatches and press reports, irritation with Hitler was not being converted into support for anything more than mild economic sanctions.[67] Furthermore, in certain French quarters there were signs by the weekend of mounting restiveness over what was increasingly being described as a retrograde attitude on the part of the Sarraut government.[68] Flandin, too, felt politically threatened by critics who not only regarded him as too anglophile, but also resented Britain's handling of Mussolini and favoured a bilateral settlement of Franco-German differences. In their eyes, the foreign minister was damned if he pressed Hitler too hard or if he yielded too readily to London.[69] Flandin may also have been aware that the British were operating in the belief that Sarraut, Mandel and Léger had adopted a far tougher attitude than could be justified by French public opinion.[70]

It is not possible to measure precisely the relative impact and importance of each of these factors. The effect was obviously cumulative, but it seems clear that domestic considerations were only of secondary importance compared with Britain's attitude and Flandin's concern that forcing action could not only destroy what remained of the Locarno pact, but also jeopardize the *entente* with England.[71] This, it was felt, would be the 'supreme disaster' for Europe as long as Hitler remained a threat.[72]

For all these reasons, Flandin decided to continue his efforts to punish Berlin for her treaty violation, but to acquiesce after he had extracted a fair price from London for failing to fulfil her Locarno obligations.[73] That price, he believed, should be a revival of the British guarantee which Clemenceau had accepted in 1919 as partial compensation for abandoning his demands for a Rhine frontier. The Locarno pact would be stripped of its vague and cumbersome League procedures and bolstered by military accords and staff talks. Flandin was even prepared to give a French guarantee to Britain in order to make the arrangement reciprocal and, therefore, more palatable to British public opinion.[74]

Flandin had no illusions about the resistance he would

have to overcome in London to achieve these aims. As early as 10 March, Eden had protested that Locarno without Germany would deprive the pact of its mutuality and amount to nothing less than a permanent Anglo-Franco-Belgian alliance.[75] London's aversion to any sort of regular or formal military contacts was one of the most consistent aspects of British foreign policy.[76] French efforts to secure such talks had been repeatedly rebuffed since 1919. Even the Belgians, whose security was a paramount British concern, were refused such talks as late as 1934.[77] Usually the reason cited was London's commitment under Locarno to be impartial in appearance as well as in fact. But neither the cabinet nor public opinion had displayed any desire for military conversations or commitments which, it was widely held, had dragged the United Kingdom into war in 1914.[78]

Meanwhile, British ministers had come up with a scheme which they hoped would prise Paris out of her intransigence by supplying the necessary vindication of international law without obliging Hitler to do any more than relocate some contingents within the Rhineland.[79] The idea was to station an international force, on the Saar model, along Germany's frontiers with France and Belgium, pending a new settlement.[80] Acceptance by Berlin, it was felt, would qualify as a contribution capable of creating the confidence required for profitable negotiations.[81] Better still, the British believed that Hitler had already approved the plan, which had been proposed to the Chancellor and Göring by *Daily Mail* correspondent Ward Price during a private 1½-hour conversation in Berlin on 13 March.[82] Hitler, who authorized Ward Price to convey this information confidentially to His Majesty's Government had even suggested that the proposed zone should be ten kilometres deep and policed by British, but not Italian, soldiers. But he also stipulated that French and Belgian soil would have to be occupied on exactly the same basis, thus ensuring full parity of treatment between Paris, Brussels and Berlin.

British ministers were enthusiastic over both the idea, which Baldwin thought would be 'very popular' at home, and the Chancellor's encouraging response.[83] But the immediate view, as pronounced by the prime minister on 14 March, was that the proposal was not yet practical politics.[84] Within twenty-four hours, however, the international force had become a major factor in the Anglo-French deliberations. The transformation was effected by Neville Chamberlain, who seized an opportunity on Sunday 15 March to lay the scheme before Flandin. The French foreign minister not only responded 'extremely well', according to the chancellor of the exchequer, but had felt '90 per cent sure' that his government would also agree, provided it were accompanied by a British promise to conclude a strictly-defined security pact.[85]

The stage now seemed set for the final phase of the search by the Locarno powers for what has been described as 'a formula which might cover their own lack of agreement'.[86] During this final, 48-hour period, Eden, Flandin, Zeeland and Grandi were closeted together for more than eleven hours, while they dissected three plans and two revisions in their struggle to resolve differences on five fundamental points. Two of these problems were rather easily overcome; two were settled after intense struggle; and one was deferred through phrasing which allowed both sides to claim success.

The latter issue focused on fortifications.[87] The French and British both agreed that their construction should be held up during the period of negotiations, but Flandin insisted, as he had done throughout, that any German move in this direction at any time would constitute a *casus foederis* for the remaining Locarno powers. As a result, he wanted provisions included which Eden feared would oblige His Majesty's Government to undergo another Rhineland crisis if Germany violated article 42 of the Versailles treaty. The foreign secretary and his cabinet colleagues also believed that it was not practical politics to expect Hitler to submit to fresh restrictions which would not only be 'continuously and surreptitiously infringed', but whose existence would render it impossible to negotiate any general settlement with Berlin.[88] In the end, however, it was agreed that the four remaining Locarno powers would 'press' for a prohibition or limitation of fortifications in a zone to be determined.[89]

The two less difficult problems dealt with the proposed international force and the French desire to involve the Hague tribunal. The dispute over the international force originated as a result of an apparent misunderstanding between Flandin and Chamberlain over whether the troops would be stationed on both sides of the frontier or only in Germany, as had been the case in the Saar.[90] It is equally

possible, however, that Flandin shifted his position when he
realized the domestic consequences of a scheme which would
place equal numbers of soldiers on French as well as German
soil. That action, in the eyes of the government's opponents,
would have lowered France to the same level as Germany. It
would also have made it considerably more difficult for Paris
to pin clear guilt on Hitler for his unilateral breach of a
freely-undertaken treaty.[91]

As a result, when the Eden and Flandin proposals were
compared, it was found that Britain was proposing to station
the international force on both sides of the frontier, while the
French were asking for the permanent presence on their side
only of contingents from Great Britain and Italy.[92] The
foreign minister insisted that the two guarantors should make
this gesture of support, otherwise he would insist that an
international force should be established exclusively on
German soil.[93] He would not even agree to a compromise
proposed by Halifax to station British and Italian troops on
his side and an international contingent in Germany —
probably because British troops would then be in both places,
thus blurring the crucial distinction between the violator and
the violated.[94]

The British, however, dismissed the idea of a permanent
troop presence on French or Belgian soil as impossible. A
military presence in France or Belgium was even more
strongly opposed in Britain than staff talks.[95] Moreover,
ministers feared approval would play into the hands of those
elements in Paris who were suspected of wanting to tie
London into a bilateral arrangement and then refuse all
negotiations. The alternative, however, was regarded as
unpromising, since it involved asking Hitler to accept the
same kind of inequality which he had repeatedly scorned.
About the only hope, it was felt, lay in persuading Berlin to
accept an international force as an earnest of her desire for
peace. Nevertheless, it seemed worth trying, if only because
Flandin and Zeeland had said that confining the international
force to German soil would considerably ease their attitude on
the other questions under discussion.[96] It was also agreed that
the Halifax scheme would be held in reserve in the event of a
German refusal.[97] But this 'clearly understood' option was
eliminated, to Eden's displeasure, on 20 March when Flandin
declared to the Chamber of Deputies that the French

government would never agree to the 'monstrous inequity' of an international force on their soil.[98]

On the issue of The Hague, it was the French and Belgians who gave way. Their draft proposals had not only invited the German government to join Paris in submitting to it the question of the incompatibility of the Franco-Soviet pact with Locarno, but had also insisted that both sides should bind themselves in advance to accept the tribunal's ruling.[99] If the judgement went against Germany, then Hitler would be expected to recall his troops from the Rhineland. Equally, if Berlin refused to have recourse to The Hague or rejected its finding, then Flandin and Zeeland said they would revert to progressive sanctions to secure the demilitarization of the Rhineland.[100] But Eden refused to accept this, and, having acquiesced on the question of the location of the proposed international force, was able to enlist Zeeland's assistance in getting Flandin to drop the punitive threat and agree that negotiations could still occur if Hitler refused to submit his complaint or if the judgement went against Germany.[101] This effectively removed the Hague procedure as a matter of importance to anyone except the French, who still insisted that Berlin be invited to submit her case to the international tribunal, simply because Paris believed Hitler's inevitable refusal would underline to world opinion the speciousness of his pretext for action.[102]

The last two problems, which were closely related, involved Flandin's continued demand for progressive sanctions if Hitler refused to vindicate international law and the Franco-Belgian desire for staff talks with Britain. After Hitler and Flandin had both apparently endorsed the international force scheme, Eden concluded that there would be no further demands for troop withdrawals and therefore no proposals which Berlin could not accept.[103] But the French foreign minister had returned to the charge on 17 March, insisting that a refusal by Hitler to accept any provisional disposition or other request concerning the Rhineland would oblige the remaining Locarno powers to 'immediately take the most effective measures, economic and financial, military, naval and air, to induce Germany to withdraw her military forces'.[104] Not only were these interim demands on Berlin to be considered as indivisible, but Paris intended that the same punitive measures should be applied if Hitler began erecting fortifications or in any way prevented or obstructed the negotiations for a fresh settlement.[105]

This declaration, which was to be embodied in a public letter of assurance from the two guarantor powers to Paris and Brussels, struck Eden as being so much like a 'dictat' that Hitler was bound to reject it out of hand.[106] Nor, in the foreign secretary's opinion, would Britain ever agree to a document which presented the Chancellor with the choice of acceptance or war.[107] This contention was hotly disputed by Flandin.[108] He recognized that the British people would never agree to impose the same kind of sanctions against Germany over the Rhineland violation as were being applied against Italy.[109] That was why Paris was only asking the Locarno powers to refuse financial accommodation to the Reich and possibly to close their ports to German shipping.[110] This statement represented a significant change of attitude, since, for the first time since 7 March, the foreign minister had spoken of imposing sanctions as an isolated measure to punish Berlin for her treaty breach, rather than as the first of several steps aimed at forcing Hitler to withdraw troops from the former demilitarized zone.[111]

This idea apparently appealed to a few British ministers, who had come by now to look upon limited sanctions as a viable alternative if Hitler remained obdurate.[112] But the majority, including the prime minister and foreign secretary, still believed that such measures would not only be unpopular with the electorate, but also counter-productive, since their imposition would almost certainly destroy all prospects for negotiations.[113] This was undoubtedly the real reason for London's refusal to endorse any embargo, but Eden was also alarmed by the possibility of escalation, since the French text of the draft letter went far beyond Flandin's moderate request.[114]

But the foreign secretary's arguments failed to mollify Flandin, whose irritation with His Majesty's Government had been smouldering for several days over Eden's efforts to promote the presence of Germany at the League council.[115] The French press, too, had manifested an 'alarming increase' in anti-British feeling, precipitated by what Flandin described as London's refusal to face her responsibility as a Locarno guarantor and her tendency to carry her mediatory rôle to the extent of consistently classing Paris and Brussels in

the same category as the guilty Germans.[116] France, he
announced on 18 March, had already given enough
ground—a sentiment echoed in Paris by Léger, who declared
to a member of the British embassy that this was 'l'heure de
Joffre, où on ne peut plus reculer'.[117] If His Majesty's Government would not accept this letter or something like it, as proof
of their determination to resist German aggression, then,
Flandin warned, he would have no choice but to leave London
immediately. To return empty-handed, he feared, would
have a serious effect on Anglo-French relations, since
Britain's opponents would not only gain the upper hand in
Paris, but also abandon sanctions against Italy and possibly
even seek to make their peace directly with Hitler.[118] Nor did
the foreign minister see how the Sarraut government could
continue imposing an embargo on Rome if London refused to
apply similar measures against Berlin.[119]

These threats spurred Zeeland into action. The Belgian
prime minister until now had supported French demands for
retribution if Germany refused to cooperate.[120] He had incorporated Flandin's letter into a Belgian compromise
project on 18 March and had even tried to persuade Eden to
accept its contents on the understanding that they would be
kept secret.[121] But now, with the discussions at the breaking
point, Zeeland undertook privately to modify the French
position.[122] This effort, while successful in securing concessions from the French on a couple of points, failed to produce
a draft letter which was in any way acceptable to British
ministers.[123] The only solution, as Eden saw it, was to make a
counter offer whose acceptance was contingent upon France
abandoning her demands for such explicit punitive provisions. That meant, the foreign secretary believed, agreeing to
Flandin's demands for immediate staff talks.[124]

During the ten days from start to finish of the Locarno
powers' deliberations, three sets of military conversations
figured in the discussions.[125] The first were consultations for
the event of unprovoked aggression by Germany during the
period required to negotiate a new settlement. The second
involved talks in case Berlin refused to cooperate or caused
the negotiations to break down. The third encompassed staff
cooperation as part of a general settlement.

There was very little argument among the negotiators over
the latter category. Eden had accepted by now, at least

privately, that Britain might have to yield to repeated Franco-Belgian demands for staff consultations which would replace the Rhine *glacis* by guaranteeing immediate assistance in the event of unprovoked German aggression.[126] The cabinet, while aware of Eden's recommendations, was not specifically asked to approve military talks as part of any proposed western settlement.[127] But it did agree that the mutual assistance pacts with Paris and Brussels to replace Locarno should provide for the effect of changed conditions in the Rhineland.[128] This gave the foreign secretary sufficient leeway to commit Britain to taking 'suitable provisions to ensure prompt action . . . as well as technical arrangements for the preparation of such measures'.[129]

The main disagreement occurred over French and Belgian demands for immediate military consultations.[130] This idea surfaced only on Tuesday, 17 March, after Flandin learned that Eden had no intention of stationing British troops exclusively on French and Belgian soil.[131] In their absence, the foreign minister had suggested that staff talks would give France some additional security for the intervening period. Flandin also wanted these consultations in order to restore domestic confidence and to serve notice on Europe that Hitler had not shaken their solidarity.[132]

Initially, Eden had attempted to avoid the question by emphasizing that the international force would supply the reassurance required by French public opinion.[133] But when that body's proposed geographical location was moved entirely on to German soil and its existence became dependent upon Hitler's approval, Flandin grew more insistent on interim staff talks.[134] His intransigence also deepened in direct proportion to Eden's assault on the draft letter, which Flandin and Zeeland regarded as the force behind their proposals to Hitler.[135] If His Majesty's Government would not accept their letter, they argued, then it was incumbent upon London to produce some suitable substitute, such as interim talks. On this point, Eden, who had benefited from Zeeland's earlier efforts with Flandin, found himself confronted not only by a determined foreign minister, but, perhaps more significantly, by a prime minister who felt that Belgium and France had gone far enough to accommodate Britain.[136] It was now London's turn to bend.

But the cabinet adamantly opposed the idea.[137] The

trouble, as ministers saw it, was that the Franco-Belgian proposal, which instructed the military staffs to prepare to fulfil 'such obligations as might devolve upon them', left entirely open the possibility that these conversations were aimed at planning joint measures for either forcing a with-drawal of German troops or obliging Hitler to comply with their other interim demands. It was further suspected that Flandin wanted to use these consultations to prepare for military action as soon as Berlin started fortifying the Rhine-land. Several ministers warned that staff talks along these lines would be 'very unacceptable' to public opinion.[138] It was even predicted that the government would be driven from office before the British people would countenance consul-tations aimed at compelling the Germans to evacuate the demilitarized zone.[139] Others argued that any interim staff talks would hopelessly prejudice the chances for a western settlement, which was, after all, the whole object of British policy.

Most ministers wanted no interim military contacts at all. But when confronted by Eden with the grave risk of the imminent breakdown of the London talks, a majority agreed to the idea of offering conversations which were limited strictly to defensive action to repel an unprovoked German attack on France or Belgium during the period of negotia-tions.[140] These talks, it was stressed, would have nothing what-ever to do with the Rhineland.[141] But even this was criticized on the grounds that public opinion would jump to the con-clusion that any staff contacts at this time were for the purpose of planning punitive action against Berlin.[142]

In spite of the foreign secretary's forceful arguments, it was not a popular decision, especially with Sir John Simon, whose opposition was so sustained and ill-concealed that Eden and Neville Chamberlain felt obliged some days later to ask Baldwin to speak to the home secretary.[143] Nor had the cabinet acted from a position of strength. On the contrary, its main consideration appears to have been to avoid the possibility that Flandin might return to Paris and pillory London for her moral and military bankruptcy.[144] This threat had already been circulating for a week, along with rumours that Britain's failure to implement her Locarno obligations might cause France to dissociate herself from Geneva and the principle of collective security and revert to her pre-war system of alliances.[145] Ministers were also disturbed, though to a lesser extent, by the prediction that such an occurrence might cause the French government to fall into the hands of a ministry anxious to ally itself directly with Germany.[146]

Eden, who had gained no small victory in persuading ministers to agree to even limited staff talks, was nevertheless worried that his colleagues had not offered enough to satisfy Flandin. With only this one concession to offer, the foreign secretary warned the cabinet that negotiations were liable to break down that night.[147] If that happened, he added, the chances of securing Germany's cooperation would also be reduced. But Flandin did not bring about a collapse. The foreign minister's aims obviously were not as far-reaching as the foreign secretary had feared, especially on the question of punishing Berlin.[148] It is also probable that Flandin did not wish to subject either the *entente* or his own career to the strain which inevitably would have resulted if he had refused all compromise and returned to Paris with nothing to show for his efforts.[149] And although the foreign minister proved less intransigent than Eden had anticipated, it is equally true that the French only pronounced themselves satisfied after London had agreed to solid security guarantees and staff talks in three contingencies.

British representatives pledged that His Majesty's Government would abide by its Locarno obligations until they were replaced by mutual assistance arrangements which London was prepared to conclude with any or all of her former Rhine pact partners.[150] This clause protected Paris and Brussels against the possibility that Berlin might prefer to wreck negotiations and prevent the completion of all mutual assistance pacts. Staff consultations were also promised to France and Belgium both during the interim and as part of the permanent settlement to expedite effective military assistance 'in case of need'. The letter, too, contained important concessions, even though Eden had managed to extract its sharpest teeth. Paris and Brussels were assured that, in the event of the failure of the conciliation effort outlined in the rest of the agreement, Britain and Italy would come immediately to their assistance in accordance with the treaty of Locarno to insure France and Belgium against unprovoked aggression. This aid was to encompass all practical measures, including staff talks, but not military assistance, which the cabinet regarded as not 'practical' in view of the weakness of Britain's armed forces.[151]

On the other hand, the letter contained no absolute commitment for Britain to join Paris and Brussels in punishing Germany if Hitler refused to cooperate. The British government also insisted that the presence of troops and fortifications in the Rhineland could not be interpreted as unprovoked aggression.[152] As Neville Chamberlain explained it, Britain was 'most certainly not . . . bound in any circumstances to invade another country in company of other nations'. Nor did the letter spell out the criteria for determining failure. But London assumed that this decision would have to be unanimous to activate her promises, which, Eden insisted, would only come into play after *all* possibility of negotiations had been exhausted.[153] Furthermore, the British had managed to clear up in their favour one of Locarno's most controversial ambiguities by getting Flandin to agree that any measures would henceforth be *jointly* decided upon. Inclusion of this word meant that Paris would no longer be able to act first and call upon her guarantors for assistance.[154] Its presence enabled Eden and Chamberlain to claim that Britain's obligations had actually been reduced or limited by the letter.[155]

The final details of the 'Text of Proposals' were settled during a session lasting until 2 a.m. on 19 March.[156] In addition to giving additional security guarantees to Paris and Brussels, the agreement covered four other areas. During the interim phase, before negotiations, the German government was invited to accept certain provisional restrictions in the Rhineland. To accommodate the international force, Berlin was asked to create a new demilitarized zone twenty kilometres deep along the frontier with France and Belgium. In the remainder of the former zone, she was requested to construct no forts, groundworks or landing strips.[157] All paramilitary forces were to be maintained on a pre-coup basis and no further troops or war material were to be sent in. This restriction constituted the first public acknowledgement of France's willingness to tolerate soldiers in the Rhineland.

If Berlin accepted these proposals, then all five Locarno powers would negotiate a western settlement which included the promised assistance pacts, mutual fortification restrictions, and revision of the Rhineland status, as well as the air and non-aggression arrangements which Hitler had offered on 7 March.[158] The Chancellor's willingness to return to the League and to conclude eastern non-aggression pacts were judged not to pertain directly to the Locarno powers. They were therefore relegated to an international conference, whose stated purpose was to discuss ways of strengthening collective security, but which also satisfied the French desire to offset Hitler's peace proposals and allowed the British to shunt Germany's colonial claims to the bottom of the agenda.[159]

Finally, the agreement supplied the League council with a draft resolution, condemning Germany's action as a 'threat to European security'. Such condemnation was important to the French, but not the British. Their main aim here was to restore to the Geneva institution some of the prestige which Eden felt had been lost as a result of the Rhineland crisis.[160] To this end, the resolution urged adoption of 'any action that may be deemed wise and effectual to safeguard the peace of nations' and proposed the creation of a committee to recommend such measures to League members.

These proposals were presented as a white paper on 20 March, after the British, French and Belgian, but not the Italian, governments had endorsed the work of their negotiators.[161] Only in Britain was there a significant split over the merits of the document. The cabinet, a large segment of the Commons and a fair number of newspapers were opposed generally by their constituents and readers, as well as a vocal minority in the dominions.[162] Typical was the complaint by South African justice minister Jan Christiaan Smuts that the powers ought to have taken Hitler at his word and immediately hammered out a peace agreement in a spirit of total equality. His sentiment was echoed throughout the United Kingdom. Canon Davey of Liverpool cathedral refused to pray a blessing on the cabinet for seeking to reimpose what he and many others regarded as 'monstrous and unjustifiable' inequalities on 'a great people' and, above all, for having suggested that Berlin should submit to the indignity of Italian soldiers policing German soil, and alongside British boys at that![163] There was also an outcry against the government for having conceded far too much to Paris when, in the eyes of many, it was the French who were thwarting the peace negotiations.[164]

Baldwin and his colleagues, on the other hand, were satisfied with the London agreement, not so much because anyone
thought it was a particularly promising plan, but because
unity had been preserved and, as Neville Chamberlain
explained, the French had made concessions at almost every
point.[165] Best of all, His Majesty's Government had managed
to escape having to fulfil any military commitments without
being forced to renege on any treaty obligations. This also
meant that the government had been spared the opprobrium
which might have been hers if the talks had failed and Flandin
had returned empty-handed to Paris.

Vansittart summarized these feelings in a personal note to
Eden on 22 March, praising the foreign secretary for having
skilfully extricated his country 'from a position in which it
might have been either dishonoured and isolated, or forced
into dangerous courses'.[166] Approval was also expressed by
Lord Robert Cecil, Sir Austen Chamberlain and *The Times,*
which described the white paper as an 'articulated series of
diplomatic devices' designed to fill the momentary void with
an offer of reasoned and conciliatory measures which
deserved a constructive answer.[167]

Neither *The Times* nor the British government expected
Hitler to accept the white paper in its entirety. The cabinet
saw almost no chance for the Hague invitation, fortifications
limitation or the unilateral international force.[168] At best, it
was hoped that Berlin's disapproval would be limited to a few
points, whereupon, as Lord Cranborne put it, 'we shall just
have to start further negotiations with the French'.[169] In other
words, the agreement was to serve only as an overture towards
Germany. Its main function, in London's eyes, had been to
prevent conflict, gain time and secure French cooperation.[170]
Eden even believed that the whole white paper proceedings
had staved off French mobilization and thereby prevented
war.[171] In this respect, the foreign secretary not only felt that
he had succeeded in bringing Paris a long way, but was also
not without hope of getting negotiations started.[172]

In France, Flandin's achievements were warmly approved.[173] Admittedly, he had surrendered more than any
other negotiator. But considering the state of the mental and
military unpreparedness in France and Britain, as well as the
francophobia and germanophilia which he had encountered
in London, the foreign minister had secured some significant

results. He had preserved for Paris the security guarantees provided by the Locarno pact and had thwarted Berlin's efforts to use the peace proposals of 7 March to split Britain from France.[174]

He had also effected an important reversal of attitude on the part of Baldwin's government, which had swung in ten days from acquiescence in the *fait accompli* to acceptance of the French thesis that Germany must make some gesture of respect for international law.[175] Moreover, if Berlin refused, British public opinion would certainly now be more receptive towards an Anglo-French effort to prevent further violations.[176] In addition, Flandin had kept faith with France's eastern allies by retaining the right to take coercive action, with the support of Belgium, Italy and Britain, as soon as Germany began fortifying the Rhineland. This was implicit, he explained, in their reaffirmation at London of Locarno's continued existence.[177] He had also shown Berlin as the villain of the piece and manoeuvred Paris into position to prevent negotiations on German terms.[178]

But the foreign minister's most significant achievement was the military guarantee, complete with staff talks, which he had been promised irrespective of Hitler's response and which was in no way encumbered by London's insistence on maintaining the old equilibrium between Paris and Berlin which had helped to stifle all hope of military contacts during the Locarno decade.[179] Better still, British support would now be immediate, since neither the mutual assistance pact nor the letter was fettered by the complicated procedures contained in Locarno. This British military guarantee, Flandin announced to the Chamber on 20 March, marked a 'decisive stage' in Anglo-French relations.[180] Maurin termed it the 'finest result' which could have been achieved in the circumstances, while a socialist member of the government declared that France had secured assurances from London 'que nous avions demandé depuis plus de 10 ans et que nous désespérions d'obtenir jamais'.[181]

As early as April 1936, the Sarraut ministry came under criticism for not having thrown the German troops out of the Rhineland.[182] But in March, as long as the risk of hostilities existed, the only dissent over French policy came largely from those who were anxious to compose with Hitler or harboured a grudge against Britain for her treatment of Mussolini, or were political foes of the foreign minister.[183] Elsewhere, Flandin's achievements were welcomed by a public whose approval of his actions was matched only by their relief at no longer having the threat of general mobilization hanging over their heads.[184]

As for the demands made on Germany, the French people appeared far less intransigent than Flandin, who insisted that a rejection by Berlin of any part of the white paper would end the period of conciliation and activate the letter with its provisions for subsequent measures.[185] Some newspapers and political leaders were willing to bend or even disregard the London arrangements, provided the Germans made some gesture to acknowledge that the force of law should prevail over the law of force. Most French men and women, however, were primarily concerned about avoiding another crisis or confrontation with Germany.

It was this sentiment, according to the Belgian ambassador, which rendered it inevitable that Flandin would be forced to make 'concessions sur concessions' in the face of continued German intransigence.[186] Moreover, as former premier Joseph Caillaux told the British embassy on 21 March, the 'vast majority' of his compatriots felt it essential to talk with Berlin.[187] Even Herriot, long acknowledged for his antipathy toward the Third Reich, admitted that, with the assurance of British assistance in hand, he was entirely disposed to seek an understanding with Hitler.[188] To the Belgians, too, the problems of punishing or even negotiating with the Germans were secondary compared to the fact that, for the first time in modern history, Britain had pledged her word in writing to a given hypothesis before the event.[189]

It would be too much to say that the white paper formalized or even symbolized a revival of the 'Entente Cordiale'.[190] The Abyssinian affair still stood between the peoples of Britain and France. Nor was it entirely accurate to suggest, as Flandin later did, that the provisions for staff talks and mutual assistance pledges converted the long-coveted Anglo-French alliance into a reality.[191] But the agreement of 19 March provided the framework for subsequent cooperation and its existence was proof that Berlin had been penalized for her action.[192] Whether the London proposals for a permanent western settlement now bore fruit depended entirely upon Hitler.

8 The agreement flounders

*It is the deliberate will of the people that the
historical decision of 7 March should remain
intact.*   GOEBBELS, 24 March 1936

For the German government, 19 March was a day of
unpleasant surprises. The League council's vote against her
had been expected, but its unanimity had come as a blow to
Berlin after her diplomatic efforts, especially with those same
powers who had urged Hitler to send a representative to
London.[1] Annoyance over this set-back, however, was minor
compared with the anger and resentment generated by the
white paper which Eden read to Ribbentrop that same
evening.

Its contents had come as a great shock after a week punctu-
ated by reports of the Locarno powers' inability to reach any
agreement. Eden's refusal to yield to French demands,
coupled with mounting public and official support across
Europe for Britain's rebuilding efforts had not only confirmed Neurath's earlier judgements, but also given rise in
Berlin to a feeling that Germany would win easily.[2] Hitler's
campaign speeches on 16 and 18 March had conveyed this
impression.[3] So had Goebbels's press.[4] Even Hoesch had
regained his composure and appeared confident that London
would resist Flandin's attempts to 'blackmail' her into a
military alliance, if only because it would be regarded as a
commitment to encirclement, which, in turn, would ruin the
prospects for negotiations.[5]

Berlin's irritation, even fury, was doubtless compounded
by her own over-confidence. These sentiments were manifested, first by the government's refusal to allow publication
of the white paper in Germany for thirty-six hours and then
by a full-throated denunciation of the document by the press
under such headlines as 'Bad Will', 'Collective Shame-
lessness' and 'Shylock's Pound of Flesh'.[6] The *Völkischer
Beobachter* condemned the plan as nothing less than 'a fresh
crime against Europe', while the *Deutsche diplomatisch-
politische Korrespondenz* called it one of the 'worst efforts of the
post-war period'.[7]

Expressions of indignation and hostility toward this 'incredible resurrection of the Versailles spirit' echoed throughout the Reich.[8] Reich Minister Rudolf Hess denounced the proposals as the product of evil-minded satirists.[9] The Auswärtiges Amt thought they 'smelt Flandin', while Hoesch, whose moderation and good sense were widely recognized, scorned the white paper as an 'abortion . . . brought to birth'.[10] Hitler's public attitude towards the agreement was expressed in promises to audiences at Hamburg and Breslau that Germany 'would go her own way alone' before she would subscribe to 'so unintelligent an action' as one which threatened to penalize a nation 'for merely claiming sovereignty in its own territory'.[11]

Officially, German rancour was focused on four points. First was Grandi's signature, which Berlin regarded as a betrayal after Mussolini had promised to go no further than to vote to acknowledge the German treaty breach.[12] Second was the draft resolution asking the League council to condemn Hitler's action and to organize against future acts of bad faith.[13] The other two were the continued demands for gestures and the prospect of an anti-German alignment, complete with staff talks, if Berlin refused to subscribe to the terms of the white paper.[14]

The Auswärtiges Amt set out almost immediately to destroy as much of the document as it could. Berlin's first outburst was against Italy for her apparent double-cross and return to the Stresa concept—a point which Flandin had underlined in his speech to the French Chamber on 20 March.[15] Attolico received on Friday a severe scolding from Bülow, who expressed 'displeasure and astonishment' at Rome's acquiescence in what he described as 'a deployment for the threat and/or application of sanctions'[16]

Mussolini's embarrassment was so acute that by Sunday evening Rome had made no fewer than six attempts to explain away Grandi's collaboration on the grounds that the ambassador had acted provisionally, or exceeded his brief, or even disobeyed orders.[17] The Auswärtiges Amt was assured by the Duce personally that Rome still fully reserved her liberty of action and would not ratify the white paper—a decision described by Baron Pompeo Aloisi, chef de cabinet in the foreign ministry, as a 'turning point' in Italian foreign policy.[18] In addition, Mussolini, Suvich and Attolico all reaffirmed

Rome's absolute opposition to any 'coercive or exceptional' measures against Germany.[19] These reassurances apparently satisfied Berlin. They also revealed the Duce's position as both awkward and vulnerable. Neurath seized the opportunity by asking Italy, in essence, to do penance by taking the lead in denouncing all the requests being made of Germany.[20] This 'psychological support', the foreign minister added, would not only be 'greatly welcomed' by Berlin, but would also be service for service in view of her benevolence towards Italy during the Abyssinian crisis.

But Mussolini, in spite of his desire for closer cooperation between the two fascist régimes, was not willing to take such a step, which almost certainly would have stung France into supporting oil sanctions.[21] Nor was the Duce ready to abandon the possibility of his return to the Stresa front, at least as a bargaining counter with London and Paris. Instead, he promised to support the German position as it developed. He was prepared to negotiate, or to repudiate the entire document, as soon as Berlin made her move. He further agreed to inform London that Rome would refuse to join any sanctions—but he did not say whether Italy would actually cast her vote against them.

The Duce, however, did not keep his promises, preferring instead to remain silent.[22] Thus, by default, the white paper was deprived of Italy's endorsement. So, too, was Berlin deprived of any active support in her campaign against the London agreement. This attitude provoked questions as to why Rome had not spoken out publicly, as pledged. But German interest flagged as events swung in her favour, making Italy's assistance both less essential and less desirable.

Berlin's second success against the white paper required no major effort on her part. Hitler, Neurath and Schacht had already provided the economic and political background which on 20 March assured the League council's hostility towards the Locarno powers' proposals, particularly the resolution condemning Germany and calling for a study of measures to enforce European security.[23]

Strong procedural objections were raised because the Locarno powers had operated alone and in secret before presenting the product of their work to the council as a *fait accompli*.[24] These tactics, Beck complained, might give the impression that the League covenant was only an annex to the

Rhineland pact.[25] Several other members challenged the
ready-made nature of the resolution as a dangerous deviation
from the council's custom of appointing a *rapporteur* or even a
committee of non-involved parties to draft measures for subsequent consideration.[26] The white paper was also opposed
for substantive reasons. The Danish foreign minister argued
that the draft resolution dealt with problems which, according
to the Covenant, ought first to be tackled by general media-
tion.[27] Beck charged that the proposed general settlement
affected nations in eastern Europe, including Poland, which
had not been consulted by the negotiators. The Poles also
warned that the draft resolution would oblige the League
council to assume responsibilities whose full consequences
could be foreseen only after thorough examination.[28]

These grievances were accompanied by an absolute determination on the part of most representatives to delay further
proceedings until they could consult their governments—and
see how Berlin would react to the white paper. Most members
insisted on adjourning for three or four days, but Edwards of
Chile declared that he could not possibly receive fresh instructions from Santiago inside nine days.[29] It required no
particular acumen to see through this discontentment. The
fact was that, apart from the Locarno powers, Litvinov and
Titulescu, no one on the council wanted to risk incurring
Hitler's wrath. Faced, therefore, with a probable public
dispute or even revolt, Eden intervened to explain that no
resolution or even draft resolution had been submitted to the
council, since Mussolini had not ratified the white paper.[30]
The London arrangements, he added, had been circulated
merely for the information of members.[31]

This announcement enabled the council to end its meeting
on Friday in good order. But the situation deteriorated over
the weekend in the face of German press reactions and diplomatic efforts ordered by Neurath, who instructed missions in
twenty-three capitals to use 'every opportunity' to stress
Berlin's displeasure on every contentious point and to warn
members of the League that the council was being confronted
with a *fait accompli* aimed at spurring them 'still further in the
direction of sanctions'.[32] This effort, however, was hardly
required, since the seven so-called neutrals of Europe had
already met and decided that the council should not be asked
to endorse, or even take note of, the white paper.[33] A 'great

many' council members were not favourable to its contents, Munch told Vansittart on 21 March, and the resulting lack of unity was bound to benefit Berlin.[34]

By Monday, the opponents of further involvement had consolidated their position to such an extent that Eden believed 'even the French could be under no illusions'.[35] It might still be possible to force through the draft resolutions, but only after what promised to be a protracted and acrimonious debate. Such discord was precisely what London and Paris did not want. Instead, Mussolini's failure to endorse the agreement was seized upon as grounds for giving no further consideration to the draft resolution.[36] With that, the London session of the League council came to an end. And, if some of the departing delegates were angry over the outcome or embittered by the blow to the League's prestige, more were perceptibly relieved to be escaping without having had to discuss or approve the 'Text of Proposals'.[37]

The refusal of League council members to become involved was doubtless inspired largely by the the intense criticism in Germany over the interim requests which the remaining Locarno powers had made to Berlin. The fact that special contributions should be asked of her as a prerequisite to negotiations was regarded as an insult to the Chancellor's good word and a demeaning exercise in vindictiveness.[38] The Hague tribunal was dismissed as incompetent to judge the political and military aspects of the German case.[39] The Auswärtiges Amt also rejected the entire interim Rhineland régime, with its 'intolerable restriction' of sovereignty, as a 'permanent wound on the European body politic'.[40] The international force was described as a 'deliberate humiliation', while Göring, Hess and a host of other German officials and editors expressed incredulity that the Italian outlaw should be asked to police the Rhineland.[41] From Frankfurt came reports that the Rhinelanders were determined to 'fight with broomsticks . . . rather than submit to such an indignity'.[42]

The German government realized that it only had to say no to these requests to bring down this particular card house. And, judging by external, as well as internal reactions to the white paper, a refusal would be widely tolerated, if not understood and accepted, in Britain and throughout most of non-aligned Europe.[43] Nor could there be any doubt, from the moment Berlin first learned of the contents of the document, that Hitler would reject it out of hand — or at least those portions which violated his concept of total equality and German sovereignty.[44] Nothing, he insisted, would induce him to deviate 'one centimetre' from this position, not even the so-called need to vindicate international law and least of all the susceptibilities of any French government. 'I will not capitulate', he declared amidst a torrent of applause during a speech in Berlin on 24 March. If other countries clung to the letter of the law, he clung to eternal morality. The only symbolic gesture forthcoming from Germany, he added, would occur at the ballot box on 29 March.[45]

At the same time, however, neither Hitler nor Neurath was prepared to allow the thread of negotiations to be broken.[46] They were fully aware that the letter, which the foreign minister described as an instrument of political pressure, carried provisions for possible punitive measures if Germany remained obdurate or caused the conciliation effort to break down.[47] It seemed unlikely that sufficient interest could be aroused in Britain or even France for any sanctions at this moment.[48] But the existence of the letter and the promise of continued Anglo-French staff consultations would certainly give Paris a lever in subsequent dealings with London, especially over the fortification of the Rhineland. A harsh reply might make His Majesty's Government both less willing and less able to deflect France in the next crisis.[49]

That was why the formal German answer to London on 24 March contained a promise to submit in one week's time a programme of counter-proposals which would outline what was possible for Berlin just as clearly as Hitler had already defined what was impossible.[50] This response was calculated, not only to avert any immediate explosion as a result of Germany's rejection of the interim proposals, but also to exacerbate a disagreement which had developed over the weekend between London and Paris over the nature of the white paper.[51]

Problems had begun to develop only hours after agreement had been reached, when Flandin declared to the French Chamber of Deputies on 20 March that the arrangements constituted an indivisible whole which Berlin was free only to accept or reject *in toto*.[52] Zeeland had made similar statements, in spite of the fact that the British had steadfastly and successfully resisted all French efforts to insert the word 'indivisible' into the agreement.[53] Moreover, as Eden pointed out to Paris, such a statement was hardly consistent with a document entitled 'Text of Proposals'.[54]

The foreign secretary's desire to correct his French and Belgian colleagues was only surpassed by his anxiety, in view of Berlin's initial reactions, to avert an early and embarrassing impasse. As a result, Ribbentrop was assured on 20 and 21 March that the white paper was 'certainly not' a 'dictat'.[55] The way was completely open for Hitler to submit counter-suggestions. Phipps, too, was instructed to emphasize how important it was to His Majesty's Government that the Chancellor returned a constructive reply.[56] According to both Poncet and Attolico, it was the ambassador's démarche, executed with Neurath on Sunday evening, which had been responsible for Berlin's spiritual revirement after 22 March, and for Hitler's decision, 'in accordance with the frequently expressed wishes of the British', to keep alive the period of negotiations by promising to submit counter-proposals.[57]

These declarations from the British, when compared with Flandin's statements reaffirming the white paper's indivisibility, revealed how much more apparent than real was the new-found unity between London and Paris.[58] The divergence was even more evident from reactions in Britain, where revulsion against the international force and the other demands on Germany elicited reassurances, both via the press and directly from Eden in the House of Commons on 23 March, as to the propositional nature of the white paper.[59] Public anger and anxiety over London's pledges to Paris had also been increased over the weekend by reports that Flandin's supporters were gloating over the 'military alliance' which the foreign minister had extracted from Britain.[60] So hostile was the feeling against the white paper that Hoesch twice compared it with the surge of opinion which had swept Sir Samuel Hoare from office some thirteen weeks earlier.[61]

Public and press anger over the Locarno arrangements and the estrangement between Britain and France must have tempted Hitler to ignore the white paper or return nothing more than a categorical rejection.[62] It even seemed possible to Poncet that the Chancellor might respond with one of his *grands gestes,* say, by withdrawing his peace proposals or renouncing his earlier promise to regard Alsace-Lorraine as French territory.[63]

But from London came warnings from such staunch friends as Major-General Lord Mottistone that the climate currently so favourable to the German thesis could shift quickly and dramatically if Berlin behaved too badly.[64] This view was seconded by Hoesch, who argued that a conciliatory reply would render it 'by no means . . . easy for any British government to pursue a foreign policy based in the main on a military alliance directed against Germany'.[65] The Auswärtiges Amt also realized that complete intransigence might have a deleterious effect on the House of Commons and on other members of the British decision-making élite, not to mention the foreign office and cabinet, where, as Hoesch continually warned, there existed a strong sense of obligation towards preserving Britain's reputation as an honourable treaty partner.[66] Nor did it seem inconceivable that British public opinion or excessive French demands might still cause the remainder of the agreement of 19 March to collapse, especially if Berlin supplied some assistance.[67]

Although the German note of 24 March made it 'unmistakably clear' that Hitler would not yield or ever accept a solution based on the white paper, Eden's disappointment was tempered by the Chancellor's promise of proposals for securing a 'real and lasting' peace.[68] Not that the foreign secretary attached any great hopes to what would be forthcoming.[69] But Berlin at least had supplied His Majesty's Government with a reply which enabled Eden to fend off Flandin for another week on the grounds that world opinion would never forgive Paris or London if they immediately terminated the period of negotiations before anyone had an opportunity to see what sort of 'genuine treaties' the Chancellor was prepared to conclude.[70]

The French had been outmanoeuvred.[71] But, in spite of demands from Léger to the British for the immediate imposition of financial sanctions, the German attitude was not the fundamental cause of French concern at this time.[72] On the contrary, the Chancellor's 'clever rather than candid' reply had only confirmed long-standing convictions that Hitler was addicted to the *fait accompli* and would take the law into his own hands whenever it suited him.[73] Many elements in France must have been pleased by Berlin's intransigence, since this not only justified their suspicions, but also enabled them to saddle Hitler with full blame for thwarting the talks which they did not particularly want anyway.[74]

What worried Paris was the possible effect of Hitler's rejection on Britain's interpretation of her white paper commitments.[75] Some correspondents, notably Pertinax in *Echo de Paris* and Geneviève Tabouis in *L'Oeuvre,* emphasized in despatches from London that Eden had no intention of backing out of the 19 March agreement.[76] The prevailing sentiment in France, however, was expressed by *Le Temps* and Count Wladimir d'Ormesson in *Figaro,* which wondered on 25 March whether the other Locarno powers would stand by the measures agreed upon six days earlier for the event of just such a German rejection.[77] This, *Le Temps* suggested, would be the decisive trial of the policy of cooperation and collective security.[78]

Anxieties such as these might not have been so openly or fervently expressed, had it not been for Eden's declaration to the House of Commons not only that the Locarno plan was composed of proposals, but that Britain had already informed the Chancellor—without the knowledge of Paris—that any constructive German gesture would be considered.[79] Had the foreign secretary not stressed this point, it seemed possible that Hitler might employ the 'indivisibility' argument to reject the entire white paper on the grounds that he could never accept foreign troops on German soil.[80] If that had occurred, London might have found herself torn between fresh French demands for sanctions in accordance with her treaty obligations, and an electorate more in sympathy with Hitler than Flandin in so far as the white paper and the Rhineland were concerned.[81]

In France, however, it seemed as if the British were seeking to encourage, or at least 'ménager', Germany, while simultaneously putting oblique pressure on Paris to make further concessions.[82] Some of this consternation stemmed from the suspicion that His Majesty's Government was faltering in the face of a burst of public pressure which seemed capable of dealing a fatal blow to the entire agreement.[83] But the bulk of French apprehensions focused on the erroneous impression that London regarded her promises to Paris and Brussels as 'negotiable'. Eden wrote a fine letter to Paris, *Intransigeant* complained on 25 March, but forgot to post it.[84] Britain, it was feared, might back out of her pledge to guarantee French soil. Nor did it seem impossible that the staff conversations and letter might be bargained away in return, say, for Germany's agreeing to drop her colonial demands, or for some vague promise of good behaviour by the Chancellor, which, like fortifications or armaments limitation, could easily be circumvented.[85]

In fact, French fears were entirely misplaced. The British cabinet consistently took the line that those parts of the White Paper which concerned France and Belgium were irrevocable 'arrangements', while the sections requiring German co-operation were 'proposals'.[86] This later became apparent, but in the heat of the pre-election atmosphere, the Sarraut government was stung into repudiating the foreign secretary's statement.[87] Flandin summoned journalists and declared that there could be no middle course.[88] France, he added, had gone to the 'utmost limit' in making concessions. As proof of Britain's good faith, Paris demanded an immediate meeting of the remaining Locarno powers, despatch of the letter, which had not yet left London, and the fixing of a firm date for the staff talks. Britain was also warned privately that France would claim her freedom of action if the London agreement were not to be effective.[89] With that, the foreign minister departed for his constituency at Yonne, thus making himself conspicuously unavailable.[90] And *Le Temps* hinted that France might be forced to look elsewhere for security if the Locarno guarantors played false with their pledges.[91]

The British government now found itself being squeezed, not just on the home front, but also from across the Channel, where, it was feared, Flandin and his colleagues might take 'the bit between their teeth' unless London did something to 'help the French to be helpful'.[92] But the thought of any consultations with Paris and Brussels at this point was most unwelcome to the foreign office, primarily because of the possibility that Flandin might seek to precipitate a fresh crisis, but also because Britain might be confronted with fresh demands for additional compensation as the price of allowing the interim phase to continue.[93]

To comfort the French and Belgians, as well as to extricate Britain and gain more time, Eden was prepared to meet their other two demands.[94] But cabinet ministers refused to act until they had had a chance to dissipate domestic criticism, particularly of the letter, which was being portrayed as the 'danger spot' of the white paper.[95] Ministers were especially concerned over public and parliamentary anxiety that Britain had entered into a new military alliance, or that Paris and Brussels so regarded the arrangements—as Lothian had stated in the House of Lords on 24 March.[96] Fears were also being voiced that the letter offered such handsome benefits for France that she might prefer to see the peace effort founder, or even sabotage it by persisting with her demands for a German gesture when she knew that none would be forthcoming.[97]

To send the letter amidst such confusion, it was argued, would almost certainly lead people to believe that His Majesty's Government was terminating the period of negotiations, when nothing could have been further from her desires or intentions.[98] The cabinet also agreed, however, that Britain would regain her own freedom if the conciliation effort failed owing to French intransigence.[99]

In addition to pacifying Paris, Eden was anxious to apply public pressure on Hitler, who had not only snubbed the white paper invitations, but also rebuffed the foreign secretary's requests of 24 and 25 March for a simple undertaking to forego fortifications during the period of negotiations.[100] Eden had even asserted that such a gesture would be treated as a voluntary and constructive contribution, rather than as an obligatory act of contrition.[101] But Berlin had not budged from her contention that London was asking her to condone an inequality and create a dangerous precedent. Neurath also argued that, by perpetuating the period of negotiations, France could deprive Germany indefinitely of her sovereign right to erect a defensive wall in the west.[102] The best Eden had to show for his efforts to secure a gesture since 12 March was an observation from Ribbentrop that permanent fortifications 'could obviously not be conjured up overnight'.[103] This, of course, was useless, since it would never satisfy Paris.

On 26 March, Eden used the occasion of the ratification debate on the white paper not only to defend London's handling of the crisis, but also to reassure the French and show beyond doubt that the current difficulties had been caused by the same power whose refusal to make any gesture to vindicate international law stood as the primary obstacle to peace negotiations.[104]

On the domestic and French fronts, Eden was about as successful as he had a right to expect. Although he had not silenced all the government's critics in Britain, he made a significant impression where it counted most—in the Commons, the clubs and the city, where, as one close observer noted, there had been a dramatic increase in the number of people who had hitherto been francophobes or germanophils, but who had reverted to being, above all, pro-British.[105] It was also reported that many of these same converts now accepted the need for a German contribution as a prerequisite to fruitful negotiations and were even prepared to accept that London's assurances to Paris were necessary, particularly after Eden had asserted to the House of Commons that the absence of compensation could easily have led to a war which inevitably would have involved Britain, since the government's obligations as a guarantor were more clear-cut than her functions as a mediator.

Anxieties were further alleviated by the foreign secretary's categorical assertion that London had taken on no fresh commitments, but had simply agreed to arrangements for more effectively fulfilling her existing obligations.[106] In this respect, the acquisition of a French guarantee to Britain proved helpful.[107] So, too, did Neville Chamberlain's observation that the letter actually had contracted, rather than expanded, London's liability, and his reassurance that Britain would continue to act as a mediator.[108]

No one criticized Britain's efforts to avoid violence, eschew sanctions and preserve peace.[109] No one in the Commons, including communist William Gallacher or opposition leaders Clement Attlee (Labour) and Sir Archibald Sinclair (Liberal), complained that Hitler had been treated too lightly.[110] There were no demands by Churchill, Sir Austen Chamberlain or anyone else for harsher action against the treaty-breaker.[111] Nor did anyone praise Flandin for having sought to set the Locarno powers on a collision course. But, equally, there was in Parliament after 26 March a far greater understanding of the extent and importance of the concessions made by Sarraut's government.[112] And although London's determination to press for a western settlement was enthusiastically endorsed, the foreign secretary and his French allies were well satisfied with the realization in the

Commons that the British were not simply 'arbiters with a fortunate destiny'.[113] Equally gratifying was the emergence of what Eden described as a healthy scepticism in the House and in some quarters of the public towards the Third Reich and the credibility of its rulers.[114]

These developments were well received in Belgium and France.[115] So was the government's assertion that nothing had happened which could be considered as freeing the Locarno signatories from any of their obligations. But Paris was most gratified by Eden's avowal to a cheering House of Commons that he had no intention of becoming the first foreign secretary to go back on a British signature.[116] This was seconded by Neville Chamberlain, who emphasized the need for a German contribution, and was accompanied by an announcement that staff talks would occur in the immediate future.[117] These 'unexpectedly definite and reassuring' references to France and her security were hailed as a major advance on 'l'accent assez terne' of Eden's earlier statements.[118] But there was also some criticism, particularly from *Le Temps*, over a suggestion by the foreign secretary that Paris, as well as Berlin, would have to adopt a more constructive attitude if negotiations were to succeed.[119]

Remarks such as these contributed to the restiveness felt by Flandin and Léger over Eden's failure to name a date for the staff talks and, especially, over London's reluctance to produce the promised letter, which Paris anxiously wanted in hand in case Hitler sprang some surprise in his forthcoming memorandum.[120] The Quai d'Orsay was doubtless also aware of the diligent efforts at this time by some elements in Britain and the dominions, particularly South Africa, to persuade His Majesty's Government that Rome's abstention had released London from her commitments of 19 March to Paris and Brussels.[121]

The weight of this argument was not insignificant, but Baldwin and his colleagues did not waver, not only because of the effect of such a tergiversation on Paris and Brussels, but also because despatch of the letter was regarded as essential 'in order to preserve a chance of inducing the French to enter upon negotiations with Germany'.[122] Nevertheless, to Flandin's chagrin and Eden's embarrassment, the cabinet refused to take any action before 31 March, partly because of the possible domestic repercussions and partly because

London feared that Hitler might charge that its transmission had ruined the diplomatic atmosphere, making it impossible for him to submit constructive counter-proposals.[123] The British government was also suspected—probably correctly—of wanting to be in a position to use the letter's delivery as a safety valve for French emotions if the Chancellor's offers contained no interim contribution.[124]

Thus, in spite of five French bids inside a week, London did not hand over the letter until 2 April, the day after Hitler's counter-proposals were published.[125] The document was accompanied by a cover note and followed by a public British declaration, emphasizing that this exchange of letters must in no circumstances be construed as Britain's reply to the latest German proposals.[126] A clear distinction was also drawn between the formality of exchanging letters and a decision, as yet to be reached, to activate the pledges contained therein.[127]

After ten days of British equivocation, the letter was received with joy, especially in Paris where Eden's studied avoidance of Corbin had re-aroused suspicions over London's intentions regarding the white paper.[128] The significance of the letter's transmission was disparaged by Dieckhoff as a mere 'bon-bon', but its arrival effectively numbed French reaction to Hitler's continued refusal to make any concessions.[129] Paris had lost her Rhine *glacis,* but few Frenchmen at that moment would have traded the arrangements with London for a restoration of the status quo in Germany's western provinces.[130] This sentiment was reinforced on 3 April when Vansittart proposed to the French chargé d'affaires that the staff talks should begin on 15 April.[131]

Although Flandin continued to press His Majesty's Government for an early meeting of the remaining Locarno powers, Eden had considerably more success in containing Paris than he had in persuading Berlin of the necessity to make some conciliatory gesture to show her respect for international law and, as the French government desired, to atone for her unilateral treaty breach.[132] Hitler, however, had no intention of yielding a particle of sovereignty at any time, but most especially at the end of an election campaign in which each of his speeches had been laced with emphatic assurances of his determination to bow to no judge other than the German people and to make no gesture other than that contained in his peace proposals.[133] Göring was even more belligerent, demanding at Berlin on 27 March to know whether Eden and his friends expected the Führer to order his Wehrmacht to pick up their weapons and walk out of the zone. If so, he bellowed, then 'they can wait until the end of the world!'[134]

Nor was there any more willingness to cooperate after Hitler received 98.8 per cent approval from German voters on 29 March.[135] On the contrary, their endorsement of the Chancellor and his Rhineland action only intensified Berlin's determination to yield to no one, not even London and least of all Paris.[136] There also existed at this time no external pressure capable of causing Hitler or Neurath seriously to consider making any concession. In spite of official French anger over Berlin's rejection of the white paper, no signs were forthcoming that Paris, now in the midst of her election campaign, would mount any punitive action over the absence of a gesture.[137]

This was especially true in the face of Britain's continued refusal to countenance the use of threats or force.[138] This omission gave every leeway to a government whose diplomatic credo was summed up by Göring some weeks earlier when he declared that 'protests are no good if they are not backed by bayonets'.[139] Moreover, as long as the British people remained so thoroughly committed to a policy of reconstruction, it seemed unlikely that they would continue for long to allow French intransigence or the demand for a German contribution to stand in the way of negotiations.[140]

Berlin's adamant refusal to make any gesture was doubtless reinforced by the realization that London was not just under heavy criticism for having acquiesced in staff talks, but actually reeling from the attack.[141] This became clear to Berlin on 25 March, when Eden asked Ribbentrop for permission to state in the House of Commons that Hitler had no objection to these conversations taking place.[142] Even the ambassador extraordinary could see from the foreign secretary's request how insecure the cabinet felt. And, whereas Ribbentrop probably did not yet know of Simon's opposition to the talks, he and Hoesch's embassy were certainly aware that press and public dissent over this pledge was increasing daily and had swept through the Commons, permeating deep into the government benches, where, according to health minister Kingsley Wood, 'The boys won't have it!'[143]

Instead of giving his blessing, as Eden had hoped, the

Chancellor categorically declared that staff talks would not only prove as fatal as they had in 1914, but also do immeasurable harm to the peace effort by encouraging French intransigents in their efforts to preserve the status quo.[144] In addition, it was argued that such consultations were totally unnecessary, since Germany's pitifully small forces could not attack anyone. In these circumstances, it was added, these talks were bound to be regarded by Berlin as both an unnecessary provocation and an attempt by her prospective treaty partners to plot against Germany before inviting her to the conference table.

Ribbentrop carried this message to all his British contacts and even to Baldwin, emphasizing that any one-sided military arrangements would be 'fraught with dangerous consequences'.[145] He also implied that the German counterproposals might be endangered and later argued that His Majesty's Government should insist as a *sine qua non* of British participation in staff talks that the French abandon their demands on Germany and promise to negotiate on the basis of the existing situation.[146] Meanwhile, Hitler was condemning secret alliances and promising the German people that he would never allow his general staff to make 'military arrangements of which the public knows nothing'.[147]

Many of these warnings struck home in the House of Commons, where Lloyd George launched a crusade against what he dramatized as a 'short-cut to war', and where no fewer than ten questions, none friendly, were asked in twelve sittings.[148] But the British government could not and would not retreat, even in the face of German insistence that military consultations might ruin the possibility of fruitful negotiations.[149] To capitulate, it was felt, would not only amount to a betrayal for the sake of a potential foe, but almost certainly precipitate precisely the sort of rash act by France which His Majesty's Government was most anxious to avoid.[150]

In these circumstances, the cabinet and foreign office did the next best thing. They deprived the talks of any real content and then set out, with the active assistance of the chiefs of staff, to ensure that Berlin, as well as British and world opinion, understood how severely limited they would be.[151] The foreign secretary and his colleagues emphasized repeatedly that the conversations covered only the period of negotiations and applied only to the event of an unprovoked act of aggression.[152] The House of Commons was further assured that London would go into talks only after Paris and Brussels had agreed formally that they involved no political undertaking or any obligation regarding the organization of national defence between the powers.[153] Eden also stressed that the cabinet regarded these consultations primarily as a device to create the confidence required to get Paris to the conference table.[154] At the same time, however, Neville Chamberlain observed that a peaceful Germany had nothing to fear from these consultations, while Eden missed no opportunity to remind Ribbentrop that the talks' origin and occurrence were a direct and indisputable result of Berlin's failure to make a simple contribution.[155]

This campaign of deflation, coupled with Hitler's continued refusal to cooperate, effectively thinned the ranks of London's domestic critics, leaving only Lloyd George, the Beaverbrook press and a few other isolationists to complain over what the *Daily Mail* described as 'military arrangements that will commit us some day to war at the call of others'.[156] Equally dramatic was the effect on Berlin. After a final attempt by Ribbentrop in the first few days of April to stop the talks, the German press adopted a nonchalant attitude towards what for the previous ten days had been portrayed as a grave British blunder.[157]

Part of the German reversal stemmed from the realization that no one could now prevent the conversations, not even the ambassador extraordinary, who, with his self-acknowledged way with the British, had apparently claimed he could.[158] Berlin must also have been impressed by the assurances from Eden and the British military that, in addition to their political insignificance, His Majesty's Government attached no military value to the talks. London planned to call up no fresh forces as a result of her interim obligations to render aid and was primarily interested only in Belgium's security.[159] Henceforth, whenever a German newspaper mentioned the topic, it was careful to explain that London had felt obliged to administer a placebo to 'calmer les nerfs' of the French. Therefore the military talks were not to be taken seriously.[160]

Nor was this assessment wide of the mark. Although Britain failed to confine the conversations to just the service attachés, she succeeded in keeping them in London and extracting so much substance that Sargent was later able to declare, without contradiction, that the talks, which took place on 15 and 16 April, were 'merely eyewash'.[161] British delegates were only allowed to give information on likely available forces and facilities required. The exchange or even discussion of operational plans was forbidden. This was confirmed to the Germans afterwards by a member of the British air ministry, who described the conference as a 'farce', since the French and Belgians had been told nothing which was not contained in the current edition of the *Air Force List*.[162]

Even so, Paris and Brussels were gratified by the fact that talks had occurred in an atmosphere of cordiality and that nothing had occurred to prevent closer and more fruitful contacts in the future.[163] The consultations had symbolized Anglo-Franco-Belgian solidarity and helped to isolate Germany as the major cause of European unrest. The French representatives also used the occasion to combat rumours circulating in Paris that Gamelin's armies had been incapable of marching to meet the German challenge of 7 March.[164] This was accomplished by asserting, and then leaking, that France was so secure from invasion that the British should direct their attention and assistance exclusively to Belgium, whose delegation had revealed that their coast was virtually unprotected.[165] London benefited, too, in at least two ways. The talks not only made the French feel less nervous generally, but also provided Paris with a fresh and closer look at her British partner's land and air weaknesses.[166] This, in turn, helped the French government to understand why Baldwin thought it would be a 'ghastly thing' if His Majesty's Government were called upon now to fulfil any of her continental commitments.[167]

The two-day staff talks in mid-April concluded the punitive phase of the crisis started on 7 March. No further demands for a gesture were made directly to Berlin, even though the absence of any concession was still regarded by the Sarraut government as a good reason for refusing to sit at the conference table with Germany.[168]

Considering France's economic weakness and political divisions, as well as the reluctance of her military leaders, the absence of any strong public support and Britain's utter opposition to sanctions, the French government could look back with satisfaction over her success in getting Germany declared a treaty violator, kept out of Locarno and visibly plotted against.[169] Hitler had escaped direct punishment, but Flandin had kept alive this possibility in connexion with any German attempt to build fortifications.[170] And, although no encirclement front had been created, the prospects for the future looked brighter, if only because Flandin's efforts had produced a greater awareness in Britain that the Chancellor's sincerity could no longer be taken for granted.[171]

The British government, on the other hand, was gratified at having escaped without having had to fight either Germany or her own public over the Rhineland. By acting both as an honest broker and as a guarantor, London had managed the crisis and the military consultations in such a way as to comfort the French, while apparently not giving Berlin cause for backing out on the negotiations, which Eden hoped could begin as soon as the French had elected a new government in early May.[172]

None of these benefits, however, could match Hitler's gains. He was not only now in full and undisputed possession of the demilitarized zone, but also the toast of Germany.[173] In exchange, he had conceded nothing and had received little more in the way of punishment than a public wrist-slap when the opposition could have employed the less-than-precise phrasing of the Locarno treaty to justify a forceful reoccupation of the Rhineland. Compared to what might have happened, the League council resolution and Locarno condemnation seemed almost trifles.[174] Nor did the gestures asked of Germany serve any punitive function, since their only apparent effect on Berlin was outrage and wounded pride, neither of which lasted more than a few days, thanks to British public reaction and bickering between London and Paris over the white paper.[175]

The Anglo-Franco-Belgian staff talks, on the other hand, were a different matter. No one in Berlin regarded these consultations, however limited, as in any way beneficial.[176] But it is difficult to gauge whether they were viewed as a defeat for anyone but Ribbentrop, to whom the phrase 'staff talks' was, according to Paul Schmidt, 'like a red rag to a bull'.[177] A week before they were held, Phipps reported that this forthcoming show of Anglo-French cooperation had intensified feelings of pessimism among moderates in the business community and Auswärtiges Amt, where legal expert Ernst Woermann described the talks as 'extremely unwelcome'.[178] The general staff was also reported to be both unhappy and very suspicious, while even some members of the Nazi party were voicing, for the first time since 7 March, their doubts about the wisdom of the denunciation of Locarno.[179]

The Auswärtiges Amt saw 'a certain element of political danger' in the fact that the talks had occurred.[180] And if the foreign minister meant what he wrote to German missions on 8 March, then the holding of these consultations represented a positive diplomatic setback for Germany, especially since they were tangible proof that Hitler had not escaped altogether unscathed from his coup.[181] However, in view of London's efforts to rob the staff talks of any practical importance, it seems unlikely that Hitler, Neurath or the party members within the government suffered any more than momentary apprehensions.[182]

By the time Hitler and the Auswärtiges Amt got round to drafting the promised counter-proposals, only two aspects of the white paper could still be regarded as potentially troublesome to the Reich. First was Britain's assistance pledge to Paris and Brussels, both for the immediate and the distant future.[183] Unlike similar promises in the Locarno treaty, these undertakings, which had survived every German criticism in mid-March, seemed beyond her influence.[184] However, Berlin had been offered the same guarantees, complete with military consultations, as part of a western settlement, whose bases had been set out largely by Hitler himself.[185] Furthermore, the new arrangements were strictly defensive, which meant that France would no longer be able to compel His Majesty's Government to join her in punitive action against Germany, as she had been entitled to do by the Rhine pact in defence of the demilitarized zone.[186] Berlin's only loss, therefore, was during the period of negotiations. But this was more apparent than real, since London had acted throughout the crisis as a brake on Paris in the face of the greatest provocation. Nor was there any sign that London or the British people would now relax after three years of seeking to moderate France's intransigent attitude towards Germany.[187]

The letter, on the other hand, could cause considerable embarrassment to Berlin in spite of London's insistence that Britain's approval was now required before any action could be initiated against Germany for causing the breakdown of the conciliation effort.[188] The letter not only perpetuated France's right under Locarno to punish Germany for her Rhineland violations, but also promised Paris a British guarantee which would not then be available to Berlin. Moreover, this guarantee contained a clause about insuring France against unprovoked aggression which could be construed as including preventive precautions, as well as repressive measures.[189]

Furthermore, in view of the anger generated in Paris over both the British and German attitudes towards the white paper, no one could rule out entirely the possibility that Flandin would precipitate a fresh crisis if Hitler's promised counter-proposals contained nothing of merit.[190] This possibility existed as long as the Sarraut ministry was in power and Great Britain, in spite of her protestations, remained a French pawn *vis-à-vis* the Rhineland. In these circumstances, it seemed preferable for Berlin to keep the period of negotiations alive — at least until May.[191] What she did then would depend upon the outcome of the French elections, Britain's attitude, and world affairs generally.[192] Nor, for that matter, can it be categorically asserted that the German government did not at this point genuinely want negotiations to produce a settlement, at least in western Europe.

These factors, coupled with Britain's desire to make a substantial attempt at a fresh settlement, rendered it a near certainty that His Majesty's Government would refuse to acknowledge the breakdown of the conciliation effort so long as there seemed any hope for negotiations.[193] Thus, from the German point of view, all that was now required to keep the letter inoperative was a set of constructive-looking counter-proposals.

9 Fait accompli

The period of so-called surprises is now over.
                    HITLER, 30 January 1937

These proposals were produced on 31 March when Hitler, fresh from his overwhelming electoral success, unveiled yet another 'great constructive' peace plan—his third inside a year.[1] It was primarily a recapitulation of all his previous propositions, with only a few new points, but the whole package was attractively presented and came complete with a timetable for achieving important initial results by 1 August. By that date, Brussels, Paris and Berlin would have concluded a 25-year non-aggression or security pact, guaranteed by Rome and London and supplemented by an air pact. Hitler also offered to accept any permanent military limitation of Germany's western frontier, so long as France and Belgium agreed to the same restrictions.

In the next phase, Germany would take up the question of non-aggression pacts with Czechoslovakia, Austria and Lithuania. Berlin and Paris would each give a sacred pledge, ratified by plebiscites, to eradicate from the education of their youth everything which might poison Franco-German relations. Meanwhile, Germany would have returned to the League and all parties would agree to be bound by the decisions of an international court of arbitration, which was to be established to ensure observance of the various agreements. From there, the peace-makers would tackle the broader tasks of checking unlimited competition in armaments, starting with naval limitation. Aerial warfare would be made more humane and heavy tanks and artillery abolished as steps towards disarmament.

The German memorandum contained no gesture of contrition, but the Chancellor did promise—provided Paris and Brussels reciprocated—that troops in the Rhineland would not be reinforced or moved closer to the frontier for four months in order to create a calmer atmosphere for negotiations.[2] Simultaneously and secretly, Blomberg forbade all uniformed German soldiers and officers from going within three miles of the land borders with France, Belgium and

Czechoslovakia, or from setting foot on the Rhine bridges linking Germany and France.[3]

Hitler also proposed the creation of a six-power commission, composed of all Locarno signatories and a disinterested neutral, to guarantee the military *status quo* along Germany's western frontier. He even offered, provided Paris and Brussels did likewise, to allow the Italian and British military attachés to investigate any alleged violations by Germany during this four-month period. This offer, coupled with Germany's willingness to give the 'fullest consideration' to the commission's conclusions, should, it was emphasized, put an end to French anxieties.[4]

Not everyone was impressed by the German plan, which was seen in some quarters as a calculated appeal to the British and French peoples, over the heads of their governments.[5] Nor were the critics confined to Whitehall and the Quai d'Orsay. This was particularly true in France, where the press was initially almost unanimous in condemning the proposals as a blatant attempt to create a *pax germanica* for Europe.[6] But to the masses, with their short memories, Hitler's latest offering looked like a practical and attainable, if not generous and sincere, proposition.[7] And its cordial reception in Britain had, according to ministerial director Hans Dieckhoff, made it 'much harder for the French to persist in their intransigent attitude'.[8]

The validity of this assessment was recognized in Paris, where even the sceptics acknowledged that the proposals could not be ignored without alienating European and world opinion.[9] It seemed in France that the Führer had scored a significant point over the opposition by giving the annoying impression that Germany alone was capable of bringing about a new order in Europe.[10] It was also clear that a flat French rejection of his proposals would redound heavily against Paris and provoke a fresh eruption of francophobia in Britain.[11] Acceptance, on the other hand, would have been politically suicidal, if only because it would have thrust Hitler into the forefront as 'le pacificateur de l'Europe'.[12]

Flandin, however, managed to avoid these pitfalls and mollify his domestic critics by producing counter-proposals which, it was argued, offered even greater prospects for achieving a genuine and lasting settlement.[13] This at least kept Paris in the game and effectively eliminated the possibility of a settlement on Hitler's terms.[14] But the French proposals achieved little else. Not only did Hitler reject them as 'a sky-scraper of pacts and visions', but they were not even taken seriously in Paris, London or Geneva and were quickly consigned to the diplomatic archives.[15]

The absence in the German proposals of any unilateral contribution was sharply criticized, not only in Paris and the French press, but also in London, where cabinet ministers complained that Berlin had, in fact, returned a negative answer to all the proposals contained in the white paper of 19 March.[16] For the next week or so, the British laboured through Ribbentrop to extract some concession on fortifications.[17] But the ambassador extraordinary would only say informally that it was technically impossible for the Reich to start fortification inside the proposed 120-day period of negotiations. Germany's national honour, he declared, prevented Berlin from accepting any inequality *vis-à-vis* France.[18] Eden even proposed that the French as well as the Germans should forego construction during the period of negotiations.[19] But Berlin refused, partly because acceptance would leave her at an obvious disadvantage and partly because Neurath anticipated that any interim renunciation would be followed by heavy outside pressure to make the obligation permanent.[20]

Moreover, as Dieckhoff observed on 2 April, with the 'most dangerous' period behind her, there was no cause for Germany to make further concessions.[21] Furthermore, and perhaps even more important, the Auswärtiges Amt was well aware that virtually no one outside the French government wanted the omission of a special German gesture to prevent the testing of Hitler's bona fides at the conference table.[22] Nowhere was this feeling stronger than in Great Britain, where the *New Statesman* predicted 'a violent revolt' in public opinion if negotiations did not now take place.[23] Even the Chancellor's detractors supported this idea. 'The best present chance', ambassador Dodd wrote, 'is to call Hitler's bluff for peace, since the powers do not seem willing or capable of calling his bluff for war.'[24] If the Chancellor's proposals proved to be 'only a façade for conquest', he added, then European and world opinion would have 'a sounder basis for common agreement and doubtless common action and meanwhile little if anything will be lost'. The ambassador's counterpart

in Vienna, G. S. Messersmith, who was a realistic and determined foe of Nazism, acknowledged as late as December 1936
that this was the only possible course of action in the circumstances.[25]

This did not prevent Paris from putting up one last show of
resistance in spite of the fact that she was, on this point, politically isolated.[26] This time Flandin's efforts were not aimed at
securing retribution from Germany for her past deeds, but at
eliciting from Great Britain some positive assurances of
support for imposing sanctions on Berlin when the next
Rhineland crisis occurred — over fortifications. This, and not
the presence of troops, the French argued, was the decisive
factor in European security. The existence of a west wall
would not only sever the lifeline to eastern Europe, but also
enormously reduce Hitler's defensive requirements and
correspondingly increase the number of men he could
employ for any offensive action.

If Britain would agree to join Paris immediately in a study
of 'all measures of coercion' to be applied in the case of a
German breach of article 42, Flandin explained to Eden on 8
April then France would be prepared to participate in peace
negotiations at the earliest possible moment.[27] But the British
would not accept this.[28] Nothing in Locarno or the agreement
of 19 March obliged them to prepare punitive action against a
potential violation. Nor did London desire to contribute to
the creation of any situation which might cause the breakdown of the conciliation effort.[29]

Such a failure was certain, Eden believed, if Hitler learned
that London and Paris were examining coercive measures
against Berlin.[30] And, although the British government still
doubted whether the French people would support sanctions
against Hitler for any activity on German soil, it seemed
inevitable that Flandin's proposals would deal a fatal blow to
London's hopes of getting Germany to the conference table.[31]
So long as Hitler acted circumspectly in the Rhineland, the
British were prepared to resist all French demands for contingency studies on the grounds that surreptitious fortification was impossible to stop and that no one in Britain would
ever endorse punitive measures against Germany for erecting
something so obviously defensive as a counterpart to the
Maginot line.

Whitehall also feared that if France forced the issue, her

actions would be seen by the British public as yet another attempt by Paris to impose her will on Berlin—and London—at the expense of German sovereignty.[32] This, it was argued, would seriously undermine the efforts of His Majesty's Government to educate public opinion to the fact that it was Hitler and no one else who had flaunted international order and obstructed the peace effort. If that occurred, then it was feared that the British people would emerge none the wiser for their Rhine experience and the government's rearmament efforts would continue to face strong opposition at home.

No sooner had Eden begun to protest, however, than Flandin observed that the problem might be overcome if Britain were prepared to contribute to a general European security arrangement.[33] It was even hinted by Paul-Boncour that Paris would not negotiate with Hitler until London had made some commitment to those countries in eastern Europe who had hitherto depended on the possibility of a French thrust into the Rhineland as their safeguard against German encroachment.[34] This was, however, exactly the sort of obligation which the British government and public had consistently refused to undertake.[35] Nor could there have been any doubt in the foreign secretary's mind as to how his colleagues would view any commitment which might precipitate a conflict with Berlin before Britain had remedied her worst military deficiencies.[36]

But instead of pressing the issue, Flandin readily agreed to a British suggestion that the desired 'compensation' for eastern Europe might conceivably be found in the Chancellor's peace scheme of 31 March.[37] The foreign minister subsequently dropped his demands regarding German fortifications in exchange for a promise that Eden would seek 'elucidation' from Berlin on certain ambiguities in the German position.[38] The French, at London's invitation, submitted a list of thirteen biting questions, including one which asked whether Berlin planned to annul its undertakings unilaterally in the future on the grounds of its peoples' 'droit vital'.[39] The essence of all but two of them was incorporated into a questionnaire, but the interrogatives were stripped of all asperity and further watered down by a British cabinet whose anxiety to avoid provoking Berlin unnecessarily was matched only by the exasperation felt over this process in Paris and in the British foreign office.[40]

The ease with which Flandin had been persuaded on 8 April to accept a compromise suggests that his concern for France's eastern allies was due in part to electoral considerations and his own realization that the French people were in no mood to prevent fortification of the Rhineland.[41] With voting less than three weeks away, Sarraut's government had come under increased attack, not only from those who wanted immediate talks with Berlin, but also from persons whose disillusionment over the presumed Anglo-French alliance had been transformed into anger over what was becoming known as a 'missed opportunity' to teach Hitler a lesson. But Flandin possessed neither the means nor the desire to force Britain to accept his proposals. He doubtless also recognized that, psychologically, the moment for action had passed.

The Eden proposal to probe further into Hitler's intentions had one merit which suited the Sarraut ministry. It would delay any negotiations for at least 6-8 weeks, since, presumably, nothing could be done until the Chancellor's replies had been examined. This meant that the French elections would be well out of the way. Even then, there were strong reasons why any French government could feel satisfied if the negotiations never did take place. As long as the powers remained in the 'interim period', Paris enjoyed all the benefits of Locarno, while Germany had only the remilitarized Rhineland. And, if London finally exhausted her patience with Hitler, the letter would be activated which gave France essentially the same guarantees as Locarno, as well as the prospect of closer military ties with Britain.[42]

On the the other hand, it seemed certain that any western settlement would not only restore to Berlin her Italian and British guarantees, but would also bring Paris little more in the way of additional reward than the promise of non-aggression from a Nazi régime whose record was so poor that it could only point to the Polish-German pact of 1934 as the sole example of its fidelity. The same argument applied to the proposed air pacts.[43] Moreover, on the basis of Britain's previous position, it was also certain that Anglo-French staff talks held under the aegis of the letter would be far more fruitful than any multilateral consultations in which London was obliged to plan simultaneously with Berlin against France and Paris against Germany.[44]

By mid-April, the diplomatic lines had been drawn. The French were not going one step out of their way to bring Hitler into any negotiations for a new Locarno. Nor was the Führer yet prepared to rejoin, at least not before he could see whether events in France and Europe made it worthwhile. The Auswärtiges Amt's attitude was also ambivalent. No one yet knew the bases for negotiations, since both Berlin and Paris had plans pending to replace the white paper's outline, which Germany had twice rejected as being contaminated by special commitments and lacking the spirit of equality which was necessary for a truly lasting peace.[45]

These obstacles did not appear so great as to discourage Eden and his colleagues from working for the remainder of 1936 to find some formula for achieving what the foreign secretary described to the Commons on 18 June as 'nothing less . . . than a European settlement and appeasement'.[46] Not all members of the cabinet believed that this pursuit had more than a remote chance of succeeding.[47] Duff Cooper even criticized the policy within the cabinet, urging instead that London ought to organize a bloc of nations to show the Germans that they could not accomplish their aims.[48]

Most ministers, however, were determined to persevere in the search for an agreement, even if it could not endure. It would be wrong, it was argued, to formulate policy on the assumption that the Germans were not genuine in their desire for a settlement.[49] Within the cabinet it was thought that this policy would appeal to public opinion, whereas the foreign office regarded the effort more as a means of showing up Hitler's insincerity and thereby reducing opposition to British rearmament.[50] In either case, the government's principal aim, as expressed by several cabinet members on 29 April, was to play for time and for peace.[51] This, it was felt, meant coming to terms with Hitler in order to fasten him down in the west until Britain's defences were secure.[52] Some cabinet ministers were even prepared to bypass Paris in their pursuit of this policy, arguing that the French would ultimately profit as much as Britain from an Anglo-German détente.[53]

But France was not pushed aside, thanks largely to the fact that the Sarraut government was replaced in May by a ministry of the popular front led by Léon Blum, whose ideas were still so deeply steeped in the dream of disarmament as to inspire Vansittart to describe him as 'naïf and weak'.[54] Nevertheless, the British felt that their chances of persuading Paris to be cooperative with London and constructive towards Berlin were greater than with almost any other French premier since Hitler had come to power.[55] Nor were they disappointed by the attitude of the Blum government, whose outstanding feature, Clerk reported in June, was an 'almost pathetic desire to be given a lead by, and be closely associated with, His Majesty's Government'.[56] But even the presence in Paris of a more amenable ministry was not enough to compensate for the loss of the demilitarized zone as a bargaining counter.

The efforts over the next twelve months to bring about negotiations were as laborious and fruitless as any chapter in Anglo-Franco-German relations between the wars. The British questionnaire was delivered on 7 May, along with an assurance by Phipps of how deeply His Majesty's Government desired an early opening of negotiations.[57] But Hitler, who only recently had campaigned heavily on a platform of peace and honour, took umbrage, not only at the suggestion that his word could be disputed, but also over what was widely regarded as the schoolmasterly nature of a document which asked, *inter alia*, if Germany intended henceforth 'to respect the existing territorial and political status of Europe'.[58] Berlin was also asked if she now regarded herself as having achieved that 'complete equality' which would enable her to conclude 'genuine treaties'.

The Chancellor's irritation found a sympathetic, albeit belated echo in Britain, where initial reactions were not critical, at least not until Berlin opened its assault on the questions, which were then described in some quarters as a tactless attempt to pillory Germany.[59] This occurred after the questionnaire had been unexpectedly published in London owing to tendentious leakages in both the French and German press.[60] Once the questions had passed into public knowledge, Germany launched a barrage of criticism.[61] The *Völkischer Beobachter* described the document as a piece of 'cat-burglary', while the *Frankfurter Zeitung* dismissed it as 'not even honourable'.[62]

Meanwhile, Hitler simply sat on the offensive document.[63] During the next few weeks, the British urged the Chancellor to expedite his answers so they could get started with preparations for the negotiations. His Majesty's Government offered to send a minister to Berlin to explain the document and its 'constructive' purpose.[64] London even betrayed signs of exasperation over the delay, which the Germans excused on a series of grounds, including the publicity given to the questionnaire and the need to see first whether Blum was desirous or capable of entering into negotiations with Berlin.[65] Hitler's only response occurred on 14 May, when he rejected any idea of temporarily foregoing the construction of fortifications by shouting at Phipps that outsiders should 'mind their own business' on matters relating to German soil.[66] Only in January 1937 did Hitler publicly acknowledge the questionnaire's existence when he told the Reichstag that no reply would be forthcoming.[67]

London was disappointed, but not surprised by Berlin's attitude. Cabinet ministers had suspected by the end of May that an answer was unlikely.[68] The effort, however, was still regarded as having been worthwhile, if only because it had silenced French demands regarding fortifications in the Rhineland and had enabled London to forestall further consideration of that thorny question while Sarraut and Flandin remained in power.[69] Once they had left office, the British were disposed to abandon the questionnaire, which was not judged to be essential to the peace effort, and push on with their attempt to bring about negotiations.[70]

The cabinet's willingness to jettison the questionnaire for the sake of German susceptibilities provoked Wigram into complaining that His Majesty's Government was exposing itself 'to what are almost impertinences'.[71] This remark is indicative of a divergence which developed between the foreign office and the cabinet in the early summer.[72] Before the coup, they were united in attempting a general settlement. During the Rhineland crisis, they worked together to avert both war and dishonour. But Hitler's refusal to be helpful convinced Vansittart, Sargent and Wigram that any agreement with Germany was unlikely.[73]

The foreign office was still willing to pursue this policy, not only to gain time, but more immediately to avoid giving Paris any opportunity to terminate the period of conciliation and bring Britain up against her obligations in the letter of 19 March.[74] If that occurred, then London would find herself committed to an Anglo-Franco-Belgian defensive alliance

against Berlin.[75] 'The die will have been cast,' Sargent
warned, 'and we shall have broken with Germany.'[76] This, it
was felt, would not only go down badly with the British
people, but could also incite Hitler to start a war before his
potential enemies became too strong and united. There was
also a strong feeling, especially among sceptics like Vansittart,
Sargent and Phipps, that London should 'ménager' Berlin
until His Majesty's Government could restore normal relations with Mussolini and thereby deprive Hitler of a potential
ally.[77] Nevertheless, the foreign office minutes at this time
reveal a fresh degree of concern over the extent to which the
cabinet seemed prepared 'to run after the Germans' in its
efforts to enlist Hitler's cooperation and demonstrate to
public opinion that London had left no stone unturned in her
efforts to secure a lasting settlement.[78]

The process of preparing the ground work for negotiations
dragged on through the summer. Meanwhile, the British,
French and Belgians consulted informally and infrequently,
usually against London's better judgement and primarily
because, as Paul-Boncour explained, the absence of any show
of unity among the remaining Locarno powers would create a
'very bad' impression in Europe.[79] Only once was there a
formal three-power meeting. It took place in London on 23
July, but only after the British had extracted a pledge from
Paris that no effort would be made to terminate the period of
conciliation.[80] Its sole purpose was to announce that Germany
and Italy would be invited to a five-power conference at an
unspecified date to discuss a western pact.

The French did attempt at that time to sound out Eden as to
Britain's attitude if the five-power meeting never took place
and, more immediately, if Hitler sent a significant number of
reinforcements into the former demilitarized zone after 1
August—the expiration date of the Chancellor's pledge not to
disturb the Rhine *status quo* for four months.[81] But the foreign
secretary refused to be drawn, insisting that another *coup de
théâtre* was not on the *tapis,* if only because the Germans were
already 'busily engaged in trying to persuade British public
opinion that they were the quietest people in the world, in
preparation for the Olympic games'. Any discussion of what
to do in the event of the failure of the proposed talks, he
added, would almost certainly prove fatal to hopes for negotiations if any leakage occurred. But the foreign secretary did

reassure the French and Belgians that London still stood by her promises of 19 March and, the case arising, would be prepared to consult with them.

The meeting of 23 July was also significant because the French, some twenty weeks and two governments after the event, finally abandoned the idea of punitive measures against Germany for her activities during March.[82] Henceforth, there would be no references in diplomatic exchanges to Berlin's treaty breach and no more demands for a gesture. In keeping with this idea of making a fresh start, Blum also acknowledged, albeit tacitly, the long-standing British contention that, since fortification could not be prevented, it was useless to talk further about imposing sanctions when Hitler began to erect his west wall. In this way, article 42 of the Versailles treaty was laid to rest alongside article 43 and the pallbearers agreed to concentrate on seeking a western settlement. It was also decided in July that nothing more should be said to Berlin about the questionnaire.[83] This break from the past was made public in an official communiqué on 23 July and by Eden four days later in the House of Commons, when he announced on behalf of his French and Belgian colleagues, 'We now look definitely to the future.'[84]

For their part, the Germans throughout the remainder of 1936 displayed a willingness in principle to cooperate in the peace effort.[85] Berlin lost no time in accepting the invitation to the five-power conference and contributed her share of suggestions regarding procedure and the agenda, as well as her ideas about the shape of the settlement.[86] But this cooperation was not based on any particular desire to see the negotiations succeed. Indeed, Neurath admitted to Hassell on 26 September that Berlin's positive responses were inspired primarily by the desire to avert the 'really serious consequences' which could occur if the other powers were able to accuse Germany of having wrecked the peace effort.[87] An 'obviously negative attitude', he feared, would ultimately strengthen ties between Paris, London and Moscow.[88]

Thus, while the Auswärtiges Amt repeatedly stressed Germany's desire for a western settlement, it simultaneously practised a policy of procrastination.[89] There was the Abyssinian problem still to be finally settled and, along with it, the question of whether Italy would participate in the negotiations. Berlin could also argue that it was necessary to see if the Blum government could survive the internal unrest and wave of strikes which had crippled France since the end of May. Summer holidays, the Olympic games in August and the party rally at Nuremberg in September kept the Auswärtiges Amt from getting down to the business of preparing for a peace conference. The Spanish civil war provided an even better reason, particularly after mid-October when Moscow began openly to send supplies to Madrid.

Even more useful in promoting delay was the question of adequate preparations. In this connexion, the Germans posed three major problems which they insisted should be thrashed out diplomatically before any conference could be convened.[90] Otherwise, Neurath argued, the powers risked an early breakdown. The first was the question of whether the agreement to replace Locarno should consist of a series of mutual assistance pacts, as France favoured, or simple non-aggression arrangements, as Hitler had consistently preferred for as long as he had been Chancellor.[91]

The second point focused on the reform of the League of Nations and its involvement in the projected settlement.[92] The Abyssinian and Rhineland affairs had demonstrated to many the need to reorganize and rejuvenate the Geneva organization, with the result that by the autumn nearly every member state had at least one proposal for its reconstitution. This confused situation, the Auswärtiges Amt argued, should be clarified before Germany could rejoin. Berlin also insisted that the proposed western pact should not in any way be linked with the League council or the Covenant.

The third and greatest difficulty involved Russia and her treaty with Paris.[93] Germany argued vehemently that there must be an absolute divorce between any western settlement and the Franco-Soviet pact. The British tried to devise safeguards against their conceivable inter-connexion, but by the end of the year it was clear that the Germans would not accept anything less than a full French repudiation of all links with Moscow. These objections were accompanied during the autumn and winter of 1936 by a worsening of relations between Berlin and Moscow, beginning with attacks on the Kremlin at the party rallies, followed by the opening of the Russian purges and then capped on 25 November by the conclusion of the German-Japanese anti-Comintern pact.[94]

Stalin was not the only person to whom Hitler and his

diplomatic tacticians owed a debt of gratitude. The king of the Belgians, Leopold III, played into German hands on 14 October when he declared his country's intention of resigning from the ranks of the great powers and retiring to a position of armed neutrality.[95] Thus, Brussels would promise to secure her territory militarily in exchange for assistance guarantees from her former Locarno partners.[96] But she would no longer be obliged to aid any power which had been invaded. The signs of a move in this direction had been detectable well before the Rhine coup, notably in connexion with the Franco-Soviet treaty and the debate over whether to renew the Franco-Belgian military pact of 1920.[97] But it was undoubtedly the events of 1936, coupled with Germany's growing strength, which had demonstrated to Brussels the hazards of remaining too closely associated with Paris and her apparent desire to encircle Berlin with the aid of Moscow.[98]

Not only did the timing of the Belgian announcement take London by surprise and infuriate Paris, but it further dislocated the British effort to arrange a conference of the former Locarno powers which had already been pushed back from mid-October as a result of Berlin's insistence that prior agreement should be reached on every contentious point.[99] Where hopes for a settlement still existed, this unilateral repudiation by Belgium of her pledged word was seen as a serious, but not fatal, setback.[100] For Hitler and his generals, however, nothing could have been more advantageous than to have Brussels split with Paris.[101] This deprived France of a direct invasion route by land into the Ruhr and reduced some 125 miles of Germany's western frontier to 'low risk'.[102] These developments also reduced Blomberg's manpower requirements for defence and increased the Wehrmacht's offensive potential by 20-30 per cent, according to German estimates.[103]

The Belgian declaration of neutrality also allowed the high command and the Todt organization to concentrate their defensive preparations on the 213-mile stretch opposite France. But, contrary to popular belief, the west wall did not spring up in 'three, four or six months', as Churchill had predicted in April 1936, or even in a year, as some Germans declared on the anniversary of the coup.[104] Berlin moved slowly, partly to avoid arousing undue anxieties, partly because time was required to draft plans and partly because of disagreements over the type of system to construct.[105] Moreover, Hitler still preferred to allocate the Reich's concrete and steel resources for other rearmament projects and even motorways, with the result that the expected completion date of the Rhineland fortifications was put back from 1942 to 1945.[106] Only in early 1938 was the erection of permanent fortifications in the western provinces made a top-priority project.[107] Until then, and for some time afterwards, France was only cut off from her eastern allies in spirit—a fact which Gamelin and his colleagues did not choose to stress.[108]

At the same time, the Belgian decision deprived Gamelin at a stroke of his main means of protecting the flat and largely unfortified northern French frontier, with its vital industrial and mining centres.[109] Even though this had been the traditional invasion route into France, Paris had not constructed fortifications opposite Belgium for several reasons, not the least of which was the expense and unsuitability of the terrain for major defensive works. But Paris had also abstained in order not to arouse suspicions in Brussels that France only valued their military agreement as providing a free pass for French armies to the Ruhr. Before October 1936, Gamelin and his predecessors had planned, on the outbreak of hostilities, to defend France—and Belgium—by marching north and taking up positions along a line from the western frontier of Luxembourg to Liège. Now Paris was presented with the choice of either extending the Maginot line—at colossal cost—some 255 miles to Dunkerque or else depending on Belgium to delay a German advance until France could respond to a request for assistance.[110] The French decided in principle to do the former, but in practice pinned their hopes on the latter.

The Belgian defection did not spell the formal end of the British effort to get negotiations started, even though the ranks had been thinned to three and the chances of success had been reduced to the barest fraction.[111] The foreign office laboured for another year in search of a basis on which talks could be held. Even in November 1937, Eden while expressing extreme scepticism about the prospects, could not quite bring himself to write off the effort entirely.[112] A month later, however, an official of the Auswärtiges Amt observed that London and Paris, while still apparently interested in an agreement with Berlin, had ceased talking in terms of a western pact.[113]

Thus, after seventeen months of planning and another twenty-one months of diplomacy, Britain's major attempt to negotiate a general settlement with the Nazi régime had yielded no tangible results. Not only had the powers not met, but the British government could not even take comfort in the thought that Hitler had been successfully cast in the eyes of people as the cause of the failure. The course of Anglo-Franco-German diplomacy since March had been too turgid and complicated, as well as uneventful. The wars in Abyssinia and Spain, the chaos in France and the purges in Russia proved much more engrossing. So, too, did the abdication of Edward VIII.

Although there is reason to believe that Hitler was in no mood in 1936 to undertake any fresh obligations at any point on the compass, his unilateral remilitarization of the Rhineland had deprived London and Paris of the one bargaining counter in their possession for which Berlin might have been willing to pay a price, if only in the shape of a western air pact. And since His Majesty's Government was not prepared to surrender any colonies, there was really very little in these various proposals to attract Hitler.[114]

Instead, the German government preferred to temporize until, as Neurath put it, 'the Rhineland had been digested'.[115] By this, he meant not only with world opinion, but also within Germany, where the army required time to absorb it into their defensive system and, equally important, to protect and mobilize the vital industrial complexes of the Rhine and Ruhr.[116] Once the western provinces were secured, Neurath added, the countries of central and eastern Europe would 'begin to feel very differently about their foreign policies and a new constellation will develop'. Meanwhile, the Chancellor had no intention of binding himself in any way which might restrict his future activities in Europe.[117] For the next twenty-two months, until the Anschluss, Hitler turned his efforts to making both the Wehrmacht and the German economy fit for war.[118]

Looking back over the events of March 1936, it is hard to escape the conclusion that there was only one winner: Germany, or, more specifically, Hitler. He had risked the most and been rewarded in kind. It would be difficult to conceive of a period between 1933 and 1939 when he as Führer and Chancellor enjoyed greater domestic popularity and support than during the months following 7 March.[119] He had successfully restored full sovereignty to the Reich and smashed the last important link in the chains which most Germans believed had been responsible for their problems since 1919. Six months after the coup, ambassador Dodd wrote that 'an overwhelming majority' of Germans would support any venture which Hitler might undertake, 'whether it be one of outright conquest or one cloaked in the guise of expelling an invader'.[120] As Hitler himself explained to Phipps, 'with dictators, nothing succeeds like success'.[121]

It has been suggested that Hitler, because he acted on 7 March against the advice of the generals and diplomats, emerged from his Rhine triumph with a contempt for their advice and for them personally.[122] But the evidence suggests that this was not an immediate effect. Hossbach, for example, has described in detail the cooperation which existed between the top military echelons and the Chancellor throughout 1937.[123] Hitler's dissatisfaction with his military advisers might be more accurately dated from the so-called Hossbach conference of 5 November 1937, when Fritsch and Blomberg protested over the Chancellor's plans for forcefully solving Germany's territorial problems by 1943-5 at the latest, or as early as 1938 if events in France or elsewhere prevented Gamelin's armies from attacking the Reich.[124]

Hitler's attitude towards the diplomatic service was certainly not wholly negative. Neurath earned his praise and he was well served by Bülow, Dieckhoff, Gaus and Hassell, as well as by most of the rest of the field staff.[125] Hitler may have felt resentful of Forster and Hoesch, as well as their service attachés, for having subjected him to strains. But if the Chancellor had felt strongly enough about their performance to want to bring the Auswärtiges Amt under closer Nazi control, he would almost certainly have made Ribbentrop the state secretary to replace Bülow, who died in June a few months before his scheduled retirement. Instead, he sent his ambassador extraordinary to London to fill the gap left by Hoesch's death on 10 April 1936.

The change in relationship which occurred as a result of the coup was in the form of increased respect which the diplomats and generals felt towards the Führer and, especially, towards his ability both to size up a situation and to await, rather than force, an opportunity for acting.[126] Nor does it seem probable that the Auswärtiges Amt or Bendlerstrasse suffered any immediate decline in Hitler's estimation as executors of policy.[127] By the same token, however, the Chancellor undoubtedly felt an even greater affinity in matters of policy formation for the advice of Göring, Goebbels and Ribbentrop, all of whom had encouraged him from the outset.[128] He also emerged from the crisis with a much stronger feeling of confidence in his own judgement.[129] These shifts, however, were not so obvious or dramatic as to discourage experienced observers such as Phipps and Vansittart, who had been attempting for nearly three years to strengthen the position of the moderates in the so-called struggle with the radicals for Hitler's ear.[130]

The failure of Britain and France to react forcefully to such a direct threat to their security as the seizure of the demilitarized zone undoubtedly influenced Hitler's attitude towards the limitations of the opposition.[131] The refusal of the Sarraut government to make good on any of its threats helped to convince the Chancellor that France would not risk an attack against Germany without British support.[132] He also assured his generals at the Hossbach conference in November 1937 that the British would not participate in any war in which Germany acted against either the Czechs or the Austrians.[133]

In the event, Hitler's assessment of Britain also proved accurate. But there are at least two reasons why it could not have been based too heavily on his experience during the Rhineland crisis. First was the distinction which the western democracies made between the unilateral repudiation of a treaty and an act of external aggression. Hitler had successfully employed this argument in 1936.[134] But, as *The Times* had stressed on 9 March, the peaceful occupation by German troops of German soil was quite different from an act 'which carries fire and sword into a neighbour's territory'.[135] The Chancellor was also aware that he had acted against articles 42 and 43 at a moment of acute military weakness for Britain, whose meagre forces were largely occupied in the Mediterranean.[136] Moreover, the British had already begun to rearm, which meant that considerations which worked to neutralize London in 1936 would no longer be so important in his envisaged attack on Czechoslovakia or Austria.[137]

The most important benefits of the remilitarization of the

Rhineland for Germany were strategical.[138] The troops at the frontier could not have prevented the French from advancing into Germany, possibly even to the Rhine.[139] But the psychological effect of their presence was real. And, given the state of mind of the French military, this represented a deterrent far beyond their actual strength, as illustrated by defence minister Edouard Daladier's assertion in November 1936 that as much as 80 per cent of the German army was concentrated on the frontiers with France, Belgium and neutral Switzerland.[140] This new situation did not, however, allow Hitler to commit aggression. The Chancellor himself estimated that the army was still at least four or even six years away from being ready for war.[141] The remilitarized Rhineland made it possible for Germany to prepare to commit aggression.[142]

In the first instance, it permitted the eventual construction of fortifications, which, in addition to furnishing protection against attack, allowed the Wehrmacht chiefs to minimize the number of troops required to hold the French front. Not only could offensive strength be thus maximized, but any western attack would be more sudden, since German troops could be concentrated closer to the frontier.[143] Even more significant was the fact that the restoration of military sovereignty in the Rhineland permitted Berlin to organize the Reich's industries for war.[144] As long as the Rhine and Ruhr had remained so vulnerable to French invasion, it had not been possible to take full advantage of their capabilities and resources, which included 80 per cent of Germany's coal production.[145] The action of 7 March enabled Hitler to launch his four-year programme, which was designed to mobilize the German economy for a large-scale war by the autumn of 1940.[146]

Although the remilitarization of the Rhineland was widely regarded in Germany as having been an unmitigated success, the unilateral repudiation of the treaty of Locarno had brought certain disadvantages. These, however, were not those which Hitler or Neurath had anticipated. There had been no imposition of economic sanctions, as the Chancellor had thought possible.[147] Nor had there been any 'automatic and general concentration' against Germany, as the foreign minister had feared.[148] Furthermore, Britain and France had not come as closely together as had seemed to be the case on 19 March.[149] But Berlin had forfeited her guarantees under Locarno from London and Rome, although this had been

offset by Britain's desire for friendship and by her determination to exercise restraint on Paris.[150] Furthermore,
Mussolini had furnished tangible evidence of his desire to
close ranks with Hitler by encouraging Vienna to sign a
gentleman's agreement with Berlin on 11 July 1936 and by
concluding in October a protocol which provided for Italo-
German collaboration on such matters as the western pact
negotiations, colonies and commercial policies in the
Danube basin.[151]

Perhaps the greatest loss suffered by Germany was to
Hitler's credibility.[152] Hassell, for example, believed that the
coup had made everyone in Europe unwilling to believe in
the sincerity of the Chancellor's assurances.[153] But this judgement was made barely a week after the event, at a moment
when distrust and anxiety were still at a high point.[154] It is also
difficult to know whether this sentiment brought many fresh
converts to the ranks of those who already suspected the Third
Reich of sinister intentions. In France it deepened existing
fears, but did not do much to eclipse the neo-fascist movement.[155] Nor did it prevent other European states, including
Russia, from entering into trade agreements, or from considering and even urging negotiations with Germany.[156]

In Britain, Eden wrote scathing comments about Hitler's
scant regard for international law and stressed that the
Chancellor had exploded the myth that his government only
repudiated forced treaties.[157] He also warned that Berlin
would break any agreement whenever it suited her to do so.[158]
But he, like most Britons, had been prepared to begin
immediate negotiations in spite of any scepticism they may
have felt about the value of German promises. It also appears
that the foreign secretary was less affected by the *fait accompli*
than by the Chancellor's subsequent refusal to make any
gesture to facilitate the early opening of talks.[159]

Eden later argued that Hitler's action had aroused resentment and created watchful foes.[160] But there remained a great
reservoir of feeling in Britain that Germany had still not been
given her chance.[161] Nor had Hitler been sufficiently exposed
to prevent the Labour party in October 1936 from approving a
resolution at the annual conference withholding its support
from the government's rearmament effort.[162] Nor was Labour
MP Sir Stafford Cripps deterred from publicly urging that
'every possible effort should be made to stop recruiting for the

armed forces'.[163] Only a clear act of aggression or blatant intimidation could cause a significant hardening against the Third Reich.[164] Once that had happened and people became acutely concerned about Hitler's intentions, the unilateral remilitarization of the Rhineland took on an importance in retrospect which had escaped most members of the British public at the time.[165]

At the official level, however, the Chancellor's coup had a negative and lasting effect. This was manifested, not so much in the diplomatic as in the military sphere. Both Paris and London felt a greater need to press ahead with rearmament as a result of the Rhineland's remilitarization and Hitler's decision of 24 August 1936 to double the army's strength by extending military service from one to two years.[166] The Blum government announced in September its intention to spend £180 million over the next four years on material for the army.[167] This was followed a month later by cabinet approval of a plan to spend a further £50 million on the air force and in December by a decision to build five battleships and ten cruisers by 1943.[168]

In Britain, the rearmament effort which was begun in 1935 had already been increased for 1936 by a further £28.5 million to £158 million.[169] In April and July, supplementary estimates totalling £20 million were announced and in October the Conservative party conference unanimously carried a resolution that one-sided disarmament was more likely to promote war than peace.[170] But, whereas the cabinet minutes from April onwards reveal a greater degree of urgency about the need to hasten rearmament, it was also clear that little more could be done until British industry had overcome a serious shortage of skilled labour and expanded its plant capacity to produce war materials.[171]

The strategical effect on France of a remilitarized Rhineland was more apparent than real in view of the fact that her military leaders had already written off the demilitarized zone, and with it, apparently, any idea of aiding their eastern allies against German aggression.[172] Indeed, many Frenchmen who originally had supported the idea of acquiring Czech and Polish divisions to help contain a weak and disarmed Germany, had by 1936 come to regard these same connexions as capable of embroiling France in a major conflict for a cause as remote to them as Danzig or the Sudeten

Germans.[173] The same reservations, magnified many times over, were felt about the Franco-Soviet pact, even though its main aim had been to keep Hitler and Stalin apart and to deprive Germany of Russian resources in time of war.[174] After March 1936, with German troops at the frontier, it would not be possible to expect as much of France.

The Rhine coup also forced the government to acknowledge that France not only did not have the army of its policy, but would henceforth be obliged to adopt the policy of its army. Since this was exclusively aimed at the defence of France, the loss of the demilitarized zone was of small importance compared to the effect on French security of Belgium's declaration of neutrality.[175] Nor was any major effort made by the high command after the coup to remedy the organizational deficiency which had made it impossible to detach a force capable of launching an immediate and sustained offensive action.[176] Indeed, the military manual which was rewritten later in 1936 still stressed, as it had in 1921, that modern firepower from prepared positions could withstand any attack almost indefinitely.[177]

The German action of 7 March was heavily felt diplomatically, especially by those who believed that France's prestige and authority had been directly challenged.[178] But, contrary to their predictions, the failure to act against Hitler did not start a gravitation of smaller powers towards Berlin. Most governments already understood the political implications for them of Germany's growing economic and military strength. They also realized that the restoration of full sovereignty to the Reich would give Berlin much greater freedom of action east of the Rhine. But in 1936, most European states were visibly relieved that Paris had not accepted the German challenge.[179]

Although some observers may have detected a serious flaw in French resolve, it was not automatically or generally concluded from her refusal to march alone in defence of articles 42 and 43 that Paris would not fulfil her obligations if Germany attacked Czechoslovakia.[180] Hitler himself was not entirely certain as late as November 1937 that France had written off the Czechs.[181] The Sarraut government had, after all, brought Europe nearer to war than it had been since 1918.[182] It was not so much France's performance during the Rhineland crisis as the internal chaos and industrial strife of

1936 and 1937, coupled with Blum's growing dependence on London, which confirmed to the British foreign office that France would not act as an independent force in east European affairs.[183] Hitler's own assertion at the Hossbach conference that Paris would not march without British support was also based heavily on the domestic turmoil which he believed was capable of causing a civil war at any time.[184]

On the positive side, the French people could be thankful that war had been averted.[185] They also proved more amenable to increased armaments expenditure.[186] The government, for its part, had reason to be satisfied that it had avoided a split with London and had retained Britain's guarantee.[187] Moreover, Paris had laid the foundation, by the terms of the letter of 19 March, for the eventual creation of a defensive bloc which would have committed London to an anti-German alliance.[188]

Her failure to bring this potential commitment to fruition, or indeed to persuade London to join in punishing Hitler, was primarily due to the refusal of His Majesty's Government to take any action which might bring war closer than 1939.[189] Any such move would have had the effect of short-changing the foreign office in its efforts to 'buy time' for the rearmament programme.[190] This consideration was paramount with Vansittart and the central department, as well as those members of the cabinet, such as Duff Cooper, who had already decided that nothing could prevent war, save perhaps Hitler's death or a miscalculation by the Führer which would give Britain and France sufficient time to become so strong that he would not dare to risk aggression.[191] To them, the state of British public opinion was important primarily in so far as it affected the rearmament effort.[192] 'We have heard far too much of this alleged public opinion.' Vansittart wrote in July 1936, 'and it has a paralysing effect.'[193]

To most cabinet ministers, however, the prospect of crossing swords with the electorate was a deterrent to action only slightly less powerful than the so-called 'empty cupboard'.[194] The British people, more than most, had succumbed to the argument that Europe had lived for the past eighteen years in the shadow of the treaty of Versailles.[195] As a result, it was felt, Germany had never been treated on a basis of mutual respect and equality. The coup of 7 March had laid to rest the last important remaining clauses of the peace treaty which had

restricted Germany's sovereignty.[196] Never again would the
leaders of the Third Reich be able to play so effectively on
domestic and world opinion by alluding to the 'Diktat' of
1919. In this respect, the abolition of articles 42 and 43 was
both a milestone and a blessing.

But this latest German violation did not evoke from the
British people any desire for punishment.[197] On the contrary,
such measures were seen as part and parcel of the French
policies which many blamed more than Hitler for the lack of
stability and security in Europe.[198] Nor did the unilateral
repudiation of a freely-negotiated treaty alter the widely-held
conviction that the leaders of the Third Reich might respond
positively if London and Paris seized the opportunity to join
with Berlin in concluding a general settlement which also
removed Germany's legitimate grievances.[199] Others agreed
with foreign office economic adviser Gladwyn Jebb, who
argued that the cancerous symptoms of Nazism would respond 'to the radio-active treatment of increased international
trade'.[200] Those who subscribed to these views were not
necessarily Nazi apologists. But there still existed in Britain at
this time an element of opinion which held that National
Socialism was a revolutionary movement whose excesses were
a tactic of necessity rather than a strategy of conviction. Now
that success had been achieved, the Reich's sovereignty had
been restored and Hitler was in firm control, the argument
continued, the Führer would pass out of his violent phase and
adopt a more conservative and constructive attitude, especially if he were assisted and guided by Great Britain.[201]

Some cabinet members, including Baldwin and Simon,
believed that Hitler would respond to the 'personal' touch
and were therefore prepared to take him at his word when he
declared that the Rhineland coup had brought the period of
surprises to an end.[202] Others were less optimistic, though
hardly more willing to face the prospect of an early war.[203]
Neville Chamberlain, for example, suspected that Berlin was
'merely playing for time until she feels strong enough to make
her next spring'.[204] But both groups, along with their counter-
parts in the foreign office, were convinced that the British
public would turn against Germany and wholeheartedly
support rearmament only after Hitler had spurned a fair offer
or had committed some other act of lawlessness for which no
excuse based on discriminatory treatment could possibly be

found.[205] There are few indications that this stage had been reached even a year after the coup.[206] At the same time, however, pro-German sentiment was never again as strong in Britain as it had been in March 1936.[207] But no one has yet determined how much of that feeling was genuine and how much was inspired by a desire to avoid war or even to repay the French for their behaviour over Abyssinia.[208] Nor is there any way of knowing what might have been the effect if public opinion had been given a strong lead by the government, both during and after the crisis.

The remilitarization of the Rhineland had brought nearer the day of reckoning, if there was to be one, since it was considered axiomatic that Hitler would not commit aggression without first having locked what at that time was most generally regarded as his back door. But the date had been advanced by a minimum. His Majesty's Government had seen to that by refusing to be drawn into sanctions of any sort and by pursuing the effort to bring about western pact negotiations far longer than could be justified by Germany's attitude.[209] This policy carried the risk that Hitler would conclude that his opponents were too spineless to stand up to him.[210] But that was a chance which the cabinet and foreign office were obliged to take at a moment when the country was judged to have 'neither the means nor the heart' to tell Germany that there was a 'definite limit beyond which Britain would not go'.[211]

The fear of setting Britain on a collision course with Germany had militated against the government becoming embroiled over the Rhineland violation. To take any punitive measures or adopt any other unfriendly attitude, it was felt, might destroy one of London's most useful assets in her efforts to gain time, namely, Hitler's interest in friendship with Britain.[212] Nor would the foreign office recommend any action which might establish a precedent that would oblige the government to resort to progressively more effective — and dangerous — measures in the face of subsequent German violations of treaties or frontiers.[213] 'We have got to be cautious, and not be carried away prematurely,' Vansittart warned in March 1936, 'or we may pay for it with our national existence.'[214] This advice was to prevail for nearly three more years.

At least five lessons are clear from the events of March 1936.

First, a nation interested in establishing or maintaining its position as a world or regional power must have the military capacity to support and enforce its policies. 'In foreign affairs,' Wigram once wrote, 'nothing is important but one's armed strength.'[215] The dilemma and frustration created by the absence of such strength was revealed by Eden during the Abyssinian affair when he declared to the House of Commons that 'you cannot close the Canal with paper boats'.[216] Equally important, a nation's armaments must be capable of performing the tasks which might be required by its leaders' foreign policy. Even more fundamental, potential enemies must not be allowed to gain any sizeable military advantage, either in terms of existing forces or, especially, in their capacity to produce war material. As long as a nation maintains its military forces and industries so that they can withstand the strain of rapid expansion and contraction, there need be no agonizing four-year lag, such as the British endured, during which the British foreign office was obliged to weigh virtually every diplomatic move on the basis of whether it would gain or lose time for rearmament.

The second point is that governments in democracies cannot afford to allow public opinion to get out of touch with the realities of the world. In the Rhineland crisis, the British government was not handicapped by public attitudes because the nation's armaments deficiencies reduced the alternatives to acquiescence. But even if the government had felt sufficiently equipped to join France in punitive measures, it is unlikely that the Baldwin cabinet could have effected any immediate reversal of the attitudes which had been developing for nearly eighteen years towards Versailles, Germany and disarmament. Uneducated opinion cannot easily or rapidly be changed unless the people can see the reasons clearly for themselves, as occurred after the Hoare-Laval agreement was made public.

The reactions to the remilitarization of the Rhineland also reinforce the validity of the observation that democracies will not normally support military measures against what they regard as an internal affair of another country, even if it involves a breach of international treaty. Such action only becomes feasible if people are convinced that their own security or interests are directly or ultimately threatened. The absence of any concentrated or sustained effort to persuade the British people of the potential menace of Nazi Germany was probably the major shortcoming of the Baldwin government.[217]

Another lesson is the importance of a sound economy in the conduct of foreign affairs. A country which cannot withstand the strain of a run on its currency or economic privation can ill afford to risk incurring international wrath. Britain discovered this during the Suez crisis in 1956 when the United States withdrew its support for the pound. Some twenty years earlier, the French did not even take the chance, partly for fear of precipitating a financial crisis which might have forced a devaluation—a decision which Paris was forced to make anyway, some six months later, as a result of internal weakness.

Finally, it is clear from the reactions to the events of 7 March that allies, both real and prospective, can dilute, as well as strengthen, the resolve of a nation. Most government leaders at this time accepted the view of their foreign-policy advisers, who, like Vansittart, regarded the German menace as a five- or even ten-year problem, which could and probably would become acute before they would be prepared to resist forcefully the realization of Nazi ambitions. Since France alone possessed neither the means nor the desire in 1936 to defeat Hitler decisively, the French government was obliged to discard any measures which could alienate her British ally and weaken the front against Germany. For their part, members of His Majesty's Government had concluded already that victory against the Third Reich would depend to a large measure on the material, financial and possibly even military support of the United States. This chain of ultimate dependence which stretched across the Channel and the Atlantic contributed to the decision to avoid a confrontation at this time.

As a result of all these factors, Hitler won in a walkover. Whether it was worth a *fait accompli* is less certain. In spite of German assertions to the contrary, the Rhine régime would almost certainly have been negotiated out of existence within another year or two. Moreover, the successful conclusion of such negotiations with London and Paris would have raised Hitler's political stature to statesmanlike levels. It would also have made it even more difficult for his opponents to arouse their publics to the threat which was being created, not only by

Germany's growing military strength, but also by a system of education and indoctrination which glorified war and demanded total obedience to the Führer.

The abolition of articles 42 and 43 brought to a close the era of Versailles. What would happen next was still not altogether clear. But there could be no doubt that, with the disappearance of the demilitarized Rhineland, Europe had lost her last guarantee against German aggression.

Appendix: Extracts from treaties and resolutions

Covenant of the League of Nations

Article 16

'1 Should any Member of the League resort to war...it shall *ipso facto* be deemed to have committed an act of war against all other Members of the League, which hereby undertake immediately to subject it to the severance of all trade or financial relations....'

'2 It shall be the duty of the Council in such cases to recommend to the several Governments concerned what effective military, naval or air force the Members of the League shall severally contribute to the armed forces to be used to protect the Covenants of the League....'

(Article 17 extended these provisions to include a resort to war by a state which was not a member of the League.)

Most non-Locarno powers argued after 7 March that they were not obliged to impose sanctions of any sort against Germany since there had been no 'resort to force'.

Treaty of Versailles (Part III, section III)

Article 42 'Germany is forbidden to maintain or construct any fortifications either on the left bank of the Rhine or on the right bank to the west of a line drawn 50 kilometres to the east of the Rhine.'

Article 43 'In the area defined above the maintenance and the assembly of armed forces, either permanently or temporarily, and military manoeuvres of any kind, as well as the upkeep of all permanent works of mobilization, are in the same way forbidden.'

Article 44 'In case Germany violates in any manner whatever the provisions of Articles 42 and 43, she shall be regarded as committing a hostile act against the Powers signatory of the present Treaty and as calculated to disturb the peace of the world.'

The treaty of Versailles contained no provisions for the enforcement of articles 42 and 43. No power was obliged to ensure that these clauses were respected after the departure from Germany of the occupation forces.

Treaty of Locarno

Article 1 'The high contracting parties collectively and severally guarantee...the observance of the stipulations of articles 42 and 43 of the said treaty [Versailles] concerning the demilitarized zone.'

Article 2 'Germany and Belgium, and also Germany and France, mutually undertake that they will not attack or invade each other or resort to war against each other.'

'This stipulation shall not, however, apply in the case of—
1 The exercise of the right of legitimate defence, that is to say, resistance to a violation of the undertaking contained in the previous paragraph or to a flagrant breach of articles 42 and 43 of the said Treaty of Versailles, if such breach constitutes an unprovoked act of aggression and by reason of the assembly of armed forces in the demilitarized zone immediate action is necessary.'

Article 4
'1 If one of the high contracting parties alleges that a violation of article 2 of the present treaty or a breach of articles 42 or 43 of the Treaty of Versailles had been or is being committed, it shall bring the question at once before the Council of the League of Nations.'
'2 As soon as the Council of the League of Nations is satisfied that such violation or breach has been committed, it will notify its finding without delay to the Powers signatory of the present treaty, who severally agree that in such case they will each of them come immediately to the assistance of the Power against whom the act complained of is directed.'
'3 In case of a flagrant violation of article 2 of the present treaty or of a flagrant breach of articles 42 or 43 of the Treaty of Versailles by one of the high contracting parties, each of the other contracting parties hereby undertakes immediately to come to the help of the party against whom such a violation or breach has been directed as soon as the said Power has been able to satisfy itself that by reason either of the crossing of the frontier or of the outbreak of hostilities or of the assembly of armed forces into the demilitarized zone immediate action is necessary.'

In 1925, when the treaty was negotiated, it was assumed that Germany would not deliberately send military forces into the Rhineland unless she was intent on attacking Paris or Brussels. The entry of armed forces into the demilitarized zone was to be the signal for Great Britain and Italy to implement their assistance obligations to defend the territorial integrity of France and Belgium.

Any other violation was to be submitted first to the League council. What happened after the council confirmed a violation had never been defined, but British legal experts acknowledged that Paris and Brussels could take any action they saw fit and call upon the Locarno guarantors to fulfil their assistance obligations.

Geneva Resolution of 17 April 1935

'Considering that the unilateral repudiation of international obligations may endanger the very existence of the League of Nations as an organization for maintaining peace and promoting security;

Decides:

That such repudiation...should...call into play all appropriate measures on the part of members of the League and within the framework of the Covenant;

Requests a committee...to propose for this purpose measures to render the Covenant more effective in the organization of collective security, and to define in particular the economic and financial measures which might be applied, should in the future a State, whether a member of the League of Nations or not, endanger peace by the unilateral repudiation of its international obligations.'

The Franco-Soviet Pact

Article 1   If either France or Russia is 'threatened with, or in danger of, aggression on the part of any European state', they undertake 'mutually to proceed to an immediate consultation as regards the measures to be taken for the enforcement of Article X of the League Covenant'.

Article 2   Each country was immediately to assist the other if either were subjected to an unprovoked aggression on the part of any European state.

Article 3   In the same circumstances, they undertook 'immediately to lend each other aid and assistance in application of Article XV of the Covenant'.

The protocol placed on record that there was to have been a tri-partite similar treaty between France, Germany and Russia, under which each would have been pledged to assist either of the others if it was subjected to aggression by the third. This, according to Berlin, was evidence that the existing pact was a military alliance directed exclusively against Germany.

The merit of the Franco-Soviet pact was claimed to be that it closed 'the gap in the Covenant' which released members from all obligations if the League council did not reach a unanimous deci-sion. Germany contended that Moscow and Paris had arrogated to themselves the right to render assistance, even if the League council could not agree or voted that an act of aggression had not been committed. This meant, in German eyes, that 'in certain circumstances', Paris would act as though the Locarno pact and League covenant were void. As a result, according to the German memorandum of 7 March, the Rhine pact had 'lost its significance and practically ceased to be'.

Notes

GUIDE TO DOCUMENTARY ABBREVIATIONS

C
: *Documents on German Foreign Policy, 1918-1945*, Series C (1933-37). C-V means volume V of the series.

CAB
: British cabinet minutes. CAB 3(36)1 means the third meeting of 1936, conclusion or topic number one.

CID
: British committee of imperial defence. Meetings are indicated as CID 42nd meeting. Papers are designated as CID 1206-B of date.

Cmd.
: British white papers or blue books.

COS
: British chiefs of staff. Meetings and papers are designated the same as for CID.

CP
: British cabinet papers. CP 42(36) of 11 Feb. 1936 indicates the 42nd paper submitted to cabinet ministers in 1936.

D
: *Documents on German Foreign Policy, 1918-1945*, Series D.

DBFP
: *Documents on British Foreign Policy, 1919-1939*, Series II.

DCM
: British cabinet's sub-committee on defence requirements (fore-runner of the DPR), with identical designations as used by the CID for its meetings and papers.

DDB
: *Documents diplomatiques belges, 1933-1939*. DDB, IV means volume IV of that series.

DDF
: *Documents diplomatiques français, 1932-1939*, 2nd series.

DO
: Dominion Office files. DO 6882A/8, meeting of 9 March, indicates the box and file number, as well as the date of the meeting.

DPR
: British cabinet's defence policy and requirements sub-committee. Designations for meetings and papers follow that used by CID.

FOL
: Foreign office library. Designates microfilmed German documents, untranslated and unpublished. FOL 63/43764 of 9 March 1936 indicates the Auswärtiges Amt file number (63) and microfilm frame numbers.

G(36)
: British cabinet sub-committee appointed in February 1936 to examine a general settlement with Germany.

Hansard
: House of Commons debates are listed as: *Hansard*, vol. 310, cols. 1459-61. House of Lords debates are cited as: *Hansard*, Lords, vol. 99, cols. 78-83.

IMT
: International Military Tribunal. *Trial of the Major War Criminals at Nuremberg*.

LNOJ	League of Nations. *Official Journal.*
L P (L)	British cabinet sub-committee created to deal with the Locarno negotiations in 1936 after the Rhineland coup.
NCA	*Nazi Conspiracy and Aggression.* Documentary evidence and guide materials for the Nuremberg prosecution.
RIIA	Royal Institute of International Affairs, London.
Survenus	*Rapport fait au nom de la commission chargée d'enquêter sur les évènements survenus en France de 1933 à 1945.*
TWC	*Trials of the War Criminals at Nuremberg.* Case 11.
USFR	*Documents in United States Foreign Relations.*

NOTE ON BRITISH FOREIGN OFFICE DOCUMENTS

A document listed as C 1610/4/18 of 10 March 1936 should be regarded as follows:
C = Central department (other departments include R = Southern N = Northern J = Abyssinia W = Western and League of Nations and A = Americas).

1610 = The number given to the document after being assigned to a department. Normally, there is only one document for one number, unless the Foreign Office replied to the incoming despatch, in which case the outgoing document carried the same number in the files.

4 = The file number attached to the document by the relevant department. New files were begun whenever a fresh topic emerged. In that case, the file number was identical with the document number, viz. C 99/99/18 began a file on the German economy in 1936 and C 3917/3917/18 began a file on German propaganda efforts in Great Britain.

In 1935, the main German file was 55; in 1936 it was 4.

18 = The country to which the document pertains. The following numbers refer to these countries:

1	Abyssinia	37	Rumania
2	Argentina	38	Russia
3	Austria	41	Spain
4	Belgium	42	Sweden
7	Bulgaria	43	Switzerland
9	Chile	44	Turkey
12	Czechoslovakia	45	U.S.A.
15	Denmark	54	Ecuador
17	France	55	Poland
18	Germany	62	Central department (general)
19	Greece	67	Southern department (general)
21	Hungary		
22	Italy	92	Yugoslavia
30	Norway	98	Western department (general)
36	Portugal		

Where no year is given with the date, 1936 is implied.

1 **The search for security, 1918-1935**

1 See, for example, Georges Clemenceau, *Grandeur and Misery of Victory* (London, 1930), pp. 107-9, 111, 182-4; Harold Nelson, *Land and Power—British and Allied Policy on Germany's Frontiers, 1916-1919* (London, 1963), p. 198; Winston Churchill, *The Second World War*, vol. I, *The Gathering Storm* (London, 1964), pp. 6-9, 50; Arnold Wolfers, *Britain and France Between Two Wars* (New York, 1940), pp. 5, 11-13; and Stephen King-Hall, *Our Own Times, 1913-1939* (London, 1941), pp. 272-3.

2 The following is based on H. W. V. Temperley, *A History of the Peace Conference of Paris*, vol. III (London, 1920), pp. 122-7; André Tardieu, *The Truth about the Treaty* (London, 1921), passim; Clemenceau, *Grandeur*, pp. 192-220, 241; Nelson, *Land and Power*, pp. 108-12, 199-206, 217, 222, 375, 377; Frank Owen, *Tempestuous Journey—Lloyd George, His Life and Times* (London, 1954), pp. 524, 545; Poitr S. Wandycz, *France and Her Eastern Allies, 1919-1925* (Minneapolis, 1962), pp. 37-9; René Albrecht-Carrié, *The Meaning of the First World War* (Englewood Cliffs, NJ, 1965), p. 98; and C2732/4/18 of 7 April 1936.

3 Wolfers, *Britain and France*, pp. 14, 23.

4 Owen, *Journey*, p. 545.

5 For the following, see Nelson, *Land and Power*, pp. 205-10, 217, 221-2; Tardieu, *Truth*, pp. 145-201; and Clemenceau, *Grandeur*, pp. 220-34.

6 Cmd 153 of 28 June 1919, pp. 206-7.

7 Ibid.; and Clemenceau, *Grandeur*, pp. 220-3, 313-14.

8 W. N. Medlicott, *Contemporary England* (London, 1967), pp. 168-9; Wolfers, *Britain and France*, pp. 43-4; and Cmd 221 of 1919.

9 The following is based on Cmd 221 of 1919; Clemenceau, *Grandeur*, pp. 220-1, 228, 300-1; Tardieu, *Truth*, pp. 202-17, 231-2; Nelson, *Land and Power*, pp. 247, 375-6; *Hansard*, vol. 310, col. 1436; C 3444/3279/4 of 15 May 1934; Owen, *Journey*, p. 545; and Wolfers, *Britain and France*, pp. 14-15n.

10 Wolfers, *Britain and France*, pp. 43-4.

11 Clemenceau, *Grandeur*, pp. 183, 225-32; Wolfers, *Britain and France*, p. 15n; and Albrecht-Carrié, *First War*, p. 128.

12 Tardieu, *Truth*, pp. 435-7; Wolfers, *Britain and France* p. 15; King-Hall, *Our Own Times*, p. 104; and Clemenceau, *Grandeur*, pp. 224-34.

13 Wolfers, *Britain and France*, p. 15; and FO 800.292, lecture by R. F. Wigram, 8 Jan 1932.

14 Wolfers, *Britain and France*, pp. 11, 16-25, 43-4, 122-3, 153-69; and René Albrecht-Carrié, *France, Europe and the Two World Wars* (Paris, 1960), pp. 103-9, 157-8.

15 C 3444/3279/4 of 15 May 1934; C 1074/270/4 of 19 Feb 1936; and C

3456/G/66 of 17 June 1936.

16 Albrecht-Carrié, *Europe,* pp. 110-16.

17 C 2656/55/18 of 28 March 1935; C 7262/92/62 of 14 Oct 1936; Paul Reynaud, *In the Thick of the Fight* (London, 1955), pp. 41-52; and William E. Scott, *Alliance against Hitler* (Durham, NC, 1962), *passim.*

18 The following is based on Clemenceau, *Grandeur,* pp. 195-217; Wolfers, *Britain and France,* pp. 26-30, 43, 55-8; Albrecht-Carrié, *Europe,* pp. 126-8, 131-5; Charles Petrie, *The Life and Letters of Austen Chamberlain,* vol. II (London, 1940), pp. 155, 249; and King-Hall, *Our Own Times,* pp. 123-30, 192-3.

19 Wolfers, *Britain and France,* p. 56.

20 This paragraph is based on Churchill, *Storm,* p. 9; Petrie, *Chamberlain,* p. 249; C-II, p. 117; Anthony Eden, *Facing the Dictators* (London, 1962), p. 93; William Strang, *Britain in World Affairs* (London, 1961), p. 299; Adolf Hitler, *Mein Kampf* (London, 1968), *passim;* Albrecht-Carrié, *Europe,* pp. 127, 133, 136-7, 147-8; Edward Grigg, *The Faith of an Englishman* (London, 1937), pp. 13-14; Robert Graves, *Goodbye to All That* (London, 1929), p. 259; King-Hall, *Our Own Times,* p. 132; and C 2732/4/18 of 7 April 1936.

21 The following is based on Austen Chamberlain, *Down the Years* (London, 1935), pp. 155-63; Petrie, *A. Chamberlain,* pp. 249-94; Albrecht-Carrié, *Europe,* pp. 138, 147-52, 156-63; Frank P. Chambers, *This Age of Conflict* (New York, 1950), pp. 121-2; Robert A. Spender, *Great Britain and the Empire* (London, 1938), pp. 665-6; Wandycz, *France,* pp. 325-7, 348-9, 359-61; and King-Hall, *Our Own Times,* pp. 121-2, 132, 268-72.

22 The following is based on Cmd 2525 of 16 Oct 1925; C-II, p. 117; C-V, pp. 8-13, 415; G(36)3, enclosure of 14 Feb 1936; CAB 15(36)1 of 5 March 1936; DDF, I, pp. 206-7, 339; DDB, III, pp. 317-19; and Eden, *Facing,* p. 342.

23 C 247/247/18 of 9 Jan 1934; and C 1994/4/18 of 14 March 1936.

24 See, for example, C 1961/20/18, minute by Wigram, 9 March 1934; C 2592/247/18 of 24 April 1934; C 3097/247/18 of 15 May 1934; C 3444/3279/4, minute by Wigram, 22 May 1934; CP 302(34) of 18 Dec 1934; CAB 3(35)2 of 14 Jan 1935; C 1149/516/4, minute by Sargent, 14 Feb 1935; C 1181/4/18 of 24 Feb 1936; C 1723/4/18 of 11 March 1936; DDB, III, pp. 317-19; DDB, IV, pp. 69-70; and Paul Hymans, *Mémoires,* II (Brussels, 1958), p. 741.

25 See, for example, DDF, I, p. 207; W 1892/10/98 of 2 March 1935; C 2483/55/18 of 22 March 1935; and Wolfers, *Britain and France,* pp. 43-4.

26 For the following, see CAB 60(33)1 of 6 Nov 1933; C 247/247/18 of 9 Jan 1934; C 4234/55/18 of 23 and 25 April 1935; C 1001/4/18, minute by Perowne, 13 Feb 1936; G(36)3, enclosure of 14 April

1936; CAB 15(36)1 of 5 March 1936; C 1994/4/18 of 14 March 1936; and Eden, *Facing,* pp. 341-2.

27 Flandin, *Survenus,* I, p. 149.

28 Clemenceau, *Grandeur,* p. 309.

29 C 4234/55/18, minute by Eden, 2 May 1935; C 247/247/18 of 9 Jan 1934; CAB 2(35)1 of 9 Jan 1935; CAB 3(35)2 of 14 Jan 1935; CID 1161-B of 8 Feb 1935; C 7698/55/18, minute by Sargent, 18 Nov 1935; and C3456/G/66 of 17 June 1936.

30 Chamberlain, *Down the Years,* p. 163; Albrecht-Carrié, *Europe,* pp. 164, 167; and King-Hall, *Our Own Times,* pp. 275-6.

31 CAB 18(36)1 of 11 March 1936.

32 CP 317(31) of 10 Dec 1931.

33 CAB 18(36)1 of 11 March 1936.

34 C 972/55/18 of 1 Feb 1935; C 3456/G/66 of 17 June 1936; and A. Chamberlain, *Down the Years,* p. 170. See also Geneviève R. Tabouis, *Perfidious Albion — Entente Cordiale* (London, 1938), pp. 237-8.

35 C 3456/G/66 of 17 June 1936; Petrie, *Chamberlain,* pp. 254-5, 263, 267, 276-7, 325; A. J. P. Taylor, *English History 1914-1945* (London, 1965), p. 366; and C 5178/55/18 of 4 July 1935.

36 C 3456/G/66 of 17 June 1936; and Wandycz, *France,* pp. 366-7.

37 Wolfers, *Britain and France,* pp. 43-4.

38 Clemenceau, *Grandeur,* pp. 300-16; Alexander Werth, *The Twilight of France, 1933-1940* (London, 1942), pp. 3, 71; Wandycz, *France,* pp. 366-8; D. W. Brogan, *The French Nation* (London, 1957), p. 266; Albrecht-Carrié, *Europe,* pp. 168-70; and Wolfers, *Britain and France,* pp. 98, 257-8.

39 Reynaud, *Thick,* pp. 81-6, 89-90; Wandycz, *France,* p. 368; Wolfers, *Britain and France,* pp. 74-75n; and Vivian Rowe, *The Great Wall of France* (London, 1959), pp. 50, 60.

40 Philip Kerr, Lothian papers, Edinburgh, vol. 324, letter from Joachim Stresemann, 29 June 1936.

41 Werth, *Twilight,* p. 71. See also René Lauret, *France and Germany* (London, 1965), p. 80; and Wandycz, *France,* pp. 327, 359, 362-3.

42 C 3444/3279/4, annex of 30 May 1934; C-I, pp. 83-4; A. J. P. Taylor, *The Origins of the Second World War* (London, 1963), p. 53; Emile Cammaerts, *Albert of Belgium* (London, 1935), pp. 357-8; and M. H. H. Macartney and Paul Cremona, *Italy's Foreign and Colonial Policy* (New York, 1938), pp. 156-7.

43 Keith Feiling, *The Life of Neville Chamberlain* (London, 1946), p. 261; and Ronald B. McCallum, *Public Opinion and the Last Peace* (London, 1944), pp. 131, 147.

44 Petrie, *Chamberlain,* pp. 278, 283; and Taylor, *English History,* pp. 215-6, 221.

45 Petrie, *Chamberlain,* p. 292.

46 CAB 60(33)1 of 6 Nov 1933. See also C 247/247/18 of 9 Jan 1934.

47 Medlicott, *Contemporary England*, pp. 209-329; Taylor, *English History*, pp. 222-368; and King-Hall, *Our Own Times*, pp. 219-519, 672-728.

48 Petrie, *Chamberlain*, pp. 256-7; Wolfers, *Britain and France*, p. 37n; and Albrecht-Carrié, *Europe*, p. 151.

49 FO 800.292, lecture by R. F. Wigram, May 1934.

50 D. W. Brogan, *The Development of Modern France, 1870-1939* (London, 1947), p. 266; Albrecht-Carrié, *Europe*, pp. 181-6; Wolfers, *Britain and France*, p. 37n; and Wandycz, *France*, p. 326. See also Petrie, *Chamberlain*, pp. 304-5.

51 Except for the Saar, which was then between régimes.

52 FO 800.292, lecture by R. F. Wigram, May 1934; Albrecht-Carrié, *Europe*, p. 186; Scott, *Alliance*, p. 7; and Wolfers, *Britain and France*, p. 65.

53 CP 82(34) of 21 March 1934; C 3097/247/18 of 17 May 1934; C 2949/55/18 of 6 April 1935; C 3438/55/18 of 25 April 1935; C 3527/55/18, minute by Sargent, 1 May 1935; C 3946/55/18, minute by Wigram, 16 May 1935; C 5454/55/18 of 9 July 1935; C 5685/55/18 of 23 July 1935; C 5607/55/18, minute by Sargent, 26 July 1935; C-I, pp. 256-60, 365, 803-4, 907-9; C-II, pp. 42, 61-2, 821-2; C-III, pp. 3, 114-15, 148-50, 218, 329-30, 544; and Wilhelm Keitel, *Generalfeldmarschall Keitel* (Göttingen, 1961), pp. 36-7.

54 CP 82(34) of 21 March 1934; CP 268(34) of 11 Oct 1934; FO. 800.292, lecture by R. F. Wigram, May 1934; C-I, pp. 256-60; and NCA, VI, p. 954. See also Robert J. O'Neill, *The German Army and the Nazi Party* (London, 1968), p. 171.

55 The following is based on FOL 9930/E694817 of 3 May 1934; IMT, IX, pp. 506-7; X, pp. 574-5; XV, pp. 347, 449-50; XIX, p. 4; and XXV, pp. 247-8; NCA, III, p. 304 and VII, p. 455; Erich von Manstein, *Aus einem Soldatenleben* (Bonn, 1958), pp. 227-9; and D. C. Watt, 'German Plans for the Reoccupation of the Rhineland: A Note,' *Journal of Contemporary History*, October 1966, pp. 193-9. See also Keitel, *Keitel*, pp. 36-7; Walter Görlitz, *The German General Staff* (London, 1953), p. 279; Maurice Gamelin, *Servir*, II (Paris, 1946), p. 214; and O'Neill, *German Army*, p. 173.

56 This plan, described in German documents as the 'Freimachung des Rheines', or 'Rheinräumung', had nothing to do with remilitarization of the western provinces, as alleged at Nuremberg. (IMT, XV, pp. 347-8; IX, pp. 506-7; and XXXVI, p. 434). See also Watt, 'German Plans,' pp. 196-8.

57 IMT, X, pp. 574-5; XIX, p. 4; XXV, pp. 247-8; NCA, VI, pp. 952-4; and Bernhard von Lossberg, *Im Wehrmachtführungsstab* (Hamburg, 1950), p. 12. See also FOL 9945/E696022-8 of 9 Oct 1934; FOL 9945/E696004-7 of 30 Oct 1934; C 235/55/18 of 31 Dec 1934; and C 1683/4/18 of 11 March 1936.

58 William L. Shirer, *The Rise and Fall of the Third Reich* (New York,

1960). p. 290; and C. Waldron Bolen, 'Hitler Remilitarizes the Rhineland,' in *Power, Public Opinion and Diplomacy* (Durham, NC, 1959), p. 246.

59 IMT, II, pp. 342-4; X, pp. 474-6; XV, pp. 445-7; XIX, p. 452; XXXIV, pp. 485-6; and NCA, I, pp. 440-1.

60 IMT, IX, pp. 284-5, 505-7; X, p. 475; XV, pp. 348, 445-8, 450; XXV, pp.247-8; E. M. Robertson, *Hitler's Pre-War Policy and Military Plans* (London, 1963), pp. 60, 89; Watt, 'German Plans,' p. 194; O'Neill, *German Army*, p. 171; and Görlitz, *General Staff*, p. 279.

61 This paragraph is based on C—I, pp. 907-9; C-II, pp. 688-9, 821-2; C-III, p. 3; C-IV, pp. 94-6, 228-9, 523, 837-8; Robertson, *Hitler's Plans*, p. 25; NCA, VII, p. 454; IMT, XV, p. 450; and Watt, 'German Plans,' p. 198.

62 C-I, pp. 907-9.

63 This paragraph is based on C-II, pp. 61-3, 821-2; C-IV, pp. 207, 229, 523, 838; FOL 9930/E694817 of 3 May 1934; VI, p. 28; NCA, VII, p. 455; IMT, IX, p. 506; XV, pp. 347, 449-50; XXXVI, p. 434; C 475/20/18 of 15 Jan 1934; C 3209/55/18, annex of 12 April 1935; C 1683/4/18 of 11 March 1936; DDF, I, pp. 113, 142, 175, 208, 246, 252, 378, 391.

64 C-III, pp. 3-4n; C-IV, pp. 96-7, 228-9, 523-4, 837-8; and DDF, I, pp. 136-8.

65 C-IV, p. 294. The police population in the demilitarized zone as of June 1935 was 35,696, or 4,196 too many. (C-IV, p. 294).

66 C-IV, pp. 94n, 229, 523. Lapo strength in the demilitarized zone as of June 1935 was 13,496.

67 C-IV, pp. 94-5; DDF, I, pp. 137-8, 151, 246; C 5420/55/18 of 12 July 1935; and Georg Tessin, *Formationsgeschichte der Wehrmacht 1933-39* (Boppard am Rhein, 1959), pp. 251, 255-6.

68 C-IV, pp. 228-9; DDF, I, pp. 137-8, 208; C 4583/20/18 of 3 July 1934; C 4297/20/18 of 5 July 1934; C 5454/55/18 of 9 July 1935; C 7664/20/18 of 14 Nov 1934; C 1683/4/18 of 11 March 1936; and Tessin, *Formationsgeschichte*, pp. 255-6.

69 DDF, I, pp. 54, 79, 136-8, 142, 151, 206-7, 277, 290, 378, 390-2; Robertson, *Hitler's Plans*, p. 25; and C 3958/85/17 of 29 June 1934.

70 C 3289/55/18, annex of 12 April 1935.

71 C 3422/55/18 of 25 April 1935; C 3596/55/18 of 1 May 1935; C 7664/20/18 of 14 Nov. 1934; and DDF, I, pp. 177, 290, 378, 392-3.

72 C-IV, p. 229; DDF, I, pp. 79, 136-8, 378; C 2897/55/18 of 5 April 1935; and C 5454/55/18 of 9 July 1935.

73 C-III, pp. 1030-1; C-IV, pp. 58, 96-7, 228-9, 522-3; IMT, XV, pp. 347-8; and Tessin, *Formationsgeschichte*, p. 251.

74 C-III, pp. 1014, 1105; C-IV, pp. 57-9, 94-6, 335-6, 837; and C 3723/55/18 of 2 May 1935.

75 C-IV, p. 837.

76 C-IV, pp. 228-9. For other expressions of army concern about the importance of scrupulously adhering to the Rhine régime, see C-IV, pp. 96-7; IMT, XV, pp. 347-8; NCA, VII, pp. 454-5; FOL 784/271668-75 of 29 April 1935; FOL 781/271680 of 9 May 1935; and Keitel, *Keitel,* pp. 36-7.

77 C-IV, pp. 837-8.

78 C-IV, pp. 96-7, 229.

79 C-IV, p. 97n. See also C-IV, pp. 229, 295n.

80 C-IV, pp. 523-4, 838.

81 C-IV, pp. 523-4; NCA, VII, p. 455; IMT, IX, p. 506; XV, p. 455; XIX, p. 4; and FOL 784/271680 of 9 May 1935. See also Watt, 'German Plans,' p. 198; and Tessin, *Formationsgeschichte,* pp. 251, 255.

82 C 151/4/18 of 9 Jan 1936 summarizes the assurances by the Chancellor and his chief advisers *vis-à-vis* the Rhine zone and Locarno.

83 Ibid.

84 C 4117/55/18 of 21 May 1935.

85 Ibid. See also C 4004/55/18, minute by Sargent, 22 May 1935; and C 4143/55/18 of 23 May 1935.

86 C-II, p. 516, C 3906/55/18 of 21 May 1935; C 151/4/18 of 9 Jan 1936; and Eden, *Facing,* pp. 62, 330, 343.

87 C 902/55/18 of 3 Feb 1935.

88 Ibid.; and C 921/55/18 of 4 Feb. 1935.

89 C-IV, p. 1166; and C 8364/55/18 of 16 Dec 1935. See also C-III, pp. 699, 1014, DDF, I, p. 193; and DDB, III, p. 450.

90 See, for example, C-II, p. 115; and C-III, pp. 544, 561, 563, 699.

91 C 8364/55/18 of 16 Dec 1935; and C 8373/55/18 of 19 Dec 1935.

92 C-IV, p. 1166; and C-III, p. 699.

93 C-III, p. 699; C-IV, p. 1164; C 2949/55/18 of 6 April 1935; C 3906/55/18 of 21 May 1935; C 3946/55/18, minute by Wigram, 16 May 1935; and Otto Meissner, *Staatssekretär unter Ebert-Hindenburg-Hitler* (Hamburg, 1950), p. 408.

94 C 3527/55/18, minute by Sargent, 1 May; C 3946/55/18, minute by Wigram, 16 May; C 5683/55/18 of 3 July; C 5333/55/18, minute by Wigram, 14 July 1935; and C 143/143/18 of 6 Jan 1936. See also C-III, p. 544.

95 For general assessments, see C 2839/111/18 of 1 April 1935; and DDF, I, pp. 183-9.

96 C 623/55/18 of 22 Jan 1935; C 2839/111/18 of 1 April 1935; and C 143/143/18 of 6 Jan 1936.

97 C 2082/55/18 of 12 March 1935; C 2949/55/18 of 6 April 1935; C 6741/55/18 of 26 Sept 1935; C 143/143/18 of 6 Jan 1936; DDF, I, p. 152; C-III, pp. 699, 1109; and O'Neill, *German Army,* p. 182.

98 FOL 7881H/E570808-23 of 28 Feb 1936; NCA, VI, pp. 1006-9; Manstein, *Soldatenleben,* pp. 226-9; C 3527/55/18, minute by Sargent, 1 May 1935; C 4585/55/18 of 31 May 1935; C 143/143/18

of 6 Jan 1936; and O'Neill, *German Army*, p. 174.

99 C 2839/111/18 of 1 April 1935; Karl Demeter, *The German Officer Corps* (London, 1965), p. 199; John Wheeler-Bennett, *The Nemesis of Power* (London, 1954), p. 335; Gerhard Ritter, *The German Resistance* (New York, 1958), pp. 73-4; Albert Kesselring, *Kesselring—A Soldier's Record* (New York, 1954), p. 17; and Görlitz, *General Staff,* p. 296.

100 C-IV, pp. 96-7, 228-9, 837-8; IMT, XV, p. 348; Görlitz, *General Staff,* p. 305; and Keitel, *Keitel,* pp. 36-7.

101 C 7833/20/18 of 19 Nov 1934; C 900/55/18 of 3 Feb 1935; C 3906/55/18 of 21 May 1935; C 6741/55/18 of 26 Sept 1935; C 151/4/18 of 9 Jan 1936; and C-III, pp. 1030-1.

102 DDF, I, pp. 86, 135, 148, 153; and Friedrich Hossbach, *Zwischen Wehrmacht und Hitler, 1934-1938* (Göttingen, 1965), p. 83. See also C 2733/4/18 of 1 April 1936; and C 2823/4/18 of 7 April 1936.

103 C-III, pp. 681, 1040, 1079; C-IV, pp. 9, 79-80, 119-20, 553-4, 558-9, 918; C 3779/55/18 of 30 April 1935; C 6741/55/18 of 26 Sept 1935; C 7984/55/18 of 30 Nov 1935; Erich Kordt, *Nicht aus den Akten* (Stuttgart, 1950), p. 109; USFR, 1935, I, p. 253; C 143/143/18 of 6 Jan 1936; and Eden, *Facing,* pp. 137-8.

104 C-IV, p. 131; C-V, p. 357; Medlicott, *Contemporary England,* p. 339; and Robertson, *Hitler's Plans,* p. 61.

105 C-IV, pp. 128-30.

106 C-IV, pp. 145, 173, 204, 472, 847, 925; C 3985/55/18 of 16 May 1935; and C 5795/55/18 of 30 July 1935.

107 C-IV, pp. 175, 206. See also Richard Freund, *Zero Hour* (London, 1936), pp. 27-8; and A. L. Kennedy, *Britain Faces Germany* (London, 1937), p. 133.

108 The following is based on C-IV, pp. 131, 142, 197-8, 203-6, 464, 492, 847-8; C 3985/55/18 of 16 May 1935; Józef Lipski, *Diplomat in Berlin* (New York, 1968), p. 207; and Gerhard Meinck, *Hitler und die deutsche Aufrüstung, 1933-1937* (Wiesbaden, 1959), p. 147.

109 C-IV, pp. 173-5; and C 4117/55/18 of 21 May 1935.

110 C-IV, pp. 202-6.

111 C-IV, p. 202.

112 C-IV, pp. 351-5, 420-2, 452-3, 455-6. See also C-IV, pp. 246-8; C 4264/55/18 of 21 May 1935; and C 4439/55/18 of 30 May 1935.

113 C-IV, pp. 491-3. See also C-IV, pp. 464, 468.

114 C 7419/6562/62 of 4 Nov. 1935; C 37/4/18 of 31 Dec 1935; C 953/4/18, C 1020/4/18, C 1051/4/18 and C 1109/4/18, all of 14-22 Feb 1936; and André François-Poncet, *The Fateful Years* (London, 1949), pp. 186-8.

115 Meissner, *Staatssekretär,* p. 408.

116 C-IV, pp. 1142-4, 1163-6.

117 For Hitler's ability to bide his time and adapt to circumstances, see Wheeler-Bennett, *Nemesis,* p. 344; Robertson, *Hitler's Plans,* p.

58; W. N. Medlicott, *The Coming of the War in 1939* (London, 1963), p. 11; and C 8198/134/18 of 10 Dec 1935.

118 C 6952/6562/62 of 5 Oct 1935.

119 C 6953/6562/62 and C 6984/6562/62, both of 10 Oct 1935.

120 J 7543/3861/1 of 2 Nov 1935; J 9206/3861/1 of 11 Dec 1935; J 9636/3861/1 of 19 Dec 1935; J 9939/1/1 of 29 Dec 1935; and J 515/15/1 of 10 Jan 1936.

121 C-IV, pp. 998-9; C 7419/6562/62 of 4 Nov 1935; Robertson, *Hitler's Plans*, p. 64; and A. J. Toynbee, *Survey of International Affairs* (London, annually), 1935, II, pp. 257-67 and 1936, pp. 252-3.

122 This paragraph is based on Cmd 5143 of 1936, pp. 85-6; G(36)4 of 2 March 1936; C 3456/G/66 of 17 June 1936; and C-IV, pp. 125-6, 137-8, 198-201, 448, 466-7, 525-7, 708. See also CP 34(35) of 1 Feb 1935; CP 43(35) of 21 Feb 1935; C 1215/55/18 of 14 Feb 1935; and C-IV, p. 488.

123 C-IV, pp. 125-6, 199, 525-7, 973; C 5708/55/18 of 1 Aug 1935; C 223/92/62 of 13 Jan 1936; and DDB, IV, pp. 39-41.

124 C-IV, pp. 914, 919, and C 8266/55/18 of 13 Dec 1935.

125 This paragraph is based on DDF, I, pp. 213, 221-7, 323, 328, 343-4; C-IV, pp. 173, 175, 919; C 902/55/18 of 2 Feb 1935; C 903/55/18 of 4 Feb 1935; C 8364/55/18 of 16 Dec 1935; C 223/92/62, minute by Wigram, 14 Jan 1936; and C 573/92/62 of 27 Jan 1936.

126 This paragraph is based on C 2839/111/18 of 1 April 1935; C 143/143/18 of 6 Jan 1936; G(36)2 of 28 Feb 1936; C-III, pp. 119-22; C-IV, pp. 55-7, 287-91, 963-7, 1010-11; DDF, I, pp. 183-5; Poncet, *Fateful*, p. 197 and *Survenus*, III, p. 767; Friedrich Hossbach, *Die Entwicklung des Oberbefehls über das Heer* (Würzburg, 1957), pp. 107-8 and *Zwischen*, p. 155; Gerhard Ritter, *German Resistance* (New York, 1958), pp. 69-73; Franz von Papen, *Memoirs* (London, 1952), pp. 277-327; Terrence Prittie, *Germans Against Hitler* (London, 1964), pp. 15-178; Admiral Karl Doenitz, *Memoirs* (London, 1959), pp. 304-5; and Hjalmar Schacht, *Account Settled* (London, 1949), pp. 192-3.

127 C 2839/111/18 of 1 April 1935; C 7889/111/18 of 27 Nov 1935; C 8198/134/18 of 10 Dec 1935; C 149/99/18 of 8 Jan 1936; DDF, I, p. 184; G(36)2 of 28 Feb 1936; and the *Economist*, 1 Feb 1936, p. 237.

128 C 7647/55/18 of 13 Nov 1935; and G(36)2 of 28 Feb 1936.

129 G(36)2 of 28 Feb 1936; C 149/99/18 of 8 Jan 1936; *The Times*, 11 Dec 1935, 13 Jan 1936 and 12 Feb 1936.

130 *The Times*, 13, 14 Jan 1936; Henri Lichtenberger, *The Third Reich* (New York, 1937), pp. 225, 229-30; C. W. Guillebaud, *The Economic Recovery of Germany* (London, 1939), pp. 97-8; and C 149/99/18 of 8 Jan 1936.

131 C 143/143/18 of 6 Jan 1936.

132 Ibid. See also C 1703/4/18 and C 1670/4/18, both of 11 March

1936; DDB, IV, p. 126; and USFR, 1936, I, pp. 193-4, 246, 259.

133 Hossbach, *Zwischen,* pp. 45, 63, 66-7, 81, 93-4, 96-7; and *Entwicklung,* p. 115; Erich Raeder, *Mein Leben,* II (Tübingen, 1957), p. 131; Doenitz, *Memoirs,* pp. 304-5; Demeter, *Officer Corps,* pp. 199-201; C 1844/4/18 of 9 April 1936; and Wheeler-Bennett, *Nemesis,* pp. 303, 335, 344.

134 In addition to the preceding citations, see Fritz von Manstein, *Verlorene Siege* (Bonn, 1955), p. 74; Kesselring, *Kesselring,* p. 17; Kordt, *Akten,* p. 126; Görlitz, *General Staff,* p. 296; and C 357/357/18 of 12 Jan 1937.

135 In addition to the preceding citations, see DDF, I, pp. 23-4; and Ian Colvin, *Vansittart in Office* (London, 1965), p. 99.

136 Peter Bor, *Gespräche mit Halder* (Wiesbaden, 1950), p. 113.

137 C-IV, pp. 780, 825-9, 835, 849-51, 859-61, 866-7, 872-4, 925-6.

138 C-IV, pp. 779-80, 825-9, 847-9, 859-61, 866-8, 925-6.

139 C-IV, pp. 745, 914, 917-19; C 6556/55/18 of 18 Sept 1935; C 8198/134/18 of 10 Dec 1935; C 8238/55/18 and C 8266/55/18, both of 13 Dec 1935; and C 8364/55/18 of 16 Dec 1935.

140 C-IV, pp. 209, 230-2, 338-9, 348, 417-19; and C 5333/55/18, minute by Wigram, 12 July 1935.

141 C-IV, pp. 808, 957, 977, 980, 1006, 1013-14, 1075-6, 1126-7; DDF, I, pp. 2, 27, 49, 163-4; C 573/92/62 of 27 Jan 1936; and CP 53(36) of 22 Feb 1936.

142 C-IV, pp. 907, 923, 928, 1044.

143 C-IV, p. 1015.

144 C-IV, pp. 695, 696, 728, 822, 1015, 1016.

145 C-IV, pp. 685, 709, 727, 732, 745, 1015-16; DDF, I, p. 186; C 7818/55/18 of 21 Nov 1935; and C 143/143/18 of 6 Jan 1936.

146 C-III, pp. 300-5; C-IV, pp. 3-5, 102-14, 130, 784, 1004-5, 1015, 1107-10.

147 C-IV, pp. 957, 959-60, 975-6, 978-80, 1004-5, 1013-14, 1035, 1108.

148 C-IV, pp. 1014-16, 1029-30, 1042-4.

149 C-IV, pp. 1014-15.

150 C 8198/134/18 of 10 Dec 1935; and C 143/143/18 of 6 Jan 1936.

2   Anglo-French anticipation, 1935-1936

1 DDF, I, pp. 8, 37-8, 53, 54, 57, 86, 92, 105, 108-9, 118, 134-5, 142; DDB, IV, pp. 46, 59; Dobler, *Survenus,* II, pp. 470-81; C 7752/55/18 of 21 Nov 1935; W 5075/79/98 of 1 Dec 1935; and C 8373/55/18 of 19 Dec 1935.

2 Ibid. See also DDF, I, pp. 152-3, 174-8; C 573/92/62 of 27 Jan 1936; and Pierre Flandin, *Politique Française* (Paris, 1947), pp. 194-5.

3 DDF, I, pp. 34, 74, 110, 153, 245-6; DDB, IV pp. 39-40, 43-4, 48-50, 54, 64, 68; C 223/92/62 and C 302/4/18, both of 14 Jan 1936; C

320/4/18 of 15 Jan 1936; Poncet, *Survenus,* III, p. 765; and C-IV, pp. 1003-5.

4 DDF, I, pp. 40-2, 71-6. See also C-IV, pp. 998-1000.

5 DDF, I, pp. 1-2, 8, 41-2, 71-6, 84-5, 91-2, 110, 141, 153; and DDB, IV, pp. 46, 52, 54-5.

6 In addition to the citations in note 1, see DDF, I, pp. 113, 151, 188, 208, 246, 251-3, 274, 280-1; and Pierre van Zuylen, *Les mains libres* (Paris, 1950), p. 344.

7 DDF, I, pp. 37-8, 52-4, 91; DDB, IV, p. 60; and R. van Overstraeten, *Albert I — Leopold III* (Bruges, 1946), p. 197.

8 DDF, I, pp. 174-6, 201-2, 205-7; C 573/92/62 of 27 Jan 1936; DDB, IV, pp. 64-7, 71-4; Flandin, *Politique Française,* pp. 195-6 and *Survenus,* I, pp. 139-40, 143; and Georges Bonnet, *Quai d'Orsay* (Isle of Man, 1965), p. 133.

9 DDF, I, pp. 2, 27, 163-4; C-IV, pp. 957, 960, 977, 980, 1013-4, 1075-6; C 435/4/18 of 20 Jan 1936; and CP 52(36) of 24 Feb 1936.

10 DDF, I, pp. 1-2.

11 DDF, I, p. 74.

12 C 556/4/18 and C 573/92/62, both of 27 Jan 1936; and Eden, *Facing,* p. 332.

13 DDF, I, pp. 105, 135, 150, 329, 344, 375, 492; and DDB, IV, pp. 49-50, 52, 54, 58, 64-5, 68.

14 C 573/92/62 of 27 Jan 1936; and Jane K. Miller, *Belgian Foreign Policy between the Wars* (New York, 1951), p. 220.

15 DDF, I, pp. 79, 177-8, 195, 208, 211, 246, 251-2, 290, 324, 378.

16 DDF, I, p. 260; and DDB, IV, pp. 85-9.

17 DDF, I, pp. 174, 287-8, 311, 316, 323-4, 328-30, 335, 343-5, 362, 371-2, 383, 399-400, 403, 405, 408, 412, 491-2; DDB, IV, pp. 74-5, 79, 84, 86-9, 110-11, 114, 129; USFR, 1936, I, pp. 200, 203, 206-7; William E. Dodd, *Ambassador Dodd's Diary* (New York, 1941), pp. 315-17, 319; C 798/4/18, C 837/4/18, C 1181/4/18, C 1250/4/18, C 1217/4/18, and C 1263/4/18, all between 10 and 28 Feb 1936.

18 Ibid. See also DDF, I, pp. 260, 334, 362, 381, 394; DDB, IV, pp. 76, 81, 84-5; USFR, 1936, I, p. 215; C 585/4/18 of 22 Jan 1936; C 573/92/62 and C 556/4/18, both of 27 Jan 1936; C 587/92/62 of 29 Jan 1936; and C 1454/4/18 and C 1474/4/18, both of 6 March 1936.

19 C 573/92/62 of 27 Jan 1936.

20 DDF, I, pp. 42, 74-5, 213, 218, 243, 250-1, 260-1, 273, 282, 294, 313, 329, 343, 362, 403.

21 DDF, I, pp. 148, 187, 260, 342-4, 354-5. See also DDB, IV, p. 88.

22 Ibid. See also DDF, I, pp. 98, 261, 300, 375, 384; and DDB, IV, pp. 73, 88.

23 DDF, I, pp. 85-6, 135, 188, 342, 384.

24 DDF, I, pp. 37-8, 53-4, 57, 86, 107, 141-2, 164, 201-2, 221, 246, 251, 323-4, 390; DDB, IV, pp. 51, 55, 59; and Gamelin, *Servir,* II, p. 195.

25 DDF, I, p. 171; and C 1081/4/18 of 20 Feb 1936. See also DDF, I, pp. 150, 188; and Ivone Kirkpatrick, *Inner Circle* (London, 1959), p. 80.
26 C 573/92/62 of 27 Jan 1936; DDF, I, pp. 171, 193, 195, 211, 251, 252, 281-2, 492.
27 C 573/92/62 of 27 Jan 1936; Flandin, *Politique Française,* pp. 194-5 and *Survenus,* I, p. 138; and Eden, *Facing,* pp. 332-3.
28 DDF, I, p. 90. See also Flandin, *Politique Française,* pp. 195-7.
29 See, for example, C 1657/55/18 of 28 Feb 1935; W 1892/10/98 of 2 March 1935; C 2456/55/18 and C 2483/55/18, both of 23 March 1935; and Poncet, *Fateful,* pp. 188-91.
30 C 2481/227/17 of 27 March 1935; C 3080/227/17 of 10 April 1935; C 3723/55/18 of 2 May 1935; C 3907/55/18 of 13 May 1935; and C-IV, pp. 57-8, 96-7, 228-9.
31 C 2144/55/18 of 17 March; and C 2456/55/18 of 23 March 1935.
32 Ibid.; C 2483/55/18 of 22 March; C 2459/55/18 of 23 March; and C 3289/55/18 of 11-14 April 1935.
33 CAB 16 (35) 1 and C 2263/55/18, both of 20 March; C 3289/55/18 of 11-14 April; Robert G. Vansittart, *The Mist Procession* (London, 1958), pp. 518-21; Eden, *Facing,* pp. 177-80; and Flandin, *Politique Française,* pp. 171-2.
34 C-IV, pp. 351-2, 420-2, 452-3, 455-6; and C 4632/55/18 of 10 June 1935.
35 DDF, I, pp. 40-2, 71-6.
36 C 1060/4/18 of 18 Feb 1936. See also C-IV, p. 1143; and *Le Temps,* 14 Feb 1936.
37 CP 166(35) of 9 Aug 1935; CAB 43(35) 1 and 2 of 24 Sept 1935; and Vansittart, *Mist,* pp. 533, 538.
38 C 6950/6562/62 of 24 Sept 1935.
39 C 6952/6562/62 of 5 Oct 1935.
40 Ibid., minutes by Vansittart, Wigram, Sargent and Hoare, 5-15 Oct 1935.
41 C 6952/6562/62, minutes by Wigram, 8 October and Wigram, 9 October.
42 C 7386/6562/62, of 31 Oct 1935. See also C 7211/6562/62, minutes by Wigram, Sargent and Vansittart, all of 19 Oct 1935.
43 C 6952/6562/62, minutes by Vansittart and Hoare, 13 and 15 Oct 1935; C 7110/6562/62, minutes by Sargent and Stanhope, 11 and 16 Oct 1935; and C 7211/6562/62, minute by Vansittart, 19 Oct 1935.
44 C 7110/6562/62, minute of 12 Oct 1935.
45 CAB 47(35)1 of 16 Oct 1935; and Feiling, *Chamberlain,* p. 268.
46 CAB 47(35)1 of 16 Oct 1935.
47 C 6562/6562/62 and C 6563/6562/62, both of 10 Sept 1935.
48 C 7698/55/18 of 15 Nov 1935.
49 C 6693/6562/62 of 26 Sept 1935. See also C 6764/6562/62 of 26 Sept 1935.

50 DDF, I, p. 275. See also Flandin, *Survenus,* I, p. 162.

51 C-IV, pp. 670-1.

52 C 763/4/18 of 7 Feb 1936; DDB, IV, pp. 71-2; and DDF, I, p. 220.

53 *Le Temps,* 8, 14 Feb 1936; DDB, III, p. 460; C 1081/4/18 of 20 Feb 1936; DDB, IV, pp. 85-9; C-IV, p. 1143; and Flandin, *Politique Française,* p. 195 and *Survenus,* I, pp. 139, 143.

54 C 2564/4/18 of 28 March 1936; C 291/4/18, minute by Wigram, 16 Jan 1936; C 1081/4/18 of 20 Feb 1936; and W. F. Knapp, 'The Rhineland Crisis of March 1936', *St Antony's Papers,* no. 5 (London, 1959), pp. 68-9.

55 The following is based on DDF, I, pp. 53, 176, 201-2, 277-8, 292-5, 302; DDB, IV, p. 43; and Poncet, *Fateful,* pp. 188-90 and *Survenus,* III, p. 766.

56 The following is based on DDF, I, pp. 53, 176, 278, 294-5 and II, p. 40; and Poncet, *Fateful,* pp. 188-90 and *Survenus,* III, p. 766.

57 DDF, I, pp. 176, 201-2, 275; C 573/92/62 of 27 Jan 1936; USFR, 1936, I, p. 41; and CAB 11(36) 2 of 26 Feb 1936.

58 DDF, I, p. 293.

59 This was a major reason for her anger over the Anglo-German naval pact of June 1935.

60 DDF, I, p. 334; and C 585/4/18, minute by Stanhope, 28 Feb 1936.

61 DDF, I, pp. 293, 294, 383.

62 DDF, I, pp. 383-4. See also DDF, I, pp. 292-3, 302.

63 DDF, II, p. 40; and Poncet, *Survenus,* III, p. 766 and *Fateful,* pp. 188-90.

64 Ibid. See also DDF, I, pp. 174, 312-13, 319-20; and DDB, IV, pp. 44-5.

65 Ibid. See also DDF, I, pp. 365-6.

66 Ibid. See also DDF, I, pp. 112, 162, 179; and DDB, IV, pp. 72-3.

67 DDF, I, p. 300. See also DDF, I, pp. 260, 344; and C 1405/4/18 of 4 March 1936.

68 DDF, I, p. 300.

69 DDF, I, pp. 112, 151, 162, 175, 239-40, 273-6, 279, 303.

70 DDF, I, pp. 148, 187, 300, 344; C-III, pp. 105, 114-15, 819; C-IV, pp. 173, 199, 202-6, 248, 401, 467, 492, 525-7, 734-5, 999, 1003-4; C 7419/6562/62 of 4 Nov 1935; C 103/92/62 of 6 Jan 1936; C 223/92/62 of 13 Jan 1936; and DDB, IV, pp. 39-40.

71 DDF, I, pp. 207, 220, 247, 277, 291; and DDB, IV, p. 87.

72 DDF, I, pp. 79, 112, 151-2, 169, 175, 207, 220, 247, 277-8, 294, 300, 301, 339; DDB, IV, pp. 65-6, 87-8; and C 1201/4/18 of 26 Feb 1936.

73 C 573/92/62 of 27 Jan 1936; C 763/4/18 of 7 Feb 1936; and DDF, I, pp. 220-1.

74 DDF, I, pp. 151-2, 174-6, 205-7, 220.

75 Ibid.; and DDF, I, pp. 278, 293-4. See also DDB, IV, pp. 64-7.

76 DDF, I, p. 313; *Le Temps,* 14, 16, 19, 20, 21, 23 Feb 1936; *The Times,* 24 Feb 1936; DDB, III, p. 460; and DDB, IV, p. 64.

77 DDF, I, pp. 85-6, 109, 148, 189, 282, 342, 344, 375, 384, 462.

78 DDF, I, pp. 78-9, 151-2, 205-7, 220, 245-7, 277-8, 299-300, 313, 317-18, 339, 397-8.

79 This paragraph is based on DDF, I, pp. 78-9, 175, 206-7, 220, 247, 277-8, 291, 317-18; Flandin, *Survenus*, I, p. 149; Sarraut, *Survenus*, III, p. 574; and Cmd 2525 of 1925.

80 DDF, I, pp. 220, 291; Sarraut, *Survenus*, III, p. 574; and Reynaud, *Thick*, pp. 128-32.

81 See note 71.

82 DDF, I, pp. 207, 220, 278, 291; and Sarraut, *Survenus*, III, p. 574.

83 DDF, I, pp. 90, 220; and DDB, IV, pp. 65, 71-2, 87. See also Flandin, *Politique Française*, p. 198 and *Survenus*, I, p. 144; Maurin, *Survenus*, IV, p. 913; and Poncet, *Fateful*, p. 190.

84 DDF, I, pp. 98, 112, 162, 175, 220, 232-3, 239-40, 242, 273-6, 279, 294, 303-4; and DDB, IV, p. 81.

85 DDB, IV, p. 72. See also DDB, IV, pp. 73, 87; and Flandin, *Survenus*, I, pp. 153, 155 and *Politique Française*, p. 208.

86 DDF, I, p. 112.

87 DDB, III, p. 450 and IV, pp. 67, 69; and DDF, I, p. 242.

88 DDF, I, pp. 112, 162, 239-40, 273-6, 279, 294; DDB, IV, pp. 71-2; and Gamelin, *Survenus*, II, p. 517.

89 DDF, I, pp. 442-3, 484-5, 503; DDB, IV, pp. 65-6, 148, 150-1; C 1734/4/18 of 11 March; C 1989/4/18 of 17 March; and *The Times*, 9 and 12 March 1936.

90 DDF, I, pp. 438, 494, 525; C 1989/4/18 of 17 March; and C 2311/4/18 of 25 March 1936.

91 DDF, I, pp. 278, 299-300, 302.

92 DDF, I, pp. 220, 278, 313, 317-8; and Flandin, *Politique Française*, pp. 96-7.

93 DDF, I, pp. 246-7, 290-3, 300-2; and Flandin, *Politique Française*, pp. 195-6.

94 DDF, I, pp. 246-7, 290-3; and Flandin, *Politique Française*, p. 195 and *Survenus*, I, p. 139.

95 DDF, I, pp. 246-7, 290-3.

96 DDF, I, p. 247.

97 DDF, I, p. 278.

98 DDF, I, pp. 290-3.

99 DDF, I, p. 292.

100 DDF, I, p. 291.

101 DDF, I, p. 301.

102 DDF, I, pp. 317-18.

103 Flandin, *Politique Française*, pp. 196-7 and *Survenus*, I, p. 144.

104 Gamelin, *Servir*, II, pp. 197-8; Flandin, *Politique Française*, p. 198; DDF, I, pp. 291-2, 300-2, 444-5; and Sarraut, *Survenus*, III, p. 645.

105 Pierre Dhers, 'Du 7 mars 1936 à l'Ile d'Yeu,' *Revue d'Histoire de la deuxième guerre mondiale*, January 1952, pp. 19-20; Richard D.

Challener, *The French Theory of the Nation in Arms* (New York, 1952), pp. 216-18; Reynaud, *Thick*, p. 93; Sarraut, *Survenus*, III, p. 645; Knapp, 'Rhineland,' p. 85; USFR, 1936. I, p. 198; and Taylor, *Origins*, p. 59.

106 Sarraut and Louis Maurin, *Survenus*, III, pp. 603, 655; Maurin, *Survenus*, IV, p. 913 and V, pp. 1266-7; and Gamelin, *Survenus*, II, pp. 447-8.

107 C 7394/20/18 of 3 Nov 1934; J 9636/3861/1 of 19 Dec 1935; DDF, I, pp. 696-700 and III, p. 66; Reynaud, *Thick*, pp. 93, 109, 121; Challener, *Nation in Arms*, pp. 216-20, 252, 270-1, 276; Sarraut, *Survenus*, III, pp. 603-4; Flandin, *Politique Française*, pp. 195-6; Paul-Marie de la Gorce, *The French Army* (London, 1961), p. 256; and Pierre Cot, *Triumph of Treason* (Chicago, 1944), p. 185.

108 Ibid. See also Maurin, *Survenus*, IV, p. 912; and Charles A. Micaud, *The French Right and Nazi Germany* (Durham, N C, 1943), p. 77.

109 Paul Reynaud, *Le problème militaire français* (Paris, 1937), p. 27 and *Survenus*, I, p. 95.

110 DDF, I, p. 300.

111 DDF, I, pp. 246-7, 290-3, 299-301, 322-3, 444. See also Knapp, 'Rhineland,' p. 85; Selby C. Davis, *The French War Machine* (London, 1937), pp. 211-12; and John Wheeler-Bennett, *Munich: Prologue to Tragedy* (New York, 1948), p. 253.

112 DDF, I, pp. 246-7, 291-2, 300, 301.

113 DDF, I, p. 300. See also DDF, I, pp. 292, 302.

114 DDF, I, p. 292. For a picture of armament requirements, see DDF, I, pp. 116-24.

115 Flandin, *Politique Française*, p. 196. See also DDF, I, p. 278.

116 DDB, IV, p. 87; and DDF, I, p. 339. See also DDF, I, p. 278.

117 C 2456/55/18 of 23 March 1935. See also DDF, I, pp. 278, 294, 317-18.

118 DDF, I, pp. 151, 278, 294.

119 DDF, I, pp. 260-1, 282, 287-8, 311, 328-30, 341-3, 362, 371, 383-4, 399-400, 403; DDB, IV, pp. 85-9, 110; USFR, 1936, I, pp. 203, 206-7, 215; and C 1181/4/18 of 24 Feb 1936.

120 DDF, I, pp. 322-3, 444; and Gamelin, *Servir*, II, pp. 198-200. See also Reynaud, *Thick*, p. 51; DDF, I, pp. 153-4; Philip C. V. Bankwitz, *Maxime Weygand and Civil-Military Relations in Modern France* (Cambridge, Mass., 1967), pp. 256, 258; and *Le Temps*, and C 1187/4/18, both of 26 Feb 1936.

121 In addition to the citations in note 119, see DDF, I, pp. 323-4, 334-5, 344, 375, 381, 394, 405, 408, 412, 450, 491-2, 668-9; DDB, IV, pp. 76, 79, 81, 109, 114, 129; C 1250/326/18 of 26 Feb 1936; Lipski, *Diplomat*, p. 249; USFR, 1936, I, p. 200; and Dodd, *Diary*, pp. 315-17, 319.

122 DDB, IV p. 72. See also DDF, I, pp. 161-2, 238-40, 242, 273-6, 279,

294, 303; and DDB, IV, pp. 67, 73, 81, 88.

123 DDB, IV, p. 73.

124 *Le Temps,* 8, 14, 16, 17, 20, 21, 23 Feb 1936; and *The Times,* 24 Feb 1936.

125 DDF, I, p. 313; DDB, III, p. 460; C-IV, p. 1143; and *Le Temps,* 14 Feb 1936. See also DDB, IV, pp. 65, 71-2; and DDF, I, p. 318.

126 The following is based on DDF, I, p. 339, DDB, IV, pp. 85-9; Flandin, *Politique Française,* pp. 196-7 and *Survenus,* I, p. 144. See also Gamelin, *Servir,* II, p. 199; and Sarraut, *Survenus,* III, p. 621.

127 DDF, I, p. 339. See also Flandin, *Politique Française,* pp. 196-7 and *Survenus,* I, p. 144; Bonnet, *Quai d'Orsay,* p. 331; and DDB, IV, p. 87.

128 R. A. C. Parker described the decision of 27 February as a 'rehearsal' for 8 March. ('France and the Rhineland Crisis,' *World Politics,* vol. VIII, 1955-6, p. 372).

129 DDB, IV, p. 86.

130 DDB, IV, pp. 86-8; and Gamelin, *Servir,* II, p. 200.

131 DDF, I, p. 339; and C 1201/4/18 of 26 Feb 1936.

132 J 1661/757/1 of 18-20 Feb 1936.

133 J 1939/757/1 and J 1971/757/1, both of 2 March.

134 CP 53(36) of 22 Feb 1936; Eden, *Facing,* pp. 326-7; and DDF, I, pp. 15, 327.

135 DDF, I, pp. 314, 367, 373, 406-8; C-IV, pp. 1121, 1165; Pompeo Aloisi, *Journal* (Paris, 1957), p. 353; DO 6109/22/17 of 29 Feb 1936; and Flandin, *Survenus,* I, p. 145 and *Politique Française,* pp. 188-9.

136 DDF, I, pp. 363, 367; Aloisi, *Journal,* pp. 350-1, 353; Basil H. Liddell-Hart, *Europe in Arms* (London, 1937), pp. 311-12; and *The Times,* 18, 19 Feb 1936.

137 CP 53(36) of 22 Feb 1936; CAB 11(36)5 of 26 Feb 1936; and Eden, *Facing,* p. 326.

138 CAB 8(36)3 of 19 Feb 1936; DO 6109/17/84 of 21 Feb 1936; CP 53(36) of 22 Feb 1936; and CAB 11(36)5 of 26 Feb 1936.

139 CAB 11 (36) 5 of 26 Feb 1936.

140 J 1939/757/1 and J 1971/757/1, both of 2 March; DDF, I, pp. 372-3; Eden, *Facing,* pp. 328-9; and C-V, pp. 7-10.

141 DDF, I, pp. 365-6; and Eden, *Facing,* pp. 328-9.

142 DDF, I, pp. 312-13, 318-19, 337; J 2061/571/1 of 28 Feb 1936; J 1977/587/1 of 2 March; *The Times,* 27, 28 Feb, 5 March 1936; Aloisi, *Journal,* p. 352; and C-IV, pp. 976, 1013, 1035, 1044, 1121, 1173.

143 DDF, I, pp. 26, 163, 318-19, 337, 396-7; J 1971/757/1 of 2 March; C 1390/4/18 and C 1391/4/18, both of 3 March; and J 2045/84/1 of 4 March.

144 DDF, I, pp. 157, 174, 221, 313, 319; Eden, *Facing,* pp. 328-9; J 1939/757/1 and J 1971/757/1, both of 2 March; C 1390/4/18 and C 1391/4/18, both of 3 March; DDB, IV, pp. 44-5; and Aloisi,

Journal, p. 352.

145 C 1391/4/18 of 3 March; and DDF, I, p. 396-8.
146 J 2045/84/1 of 4 March; and DDF, I, p. 398.
147 Eden, *Facing,* p. 328; and CAB 15(36)1 of 5 March.
148 CAB 15(36)1 of 5 March.
149 This paragraph is based on CAB 15(36)1 of 5 March.
150 Ibid.; C 1672/4/18 of 10 March; and LP (L) 4th meeting, 16 March 1936.
151 CP 302(34) of 18 Dec 1934; and CP 6(35) and CAB 2(35)1, both of 9 Jan 1935.
152 CAB 2(35)2 of 14 Jan 1935.
153 *Hansard,* vol. 292, col. 2339; CP 82(34) of 21 March; C 1804/20/18, minute by Wigram, 27 March; CP 104(34) of 9 April; C 3445/3279/4, minute by Wigram, 22 May; CAB 26(34)4 of 27 June; CAB 27(34)4 of 4 July; CP 175(34) of 9 July; CAB 28(34)2 of 11 July; C 5223/3279/4 of 30 July 1934; and C 3456/G/66 of 17 June 1936.
154 W 2991/10/98, minute of 18 March 1935.
155 CAB 2(35)1 of 9 Jan 1935; CAB 3(35)2 of 14 Jan 1935; C 2483/55/18 of 22 March; C 2456/55/18 and C 2459/55/18, both of 23 March; CP 79(35) and C 2928/55/18, both of 5 April; and CAB 30(35)1 of 8 April.
156 C 2459/55/18, minute by Sargent, 26 March; C 3289/55/18 of 11-14 April; and C 3779/55/18 of 30 April 1935.
157 *Hansard,* vol. 308, col. 918.
158 See, for example, C 1657/55/18 of 28 Feb 1935; C 2456/55/18 and C 2459/55/18, both of 23 March 1935; C 6962/6562/62, minutes by Wigram, Sargent and Vansittart, 8-13 Oct 1935; and C 435/4/18 of 20 Jan 1936.
159 C 1804/20/18, minutes by Wigram, Sargent, Vansittart, all of 27 March 1934.
160 C 1145/516/4, minute by Wigram, 13 Feb 1935.
161 C 1149/516/4, minutes by Wigram, 13 Feb 1935 and Vansittart, 14 Feb 1935; C 1464/516/4, minutes by Wigram, 25 Feb 1935 and Vansittart, 28 Feb 1935; and C 2696/55/18 of 14 March 1935.
162 C 1149/516/4, minute of 14 Feb 1935.
163 C 1149/516/4, minute of 13 Feb 1935.
164 CAB 16(35)1 and annex I, both of 20 March 1935; and C 2413/55/18 of 22 March 1935. See also C 1657/55/18 of 28 Feb 1935.
165 C 921/55/18 of 4 Feb 1935; C 1920/55/18 of 7 March 1935; C 1991/55/18 of 11 March; C 1905/55/18, minute by Sargent, 13 March; and C 2717/55/18 of 25 March.
166 CAB 3(35)2 of 14 Jan 1935; C 1149/516/4, minute by Sargent, 14 Feb 1935; and C 1464/516/4, minute by Wigram, 25 Feb 1935.
167 W. N. Medlicott, *Britain and Germany: The Search for Agreement,*

1930-1937 (London, 1969), pp. 9-18; William Strang, *Home and Abroad* (London, 1956) p. 122; E. H. Carr, *International Relations between the Two Wars, 1919-1939* (London, 1947), pp. 220-1; and C 972/55/18 of 1 Feb 1935.

168 CAB 15(35)1 of 18 March; CAB 16(35)1 of 20 March; CP 69(35) of 25-26 March; and C 3779/55/18 of 30 April 1935.

169 See, for example CP 302(34) of 18 Dec 1934; C 921/55/18, minute by Vansittart, 5 Feb 1935; C 3946/55/18, minute by Wigram, 16 May 1935; C 5685/55/18 of 23 July 1935; and C 7752/55/18 of 21 Nov 1935.

170 C 2949/55/18 of 6 April 1935. See also C 2413/55/18 of 22 March; C 3779/55/18 of 30 April; C 3621/55/18 of 2 May; and C 7752/55/18 of 21 Nov 1935.

171 C 1657/55/18 of 28 Feb 1935. The issue was not raised.

172 LNOJ, Special Supplement No. 138, pp. 43-6; C 7752/55/18 of 21 Nov 1935; Eden, *Facing,* pp. 260-3; C-IV, pp. 627, 629-30; G. M. Young, *Stanley Baldwin* (London, 1952), p. 210; and Vansittart, *Mist,* pp. 531-2.

173 C 6693/6562/62 of 26 Sept 1935.

174 C 6952/6562/62, minutes by Wigram, Vansittart and Hoare, 8-15 Oct 1935; C 7752/55/18 and C 7762/55/18, both of 21 Nov 1935; C 8523/55/18 of 22 Nov 1935; and C 8524/55/18 and W 5075/79/98, both of 1 Dec 1935.

175 The following is based on the preceding citations and C 585/4/18 of 22 Jan 1936; CP 13(36) of 17 Jan 1936; and CP 42(36) of 11 Feb 1936.

176 CP 42(36) of 3 Feb 1936.

177 C 7752/55/18 of 21 Nov 1935; W1274/79/98 of 4 Feb 1936; CAB 4(36)1 of 5 Feb 1936; CP 42(36) of 3 and 11 Feb 1936; G(36)1st meeting, 17 Feb 1936; and C 750/4/18 of 24 Feb 1936.

178 CP 39(36) of 10 Feb 1936 (quoting Hitler); and CP 42(36) of 3 Feb 1936.

179 CP 42(36) of 3 Feb 1936; and C 8998/8998/18 of 31 Dec 1936.

180 The following is based on C 7837/6562/62 of 7 Nov 1935; C 7752/-55/18 of 21 Nov 1935; W 5075/79/98 of 1 Dec 1935; C 585/4/18, minutes by Carr, Strang, Vansittart, Stanhope and Cranborne, 30, 31 January, 3, 28 February and 4 March 1936; CP 42(36) of 3 Feb 1936; and C 998/4/18 of 15 Feb 1936.

181 C 585/4/18, minute of 3 Feb 1936.

182 In addition to the citations in note 180, see C 6952/6562/62, minute by Wigram, 8 Oct 1935; C 8523/55/18 of 22 Nov 1935; G(36)1st meeting, 17 Feb 1936; and DDF, I, p. 276.

183 Ibid. See also CP 42(36) of 3 Feb 1936; C 924/4/18, minute by Wigram, 18 Feb 1936; and G(36)6 of 24 Feb 1936.

184 C 3258/55/18 of 8 April 1935; and C 3779/55/18 of 30 April 1935.

185 C 2949/55/18 of 6 April 1935.

186 C 7752/55/18 of 21 Nov 1935; and C 8524/55/18 of 1 Dec 1935.
187 C 8524/55/18 of 1 Dec 1935; C 151/4/18, minute by Wigram, 9 Jan 1936; and C 157/4/18, minute by Wigram, 10 Jan 1936.
188 C 291/4/18, minute by Wigram, 16 Jan 1936.
189 Ibid. See also C 151/4/18, minute by Wigram, 9 Jan 1936; and C 157/4/18, minute by Wigram, 10 Jan 1936.
190 C 4143/55/18 of 23 May 1935.
191 C 3422/55/18 of 25 April 1935; C 5454/55/18 of 9 July 1935; C 4/4/18 of 30 Dec 1935; C 573/92/62 of 27 Jan 1936; and C 1181/4/18 of 24 Feb 1936.
192 C 902/55/18 of 3 Feb 1935; C 921/55/18 of 4 Feb 1935; C 5685/55/18 of 23 July 1935; C 7752/55/18, minute by Sargent and C 7931/55/18, both of 21 Nov 1935; C 8198/134/18 of 10 Dec 1935; C 8329/55/18 of 16 Dec 1935; and C 8373/55/18, minute by Wigram, 21 Dec 1935.
193 G(36)3 of 14 Feb 1936. See also C 291/4/18, minute by Wigram, 16 Jan 1936; C 587/92/62 of 29 Jan 1936; and R 759/125/67, minutes by Carr and Wigram, both of 10 Feb 1936.
194 C 7110/6562/62, minute by Wigram, 10 Oct 1935; and C 7717/33/17, minute by Wigram, 20 Nov 1935.
195 C 7110/6562/62 of 7 Oct 1935; and C 7315/5527/17 of 25 Oct 1935.
196 C 5683/55/18 of 3 July 1935; and C 5685/55/18 of 23 July 1935.
197 C 7211/6562/62, minute of 19 Oct 1935; C 418/4/18 of 20 Jan 1936; and Vansittart, *Mist,* pp. 489, 505.
198 C 3946/55/18, minute by Wigram, 16 May 1935; J 9206/3861/1 of 11 Dec 1935; C 797/172/17 of 8 Feb 1936; CP 42(36) of 3 Feb 1936; and CAB 15(36)1 of 5 March 1936.
199 G(36)3 of 14 Feb 1936; CP 73(36) of 8 March and CAB 16(36)1 of 9 March 1936.
200 G(36)3 of 14 Feb 1936.
201 See, for example C 6562/6562/62 of 10 Sept 1935; C 6952/6562/62 of 5 Oct 1935; and A 1537/4/45 of 21 Feb 1936.
202 C 418/4/18, minute by Vansittart, 20 Jan 1936; C 1010/1/17 of 18 Feb 1936; G(36)2 of 14 Feb 1936; and C 3289/55/18 of 11-14 April 1935.
203 G(36)3 of 14 Feb 1936.
204 C 585/4/18, minutes by Strang, Stanhope and Cranborne, 31 January, 28 February and 4 March 1936; C 979/4/18 of 3 Feb 1936; CP 42(36) of 3 and 11 Feb 1936; and G(36)3 of 14 Feb 1936.
205 Ibid. See also C 151/4/18, minute by Wigram, 9 Jan 1936; C 682/4/18 of 21 Jan 1936; C 998/4/18 of 15 Feb 1936; and C 750/4/18 of 24 Feb 1936.
206 This is based on C 291/4/18, minute by Wigram, 16 Jan 1936; C 573/92/62 of 27 Jan 1936; C 585/4/18, minutes by Stanhope, 28 Feb 1936 and Cranborne, 4 March 1936; CP 42(36) of 3 Feb 1936; C 796/4/18 of 10 Feb 1936; G(36)1st meeting, 17 Feb 1936; A

1537/4/45 of 21 Feb 1936; C 1028/4/18 of 24 Feb 1936; and C 1305/4/18, minute by Wigram, 3 March 1936.

207 See, for example C 585/4/18, minute by Strang, 31 Jan 1936; CP 42(36) of 3 Feb 1936; G(36)3 of 14 Feb 1936; and Medlicott, *Search*, pp. 21-3.

208 C 8373/55/18 of 19 Dec 1935; C 7752/55/18 of 21 Nov 1935; C 807/4/18 of 31 Jan 1936; and CP 42(36) of 3 Feb 1936.

209 C 807/4/18 of 31 Jan 1936; G(36)6 of 27 Feb 1936.

210 For a sample during pre-coup 1936, see C 157/4/18, C 585/4/18, C 573/92/62, C 587/92/62, CP 42(36), C 750/4/18, G(36)3, C 1073/4/18, C 1081/4/18, C 1181/4/18, C 1250/4/18, C 1217/4/18, C 1263/4/18, C 1257/4/18, C 1351/4/18, C 1404/4/18, CAB 15(36)1, C 1454/4/18, C 1457/4/18; and DDB,IV, pp. 55, 76, 82, 89, 110-11, 114.

211 CP 42(36) of 3 Feb 1936.

212 C 8524/55/18 of 1 Dec 1935; C 151/4/18, minute of 10 Jan 1936; C 585/4/18, minute of 3 Feb 1936; and CP 42(36) of 3 Feb 1936.

213 C 62/1/17, minute of 6 Jan 1936; C 157/4/18, minute of 10 Jan 1936; C 291/4/18, minute of 16 Jan 1936; and C 979/4/18 of 3 Feb 1936.

214 C 8267/55/18 of 13 Dec 1935; C 8329/55/18 and C 8329/55/18, minute by Wigram, both of 16 Dec 1935; and C 8373/55/18 of 19 Dec 1935.

215 C 8267/55/18 of 13 Dec 1935; and C 8373/55/18 of 19 Dec 1935.

216 C 62/1/17, minute of 6 Jan 1936; and C 157/4/18, minute of 10 Jan 1936.

217 Ibid.; C 151/4/18, minute of 9 Jan 1936; C 291/4/18, minute of 16 Jan 1936; C 796/4/18 of 10 Feb 1936; and C 750/4/18, minute of 11 Feb 1936.

218 C 8329/55/18, minute of 16 Dec 1935; and C 151/4/18, minute of 9 Jan 1936.

219 C 583/4/18 and C 584/4/18, both of 27 Jan 1936.

220 C 151/4/18 of 9 Jan 1936.

221 CP 13(36) of 9 and 17 Jan 1936; and C 7647/55/18 of 13 Nov 1935.

222 C 291/4/18, minute of 9 Jan 1936; C 682/4/18 of 21 and 23 Jan 1936; and C 998/4/18 of 15 Feb 1936.

223 C 291/4/18, minute of 9 Jan 1936.

224 C-IV, pp. 1089, 1137, 1139.

225 C 4/4/18 of 30 Dec 1935.

226 C 8373/55/18 of 19 Dec 1935. See also C 585/4/18 of 22 Jan 1936.

227 R 1457/341/22 of 4 March. See also C 6741/55/18, C 7005/134/18, C 7752/55/18 of 1935; C 503/4/18, J 872/561/1, C 933/4/18, C 720/4/18, R 681/125/67, C 799/4/18, C 852/4/18 and C 1350/4/18 of 1936.

228 Ibid.

229 C 3289/55/18 of 11-14 April; and C 3779/55/18 of 30 April 1935.

230 D. C. Watt, 'The Anglo-German Naval Agreement of 1935,' *Journal of Modern History,* June 1956, pp. 155-75; G(36)4 of 2 March 1936; C-IV, pp. 1052-9; and C 3456/G/66 of 17 June 1936.

231 C-IV, pp. 1002-4, 1123-6, 1149, 1187-90, 1198-1200, 1209-10, 1214-19, 1221-3; C 8329/55/18 of 8 Jan 1936; and C 248/4/18 and C 249/92/62, both of 14 Jan 1936.

232 C 92/92/62 of 6 Jan 1936; C 8329/55/18 of 8 Jan 1936; J 436/15/1 of 13 Jan 1936; C 249/92/62 and J 681/15/1, both of 14 Jan 1936; C 271/92/62 of 15 Jan 1936; C 556/92/62 of 27 Jan 1936; and C-IV, pp. 972-3, 1003-4.

233 C-IV, pp. 1136-9, 1147-9, 1207-8; C 799/4/18 of 10 Feb 1936; CAB 6(36)3 of 12 Feb 1936; C 850/4/18 of 12 Feb 1936; C 1014/4/18 of 15 Feb 1936; and C 1257/4/18 of 27 Feb 1936.

234 C-IV, pp. 1088-9.

235 *Hansard,* vol. 309, cols. 85-7. See also C 850/4/18, minute by Eden, 13 Feb 1936; and C-IV, p. 1207.

236 C-IV, pp. 1088-9, 1136-8, C 835/4/18 of 4 Feb 1936; and C 850/4/18 of 12 Feb 1936.

237 C-IV, pp. 1147-8, 1208; C 1014/4/18 of 15 Feb 1936; and C 1257/4/18 of 27 Feb 1936.

238 C 979/4/18 of 3 Feb 1936; N 515/187/38, minute by Eden, 6 Feb 1936; CAB 6(36)7 of 12 Feb 1936; CP 32(36) of 11 Feb 1936; C 998/4/18 of 15 Feb 1936; and CAB 11(36)6 of 26 Feb 1936.

239 C-IV, pp. 1141, 1147; C 853/4/18 of 11 Feb 1936; C 850/4/18, minute by Wigram, 12 Feb 1936; and C 998/4/18 of 15 Feb 1936.

240 C-IV, p. 1138; C 850/4/18, minute by Wigram, 12 Feb 1936; and C 998/4/18 of 15 Feb 1936.

241 C 573/92/62 of 27 Jan 1936; A 1537/4/45 of 21 Feb 1936; DDF, I, pp. 168, 295; and C-IV, pp. 1123-6, 1164, 1198-1200, 1209-10, 1214-17.

242 *Hansard,* vol. 308, col. 918.

243 C-IV, pp. 1135-9; C 973/4/18 of 3 Feb 1936; CAB 6(36)2 of 12 Feb 1936; and G(36) 1st meeting, 17 Feb 1936.

244 G(36)2 of 14 Feb 1936.

245 G(36) 1st meeting, 17 Feb 1936.

246 Ibid.; and G(36)3 of 14 Feb 1936.

247 This paragraph is based on G(36) 1st meeting, 17 Feb 1936; C 998/4/18 of 15 Feb 1936; and C 750/4/18 of 24 Feb 1936.

248 C 750/4/18 of 24 Feb 1936. See also notes 180-2.

249 See also CP 42(36) of 3 Feb 1936; and W 1274/79/98 of 4 Feb 1936.

250 G(36)3 of 14 Feb 1936.

251 C 750/4/18 of 24 Feb 1936.

252 Ibid. See also CP 42(36) of 3 and 11 Feb 1936; CAB 4(36)1 of 5 Feb 1936; G(36)3 of 14 Feb 1936; and G(36) 1st meeting, 17 Feb 1936.

253 G(36) 1st meeting, 17 Feb 1936.

254 C 7753/55/18 of 21 Nov 1935; and CP 42(36) of 3 Feb 1936.

255 C 750/4/18 of 24 Feb 1936.

256 C 1181/4/18 of 3 March 1936; and DDB, IV, pp. 76-83.

257 C 1073/4/18 of 19 Feb 1936; and C 1217/4/18 of 27 Feb 1936.

258 C 750/4/18 of 24 Feb 1936.

259 C 998/4/18 of 15 Feb 1936; G(36) 1st meeting, 17 Feb 1936; C 750/
     4/18 of 24 Feb 1936; and C 1257/4/18, minute by Wigram, 28 Feb
     1936.

260 CP 42(36) of 3 Feb 1936; G(36) 1st meeting, 17 Feb 1936; and C
     750/4/18 and C 1028/4/18, memo by Owen St Clair O'Malley,
     both of 24 Feb 1936.

261 See, for example, C 435/4/18 of 20 Jan 1936; C 573/92/62 of 27 Jan
     1936; C 859/4/18 of 12 Feb 1936; and G(36)3 of 14 Feb 1936.

262 C 1/1/17, minutes by Wigram, Sargent, Vansittart and Eden, 1
     and 2 Jan 1936; C 156/4/18, minute by Sargent, 18 Jan 1936; C
     359/1/17, minute by Wigram, 18 Jan 1936; and C-IV, p. 1137.

263 C 656/1/17 of 31 Jan 1936; and C 688/1/17 of 2 Feb 1936.

264 C 573/92/62 of 26 Jan 1936; C 763/4/18 of 7 and 13 Feb 1936; C
     796/4/18 of 10 Feb 1936; and G(36)3 of 14 Feb 1936.

265 Ibid.; and C 151/4/18, minute by Wigram, 9 Jan 1936.

266 C 435/4/18 of 20 Jan 1936; and C 573/92/62 of 27 Jan 1936.

267 Hansard, vol. 308, col. 918; DDB, IV, pp. 72-3; and C 1181/4/18 of
     24 Feb 1936. See also USFR, 1936, I, p. 60; Le Temps, 14, 16, 20, 21,
     and 23 Feb 1936; and C-IV, p. 1140.

268 C 763/4/18 of 13 Feb 1936. See also C 763/4/18 of 7 Feb 1936.

269 G(36)3 of 14 Feb 1936; C 1390/4/18, C 1391/4/18 and C 1485/4/18,
     all of 3 March 1936. See also C 1405/4/18 of 4 March; and CAB
     15(36)1 of 5 March 1936.

270 CAB 3(35)1 of 14 Jan 1935; and G(36)3 of 14 Feb 1936.

271 CAB 15(36)1 of 5 March 1936.

272 Deliberate leakages were at this time considered as part of
     French diplomacy. See C 998/4/18 of 15 Feb 1936; C 750/4/18 and
     C 1028/4/18, both of 24 Feb 1936; and CAB 15(36)1 of 5 March
     1936.

273 This paragraph is based on C 1405/4/18 of 4 March; and CAB
     15(36)1 of 5 March. See also C 1028/4/18 of 24 Feb 1936.

274 The British had made this same point with Paris during their
     efforts in autumn 1935 to secure French support in the Medi-
     terranean crisis.

275 CAB 15(36)1 of 5 March; Eden, Facing, pp. 329, 337-8; and C
     1485/4/18 of 3 March 1936.

276 Ibid.; C 796/4/18 of 10 Feb 1936; and G(36)3 of 14 Feb 1936.

277 CAB 15(36)1 of 5 March. See also C-IV, pp. 914, 919; C 8266/55/18
     of 13 Dec 1935; C 796/4/18 of 10 Feb 1936; and G(36)4 of 2 March
     1936.

278 CAB 15(36)1 of 5 March. See also C-V, pp. 24-6; Eden, Facing, p.
     338; and C 1405/4/18 of 4 March 1936.

279 C 750/4/18 of 24 Feb 1936. The last three of nine reports were submitted on 2 March.

280 CAB 15(36)1 of 5 March 1936. See also C 796/4/18 of 10 Feb 1936.

281 Eden, *Facing*, p. 338; and C 796/4/18 of 10 Feb 1936.

282 C 1450/4/18 of 6 March; and C-V, pp. 24-6. See also C 1537/4/18 of 5 or 6 March; CP 73(36) of 8 March; and Eden, *Facing*, p. 338.

283 For Neurath's reservations about the Rhine coup, see chapter 3.

284 Albert Speer, *Inside the Third Reich* (London, 1971), p. 72; Lossberg, *Wehrmachtführungsstab*, p. 11; Hans Frank, *Im Angesicht des Galgens* (Munich, 1953), p. 211; Kurt von Schuschnigg, *Requiem in Rot-Weiss-Rot* (Zürich, 1946), p. 43; RIIA, Documents, 1937, p. 162; Paul Schmidt, *Statist auf diplomatischer Bühne* (Bonn, 1949), p. 320; Hugh Trevor—Roper, *Hitler's Table Talk* (London, 1953), p. 259; and DBFP, 1938, I, p. 177.

3   Hitler prepares another surprise

1 Hossbach, *Zwischen*, p. 97; C-IV, pp. 1142-4; and Dirk Forster, letter to *Wiener Library Bulletin*, vol. X, nos. 5-6, p. 48.

2 C-IV, pp. 173, 175, 1142, 1166; C 902/55/18 of 2 Feb 1935; C 921/55/18 of 4 Feb 1935; DDF, I, pp. 416-17; Joachim von Ribbentrop, *The Ribbentrop Memoirs* (London, 1954), p. 52; Dodd, *Diary*, p. 351; Max Braubach, 'Der Einmarsch deutscher Truppen in die entmilitarisierte Zone,' *Arbeitsgemeinschaft für Forschung des Landes Nordrhein-Westfalen*, vol. 54 (Köln, 1956), p. 12.

3 C-IV, p. 1142. See also Kurt von Schuschnigg, *The Brutal Takeover* (London, 1969), p. 58.

4 DDF, I, pp. 183-9, 465; G(36)2 of 28 Feb 1936; *Economist*, 1 Feb 1936, p. 237; and *Survey*, 1936, p. 259.

5 FOL 769/270931-47 of 5 and 19 Feb 1936; DDF, I, pp. 86, 177-8, 500-1, 537; C 642/4/18 of 30 Jan 1936; and *The Times*, 11 Jan and 26 Feb 1936.

6 C 414/86/18 of 18 Jan 1936.

7 FOL 769/270934-47 of 5 Feb 1936; CP 268(34) of 11 Oct 1934; C 235/55/18 of 7 Jan 1935; C 476/4/18 of 21 Jan 1936; C 5270/99/18 of 20 July 1936; DDF, I, pp. 177-8; and Dobler, *Survenus*, II, p. 477.

8 FOL 769/270931-47 of 5 and 19 Feb 1936; DDF, I, pp. 86, 135, 177-8, 500-1, 537-8; *The Times*, 11 Jan 1936, 26 Feb and 9 March 1936; Fritz Thyssen, *I Paid Hitler* (London, 1959), p. 173; and Dobler, *Survenus*, II, p. 477.

9 C-IV, pp. 918, 1142; C-V, pp. 12, 23; DDF, I, pp. 86, 148, 152-4, 258-9, 274; USFR, 1936, I, p. 193; C 953/4/18 of 14 Feb 1936; C 1051/4/18 of 18 Feb; R 1983/1162/12 of 3 April; and C 2737/4/18

of 6 April 1936.

10 IMT, XVI, pp. 627-8. Robertson calls the Czech-Soviet agreement of 16 May 1935 the 'key to an understanding of Hitler's real objections' (*Hitler's Plans*, p. 62). See also IMT, X, p. 94; and W. Förster, *Generaloberst Ludwig Beck* (Munich, 1953) p. 57.

11 See, for example, C-IV, pp. 672-3; C 7508/134/18 of 6 Nov 1935; C 7873/227/17 of 26 Nov 1935; C 143/143/18 of 6 Jan 1936; C 895/4/18 of 13 Feb 1936; DDF, I, pp. 117, 122, 505; and USFR, 1936, I, pp. 192, 238.

12 In addition to the previous citations, see DDF, I, p. 90; C 435/4/18 of 20 Jan 1936; C 1167/4/18 of 7 Feb 1936; and CID 1216-B of 4 March 1936.

13 See, especially, Alan S. Milward, *The German Economy at War* (London, 1965), p. 2; Burton Klein, *Germany's Economic Preparedness for War* (Cambridge, Mass., 1959), pp. 16-17; Albert Müller, *Hitler's Stossarmee* (Paris, 1936); and Georges Castellan, *Le réarmament clandestin du Reich, 1930-1935* (Paris, 1954).

14 For a sample, see C 2481/227/17 of 23 March 1935; C 7873/227/17 of 26 Nov 1935; C 895/4/18 of 13 Feb 1936; DDF, I, pp. 117, 122, 505; Gamelin, *Servir,* II, p. 201; and John Erickson, *The Soviet High Command* (London, 1962), p. 404.

15 C-IV, p. 1142.

16 Ibid. See also FOL 7469H/H183728-30 of 20 Jan 1936; FOL 5669H/H015818-23 of 4 Feb 1936; C 7873/227/17 of 26 Nov 1935; and Jane Degras (ed.), *Soviet Documents on Foreign Policy, 1917-1941* (London, 1953), III, p. 125.

17 This paragraph is based on C 143/143/18 of 6 Jan 1936; C 357/357/18 of 12 Jan 1937; DDF, I, pp. 23-4, 183-5; Hossbach, *Zwischen,* pp. 38-9, 81; Poncet, *Fateful,* p. 197; Shirer, *Rise and Fall,* p. 231; Schacht, *Account Settled,* pp. 192-3, 206; and Otto Dietrich, *Zwölf Jahre mit Hitler* (Munich, 1955), p. 44.

18 C 2839/111/18 of 1 April 1935; and C 143/143/18 of 6 Jan 1936. See also E. M. Robertson, 'Zur Wiederbesetzung des Rheinlandes 1936,' *Vierteljahreshefte für Zeitgeschichte,* April 1962, p. 204; and K. H. Abshagen, *Canaris* (London, 1956), p. 107.

19 Hossbach, *Zwischen,* p. 38.

20 DDF, I, pp. 92, 410, 621; C-IV, pp. 173, 175; Dobler, *Survenus,* III, p. 474; DDB, III, p. 450; C 470/4/18 of 20 Jan 1936; and Poncet, *Fateful,* p. 180.

21 See, for example, C 1670/4/18 of 11 March 1936; C 3010/86/18 of 14 April 1936; IMT, XVI, pp. 625, 628; DDF, I, pp. 178, 708; and DDB, IV, p. 201.

22 C 1670/4/18 of 11 March 1936; C-III, pp. 105n, 115, 698; C-V, pp. 12, 417; FOL 7629H/E545268-71 of 16 Jan 1936; DDF, I, pp. 92, 198, 213, 277; DDB, IV, pp. 39-40; and USFR, 1936, I, p. 261.

23 Robertson, *Vierteljahreshefte,* pp. 203-4; USFR, 1936, I, pp. 222-3,

226; C 1619/4/18 of 10 March; C 2733/4/18 of 2 April; C 3238/4/18 of 19 April 1936; and DDF, I, p. 690.

24 C-IV, pp. 1142, 1164; and IMT, XVII, pp. 41-2.

25 C-IV, pp. 957, 960, 977, 980, 1013-14, 1017, 1075-6, 1142-3, 1163-5; DDF, I. pp. 2, 27, 163-4, 418, 464; C 470/4/18 of 20 Jan 1936; USFR, 1936, I, p. 206; Lipski, *Diplomat,* p. 251; and Poncet, *Fateful,* p. 193.

26 C-IV, *passim,* but especially, pp. 533, 685, 696, 727-8, 732, 734, 745-6, 784-5, 795, 797n-9, 817-19, 822-4, 958-9, 975, 1015; and C-V, pp. 15, 48-9.

27 C-IV, pp. 1034, 1044, 1073, 1143-4.

28 C-IV, pp. 907, 916, 921-4, 1064; C-V, p. 423; DDF, I, p. 464; C 235/1/17 of 13 Jan 1936; and Eden, *Facing,* pp. 316-17, 336, 353.

29 C-IV, pp. 735-6; C-V, p. 57; CAB 47(35)1 of 16 Oct 1935; CAB 56(35) of 18 Dec 1935; Samuel Hoare, *Nine Troubled Years* (London, 1954), p. 191; Feiling, *Chamberlain,* pp. 268, 271; and Flandin, *Politique Française,* p. 187.

30 Ibid. See also DDF, I, pp. 112, 162, 232-3, 275-6, 279, 303-4; DDB, IV, pp. 67, 69, 71-3, 81; and C 223/92/62 of 14 Jan 1936.

31 C-IV, p. 1142. See also C-V, pp. 297-301; and DDF, I, p. 463.

32 C-IV, pp. 745, 914, 917-19; C-V, p. 57; C 1905/4/18 of 8 March; C 1595/4/18 of 9 March; DDF, I, p. 164; USFR, 1936, I, pp. 241-2; Leopold S. Amery, *My Political Life,* III (London, 1955), pp. 188-9; and F. S. Northedge, *The Troubled Giant* (London, 1966), p. 426.

33 C-IV, p. 131; C-V, pp. 12, 15-17; Robertson, *Hitler's Plans,* p. 60; Lipski, *Diplomat,* p. 207; Kordt, *Akten,* p. 130; Meinck, *Aufrüstung,* p. 147; IMT, XVII, p. 124; and DDB, IV, p. 201.

34 C-IV, pp. 1142, 1165; and Robertson, *Vierteljahreshefte,* p. 204.

35 For German arguments against staff talks, see C-IV, pp. 959, 1005; DDF, I, pp. 16-17, 24-5, 31-4, 41, 72, 84-5, 111-12, 141, 148, 230, 274; DDB, IV, pp. 37, 52; C 103/92/62 of 6 Jan 1936; C 151/4/18 of 9 Jan; C 223/92/62 of 13 Jan; and C 250/92/62 and C 256/92/62, both of 14 Jan 1936.

36 C-IV, p. 1142.

37 See, for example, C-IV, pp. 533, 628, 685, 918-19, 958, 974, 1024, 1063-5, 1069, 1071, 1142; C-V, pp. 79, 159, 184; Kordt, *Akten,* p. 128; IMT, XVI, p. 626; XIX, p. 273; W 3359/403/36 of 7 April 1936; and N 2767/1091/42 of 8 May 1936.

38 See, for example, USFR, 1936, I, p. 268.

39 Forster, *Bulletin,* p. 48.

40 C-V, pp. 5-6, 14-15, 47-8, 136-40; G(36)3 of 14 Feb 1936; CP 73(36) of 8 March; Joseph Paul-Boncour, *Entre deux guerres,* III (Paris, 1946), p. 32; and Eden, *Facing,* p. 353.

41 C-V, p. 424. See also C-IV, pp. 1112-13, 1143; FOL 5669H/ H015800-2 of 17 Jan 1936; FOL 7881H/E570767-70 of 4 Feb 1936; FOL 5669H/H015881-5 of 28 Feb 1936; and Lipski, *Diplomat,* p.

253.

42 C-IV, p. 1143; DDF, I, pp. 42, 173, 339-40, 371; DDB, IV, pp. 83-5, 89; FOL 6710/E506192-4 of 21 Feb 1936; and *The Times,* 13 Feb 1936.

43 C-IV, pp. 1142, 1164; and Forster, *Bulletin,* p. 48.

44 Ibid. See also FOL 7881H/E570820-2 of 1 Feb 1936; FOL 6710/E506192-4 of 21 Feb 1936; C-IV, pp. 1034, 1044, 1112, 1113n; DDF, I, p. 463; DDB, IV, pp. 69, 73; and Count Jean Szembek, *Journal, 1933-1939* (Paris, 1952), p. 156.

45 C-IV, p. 1142; C-V, pp. 422-4; and Forster, *Bulletin,* p. 48. See also C-IV, pp. 824, 829, 851, 916-17, 926; DDF, I, p. 160; FOL 5669H/H015818-23 of 4 Feb 1936; Vladimir Potiemkine (ed.), *Histoire de la Diplomatie,* III (Paris, 1947), pp. 570-1; and Micaud, *French Right,* pp. 74-84, 99-100.

46 C-IV, p. 1142; C-V, p. 424; USFR, 1936, I, p. 187; Poncet, *Fateful,* p. 193; Reynaud, *Thick,* p. 119; *Le Temps,* 25 Jan 1936; C 688/1/17 of 2 Feb; C 1010/1/17 of 18 Feb 1936; and Micaud, *French Right,* p. 119.

47 *Le Temps,* 14, 15 Feb 1936; Georges Lefranc, *Le Mouvement socialiste sous la IIIe République* (Paris, 1963), pp. 319-20; Joel G. Colton, *Léon Blum* (New York, 1966), pp. 115-22; Blum, *Survenus,* I, p. 126; and Micaud, *French Right,* pp. 80-1, 99-101.

48 C 1010/1/17 of 18 Feb 1936; and Lefranc, *Mouvement socialiste,* p. 320.

49 Ibid.; Colton, *Blum,* pp. 116-17; Pierre Maillaud, *France* (London, 1942) pp. 86-90; and J. P. T. Bury, *France 1814-1940* (London, 1962), pp. 274-6.

50 Forster, *Bulletin,* p. 48. Forster dated this meeting 12 February, but this may be a week too early, since Blomberg, whom he listed as a participant, was in Garmisch on that day.

51 C-IV, pp. 851, 859, 1034, 1142. See also Micaud, *French Right,* pp. 87-101; and Geneviève R. Tabouis, *Blackmail or War* (London, 1938), pp. 119-20.

52 C-IV, pp. 916-17. Köster died in Paris on 31 Dec 1935, leaving Forster as the chief of mission until 22 April 1936.

53 C-IV, p. 926.

54 For the ratification debate, see *The Times* and *Le Temps,* 11-29 Feb 1936; Micaud, *French Right,* pp. 69-84; Scott, *Alliance,* pp. 264-5; Werth, *Twilight,* pp. 66-8; and C 839, C 887, C 999, C 1076, C 1182, C 1197 and C 1200/4/18, all between 11 and 26 Feb 1936.

55 *Le Temps,* 20 Feb 1936; and Jacques Benoist-Mechin, *Histoire de l'armée allemande depuis l'armistice,* III (Paris, 1938), p. 641.

56 Micaud, *French Right,* p. 78.

57 Reynaud, *Thick,* p. 123.

58 Micaud, *French Right,* p. 78.

59 Micaud, *French Right,* pp. 70-1, 74, 78, 84.

60 FOL 5669H/H015818-23 of 4 Feb 1936. See also C-IV, pp. 851, 859, 916, 926, 1034, 1044, 1164; and Pierre Lazareff, *Dernière édition* (Montreal, 1942), p. 301.
61 Micaud, *French Right*, pp. 77-8.
62 C-IV, pp. 1142.
63 Dodd, *Diary*, p. 314.
64 C-IV, p. 1142. See also C-IV, pp. 20, 822, 1011, 1025, 1065-6, 1071, 1140; Gustav Hilger and Alfred G. Meyer, *The Incompatible Allies* (New York, 1953), pp. 277, 283-4; Max Beloff, *The Foreign Policy of Soviet Russia, 1929-1941* (London, 1949), II, p. 50; and USFR, *Soviet Union*, pp. 285-6.
65 C-IV, pp. 1142, 1164.
66 C-IV, pp. 923-4, 1112, 1142, 1165; FOL 7881H/E570820-2 of 1, 28 Feb 1936; FOL 5669H/H015818-23 of 4 Feb; FOL 7881H/E570773 of 6 Feb; FOL 7469H/H183740-5 of 17 Feb; and FOL 6710/ E506192-4 of 21 Feb 1936.
67 C-IV, pp. 1142, 1164; and IMT,XVII, pp. 41-2.
68 C-IV, pp. 670-1, 674-5, 682-3, 706-7, 734, 807, 904-8, 921-4, 1017, 1024, 1040, 1062-8, 1071-2, 1089, 1142, 1147-9; and C-V, pp. 106, 120, 194.
69 C-IV, p. 1142.
70 Cmd 4827 of 1 March 1935. For other examples of Germany's knowledge of British military weakness, see FOL 7469H/ H183728-30 of 20 Jan 1936; and FOL 7469H/H183758-9 of 29 Feb 1936.
71 C-IV, p. 918.
72 *Daily Mail*, 24 Jan 1936; *Morning Post*, 16 Jan and 3 Feb 1936; *Manchester Guardian*, 17 Feb 1936. See also Thomas Jones, *A Diary with Letters* (London, 1954), p. 160; and Vansittart, *Mist*, p. 543.
73 *Morning Post*, 16-18 Jan 1936; FOL 7469H/H183728-36 of 16-18 Jan 1936; and C 416/92/62 of 20 Jan 1936.
74 C-IV, pp. 923, 1065.
75 C-IV, pp. 923-4, 1064, 1142; *Hansard*, vol. 308, cols. 1360-2; FOL 7469H/H183740-5 of 17 Feb; FOL 6710/E506192-4 of 21 Feb 1936; and Ivone Kirkpatrick, *Mussolini* (London, 1964), p. 316.
76 C-IV, pp. 1024, 1062-4; FOL 7881H/E570820-2 of 1 and 28 Feb 1936; Lord Londonderry, *Ourselves and Germany* (London, 1938), pp. 86, 104-5; USFR, 1936. I, p. 188; Ribbentrop, *Ribbentrop*, p. 52; Michael Astor, *Tribal Feeling* (London, 1963), p. 145; and DDF, I, pp. 303-4.
77 C-IV, pp. 1061-72.
78 C-IV, p. 1040.
79 C-IV, pp. 972-3, 1003-4, 1136-9, 1142, 1148-9, 1207-8.
80 C-IV, pp. 1135-9, 1147-9, 1164, 1207-8.
81 *Hansard*, vol. 308, col. 918; and C-IV, pp. 1120, 1140, 1143, 1166.
82 FOL 7881H/E570820-2 of 28 Feb 1936.

83 Ibid. See also *Sunday Referee,* 16 Feb 1936; DDF, I, pp. 198, 213, 273, 303-4; DDB, IV, p. 73; Londonderry, *Ourselves,* pp. 82-110; C 969/4/18 of 11 Feb 1936; and C 1814/4/18 of 9 March 1936.

84 C-IV, pp. 923-4, 1017, 1142; C-V, pp. 239, 293-4; FOL 7469H/ H183740-5 of 17 Feb 1936; FOL 6710/E506192-4 of 21 Feb 1936; DDB, IV, p. 73; DDF, I, pp. 213, 277; *Le Temps,* 17 Feb 1936; and Ribbentrop, *Ribbentrop,* p. 52.

85 Hossbach, *Zwischen,* p. 97; IMT, IX, p. 505; Braubach, *Einmarsch,* pp. 12-14; Londonderry, *Ourselves,* p. 114; and O'Neill, *German Army,* p. 182.

86 Ribbentrop's clumsy flattery of Hitler made 'einen fatalen Eindruck' on Hassell. (Robertson, *Vierteljahreshefte,* p. 203).

87 C 1396/4/18 of 4 March 1936; C 1483/4/18 of 7 March; R 1371/ 1162/12 of 8 March; C 1619/4/18 and C 1672/4/18, both of 10 March; DDF, I, pp. 762-3; II, p. 88; USFR, 1936, I, p. 236; and Speer, *Inside,* pp. 35, 122.

88 C-IV, p. 1142; and Robertson, *Vierteljahreshefte,* p. 204.

89 Robertson, *Vierteljahreshefte,* p. 204.

90 Braubach, *Einmarsch,* p. 13.

91 See, for example, Forster, *Bulletin,* p. 48; Robertson, *Vierteljahreshefte,* pp. 203-4; C-IV, pp. 1142-4, 1164-6; and Hossbach, *Zwischen,* pp. 30-1.

92 Hossbach, *Zwischen,* p. 97; and C-IV, p. 1142.

93 Hossbach, *Zwischen,* p. 97.

94 Ibid.; and DDF, I, p. 298. See also Robertson, *Vierteljahreshefte,* p. 203.

95 Hassell had the impression Hitler was over 50 per cent decided by the time they spoke in Munich on 14 February. (Robertson, *Vierteljahreshefte,* p. 203).

96 C-IV, p. 1164; and IMT, XVII, pp. 41-2. See also Forster, *Bulletin,* p. 48; Robertson, *Vierteljahreshefte,* pp. 203-4; and C-IV, pp. 1142-4.

97 IMT, XVI, p. 625; DDB, IV, p. 201; C-IV, pp. 1164-6; C-V, pp. 12, 15-17; and Robertson, *Vierteljahreshefte,* p. 204.

98 C-V, pp. 13, 56-8, 68; DDF, I, pp. 384, 411; DDB, IV, pp. 201, 320-1; USFR, 1936, I, p. 269; and C 1610/4/18 of 10 March.

99 DDF, I, p. 411; C 1605/4/18 of 9 March; and C 2607/86/18 of 31 March 1936.

100 C-IV, p. 1164. See also Robertson, *Vierteljahreshefte,* pp. 203-4.

101 Neurath testified at Nuremberg that he merely described the situation as he saw it. He also described the act itself as a dynamic development. (IMT, XVII, pp. 41-2).

102 C-IV, pp. 1164-6; and Robertson, *Vierteljahreshefte,* p. 204.

103 C-IV, p. 1166.

104 C-IV, p. 1164; and Robertson, *Vierteljahreshefte,* p. 204.

105 Robertson, *Vierteljahreshefte,* p. 204. See also Schwerin von

Krosigk, *Es geschah in Deutschland* (Tübingen, 1951), p. 311.
106 Forster, *Bulletin,* p. 48. Forster said that Hitler grew steadily more sarcastic when the chargé d'affaires urged negotiations.
107 Hitler was not known to favour those who argued against him. (Dietrich, *Zwölf Jahre,* p. 45; Hossbach, *Zwischen,* pp. 30-1; and Rudolf Rahn, *Ruheloses Leben* (Düsseldorf, 1950), pp. 83-4).
108 See, for example, DDF, I, pp. 632-3; *The Times,* 14 March and 23 April 1936; C 1831/4/18 of 9 March; C 1939/4/18 of 14 March; C 2029/4/18 of 18 March; and C 4806/4/18 of 2 July 1936.
109 C-IV, p. 1143.
110 C-IV, pp. 1143-4, 1165-6.
111 C-IV, pp. 1165-6, 1170-1; and R 1092/230/22 of 22 Feb 1936.
112 C-IV, pp. 1142-3.
113 C-IV, pp. 1142, 1144.
114 C-IV, p. 1144.
115 C-IV, pp. 1142-4; Hossbach, *Zwischen,* p. 97; and Robertson, *Vierteljahreshefte,* pp. 202-3.
116 C-IV, pp. 1143-4, 1164-5.
117 C-IV, pp. 1164-5.
118 Hossbach, *Zwischen,* p. 97.
119 C-IV, pp. 1159-62, 1163n, 1164; FOL M281/M011520 of 19 Feb 1936; and Robertson, *Vierteljahreshefte,* p. 203.
120 C-IV, pp. 1143, 1160-2.
121 C-IV, pp. 927-8, 958, 977, 983, 1034-5, 1143, 1160-3, 1166, 1213; C-V, pp. 71-2, 472; and Jürgen Gehl, *Austria, Germany and Anschluss, 1931-1938* (London, 1963), p. 123.
122 Ibid. See also R 1724/458/22 of 21 March 1936; and R 3151/241/22 of 9 June 1936.
123 C-IV, pp. 1143, 1159-73; R 1088/1088/22 of 22 Feb 1936; and R 3171/3171/22 of 3 May 1937.
124 C-IV, pp. 1160, 1163-4, 1166, 1171-3; and FOL 3175H/D682458 of 14 Feb 1936.
125 See, for example, C-IV, pp. 697, 958, 978-80, 1004, 1013, 1014-16, 1027, 1029-30, 1140, 1143, 1166, 1175; R 1457/341/22 of 4 March 1936; and Dodd, *Diary,* p. 331.
126 C-IV, pp. 1143-4.
127 C-IV, pp. 1164-5, 1170-5.
128 C-IV, p. 1164.
129 C-IV, pp. 1173-5.
130 C-IV, p. 1175.
131 C-IV, pp. 1166, 1173-5.
132 C-V, pp. 36-8, 51-2, 71-2. See also Hubert Lagardelle, *Mission à Rome* (Paris, 1955), p. 229; USFR, 1936, I, p. 208; and DDF, I, pp. 464, 484.
133 C 1332/4/18 of 27 Feb 1936.
134 C-IV, pp. 1202-4.

135 C-IV, pp. 1204, 1211-14, 1220; and C-V, p. 21.
136 Suvich, who made six changes to suit Hassell, claimed that Mussolini had instructed him to draft the memorandum on the basis of a four-word explanation. (C-IV, pp. 1202, 1212).
137 C-IV, pp. 1219-20; and C-V, pp. 20-1.
138 See, for example, C-III, pp. 926, 1109; C-IV, p. 1015; and C-V, p. 423.
139 C-IV, p. 1015.
140 Joseph Beck, *Final Report* (New York, 1957), pp. 254-5, 261; C-V, p. 366; DDF, I, pp. 152-4, 356, 376-7 and II, pp. 35-6, 121; Szembek, *Journal,* pp. 117-18; Léon Noël, *L'agression allemande contre la Pologne* (Paris, 1946), pp. 88-9; C 995/4/18 of 15 Feb 1936; Beloff, *Soviet Policy,* I. p. 157; and Gotthold Rhode, 'Aussenminister Josef Beck und Staatssekretär Graf Szembek,' *Vierteljahreshefte für Zeitgeschichte,* January 1954, p. 93.
141 C 810/33/55 of 4 Feb 1936; C 1162/33/55 of 1 Feb; C 3365/33/55 of 24 April; and C 3649/33/55 of 13 May 1936.
142 Ibid. See also C-III, docs. 244, 248, 308, 391, 485, 500; C-IV, docs. 4, 80, 86, 97, 150, 442, 443, 454, 499, 546; C 341/341/44 of 1 Jan 1937; and C 357/357/18 of 12 Jan 1937.
143 C-IV, pp. 815-16, 868, 901-2, 929, 935, 1037, 1049-51, 1087, 1117, 1146-7; C-V, p. 90n; DDF, I, pp. 214, 254, 336; and Szembek, *Journal,* pp. 123-4, 140-1, 148, 155, 159.
144 *Central European Observer,* 7 Feb 1936, p. 34; and Robert Machray, *The Poland of Pilsudski* (London, 1936), p. 439. See also C-IV, pp. 457-8, 1201.
145 C-IV, p. 1201; and DDF, I, pp. 315-16.
146 C-IV, p. 1147n. See also C-IV, pp. 930, 1037, 1049-51, 1146-7; and Szembek, *Journal,* pp. 154-5.
147 C-IV, p. 1201.
148 Szembek, *Journal,* p. 161; and Polish White Book, p. 31.
149 C-IV, p. 1201; Szembek, *Journal,* p. 443; and C 1600/4/18 of 9 March 1936.
150 C-IV, p. 1202,; and Szembek, *Journal,* pp. 152-3.
151 See, for example, C-IV, pp. 1201-2; *The Times,* 25 Feb 1936; C 1600/4/18 of 9 March; C 5268/49/55 of 15 July 1936; and Machray, *Poland,* p. 443.
152 C-IV, pp. 1186-90, 1209-10.
153 C-IV, pp. 917-18, 979, 1002-4, 1008, 1038-40, 1198; C 573/92/62 of 27 Jan 1936; CAB 3(36)4 of 29 Jan 1936; C 657/4/18 of 3 Feb 1936; CAB 4(36)3 of 5 Feb 1936; A 1537/4/45 of 21 Feb 1936; G(36)9 of 2 March 1936 and USFR, 1936, I, pp. 58-60.
154 C-IV, pp. 1209-10, 1217-18.
155 C-IV, pp. 1187-90, 1198-1200, 1209-10, 1214-18; C-V, pp. 22, 28-9, 41-2, 73-5.
156 C-V, pp. 9, 24, 74-5, 188-90; and CAB 20(36)5 of 16 March 1936.

157 C-V, p. 9.
158 C-IV, pp. 1207-8; C 1257/4/18 of 27 Feb 1936; C 1286/4/18 of 28 Feb 1936; and DDF, I, p. 359.
159 C-IV, p. 1186.
160 See, for example C-IV, pp. 1164-6; and Robertson, *Vierteljahreshefte*, p. 204.
161 C-IV, pp. 1207-8; and C 1257/4/18 of 27 Feb 1936.
162 C-IV, p. 1164.
163 C-IV, pp. 1207-8. See also C-V, pp. 9, 24-6; and CAB 15(36)1 of 5 March.
164 CP 73(36) of 8 March; and CAB 16(36)1 of 9 March.
165 C-IV, p. 1208.
166 C-V, pp. 24-6; and C 1450/4/18 of 6 March. Hitler had consistently rejected French demands that an air pact be accompanied by limitation, arguing that only Berlin could judge German requirements.
167 C 968/4/18 of 11 Feb 1936; DDF, I, pp. 190-1; and Aloisi, *Journal*, pp. 350-3.
168 C-IV, pp. 131, 142, 145, 173, 197-8, 203-6, 464, 472, 492, 847-8, 925, 1142; Ribbentrop, *Ribbentrop*, p. 52; Meinck, *Aufrüstung*, pp. 147-8; Robertson, *Hitler's Plans*, pp. 60-2; Kordt, *Akten*, p. 130; Meissner, *Staatssekretär*, p. 408; and C 3527/55/18, minute by Sargent, 1 May 1935.
169 C-IV, pp. 131, 202-6, 491-2; and DDF, I, pp. 656, 690.
170 DDF, I, pp. 153, 229-30, 256-9, 267, 281, 286-7, 304, 341; and C 953/4/18, C 1020/4/18, C 1051/4/18, C 1123/4/18, all between 14 and 22 Feb 1936.
171 DDF, I, pp. 322-5, 444; C 1182/4/18 of 25 Feb 1936; C 1197/4/18 and *The Times*, both of 26 Feb 1936; and Gamelin, *Servir*, II, p. 200.
172 DDF, I, pp. 328-9, 343-4, 371, 383-4, 395, 397-8, 403; and C 1263/-4/18 of 28 Feb 1936.
173 C 799/4/18 of 10 Feb 1936; C 852/4/18 and C 853/4/18, both of 11 Feb; C 1193/4/18 of 26 Feb; C 1408/4/18 of 3 March; C 1538/4/18 of 9 March; DDF, I, pp. 264, 267; DDB, IV, p. 37; and *The Times*, 5, 12, 22 Feb 1936.
174 DDF, I, pp. 288, 306, 333, 341; and C 1236/4/18 of 26 Feb 1936.
175 DDF, I, pp. 250-1, 305-7.
176 Ibid. See also C 953/4/18 of 14 Feb 1936; C 1020/4/18 of 17 Feb 1936; and *Le Temps*, 15 Feb 1936.
177 C 1051/4/18 of 18 Feb 1936; C 1236/4/18 of 22 Feb 1936; C 1295/-4/18 of 28 Feb 1936; DDF, I, pp. 285-7, 322-5, 333, 341; and *Le Temps*, 19, 21, 27, 28 Feb 1936.
178 DDF, I, pp. 288, 306, 333, 341; and C 1236/4/18 of 26 Feb 1936.
179 DDF, I, p. 359; and C 1286/4/18 of 28 Feb 1936.
180 *The Times*, 29 Feb 1936; *New York Times*, 1 March 1936; and DDF,

I, pp. 324-5, 333, 341, 375.

181 DDF, I, pp. 329, 334-5, 341, 343-4, 359, 362, 381, 394, 400; DDB, IV, pp. 75-6, 79, 81, 84-6, 88-9, 110-11, 114; Lipski, *Diplomat*, p. 249; and C 1454/4/18, and C 1474/4/18, both of 6 March.

182 C 1267/4/18 of 28 Feb 1936. See also Otto Abetz, *Das offene Problem* (Cologne, 1951), pp. 78-9; Meissner, *Staatssekretär*, p. 409; Meinck, *Aufrüstung*, p. 157; and IMT, XVI, p. 626.

183 See citations in note 182.

184 Micaud, *French Right*, p. 75n; C 1305/4/18 of 2 March; FOL 5669H/H015903-17 of 29 Feb 1936; *The Times*, 2 March; and *Le Temps*, 1 and 3 March.

185 Werth, *Twilight*, p. 69; FOL 5669H/H015928 of 3 March; *The Times*, 4 March; DDF, I, p. 361; and C-V, p. 9.

186 Abetz, *Problem*, pp. 78-9; Lazareff, *Dernière édition*, pp. 273-4; DDF, I, p. 386; Reynaud, *La France*, I, p. 121 and *Survenus*, I, p. 90; C-V, p. 17; and Norman H. Baynes (ed.), *The Speeches of Adolf Hitler*, II (London, 1942), pp. 1266-71.

187 C-IV, p. 1165, 1184-5; and C-V, pp. 12-15, 18, 72.

188 C-IV, pp. 1142-4; and Forster, *Bulletin*, p. 48.

189 C-IV, pp. 1135-9, 1143, 1186; and Forster, *Bulletin*, p. 48.

190 C-IV, p. 1165; and C-V, pp. 12, 14. See also USFR, 1936, I, pp. 215, 223; *The Times, The History of the Times*, IV, 2 (London, 1952), p. 900; Eden, *Facing*, p. 340; Kordt, *Akten*, p. 130; DDB, IV, p. 202; Meissner, *Staatssekretär*, p. 411; and *Survey*, 1936, p. 277.

191 C-V, pp. 14-15. Eden said almost the same thing in his appreciation of the situation on 8 March. (CP 73(36) of 8 March).

192 See, for example C 1486/4/18, C 1487/4/18 and C 1488/4/18, all of 7 March 1936; and DDB, IV, pp. 98, 103.

193 C-V, pp. 18, 23.

194 Londonderry, *Ourselves*, pp. 86-7; C-V, pp. 69, 105-6; DDF, I, pp. 416-17; and CP 73(36) and C 1533/4/18, both of 8 March 1936.

195 C-V, pp. 12, 18, 23. See also: FOL 63/43630-31 of 6 March.

196 See, for example, C 803/55/18 of 3 Feb 1935; C-IV, pp. 1052-9; CP 73(36) of 8 March; and Dodd, *Diary*, p. 319.

197 C-II, p. 1; C-IV, pp. 172, 176; and C-V, pp. 18-19, 78-9.

198 C-V, pp. 12, 19.

199 Ribbentrop, *Ribbentrop*, p. 53. See also Kordt, *Akten*, pp. 130-1.

200 C-V, pp. 12-13. The Versailles treaty had internationalized all Germany's major waterways and divested her of all colonies.

201 C-V, p. 19.

202 C-V, pp. 15, 19, 37, 48, 55-6; and DDF, I, p. 515.

203 C-IV, p. 1165.

204 Ribbentrop, *Ribbentrop*, p. 53.

205 Neurath told Dodd on 29 February that the idea was under discussion. (Dodd, *Diary*, pp. 315-16; and DDF, I, pp. 403-4).

206 DDF, I, p. 400; *The Times*, 5 and 9 March; DDB, IV, p. 202; FOL

8604H/E603809-10 of 29 Feb 1936; and C 3144/86/18 of 15 April 1936.

207 Robertson, *Vierteljahreshefte*, p. 205.

208 C-V, pp. 13-14.

209 C-V, pp. 14-15.

210 Robertson, *Vierteljahreshefte*, p. 203.

211 See, for example, C 1657/4/18, C 1765/4/18, C 1792/4/18, C 1884/4/18, C 1983/4/18, C 2051/4/18, C 2075/4/18, C 2175/4/18, C 2248/4/18, C 2276/4/18, C 2277/4/18, C 2346/4/18 and C 2604/-4/18, all between 11 and 31 March; *The Times*, 13-26 March; DDF, I, p. 708; and USFR, 1936, I, p. 271.

212 Robertson, *Vierteljahreshefte*, pp. 203-4.

213 In addition to the citations in note 211, see C 1737/4/18 of 12 March; C 2015/4/18 of 17 March; C 2186/4/18 of 21 March; C 2208/4/18 of 23 March; C-V, pp. 286-7; and RIIA, *Survey*, 1936, p. 285.

214 Such non-physical solutions were widely discussed before 7 March. See DDF, I, pp. 54, 75, 79, 91, 105, 136-8, 175, 207, 232, 246-7, 277, 299; DDB, IV, pp. 60, 64-6, 88; C 796/4/18 of 10 Feb 1936; G(36)3 of 14 Feb 1936, and C 1405/4/18 of 4 March 1936.

215 See, for example, DDF, I, pp. 107-8, 177-8, 390-3, 499-501; Dobler, *Survenus*, II, pp. 470-81; and C 3289/55/18, annex IV of 12 April 1935.

216 See, for example, DDF, I, pp. 54, 105, 112, 246, 274-7, 294, 303.

217 Baynes, *Hitler's Speeches*, II, pp. 1271-93.

218 C-V, pp. 11, 23.

219 C-V, pp. 13-14, 47; FOL 5669H/H015818-23 of 4 Feb 1936; USFR, 1936, I, pp. 268-9; and Görlitz, *General Staff*, p. 307.

220 C-V, pp. 5-6, 137, 415. It was undoubtedly advice from the foreign ministry which showed Hitler how he could remilitarize without committing a flagrant violation.

221 C-V, pp. 13-14, 137, 415.

222 C-V, pp. 14, 47, 136-40.

223 C-IV, p. 1142.

224 FOL 9944/E695952-61 of 3 March; and C-V, pp. 14, 44-5, 142-3, 151, 191n.

225 In addition to the citations in note 224, see FOL 6710/E506489 of 11 March; and Tessin, *Formationsgeschichte*, pp. 31, 256.

226 FOL 9944/E695955 of 2 March; and IMT, X, pp. 485-6.

227 FOL 9944/E695952-61 of 3 March; and Tessin, *Formationsgeschichte, passim*.

228 There is no evidence either way, but this certainly was the post-coup effect on Paris and London. (DDF, I, pp. 414-15; and Eden, *Facing*, p. 367).

229 For military anxieties about the operation, see IMT, XV, pp. 351-2 and XX, p. 603; NCA, V, p. 1102; Hossbach, *Zwischen*, p. 97

and *Entwicklung,* p. 115; Förster, *Beck,* pp. 56-7; Robertson, *Vierteljahreshefte,* pp. 203-4; Lossberg, *Wehrmachtführungsstab,* p. 11; and Keitel, *Keitel,* pp. 36-7.

230 IMT, XX, p. 603; Görlitz, *General Staff,* p. 307; Wheeler-Bennett, *Nemesis,* p. 352; and Gordon A. Craig, *Politics of the Prussian Army* (Oxford, 1955), p. 486.

231 The following is based on FOL 9944/E695952-61 of 3 March 1936; Watt, 'German Plans,' pp. 193-9; O'Neill, *German Army,* pp. 171-4; Manstein, *Soldatenleben,* pp. 226-8; and Siegfried Westphal, *The German Army in the West* (London, 1951), pp. 40-1.

232 In addition to the citations in note 231, see Tessin, *Formationsgeschichte,* pp. 23-7, 31, 255-6.

233 In addition to the citations in note 231, see NCA, VI, pp. 952-4, 1006-9 and VII, pp. 451-5; TWC, X, pp.475-6; IMT, XV, pp. 351-2, XXIV, pp. 487-91, 644-7 and XXXVI, p. 435; FOL 9930/E694817 of 3 May 1934; FOL 8845/E696004-7 of 30 Oct 1934; and C-III, pp. 1016-17, 1109-10.

234 FOL 9944/E695952-61 of 3 March.

235 Ibid. See also Hossbach, *Zwischen,* p. 97.

236 In addition to the citations in note 235, see IMT, X, pp. 484-6, 575; and Lossberg, *Wehrmachtführungsstab,* pp. 12-13.

237 IMT, XXXIV, pp. 644-7; FOL 9944/E695952-61 of 3 March; and Watt, 'German Plans,' pp. 197-9.

238 Ibid.; and FOL 9944/E696004-7 of 30 Oct 1934.

239 IMT, XXXIV, p. 645; and FOL 9944H/E695952-61 of 3 March 1936.

240 C-IV, pp. 294-5; NCA, VI, pp. 952-4; VII, pp. 451-5; FOL 9930/E694817 of 3 May 1934; and Watt, 'German Plans,' pp. 197-9.

241 NCA, VI, pp. 952-4. See also C-II, p. 42n; FOL 9930/E694817 of 3 May 1934; and NCA, VII, pp. 454-5. On 21 July 1935, the Lapo in the zone were told that, in the event of invasion, all of the Reich's *Machtmittel* would be employed in defence. (Tessin, *Formationsgeschichte,* p. 255).

242 FOL 9944H/E695942-4, 945-7, 948, all of 6 March 1936; and FOL 9944H/E695950-1 of 7 March 1936.

243 Schmidt, *Statist,* p. 320; Schuschnigg, *Requiem,* p. 43; Trevor-Roper, *Table Talk,* p. 259; Hans Frank, *Im Angesicht des Galgens* (Munich, 1953), p. 211; and Kurt Assman, *Deutsche Schicksalsjahre* (Wiesbaden, 1950), p. 45.

244 Waldemar Erfurth, *Geschichte des Deutschen Generalstabs* (Göttigen, 1960), II, p. 201; Bor, *Halder,* p. 111; and IMT, XX, pp. 603-4.

245 Schuschnigg, *Requiem,* p. 43.

246 In addition to the citations in notes 231 and 233, see IMT, X, pp. 475, 575; NCA, X, pp. 484-6; FOL 9945/E695989-91 of 13 Oct 1934; FOL 9945/E696022-8 of 9 Oct 1934; and FOL 9945/E696061 of 12

March 1935.

247 C 4279/4/18 of 12 June 1936; and Eden, *Facing,* p. 340.

248 See notes 253 and 255.

249 C-IV, pp. 1142, 1164-6; and Robertson, *Vierteljahreshefte,* p. 204.

250 C-IV, p. 1165; and Robertson, *Vierteljahreshefte,* p. 204.

251 Robertson, *Vierteljahreshefte,* p. 204.

252 This paragraph is based on DDF, I, pp. 287-409; DDB, IV, pp. 74-114; C 1181/4/18, C 1217/4/18, C 1263/4/18, C 1454/4/18 and C 1474/4/18, all between 24 February and 6 March; USFR, 1936, I, pp. 200, 206-7; Lipski, *Diplomat,* p. 249; and Dodd, *Diary,* pp. 315-17, 319.

253 See, for example, DDF, I, pp. 38, 52, 303-4, 412; Dobler, *Survenus,* II, pp. 469-81; and various British and French newspapers, including *The Times, Daily Telegraph, Manchester Guardian* and *Le Temps.*

254 In the ten weeks prior to the coup, no fewer than nine assurances were given by the Auswärtiges Amt.

255 For a sample, see DDF, I, pp. 328-9, 362, 375, 394, 403-4; DDB, IV, pp. 75-6, 81, 88-9, 110-11; C 1181/4/18 of 24 Feb 1936; and C 1404/4/18 of 4 March 1936.

256 They were Göring, Goebbels, Ribbentrop, Neurath, Bülow, Fritsch, Blomberg, Hassell and Forster.

257 Forster, *Bulletin,* p. 48.

258 C 1892/4/18 of 13 March; C-IV, p. 1063; Geyr von Schweppenburg, *The Critical Years* (London, 1952), pp. 54-5; and Kordt, *Akten,* p. 148.

259 FOL 6710/E506196-207 of 5 March; and C-V, pp. 11, 19-20, 22-4, 71.

260 Braubach, *Einmarsch,* p. 18.

261 TWC, X, pp. 484-6; IMT, XX, p. 603; FOL 9944/E695956 of 3 March; and Manstein, *Soldatenleben,* pp. 236-7.

262 FOL 9944/E695956 of 3 March; and FOL 9944/E695941 of 5 March 1936.

263 Lossberg, *Wehrmachtführungsstab,* p. 11.

264 Heinrich Hoffman, *Hitler Was My Friend* (London, 1955), pp. 82-3; H. S. Hegner, *Die Reichskanzlei* (Frankfurt, 1959), p. 200; and Eugen Hadamovsky, *Hitler kämpft um den Frieden Europas* (Munich, 1936), pp. 41-3.

265 C-V, pp. 26-8; IMT, XI, p. 39; and Meissner, *Staatssekretär,* p. 411.

266 This paragraph is based on Hossbach, *Zwischen,* pp. 97-8.

267 C-V, pp. 9-10; DDF, I, pp. 385, 401, 702; C 1448/4/18 of 6 March; and C 3144/86/18 of 15 April 1936.

268 DDF, I, p. 394; and Ribbentrop, *Ribbentrop,* p. 52.

269 C-V, pp. 29-31; DDB, IV, pp. 111-12; DDF, I, pp. 410-11; and C 1483/4/18 of 7 March.

270 Baynes, *Hitler's Speeches,* II, pp. 1271-93; and *The Times,* 9 March.

271 Eden, *Facing*, p. 340.
272 C-IV, p. 1166.
273 Ibid.

4 'Aucune action isolée'

1 Gamelin, *Servir*, II, pp. 201-2; Sarraut, *Survenus*, III, pp. 575, 622; Flandin, *Survenus*, I, pp. 148-9 and *Politique Française*, p. 198; Lebrun, *Survenus*, IV, p. 962; and DDF, I, p. 444.
2 C 1520/4/18 of 8 March; and *Le Temps*, 9 March.
3 DDF, I, p. 445; Gamelin, *Servir*, II, pp. 201-2; and Sarraut, *Survenus*, III, p. 622.
4 Lazareff, *Dernière édition*, p. 302; and Sarraut, *Survenus*, III, p. 582.
5 No minutes were kept of French cabinet meetings. For the problem of documentation, see DDF, I, pp. vii-xiv.
6 Lazareff, *Dernière édition*, pp. 302-3; Sarraut, *Survenus*, III, p. 582; and Gamelin, *Servir*, II, p. 201. Accounts of this Cabinet meeting may be found in Sarraut, *Survenus*, III, pp. 576, 581-4, 643; Lazareff, *Dernière édition*, pp. 302-5; Flandin, *Politique Française*, pp. 198-9 and *Survenus*, I, pp. 148-9; Paul-Boncour, *Entre deux*, III, pp. 33-8 and *Survenus*, III, pp. 798-800; Maurin, *Survenus*, IV, pp. 907-9; Gamelin, *Servir*, II, p. 203; Jean Zay, *Souvenirs et solitude* (Paris, 1945), pp. 65-7; Bonnet, *Quai d'Orsay*, pp. 134-5; and Reynaud, *Thick*, pp. 128-9.
7 Paul-Boncour, *Entre deux*, III, pp. 32, 37-8 and *Survenus*, III, pp. 798-9; Flandin, *Survenus*, I, p. 149 and *Politique Française*, p. 199; Zay, *Souvenirs*, p. 66; and Sarraut, *Survenus*, III, pp. 574-5, 582-3. Others who have been named as partisans of action include Flandin, Henri Guernut and Yvon Delbos.
8 Lazareff, *Dernière édition*, p. 302. See also Flandin, *Politique Française*, pp. 196, 198, 200, 205 and *Survenus*, I, p. 149; DDF, I, pp. 426-7; and Sarraut, *Survenus*, III, pp. 575-6, 582-3, 599, 668.
9 C 2564/4/18 of 28 March 1936; C 1903/1903/17 of 30 Jan 1937; Bury, *France*, pp. 273-6, 280; USFR, 1936, I, pp. 202, 306; and François Goguel, *La Politique des Partis*, II (Paris, 1958), p. 161.
10 DDF, I, pp. 246-7, 290-3, 299-300, 444-6, 522-3; DDB, IV, pp. 178, 180; Lazareff, *Dernière édition*, pp. 303-4; Zay, *Souvenirs*, pp. 66-7; and Paul-Boncour, *Survenus*, III, p. 799.
11 DDF, I, pp. 504-6, 696-700 and II, pp. 184-6; Sarraut, *Survenus*, III, pp. 602-3, 605, 621, 623; Gamelin, *Servir*, II, pp. 204-12 and *Survenus*, II, pp. 390, 448, 450; Flandin, *Politique Française*, pp. 195-9; and Maurin, *Survenus*, IV, p. 910.
12 DDF, I, p. 698; and *Survenus*, III, pp. 644-5.
13 In addition to citations in note 11, see Tony Albord, 'Les

relations de la politique et de la strategie', *La Défense Nationale* (Paris, 1958), p. 291 and *Survenus*, V, pp. 1256-7; and DDF, I, pp. 291-2.

14 DDF, I, p. 699.
15 DDF, II, p. 186.
16 Sarraut, *Survenus*, III, pp. 621, 644-5; Flandin, *Politique Française*, p. 196; DDF, III, p. 66; and C 2498/4/18 of 30 March 1936.
17 This paragraph is based on DDF, I, pp. 444, 698-9 and II, pp. 184-6, 569-76 and III, pp. 17-23; Challener, *Nation in Arms*, pp. 216-20, 252, 264, 266-76; Sarraut, *Survenus*, III, pp. 603-4, 645; Reynaud, *Thick*, pp. 93, 109, 119-21; and Gorce, *French Army*, pp. 255-6.
18 DDF, I, pp. 300, 444, 502-6, 522-3, 697, 699-700 and II, pp. 47-8; Sarraut, *Survenus*, III, pp. 583, 643; Gamelin, *Servir*, II, pp. 201, 204 and *Survenus*, II, pp. 388, 450; and Maurin, *Survenus*, IV, pp. 907-8, 919 and V, pp. 1266-7.
19 DDF, I, p. 444.
20 Maurin, *Survenus*, IV, p. 908.
21 DDF, I, pp. 504-6, 696-700; Gamelin, *Survenus*, II, pp. 390-2; and *Survenus*, II, pp. 389-90; and Maurin, *Survenus*, V, pp. 1266-7.
22 Maurin, *Survenus*, V, p. 1266; and DDF, I, pp. 505, 698.
23 Maurin, *Survenus*, IV, p. 908 and V, p. 1266; DDF, I, pp. 444, 505, 698-9; Lazareff, *Dernière édition*, p. 303; and Sarraut, *Survenus*, III, pp. 583, 602, 621, 643.
24 Maurin, *Survenus*, IV, pp. 807-8 and V, pp. 1266-7; and Gamelin, *Servir*, II, p. 201.
25 This paragraph is based on DDF, I, pp. 504-6, 697n, 699; Gamelin, *Servir*, II, pp. 189, 201, 205, 208-11, 214 and *Survenus*, II, pp. 389, 450; and C 1795/4/18 of 12 March 1936. Figures here are all French estimates.
26 These included NSKK, 30,000; SS, 25,000; and SA, 150,000.
27 DDF, I, pp. 247, 291, 300-1, 444, 504-6, 697-700; Gamelin, *Servir*, II, pp. 208-11; Maurin, *Survenus*, V, p. 1266; and C 2203/4/18 of 21 March 1936.
28 DDF, I, p. 700.
29 DDB, IV, p. 177.
30 Ibid. See also DDF, I, pp. 116-24, 219-21, 319, 696-700; Maurin, *Survenus*, V, p. 1266; and Gamelin, *Servir*, I, p. 367 and II, p. 201.
31 Maurin, *Survenus*, IV, p. 908; Gamelin, *Servir*, II, p. 201 and *Survenus*, II, pp. 389-90; and Sarraut, *Survenus*, III, pp. 644-5.
32 Maurin, *Survenus*, IV, p. 908; Lebrun, *Survenus*, IV, p. 962; DDF, I, pp. 444, 551, 698-700; and Challener, *Nation in Arms*, pp. 268-75.
33 Gamelin, *Servir*, II, p. 214 and *Survenus*, II, p. 450; and DDF, I, pp. 444, 696-700.
34 C 7394/20/18 of 3 Nov 1934; C 2928/55/18 of 5 April 1935; and C 2106/227/17 of 15 March 1935.

35 Gamelin, *Servir*, II, p. 199. See also DDF, I, pp. 391, 505, 698, 700; Gamelin, *Servir*, II, pp. 189, 204, 210 and *Survenus*, II, pp. 389-90; and Maurin, *Survenus*, V, p. 1266.

36 DDF, I, pp. 117, 121-2; C 895/4/18 of 13 Feb 1936; and Sarraut, *Survenus*, III, p. 608.

37 DDF, I, p. 505; and Gamelin, *Servir*, II, p. 210. Of these, 600,000 were regulars, 100,000 auxiliary and military police, and 300,000 in the labour service.

38 This paragraph is based on DDF, I, pp. 117-18, 121-2, 221, 700 and II, pp. 47, 536-7, 570-6; C 4413/55/18 of 30 May 1935; C 895/4/18 of 13 Feb 1936; Sarraut, *Survenus*, III, pp. 603-4, 605-9, 611-15; DDB, IV, p. 178; Gamelin, *Servir*, I, p. 367 and II, pp. 194, 201, 212; and Overstraeten, *Albert*, p. 214.

39 In addition, see Jacomet, *Survenus*, I, pp. 189-97; Challener, *Nation in Arms*, p. 224; DDF, III, pp. 311-14; and C 5356/4/18 of 3 July 1936.

40 Gamelin, *Servir*, I, p. 367 and II, p. 212; DDF, I, p. 700; and Sarraut, *Survenus*, III, pp. 613-14.

41 DDF, I, p. 698.

42 Sarraut, *Survenus*, III, pp. 613-14 (quoting Fabry, who served under Laval in 1935-6).

43 Zay, *Souvenirs*, p. 66. See also DDB, IV, pp. 178-80.

44 DDF, I, p. 698.

45 DDB, IV, p. 180.

46 DDB, IV, p. 178.

47 Fabry, quoted by Sarraut, *Survenus*, III, p. 613.

48 Jacomet, *Survenus*, I, pp. 193, 197; and Cot, *Triumph*, p. 183.

49 DDB, IV, p. 178. See also DDF, I, pp. 116-20, 122, 700 and III, pp. 311-14; and Gamelin, *Servir*, I, p. 367 and II, pp. 194, 212.

50 For a general picture, see C 2928/55/18 of 5 April 1935; C 4413/55/18 of 30 May 1935; Dufieux, *Survenus*, IV, pp. 886-93; Jacomet, *Survenus*, I, pp. 191-3; Sarraut, *Survenus*, III, pp. 611-15; and Gorce, *French Army*, p. 255.

51 In addition to the citations in note 50, see DDF, I, p. 119.

52 Jacomet, *Survenus*, I, p. 193; and Sarraut, *Survenus*, III, p. 613.

53 Fabry, quoted by Sarraut, *Survenus*, III, p. 613; and DDF, I, p. 119.

54 Generals Dufieux and Velpry, *Survenus*, IV, pp. 887-93.

55 Velpry, quoted by Dufieux, *Survenus*, IV, pp. 887-8.

56 Jacomet, *Survenus*, I, p. 193. See also Keller, quoted by Sarraut, *Survenus*, III, p. 611; and Dufieux, *Survenus*, IV, p. 893.

57 Sarraut, *Survenus*, III, p. 611; DDF, I, pp. 118-19; and Velpry, quoted by Dufieux, *Survenus*, IV, p. 893.

58 Fabry, quoted by Sarraut, *Survenus*, III, p. 613; and Velpry, quoted by Dufieux, *Survenus*, IV, p. 893.

59 Between January and June 1936, German first-line strength was

estimated in France at 600, 650, 900, 1,380 and 1,500 machines, but not in that order. (DDF, I, p. 90; II, pp. 48, 465; CID 1216-B of 4 March 1936; and C 4103/4/18 of 5 June 1936).

60 DDF, III, p. 66; Sarraut, *Survenus,* III, p. 619; C 6704/55/18 of 9 Sept 1935; C 435/4/18 of 20 Jan 1936; C 1167/4/18 of 7 Feb; CID 1216-B of 4 March; CID 1218-B of 11 March; and CID 1284-B of 30 Nov 1936.

61 C 6704/55/18 of 9 Sept 1935; and C 5391/172/17 of 15 July 1936.

62 The following is based on C 2928/55/18 of 5 April 1935; C 4104/55/18 of 25 May 1935; C 6985/227/17 of 8 Oct 1935; C 1167/4/18 of 7 Feb 1936; C 4182/172/17 of 9 June 1936; C 4181/172/17 of 12 June 1936; C 5391/172/17 of 15 July 1936; and DDF, II, pp. 464-7 and III, pp. 66-7.

63 C 4274/3928/18, minute by Wigram, 16 June 1936. See also C 6704/55/18 of 9 Sept 1935; and DDF, II, p. 66.

64 See, for example, Klein, *Economic Preparedness, passim;* and Milward, *German Economy, passim.*

65 C 3663/85/17 of 9 June 1934; C 3827/85/17 of 14 June 1934; C 3958/85/17 of 20 June 1934; C 4297/20/18 of 5 July 1934; C 7890/85/17 of 21 Nov 1934; and C-III, pp. 543-4, 563.

66 C 7873/227/17 of 26 Nov 1935; C 895/4/18 of 13 Feb 1936; DDF, I, pp. 117, 122, 505; and Gamelin, *Survenus,* II, p. 389.

67 Klein, *Economic Preparedness,* p. 17; Sarraut, *Survenus,* III, pp. 561, 603-4, 622, 646, 651, 657; DDF, I, pp. 505, 697; Maurin, *Survenus,* IV, p. 908; and Gamelin, *Servir,* II, p. 201.

68 This paragraph is based on DDF, I, pp. 300, 444, 504-6, 512, 517, 697-700; DDB, IV, pp. 106, 177, 179; and C 435/4/18 of 20 Jan 1936.

69 See also Overstraeten, *Albert,* p. 214.

70 *Survenus,* III, p. 603. See also Sarraut, *Survenus,* III, pp. 561, 646, 657; and Albord, 'Les relations,' p. 291 and *Survenus,* III, pp. 644-5.

71 Sarraut, *Survenus,* III, pp. 602, 605, 623; Maurin, *Survenus,* IV, pp. 910, 919 and V, p. 1267; and Gamelin, *Servir,* II, pp. 205-7 and *Survenus,* II, p. 449.

72 DDF, I, pp. 504-6; Gamelin, *Servir,* II, p. 213; and Sarraut, *Survenus,* III, pp. 583, 604-5, 622-3, 646, 651.

73 This paragraph is based on Lazareff, *Dernière édition,* pp. 302-4; Zay, *Souvenirs,* p. 66; Flandin, *Politique Française,* pp. 196, 198-9; Reynaud, *La France,* p. 354; Paul-Boncour, *Entre deux,* III, pp. 29, 33-4 and *Survenus,* III, p. 799; and Sarraut, *Survenus,* III, pp. 561, 583, 603-5, 643, 651.

74 In addition to the citations in note 73, see DDB, IV, pp. 178-80; and Maurin, *Survenus,* IV, pp. 910, 919 and V, p. 1269.

75 See also DDF, I, pp. 502-3, 506, 699; Gamelin, *Servir,* II, pp. 205-7; and Sarraut, *Survenus,* III, pp. 602, 623.

76 In addition to the citations in note 73, see Maurin, *Survenus*, IV, pp. 919-20; Bonnet, *Quai d'Orsay*, pp. 138, 141; and Pierre Dhers, 'Du 7 mars 1936 à l'Ile d'Yeu,' *Revue d' Histoire*, January 1952, p. 20.

77 Lazareff, *Dernière édition*, p. 303. Sarraut described Déat's arguments as a decisive factor against action. (Ibid.)

78 Paul-Boncour, *Survenus*, III, p. 798; Reynaud, *Le probleme militaire français* (Paris, 1937), p. 66; Flandin, *Survenus*, I, pp. 149, 151-2; Gamelin, *Servir*, II, p. 212; Poncet, *Fateful*, p. 196; and Tabouis, *Blackmail*, p. 133.

79 The next two paragraphs are based on J 9978/1/1 of 30 Dec 1935; C 656/1/17 of 31 Jan 1936; C 1903/1903/17 of 30 Jan 1937; C-IV, p. 824; C-V, p. 422; DDF, I, pp. 160, 699; Reynaud, *Thick*, p. 119; and Bury, *France*, p. 280.

80 One French historian described the economic and financial situation in the spring of 1936 as the worst since 1929 (Gorce, *French Army*, p. 263).

81 DDF, I, pp. 698, 700; and DDB, IV, pp. 178, 180.

82 DDF, I, p. 699; Gamelin, *Servir*, II, p. 210; J 9978/1/1 of 30 Dec 1935; *Survey*, 1936, p. 266n; and the *Economist*, 25 Jan 1936, p. 175.

83 C 455/1/17 of 21 Jan 1936; C 477/1/17 of 23 Jan 1936; and the *Economist*, 25 Jan 1936, p. 180.

84 C 656/1/17 of 31 Jan 1936; C 688/1/17 of 2 Feb 1936; and *Le Temps*, 31 Jan 1936.

85 The franc's vulnerability was underlined by the fact that in February 1936 Paris requested and received a £40 million credit from British sources.

86 This paragraph is based on Maurin, *Survenus*, IV, pp. 907, 914; and Gamelin, *Servir*, II, p. 203.

87 DDF, I, p. 300; and Maurin, *Survenus*, IV, p. 907.

88 Reynaud, *La France*, p. 354 and *Thick*, p. 128 (quoting Maurin).

89 Maurin, *Survenus*, IV, pp. 907-9; and Gamelin, *Servir*, II, p. 203.

90 Lazareff, *Dernière édition*, p. 305; and Zay, *Souvenirs*, p. 66. See also Gamelin, *Servir*, II, p. 212; Reynaud, *Thick*, pp. 132, 134; USFR, 1936, I, p. 156; and Tabouis, *Blackmail*, p. 131.

91 DDF, I, pp. 339, 428, 493-4; and DDB, IV, pp. 125-6.

92 See, for example, DDF, I, pp. 291-3, 300, 302.

93 DDF, I, p. 300.

94 This paragraph is based on DDB, IV, p. 148; Sarraut, *Survenus*, III, pp. 573, 602-3; Flandin, *Politique Française*, p. 199; Paul-Boncour, *Entre deux*, III, p. 34 and *Survenus*, III, p. 799; Henri de Kérillis and Raymond Cartier, *Kérillis on the Causes of War* (London, 1939), p. 5; C-V, pp. 131-2, 141, 424; and Zay, *Souvenirs*, p. 66.

95 This group may have been encouraged by Poncet's reports of opposition to the coup from within the German government.

(DDF, I, pp. 460, 462, 468, 482).

96 Flandin, *Politique Française,* pp. 198-208; DDF, I, pp. 339, 437-8, 494, 501-2; and DDB, IV, pp. 104-6, 125-7, 132-40.

97 Gamelin, *Servir,* II, pp. 176, 202, 213; DDB, IV, pp. 64-7, 71-3, 87-9, 146-51; DDF, I, p. 503; and C 1734/4/18 of 11 March 1936.

98 In addition to citations in the two preceding notes, see DDF, I, pp. 428, 525; C 1614/4/18 and C 1673/4/18, both of 10 March; and C 1989/4/18 of 17 March 1936.

99 Flandin, *Survenus,* I, p. 149; and Sarraut, *Survenus,* III, pp. 574-5.

100 Flandin, *Politique Française,* p. 204; Paul-Boncour, *Survenus,* III, p. 798; and Sarraut, *Survenus,* III, pp. 574, 582-3.

101 C 1673/4/18 of 10 March 1936.

102 This paragraph is largely based on Flandin's subsequent behaviour, but in addition, see Flandin, *Politique Française,* pp. 198, 202, 205, 208-10, 212 and *Survenus,* I, pp. 142, 148-9, 153, 155, 158; DDF, I, pp. 151, 207, 220, 277-8; DDB, IV, pp. 71-2, 105, 126; and C 573/92/62 of 27 Jan 1936.

103 Paul-Boncour agreed that 'it would have been unwise to come to any decision against the will of Great Britain', (*Entre deux,* III, p. 36).

104 Reynaud, *La France,* p. 354 and *Thick,* p. 129; and Paul-Boncour, *Entre deux,* III, p. 35 and *Survenus,* III, p. 799.

105 See, for example, DDF, I, pp. 427-8, 437-8, 484-5, 493-4, 525; DDB, IV, pp. 125-7; and C 1614/4/18 and C 1673/4/18, both of 10 March.

106 This argument can be supported by the frequent assertions that Britain's reticence was a decisive factor in dissuading Paris from action. See, for example, Sarraut, *Survenus,* III, pp. 582-93, 602, 617, 647, 651, 668; and Flandin, *Survenus,* I, pp. 149, 159 and *Politique Française,* p. 202.

107 R 1305/137/7 of 22 Feb 1936; Elizabeth R. Cameron, *Prologue to Appeasement* (Washington, DC, 1942), pp. 179-81; and Kérillis, *Kérillis,* p. 5.

108 This paragraph is based on DDF, I, pp. 44-8, 112, 161-2, 175, 232-3, 239-40, 273-6, 303; DDB, IV, pp. 67, 71-4, 87-9, 126; C 573/92/62 of 27 Jan 1936; Flandin, *Politique Française,* pp. 201, 203; and USFR, 1936, I, p. 216.

109 DDF, I, pp. 413-14, 426-7; C 1486/4/18 and C 1490/4/18, both of 7 March; C 1530/4/18 of 8 March; Flandin, *Politique Française,* pp. 201-3; and USFR, 1936, I, p. 214.

110 DDF, I, p. 427.

111 DDF, I, p. 532; Flandin, *Politique Française,* p. 201 and *Survenus,* I, p. 148; Sarraut, *Survenus,* III, p. 593; USFR, 1936, I, p. 242; and *Le Temps* and *The Times* 9 and 10 March (press extracts).

112 DDF, I, pp. 427-8.

113 DDF, I, pp. 450-1, 455; and *Hansard,* vol. 308, cols. 1808-13.

114 This paragraph is based on DDF, I, pp. 415, 484-5, 493-4, 525; DDB, IV, pp. 147-51; Flandin, *Survenus,* I, p. 150; Sarraut, *Survenus,* III, pp. 587, 602; C 1676/4/18 and C 1674/4/18, both of 10 March; C 1734/4/18 of 11 March 1936; and *Le Temps* 10, 11 March 1936.

115 *Hansard,* vol. 308, cols. 1808-13. See also DDF, I, p. 493.

116 In addition see Flandin, *Politique Française,* pp. 208-9; C 1543/4/18 of 9 March; C 1832/4/18 and C 1965/4/18, both of 13 March; C 1962/4/18 of 17 March; and C 2068/4/18 of 18 March 1936.

117 USFR, 1936, I, p. 233. This was also Zeeland's primary objective. (C 1672/4/18 of 10 March; and USFR, 1936, I, p. 243).

118 DDF, I, pp. 428, 438, 494; and DDB, IV, pp. 125-7.

119 In addition to relevant citations in earlier chapters, see CP 73(36) of 8 March; C 1595/4/18 of 9 March; C 1614/4/18 and C 1672/4/18, both of 10 March; C 1679/4/18 of 11 March; DDB, IV, pp. 72-3; and USFR, 1936, I, p. 708.

120 C 1513/4/18 and FOL 6710/E506344-6, both of 8 March; C 1676/4/18 of 10 March; *Le Temps* 8 and 9 March (quoting other press reaction); C 2202/4/18 of 21 March; Flandin, *Survenus,* I, p. 151 and *Politique Française,* p. 199; Sarraut, *Survenus,* III, pp. 565-7, 569, 593; and Reynaud, *Thick,* p. 127.

121 Quoted in *Le Temps* 11 March; and C 1676/4/18 of 10 March.

122 Quoted in *Le Temps,* 9 and 11 March.

123 C 1513/4/18 of 8 March; *Le Temps* (press extracts), 9, 11 and 13 March; C 1543/4/18 of 9 March; and C 1678/4/18 of 11 March.

124 C 1543/4/18 of 9 March; C 2564/4/18 of 28 March; and FOL 6710/E506344-6 of 8 March.

125 C 1543/4/18 of 9 March; C 1676/4/18 of 10 March; C 1744/4/18 of 12 March; *Le Temps* 11 and 12 March; and Sarraut, *Survenus,* III, pp. 565, 569, 593.

126 C 1513/4/18 of 8 March; and *Le Temps* (press extracts), 9 and 10 March.

127 In addition to the citations in note 120, see C 1755/4/18 of 12 March; C 1949/4/18 of 16 March; C 1987/4/18 of 17 March; C 2564/4/18 of 28 March; Flandin, *Survenus,* I, p. 149; Dobler, *Survenus,* II, p. 482; Goguel, *Politique,* p. 161; Bonnet, *Quai d'Orsay,* pp. 138, 142; and C-V, pp. 60, 120, 131, 181.

128 C 1544/4/18 of 9 March; C 1877/4/18 of 12 March; C 2003/9/17 of 13 March; C 2236/9/17 of 20 March; and C 2638/4/18 of 2 April 1936.

129 Flandin, *Politique Française,* p. 199.

130 C 1693/4/18 of 11 March; *Le Temps,* 12 March; and Sarraut, *Survenus,* III, p. 567.

131 Flandin, *Politique Française,* p, 201; Irving M. Gibson, *Maginot and Liddell Hart* (Princeton, NJ 1943), p. 372; Werth, *Twilight,* p. 201; and *Matin,* quoted by *Le Temps,* 9 March 1936.

132 C 1513/4/18 of 8 March; Reynaud, *Thick,* p. 127 and *Survenus,* I, p. 151; C 2202/4/18 of 21 March; Flandin, *Politique Française,* p. 201; and DDB, IV, p. 69.

133 The following is based on C 1502/4/18 and *The Times,* both of 9 March; *Le Temps,* 10 March; Sarraut, *Survenus,* III, pp. 570, 584-5; and Flandin, *Politique Française,* p. 201 and *Survenus,* I, p. 151.

134 C 1543/4/18 and C 1544/4/18, both of 9 March; C 1676/4/18 of 10 March; *Le Temps,* 10 and 11 March; Flandin, *Politique Française,* p. 201; Sarraut, *Survenus,* III, pp. 566, 654-5; and Dhers, 'Du 7 mars 1936,' p. 20.

135 In addition to the citations in note 134, see C 1678/4/18 of 11 March; and C 1744/4/18 and C 1877/4/18, both of 12 March.

136 C 1544/4/18 of 9 March; C 1676/4/18 of 10 March; C 1743/4/18 of 12 March; C 2564/4/18 of 28 March; Zay, *Souvenirs,* p. 67; Micaud, *French Right,* pp. 100-2; Reynaud, *Thick,* p. 127; E. R. Tannenbaum, *The Action Française* (New York, 1962), pp. 215-16; and *Le Temps,* 10 March.

137 Lazareff, *Dernière édition,* p. 305.

138 Sarraut, *Survenus,* III, pp. 567, 569-70.

139 C 1678/4/18 of 11 March.

140 Flandin, *Survenus,* I, p. 192; Sarraut, *Survenus,* III, pp. 565, 567-9; *Le Temps,* 11 March; C 1693/4/18 of 11 March; and Peter J. Larmour, *The French Radical Party in the 1930s* (Stanford, Calif., 1964), p. 198.

141 Sarraut, *Survenus,* III, pp. 566, 569, 647-8, 654-5; Flandin, *Politique Française,* p. 199; Micaud, *French Right,* pp. 99-103; *Jour,* quoted by *Le Temps,* 12 March.

142 This paragraph is based on Flandin, *Politique Française,* pp. 199-202, and *Survenus,* I, p. 136; Sarraut, *Survenus,* III. pp. 566, 647-8; Micaud, *French Right,* pp. 99-100, 105-6; Goguel, *Politique,* pp. 160-1; Reynaud, *Thick,* p. 119; Tannenbaum, *Action Française,* pp. 217-18; Tabouis, *Blackmail,* p. 133; C-V, p. 422; DDB, IV, p. 149; and C 1513/4/18 of 8 March.

143 Flandin, *Politique Française,* pp. 200-1; Sarraut, *Survenus,* III, pp. 569-70, 647-8; C-V, pp. 120-1, 199, 425; and C 2564/4/18 of 28 March.

144 Flandin, *Politique Française,* pp. 201-2.

145 Flandin, *Politique Française,* pp. 199-202 and *Survenus,* I, pp. 136, 149, 151-2; and Sarraut, *Survenus,* III, pp. 561-2, 647-8, 651, 654-5.

146 C 1614/4/18 of 10 March; and C 1734/4/18 of 11 March.

147 CAB 18(36)1 of 11 March; C 1755/4/18 of 12 March; C 1886/4/18 of 14 March; C 1949/4/18 of 16 March; C 1987/4/18 of 17 March; C 2048/4/18 of 18 March; C 2564/4/18 of 28 March; and USFR, 1936, I, pp. 235-6.

148 DDF, I, pp. 437-8, 483-5, 493-4; DDB, IV, pp. 125-7, 147-51; USFR, 1936, I, pp. 217, 234-6; and C 1734/4/18 of 11 March.

149 See, for example, DDF, I, pp. 440-1, 448-9, 469-70, 476-7, 481, 487-90, 498-9, 516-17, 519-21, 528, 546, 572-3; and DDB, IV, pp. 148-50.

150 DDF, I, pp. 419, 453-4, 485-6, 496-7, 517-18, 547; DDB, IV, pp. 148-9; Edouard Beneš, *Memoirs of Dr Edouard Beneš* (London, 1954), pp. 12-13; and Sarraut, *Survenus,* III, pp. 585, 668.

151 DDF, I, pp. 415-16, 435-6, 476-7, 489; C 1503/4/18 of 8 March; and Noël, *Agression*, p. 125.

152 DDF, I, pp. 476, 546, 670; C 1699/4/18 of 11 March; C 1854/4/18 and C 1932/4/18, both of 13 March; USFR, 1936, I, p. 252; and C-V, pp. 153, 302.

153 DDF, I, p. 462. For the Rumanian attitude, see DDF, I, pp. 420-1, 435-6, 570, 585-6, 646-7; and II, p. 272; C 1832/4/18 of 13 March; USFR, 1936, I, pp. 227-8, 236; DDB, IV, p. 149; and C-V, pp. 63, 175.

154 DDF, I, p. 421.

155 DDF, I, p. 436.

156 Noël, *Agression,* p. 129.

157 DDF, I, pp. 376-7, 415-16, 440, 526, 528; C 1503/4/18 of 8 March; C 1717/4/18 of 11 March; C 1900/4/18 of 15 March; C-V, pp. 88-9; Joseph Beck, *Final Report* (New York, 1957), pp. 109-12, 261, Szembek, *Journal,* pp. 159, 162-3, 165-70; Dodd, *Diary,* pp. 321-2; and USFR, 1936, I, pp. 239, 241.

158 DDF, I, pp. 436-7, 488, 571; C 1614/4/18 of 10 March; LP (L) 3rd meeting, 14 March; and C 1989/4/18 of 17 March.

159 DDB, IV, pp. 131, 149; DDF, I, pp. 433-7, 488, 528, 639-41; Beck, *Final Report,* pp. 110-11; C 1498/4/18 of 8 March; and Noël, *Agression,* p. 136.

160 DDF, I, p. 571; and C 1900/4/18 of 15 March. See also DDF, I, pp. 638-40, 724-5 and II, pp. 90-1; Flandin, *Politique Française,* p. 206; and Noël, *Agression,* pp. 125-9, 137.

161 DDF, I, p. 439.

162 USFR, 1936, I, p. 212.

163 See, for example, J. B. Duroselle, *Histoire diplomatique* (Paris, 1953), p. 218n; Reynaud, *Thick,* p. 132; *Survey,* 1936, p. 272; Chambers, *Conflict,* p. 394; and Hugh Dalton diaries, 11 March 1936.

164 USFR, 1936, I, p. 212.

165 Gamelin, *Survenus,* II, p. 450.

166 Sarraut, *Survenus,* II, pp. 585, 668.

167 Bonnet, *Quai d'Orsay,* p. 317; Beneš, *Memoirs,* pp. 12-13; Noël, *Agression,* p. 132; and C 4949/3928/18 of 7 July 1936.

168 C 1614/4/18 of 10 March. See also DDF, I, pp. 439, 481; and DDB, IV, p. 149.

169 DDF, I, p. 448. See also DDF, I, pp. 423, 490-91.

170 DDF, I, pp. 449, 513; Aloisi, *Journal,* p. 356; C-V, p. 66; and C

1595/4/18 of 9 March.

171 DDF, I, p. 494; C 1614/4/18 of 10 March; C 1734/4/18 of 11 March, DDB, IV, pp. 106, 149-50; Flandin, *Politique Française*, p. 202; Aloisi, *Journal*, p. 363; and USFR, 1936, I, p. 217.

172 C 1614/4/18 of 10 March. See also DDB, IV, pp. 126, 148-152; and C 1734/4/18 of 11 March.

173 The following is based on DDF, I, pp. 437-8, 483-5, 493-4, 525; DDB, IV, p. 127; USFR, 1936, I, pp. 217-18; C 1940/4/18 of 12 March; and Flandin, *Politique Française*, p. 203.

174 USFR, 1936, I, p. 217.

175 Ibid. See also DDF, I, pp. 237, 424; CAB 11(36)5 of 26 Feb 1936; CAB 18(36)1 of 11 March; C 8998/8998/18 of 31 Dec 1936; and Eden, *Facing*, pp. 241, 257, 283, 318, 525-5.

176 USFR, 1936, I, pp. 218, 228, 234-5, 244-5; and Cordell Hull, *Memoirs of Cordell Hull* (New York, 1948), I, p. 453.

177 C 1810/4/18 of 13 March; C 2348/4/18 of 17 March; C 2383/4/18 of 18 March; J. V. Compton, *Swastika and the Eagle* (Boston, 1967), p. 58; DDF, I, pp. 456-8, 609-10; C-V, pp. 66-7; and FOL 6710: E506390, E506757, E506836, E507458 and E508297, all between 8 and 26 March.

178 DDF, I, pp. 484-5. See also DDF, I, p. 438.

179 DDF, I, pp. 496-7, 517-18, 547.

180 *Le Temps*, and FOL 6710/E506910, both of 13 March; C-V, pp. 106-7, 133, 149-50; R 1579/125/67 of 17 March; and Robert Machray, *Struggle for the Danube and the Little Entente* (London, 1938), p. 214.

181 C-V, pp. 133, 135-6, 149-50, 153; FOL 6710/E506879, FOL 6710/E506910 and C 1766/4/18, all of 13 March; FOL 6710/E507353 of 17 March; and *The Times*, 17, 18 March 1936.

182 C 1734/4/18 of 11 March; C 1940/4/18 of 12 March; DDB, IV, p. 149; and USFR, 1936, I, pp. 235, 236.

183 DDF, I, p. 525; DDB, IV, pp. 148-50; USFR, 1936, I, pp. 242, 268; C 1734/4/18 of 11 March; C 1806/4/18 of 12 March; and C 1989/4/18 of 17 March.

184 DDF, I, p. 525. See also DDB, IV, pp. 127, 151.

185 C 1596/4/18 of 9 March; C 1647/4/18 of 10 March; FOL 6710/E506967-75 of 12 March; C-V, pp. 84-5; Flandin, *Survenus*, I, p. 149; and Sarraut, *Survenus*, III, pp. 602, 623.

186 C 1657/4/18 of 10 March.

187 C 1507/4/18 of 8 March; C 1647/4/18 of 10 March; FOL 6710: E506967-75 of 12 March and E507214-20 of 14 March; DDF, I, pp. 608-9; and Sarraut, *Survenus*, III, pp. 585-6.

188 DDB, III, pp. 457-60; DDF, I, p. 398; Overstraeten, *Albert*, pp. 189, 199-211; Sarraut, *Survenus*, III, pp. 457-60; and Flandin, *Politique Française*, p 200.

189 C 1074/270/4 of 19 Feb 1936; C 1126/270/4 of 22 Feb 1936; C

1261/270/4 of 28 Feb 1936; C 1424/270/4 of 5 March 1936; and Miller, *Belgian,* pp. 219-20.

190 DDB, IV, pp. 92, 134; C-V, pp. 31-2, 85; and C 1613/4/18 of 10 March.

191 DDF, I, pp. 608-9; Szembek, *Journal,* p. 166; and C 3456/G/66 of 17 June 1936.

192 DDB, III, pp. 474-9, 482-4; DDF, I, pp. 396, 608-9; Miller, *Belgian,* pp. 195-232; Theodore Draper, *Six Weeks War* (London, 1946), p. 11; and Zuylen, *Mains libres,* pp. 336-7. 367.

193 C 1613/4/18, C 1614/4/18, C 1672/4/18 and C 1673/4/18, all of 10 March; DDB, IV, pp. 127, 140; DDF, I, pp. 414-15; and USFR, 1936, I, pp. 234, 248.

194 DDB, IV, pp. 100-1, 107-8, 115-17, 119-22; DDF, I, pp. 432, 440; and C 1688/4/18 and C 1495/4/18, both of 7 March.

195 C 1614/4/18 and C 1672/4/18, both of 10 March; DDB, IV, pp. 140, 143; DDF, I, pp. 493-4; Zuylen, *Mains libres,* pp. 350-3; and J. Wullus-Rudiger, *Les origines internationales du drame belge de 1940* (Brussels, 1950), p. 55.

196 CAB 18(36)1 of 11 March. See also C 1614/4/18 and C 1673/4/18, both of 10 March; and USFR, 1936, I, p. 234.

197 DDB, IV, pp. 140, 147-8.

198 C 1614/4/18 and C 1672/4/18, both of 10 March; C 1805/4/18 of 13 March; and DDB, IV, pp. 140-3.

199 In addition to the citations in note 198, see C 1742/4/18 of 11 March; and DDB, IV, pp. 147-51.

200 C 1835/4/18 of 13 March; C 1985/4/18 of 17 March; DDF, I, pp. 439-43; DDB, IV, pp. 134-5, 139-40, 147-51; and USFR, 1936, I, pp. 248-9.

201 DDB, IV, pp. 140-3; DDF, II, pp. 52-3; USFR, 1936, I, pp. 242, 272; C-V, pp. 84-5; C 1543/4/18 of 9 March; and C 1672/4/18 of 10 March.

202 This paragraph is based on C 1614/4/18 and C 1673/4/18, both of 10 March; C 1806/4/18 of 12 March; C 1965/4/18 of 13 March; C 1962/4/18 of 17 March; DDF, I, pp. 493-4, 501-2; and DDB, IV, pp. 105, 126. See also Flandin, *Politique Française,* pp. 204-5; and USFR, 1936, I, p. 229.

203 C 1673/4/18 of 10 March; C 1806/4/18 of 12 March; and DDB, IV, pp. 105, 132-8.

204 DDF, I, pp. 441, 448-9, 463, 489-90, 498, 499, 516-17, 572-3, 639-40; DDB, IV, pp. 149-50, 152-3, 156-7; C 1614/4/18 and C 1673/4/18, both of 10 March; C 1734/4/18 of 11 March; Sarraut, *Survenus,* III, p. 564; and Flandin, *Survenus,* I, p. 153.

205 C 1614/4/18 and C 1673/4/18, both of 10 March; C 1806/4/18 of 12 March; C 1965/4/18 of 13 March; and C 1962/4/18 of 17 March.

206 C 1614/4/18 of 10 March; C 1734/4/18 of 10 March; C 2069/4/18 of 18 March; and DDB, IV, pp. 126, 150.

207 DDF, I, pp. 501-2; Gamelin, *Servir,* II, pp. 203-4 and *Survenus,* II, p. 449; Sarraut, *Survenus,* III, p. 602; Maurin, *Survenus,* IV, pp. 910, 919 and V, p. 1267.

208 DDF, I, pp. 502-3, 522-3; and Maurin, *Survenus,* IV, pp. 910, 919.

209 DDF, I, p. 522.

210 DDF, I, pp. 522-3.

211 The following is based on DDF, I, pp. 504-6; Gamelin, *Servir,* II, pp. 204-11 and *Survenus,* II, pp. 390, 392, 449; and Maurin, *Survenus,* IV, pp. 910, 919.

212 In addition to the citations in note 211, see Sarraut, *Survenus,* III, p. 623; and Albord, 'Les relations,' p. 623.

213 Sarraut, *Survenus,* III, pp. 561, 602-6, 623, 657, 668; DDF, II, p. 186n; and Flandin, *Politique Française,* pp. 196, 199, 205.

214 In this connexion, however, Poncet's reports tend to support the Gamelin-Maurin thesis that Germany would resist (DDF, I, pp. 464, 512, 517).

215 DDF, I, p. 503; DDB, IV, pp. 126, 150-1; C 1614/4/18 and C 1673/4/18, both of 10 March; C 1734/4/18 of 11 March; C 1965/4/18 of 13 March; C 2069/4/18 of 18 March; and USFR, 1936, I, p. 269.

216 DDF, I, pp. 244-5, 442-3, 460, 463, 468, 482; Dobler, *Survenus,* II, pp. 486-8; and DDB, IV, pp. 126, 150.

217 DDB, IV, pp. 126, 150; DDF, I, p. 463; USFR, 1936, I, p. 269; and Feiling, *Chamberlain,* p. 279.

218 DDB, IV, pp. 126, 150; C 1616/4/18 of 10 March; C 1734/4/18 of 11 March; Robert Boothby, *I Fight to Live* (London, 1947), p. 136; and Nigel Nicolson (ed.), *Harold Nicolson — Diaries and Letters, 1930-1939* (London, 1966), p. 251.

219 DDB, IV, pp. 106, 150-1; and DDF, I, p. 464.

220 DDB, IV, p. 150.

221 DDB, IV, p. 126.

222 DDF, I, pp. 460, 468, 482, 503, 512, 533-4, 539, 544; C 1672/4/18 of 10 March; and USFR, 1936, I, pp. 236, 238.

223 The following is based on C 1614/4/18 and C 1673/4/18, both of 10 March; DDB, IV, pp. 132-40; and DDF, I, pp. 493-4. See also Eden, *Facing,* pp. 347-52; Flandin, *Politique Française,* pp. 202-4 and *Survenus,* I, p. 151; and CAB 18(36)1 of 11 March.

224 C 1673/4/18 of 10 March, and DDB, IV, p. 134.

225 C 1614/4/18 of 10 March.

226 This paragraph is based on C 1672/4/18 of 10 March; DDB, IV, p. 143; and the citations in note 223.

227 C 1614/4/18 of 10 March; and DDB, IV, pp. 140, 143.

228 DDB, IV, pp. 140, 143. Léger agreed that the worst policy would be a 'coup de poing dans l'oreiller', (DDB, IV, p. 66).

229 DDB, IV, pp. 143, 151.

230 DDF, I, p. 525; C 1734/4/18 of 11 March; DDB, IV, pp. 148-9, 151; and Schuschnigg, *Requiem,* p. 16.

231 This paragraph is based on C 1614/4/18, C 1672/4/18 and C 1673/4/18, all of 10 March; DDB, IV, pp. 138-43; and Eden, *Facing*, pp. 348-51.

232 C 1614/4/18 and C 1672/4/18, both of 10 March; DDB, IV, pp. 141, 143; and DDF, I, p. 493.

233 C 1615/4/18 of 10 March.

234 C 2192/4/18 of 20 March. See also Churchill, *Storm*, p. 171; Colvin, *Vansittart*, p. 98; Valentine Lawford, *Bound for Diplomacy* (London, 1963), p. 277; A. H. Furnia, *The Diplomacy of Appeasement* (Washington, 1960), p. 194; USFR, 1936, I, p. 264; and Sarraut, *Survenus*, III, p. 593.

235 Parker, for example, argued that Flandin's departure signalized the 'abandonment by France of any opportunity she had to force back the Germans' (Parker, *Rhineland*, p. 359).

236 Flandin, *Politique Française*, p. 205; C 1940/4/18 of 12 March; C 1678/4/18 of 11 March; USFR, 1936, I, pp. 235, 241-3; C 1734/4/18 of 11 March; DDF, I, pp. 501-3; Feiling, *Chamberlain*, p. 279; Paul-Boncour, *Entre deux*, III, p. 39; Jones, *Diary*, p. 182; and Churchill, *Storm*, p. 172.

237 DDF, I, pp. 246-7, 290-3, 300-1, 437-8, 444, 504-6, 696-700; and DDB, IV, pp. 65, 87-9.

238 Flandin, *Politique Française*, p. 205.

239 Flandin, *Politique Française*, pp. 205, 208, and *Survenus*, I, pp.. 154-5; and France, Chambre des Députés, *Journal official*, 26 Jan 1937, p. 170.

240 See, for example, DDB, IV, pp. 66, 88, 126, 140, 143; C 1614/4/18 of 10 March; and USFR, 1936, I, p. 269.

241 Flandin, *Politique Française*, p. 208 and *Survenus*, I, pp. 154-5.

242 DDF, I, p. 494; DDB, IV, pp. 147-51; C 1673/4/18 of 10 March; C 1806/4/18 of 12 March; C 1965/4/18 of 13 March; and C 1918/4/18 of 15 March.

243 See, for example, C 1940/4/18, minute by Vansittart, 12 March; and C 2048/4/18, minute by Vansittart, 19 March 1936.

244 Eden, *Facing*, p. 352.

245 C 1614/4/18 of 10 March; and CAB 18(36)1 of 11 March.

5 **Britain rejects force**

1 CP 73(36) of 8 March. Brussels, too, was reportedly taking events in stride (C 1495/4/18 of 7 March; and C 1506/4/18 of 8 March).

2 C 1489/4/18 of 7 March; C 1513/4/18 of 8 March; C 1544/4/18 of 9 March; and C 1693/4/18 of 11 March.

3 Ibid. See also C 1543/4/18 of 9 March; and C 1676/4/18 of 10 March.

4 C 1490/4/18 and C 1486/4/18, both of 7 March; C 1505/4/18 of 8 March; and Eden, *Facing*, p. 344.

5 C 1490/4/18 of 7 March; and C 1500/4/18, C 1504/4/18, C 1520/
   4/18 and CP 73(36), all of 8 March.
6 C 1490/4/18 and C 1491/4/18, both of 7 March. See also DDB, IV,
   p. 105; and C 1529/4/18 of 9 March.
7 DDB, IV, pp. 101, 108, 119-21; and C 1495/4/18 of 8 March.
8 C 1490/4/18 and C 1491/4/18, both of 7 March; C 1501/4/18 and
   C 1509/4/18, both of 8 March; and C 1850/4/18 of 13 March.
9 C 1490/4/18 of 7 March; C 1505/4/18 and C 1520/4/18, both of 8
   March; and C 1508/4/18 of 9 March.
10 C 1490/4/18 of 7 March; C 1505/4/18 and C 1530/4/18, both of 8
   March; DDF, I, pp. 427-8, 431-2; DDB, IV, pp. 119-20, 125-7; and
   Sarraut, *Survenus*, III, pp. 591-2. See also Eden, *Facing*, p. 346; and
   DO 6882A/8 of 9 March.
11 CP 73(36) of 8 March; C 1615/4/18 of 10 March; *Hansard*, vol. 308,
   cols. 1812-13; and DDB, IV, p. 121.
12 CP 73(36) of 8 March; and Eden, *Facing*, p. 342.
13 Eden, *Facing*, pp. 338, 341-2, 353, 367; CAB 18(36)1 of 11 March;
   and Alfred Duff Cooper, *Old Men Forget* (London, 1954), p. 204.
14 DO 6882A/8, meeting of 9 March; and CAB 16(36)1 of 9 March.
15 C 1498/4/18, C 1503/4/18, C 1512/4/18 and C 1622/4/18, all of 8
   March; DO 6882A/8, C 1592/4/18, C 1598/4/18, C 1604/4/18, C
   1623/4/18 and C 1624/4/18, all of 9 March; and Eden, *Facing*,
   p. 367.
16 Eden, *Facing*, p. 347; CAB 16(36)1 of 9 March; Earl of Birkenhead, *Halifax* (London, 1965), p. 351; and DO 6882A/8, meeting
   of 9 March.
17 CP 73(36) of 8 March.
18 C 763/4/18 of 7 Feb 1936.
19 CP 73(36) of 8 March. See also C 1181/4/18, encl. of 30 Jan 1936;
   G(36)3, annex of 14 Feb 1936; and C 1440/4/18 of 4 March 1936.
20 CP 73(36) of 8 March.
21 Ibid.
22 C 1488/4/18 of 7 March. See also C 1487/4/18 and C 1480/4/18,
   both of 7 March; CP 73(36) of 8 March; DDB, IV, pp. 98-9; and
   DDF, I, pp. 414, 427.
23 C 1490/4/18 of 7 March; CP 73(36) of 8 March ; C 1602/4/18 of 9
   March; Colvin, *Vansittart*, p. 97; and Poncet, *Fateful*, p. 196.
24 C 1486/4/18 of 7 March.
25 C 1480/4/18, C 1486/4/18, C 1487/4/18 and C 1488/4/18, all of 7
   March; C-V, p. 42; DDB, IV, p. 98; *Hansard*, vol. 308, cols. 1810-
   11; and Eden, *Facing*, pp. 340, 366.
26 See, for example, C 366/55/18, minute by Sargent, 16 Jan 1935; C
   1480/4/18 of 7 March 1936; C 1533/4/18 of 9 March; and Vansittart, *Mist*, p. 511.
27 C-V, pp. 14, 42; and C 1480/4/18 of 7 March.
28 CP 73(36) of 8 March.

29 See minutes by Carr, Sargent, Strang, Wigram, Stanhope and Cranborne in connexion with C 585/4/18, R 579/125/67 and C 924/97/18 of January and February, 1936.

30 C 8373/55/18 of 19 Dec 1935; CP 15(36) of 17 Jan 1936; C 1137/4/18 of 25 Feb 1936; CP 73(36) of 8 March; and C 1831/4/18 of 9 March.

31 CP 73(36) of 8 March.

32 *Hansard*, vol. 308, cols. 1812-3; *The Times*, 10 and 11 March; C 1616/4/18 of 9 March; C 1647/4/18 of 10 March; and C 2105/4/18 of 11 March.

33 *Hansard*, vol. 308, cols. 1840-1.

34 CAB 18(36)1 of 11 March. See also DO 6882A/8, meeting of 11 March.

35 Ibid. See also C 1940/4/18, minute by Vansittart, 12 March.

36 CAB 18(36)1 and DO 6882A/8, meeting, both of 11 March. See also LP(L) 1st meeting, 13 March.

37 This paragraph is based on C 1670/4/18 and CAB 18(36)1, both of 11 March; C 1740/4/18 and C 1806/4/18, both of 12 March; LP(L) 2nd meeting and C 1817/4/18, both of 13 March; C 1856/4/18 of 14 March; C 1889/4/18 of 15 March; CAB 20(36)3 of 16 March; DO 6882A/8, meetings of 11 and 16 March; and Eden, *Facing*, pp. 353, 367.

38 Feiling, *Chamberlain*, p. 279.

39 CAB 18(36)1 of 11 March; LP(L) 1st and 2nd meetings, both of 13 March; C 1965/4/18 of 13 March, CAB 20(36)3 of 16 March; Eden, *Facing*, p. 367; and Eustace Percy, *Some Memories* (London, 1958), p. 185.

40 C 1670/4/18, minute by Charles W. Baxter, 11 March. See also C 1614/4/18 of 10 March; C 1983/4/18, minute by Valentine Lawford, 18 March; C 2239/4/18, minute by Wigram, 24 March; Zuylen, *Mains libres*, p. 353; Colvin, *Vansittart*, pp. 101-2; and Strang, *Home and Abroad*, p. 122.

41 C 1533/4/18 of 9 March; CAB 18(36)1 of 11 March; DO 6882A/8, meeting of 16 March; C 1906/4/18, minute by Sargent, 18 March; and CAB 23(36)1 of 19 March.

42 CP 85(36) of 19 March. See also C 1883/99/18, minute by Sargent, 17 March.

43 CP 73(36) of 8 March; C 1533/4/18 of 9 March; CAB 18(36)1, DO 6882A/8, meeting, and C 1670/4/18, minute by Baxter, all of 11 March; C 1806/4/18 of 12 March; and LP(L) 2nd meeting, C 1965/4/18 and C 1893/4/18, all of 13 March.

44 This paragraph is based on C 1614/4/18 of 10 March; C 1670/4/18 of 11 March; C 1827/4/18 of 13 March, and C 1856/4/18 of 14 March.

45 See also C 1703/4/18 of 11 March; C 1939/4/18 of 14 March; and C 1983/4/18 of 16 March.

46 C 623/55/18 of 22 Jan 1935; C 5685/55/18 of 23 July 1935; and C 7508/134/18 of 6 Nov 1935.

47 For example, see C 623/55/18, C 2727/55/18, C 3704/55/18, C 5178/55/18, C 5680/55/18, C 7508/134/18, C 7931/55/18 and DCM(32)145, all of 1935; and CP 42(36) of 3 Feb 1936.

48 C 1682/4/18 of 11 March. See also C 143/143/18 of 6 Jan 1936.

49 C 1682/4/18 of 11 March; and R 2401/73/3, minute by Wigram, 29 April 1936.

50 C 1817/4/18 of 13 March; and R 2589/73/3 of 5 May 1936. See also C 1533/4/18 of 8 March; C 1610/4/18 of 10 March; C 1658/4/18 of 11 March; and C 1740/4/18 of 12 March.

51 CAB 18(36)1 of 11 March. For Britain's rearmament problems and progress, see CP 85, CP 100, CP 103, CP 106, CP 166 and CAB 50(35)2, all of 1935; CP 26, CP 27 and CAB 55(36)13, all of 1936; Franklyn A. Johnson, *Defence by Committee* (London, 1960), pp. 224-6, 229; W. K. Hancock and M. M. Gowing, *British War Economy* (London, 1949), pp. 52-5, 63-4; M. M. Postan, *British War Production* (London, 1952), pp. 2, 6; and A. E. M. Chatfield, *The Navy and Defence*, II, *It Might Happen Again* (London, 1947), pp. 77-84, 89, 115, 165-6.

52 CP 167(31) of 7 July 1931; *Hansard*, vol. 309, cols. 1989-92, 2004-5; Hoare, *Nine Years*, pp. 112-13; Vansittart, *Mist*, pp. 333, 351, 385; and Churchill, *Storm*, pp. 25-7, 40, 42-3.

53 Vansittart, *Mist*, pp. 418, 444, 508-10; Feiling, *Chamberlain*, p. 262; Colin R. Coote, *Companion of Honour: The Story of Walter Elliot* (London, 1965), pp. 150-1; Hugh Dalton, *Memoirs*, vol. II, *The Fateful Years* (London, 1957), pp. 87, 90, 97, 132; CAB 18(36)1 of 11 March; *Hansard*, vol. 309, cols. 1841-2, 1877, 1982, 1997, 2046-7, 2051, 2075-7; vol. 317, cols. 1143-5; and Labour Party Annual Report, 1936, pp. 110, 182-207.

54 CAB 18(36)1 of 11 March. See also CAB 15(36)1 of 5 March 1936.

55 The following discussion of British arms weakness is based on CP 105(36) annex and enclosure, 16 and 18 March; AIR.9.73, folder 12; COS 166th meeting, 12 March; and L P (L)1st meeting, 13 March.

56 CP 81(36) of 18 March.

57 Ibid. See also C 5178/55/18 of 4 July 1935; and CP 58(37) of 11 Feb 1937.

58 CAB 20(36)7 of 16 March 1936.

59 COS 166th meeting, 12 March; and *Hansard*, vol. 309, cols. 2335-6, 2353.

60 Britain's total number of tanks in 1936 was 375, of which 304 were obsolete, 2 were experimental and 69 were armed only with machine guns. (Postan, *War Production*, p. 7; and R. J. Minney, *Private Papers of Hore-Belisha* (London, 1960), p. 37).

61 CP 105(36) of 16 March 1936; CID 271st meeting, 14 Oct 1935;

DPR 15th meeting, 6 Dec 1935; Jones, *Diary*, p. 160; Postan, *War Production*, p. 7; Halifax, *Fulness of Days* (London, 1957), p. 182; CP 58(37) of 11 Feb 1937; and *Hansard*, vol. 309, col. 1911.

62 CP 105(36) of 16 March 1936; DPR 79 of 5 Feb 1936; CAB 11(36)5 of 26 Feb 1936; and DPR, 19th meeting, 3 March 1936.

63 CAB 20(36)7 of 16 March; CP 105(36) of 16 March; and AIR 9 73, folder 12.

64 CID 268th meeting, 25 Feb 1936; CID 1216-B of 4 March 1936; CID 1241-B of 12 June 1936; CID 282nd meeting, 8 Oct 1936; *Hansard*, vol. 309, col. 2059; *The Times*, 2 May, 8 June 1936; Dalton, *Fateful*, II, p. 88; Hoare, *Nine Years*, pp. 117-18; Eden, *Facing*, pp. 182-6; Nicolson, *Diaries*, p. 272; and Medlicott, *Contemporary England*, p. 337.

65 CP 105(36) annex and encl., 16 and 18 March; CAB 18(36)1 of 11 March; LP(L) 1st and 2nd meetings, 13 March; Eden, *Facing*, pp. 481-3, 491-5; Amery, *Political Life*, III, p. 183; and Medlicott, *Contemporary England*, pp. 337-8.

66 CID 268th meeting, 25 Feb 1936; *Hansard*, vol. 309, cols. 1850, 2051; *Hansard*, Lords, vol. 100, cols, 51-2, 133; Taylor, *English History*, pp. 96, 229-31, 364, 390-1; Colvin, *Vansittart*, p. 120; and P. R. C. Groves, *Behind the Smoke Screen* (London, 1934), pp. 161, 177-8, 336.

67 See, for example, CID 270th and 271st meetings, CAB 50(35)2, CP 85(35), C 3228/55/18, C 4174/55/18, C 8332/55/18 and J 9156/3861/1, all of 1935; and CID 1238-B, CID 1284-B, CID 282nd meeting and C 1603/4/18, all of 1936.

68 Ibid. See also C 2717/55/18, minute by Creswell, 3 April 1935; and CID 1238-B, minute by Vansittart, 18 June 1936.

69 CID 1161-B and CID 268th meeting, both of 1935; CP 26(36) annex of 21 Nov 1935; C 4922/3928/18 of 27 June 1936; and CP 58(37) of 11 Feb 1937.

70 C 1533/4/18 of 9 March.

71 LP(L) 4th meeting, 16 March.

72 CP 26(36), encl. of 21 Nov 1935. See also CID 269th meeting, 16 April 1935; and C 5685/55/18 of 23 July 1935.

73 DCM(32)145 of 7 June 1935; CP 25(36) encl. of 21 Nov 1935; CP 12(36) of 17 Jan 1936; and DDF, I, p. 480.

74 CAB 3(36)6 of 29 Jan 1936. See also R 2416/226/22 of 23 April 1936.

75 CID 266th meeting, 22 Nov 1934; CID 1161-B of 8 Feb 1935; CID 1187-B of 29 April 1935; and DCM(32)145 of 7 June 1935.

76 DPR 19th meeting, 3 March 1936. See also LP(L) 4th meeting, 16 March.

77 CP 12(36) of 17 Jan 1936; and CP 26(36) encl. of 21 Nov 1935. See also Medlicott, *Coming of War*, p. 9; and DPR 79 of 5 Feb 1936.

78 Admiral Chatfield feared the loss of even some old ships would

have had a 'very serious' effect, while Vansittart believed that Britain would have lost the second war 'if we had spent our small naval margins prematurely'. (Chatfield, *It Might Happen*, pp. 89, 115; and Vansittart, *Mist*, p. 523).

79 CP 166(35) of 9 Aug 1935; J 4889/3861/1 of 16 Sept 1935; CAB 50(35)2 of 2 Dec 1935; and Hoare, *Nine Years*, p. 191.

80 For a picture of the bottlenecks plaguing British arms production, see C 3770/55/18, C 5119/55/18, CID 271st meeting, all of 1935; *Hansard*, vol. 309, cols. 1989-92, 2004-5; vol. 312, cols. 1399-1435; vol. 315, cols. 59-62; and vol. 318, cols. 389, 1257.

81 *Hansard*, vol. 309, col. 2006. In reality, Germany's total expenditure on arms between March 1933 and March 1936 was £667 million.

82 *Hansard*, vol. 309, cols. 2006-7. Britain's total defence outlay for the fiscal year ending 31 March 1936 was £362,442,000.

83 C 1595/4/18 of 9 March; C 1614/4/18 and C 1626/4/18, both of 10 March; LP(L) 2nd meeting, 13 March; and Eden, *Facing*, pp. 343, 350.

84 C 1529/4/18 of 9 March; C 1614/4/18 of 10 March; LP(L) 2nd meeting, 13 March; DDB, IV, pp. 126, 149; DDF, I, pp. 448-9, 549-52, 688, 705-6; USFR, 1936, I, p. 217; and Eden, *Facing*, pp. 350, 360.

85 See, for example, Amery, *Political Life*, III, pp. 188-9; Birkenhead, *Halifax*, p. 351; M. D. Stocks, *Eleanor Rathbone* (London, 1949), pp. 234-5; *Hansard*, vol. 310, cols. 1508, 2543-4; Eden, *Facing*, pp. 336-8; C 1028/4/18 of 24 Feb 1936; and C 2567/4/18 of 31 March.

86 See, for example, C 1079/4/18, C 1498/4/18, R 1564/125/67, C 1623/4/18, C 1699/4/18, C 1700/4/18, C 1717/4/18, C 1819/4/18, C 1820/4/18, C 1860/4/18, C 1900/4/18, C 1967/4/18, C 2249/4/18 and C 2348/4/18, all 8-17 March.

87 In addition to the preceding citations, see R 1647/444/7, C 1713/4/18, C 1724/4/18, C 1725/4/18, C 1766/4/18, C 1854/4/18, C 1893/4/18, C 1924/4/18, C 1932/4/18 and C 1972/4/18, all between 11 and 17 March.

88 C 1699/4/18 of 11 March; C 1854/4/18 and C 1932/4/18, both of 13 March; and R 1667/1162/12 of 17 March.

89 CP 85(36) of 12 March; C 1832/4/18 of 13 March; and C 2567/4/18 of 31 March.

90 C 1498/4/18 of 8 March; LP(L) 3rd meeting, 14 March; and C 1989/4/18 of 17 March.

91 CP 105(36) annex and encl., 16 and 18 March; and LP(L) 1st meeting, 13 March.

92 C 1356/270/4 of 6 March 1936; C 3500/3398/4 of 26 April 1935; CP 58(37) of 11 Feb 1937; and DO 6882A/8 of 20 March.

93 C 1809/4/18 and R 1785/1162/12, both of 13 March; and C

4949/3928/18 of 7 July 1936. See also R 1646/1162/12 of 17 March.

94 G(36)6 of 27 Feb 1936. See also R 1643/1162/12 of 17 March 1936.

95 R 1023/125/67, minute by O'Malley, 21 Feb 1936; and G(36)6 of 27 Feb 1936.

96 C 1512/4/18 of 8 March; and C 1602/4/18 of 9 March.

97 C 1716/4/18 of 10 March.

98 C 1512/4/18 of 8 March; C 1659/4/18 of 10 March; C 1903/4/18 of 15 March; and C 1936/4/18 of 16 March.

99 DO 6882A/8, meeting of 16 March; CP 85(36) of 12 March; C 1893/4/18 of 13 March; and C 1936/4/18 of 16 March. See also Erickson, *Soviet High Command,* p. 416; and Beloff, *Soviet Foreign Policy,* II, p. 50.

100 DO 6882A/8, meeting of 16 March.

101 R 1983/1162/12 of 3 April 1936; C 5356/55/18 of 3 July 1936; and CP 58(37) of 11 Feb 1937. See also C 5685/55/18 of 23 July 1935; and R 730/125/67 of 7 Feb 1936.

102 In addition to the citations in note 101, see C 2819/55/18 of 2 April 1935; C 1595/4/18 of 9 March 1936; and N 6375/136/38 of 18 Dec 1936.

103 C 52/52/55 of 1 Jan 1936; R 1983/1162/12 of 3 April 1936; N 2609/307/38 of 1 May 1936; C 7389/92/62, minute by N. J. A. Cheetham, 27 Oct 1936; and N 6375/136/38 of 18 Dec 1936.

104 USFR, 1936, I, p. 213.

105 For a sample of British discussion of French fighting capacity, see C 4413/55/18, C 6985/227/17 and C 7873/221/17 of 1935; C 797/172/17, C 1167/4/18, C 4274/3928/18, C 5356/4/18 and C 7388/4/18 of 1936; and CP 58(37) of 11 Feb 1937.

106 C 5683/55/18 of 10 July 1936.

107 C 5356/4/18 of 3 July 1936.

108 CP 58(37) of 11 Feb 1937.

109 For a sample of British assessments of French air strength and capacity, see C 2928/55/18, C 6704/55/18 and CID 271st meeting of 1935; C 435/4/18, C 4182/172/17, C 4274/3928/18 and C 5391/-172/17 of 1936.

110 Medlicott, *Contemporary England,* p. 338.

111 For a sample, see *The Times,* 9-31 March; RIIA, *Germany and the Rhineland,* symposia at Chatham House (London, 1936), pp. 4-61; Colin R. Coote, *A Companion of Honour: The Story of Walter Elliot* (London, 1965), p. 155; Harold Macmillan, *Winds of Change* (London, 1966), pp. 460-5; Colin Cross, *Philip Snowden* (London, 1963), p. 339; J. R. Clynes, *Memoirs,* II (London, 1937), pp. 232-3; Dalton, *Memoirs,* II, p. 88; and C-V, *passim.*

112 For the impact of public opinion on the government, see CAB 18(36)1 of 11 March; LP(L) 2nd meeting, 13 March; Eden, *Facing,* pp. 338, 340, 343, 346, 353, 367; Feiling, *Chamberlain,* p. 279; John Simon, *Retrospect* (London, 1952), p. 215; Halifax, *Fulness,* p. 197;

Young, *Baldwin,* pp. 223-4; Cooper, *Old Men,* p. 196; Walter M. Citrine, *Men and Work* (London, 1964), p. 356; and Percy, *Memories,* p. 184.

113 In addition to the citations in notes 111 and 112, see *Hansard,* vol. 309, cols. 1863, 1877, 1926-7, 2035; *Hansard,* Lords, vol. 99, col. 968 and vol. 100, cols. 26, 193, 253, 547-8, 551-3; C 1831/4/18 of 9 March; C 1720/4/18 of 11 March; C 1938/4/18 of 12 March; and C 2802/4/18 of 13 March.

114 CAB 18(36)1 of 11 March; LP(L)1st meeting, 13 March, C 1643/4/18 of 9 March; C 1818/4/18, minute by Lawford, 14 March; Eden, *Facing,* pp. 353, 367; Feiling, *Chamberlain,* p. 280; and *Hansard,* vol. 309, cols. 1841-3, 1982, 1997-2002, 2046-7.

115 In addition to the preceding citations, see Birkenhead, *Halifax,* p. 351; Stocks, *Rathbone,* pp. 234-5; Amery, *Political Life,* III, pp. 188-9; Robert Cecil, *Great Experiment* (London, 1941), p. 277; and Jones, *Diary,* pp. 187-8.

116 Jones, *Diary,* p. 183; Alan C. Johnson, *Viscount Halifax* (London, 1941), p. 394; Philip Gibbs, *Ordeal in England* (London, 1937), pp. 229-31; J. R. M. Butler, *Lord Lothian, 1882-1940* (London, 1960), p. vi; and *Hansard,* Lords, vol. 100, col. 26.

117 A. Chamberlain papers, 41/3/27, letter to V. d'Ormesson, 28 March 1936; *Survey,* 1936, pp. 277, 280; Amery, *Political Life,* II, pp. 189, 193; C 2086/4/18, minute by Cranborne, 17 March; C 1912/4/18, minute by Sargent, 18 March; *Hansard,* vol. 310, col. 1493; *Hansard,* Lords, vol. 99, col. 968 and vol. 100, cols. 254, 556; Grigg, *Faith,* pp. 312-13; Clynes, *Memoirs,* II, p. 231; and Londonderry, *Ourselves,* pp. 21, 129.

118 This paragraph is based on *The Times* and *Le Temps* (and press extracts), both 9-14 March; C-V, pp. 59, 93; C 2105/4/18 of 11 March; Colin R. Coote, *Editorial* (London, 1965), p. 173; Eden, *Facing,* p. 346; and Vansittart, *Lessons,* p. 571.

119 *The Times,* 9 March; Jones, *Diary,* pp. 179-81; CP 73(36) of 8 March; Butler, *Lothian,* pp. 212-13; Astor, *Tribal Feeling,* pp. 136-47; C-V, p. 103; Margaret George, *The Warped Vision* (Pittsburgh, 1965), p. 77n; and Eden, *Facing,* pp. 336-7, 343-4, 347.

120 The following is based on: C 1643/4/18 of 9 March; C 1714/1714/18 and C 1715/1714/18, both of 9 March; C 1720/1714/18 of 11 March; C 2802/4/18, minute by Wigram of 13 March; C 1818/4/18, minute by Lawford, 14 March; CAB 18(36)1 of 11 March; LP(L)1st meeting, 13 March; *The Times,* 9-19 March; and Eden, *Facing,* pp. 338, 343, 353, 367.

121 In addition, see C 1643/4/18 and C 1831/4/18, both of 9 March; C 1865/4/18 of 12 March; *Hansard,* vol. 309, cols. 1862, 1964, 1926, 2035-7; *Hansard,* Lords, vol. 99, col. 968; Jones, *Diary,* pp. 180-3; and RIIA, *Rhineland,* pp. 38, 40-2.

122 *Hansard,* vol. 309, col. 2035.

123 C. L. Mount, *Britain between Wars, 1918-1940* (London, 1940), p. 564.

124 C 1616/4/18 of 9 March; DO 6882A/8, meetings of 9, 11, 13, 16, 19 and 20 March; CAB 20(36)3 of 16 March; and Vansittart, *Mist,* p. 529.

125 Vincent Massey, *What's Past Is Prologue* (London, 1963), pp. 229-31; and DO 6882A/8 of 11 March. See also James Eayrs, *In Defence of Canada,* II (Toronto, 1965), p. 50.

126 DO 6882A/8, meeting of 14 March. See also Nicholas Mansergh, *Survey of British Commonwealth Affairs,* III (London, 1952), p. 234; Oswald Pirow, *James B. M. Hertzog* (London, 1958), pp. 221-3; and D. C. Watt, 'South African Attempts to Mediate between Britain and Germany, 1935-1938', *Studies in International History* (London, 1967), pp. 406-7.

127 Massey, *Prologue,* pp. 231-2; C 2074/4/18 of 17 March; Carter, *Commonwealth,* pp. 233-4; Eayrs, *Defence,* II, p. 52; and Bruce Hutchison, *Mackenzie King* (London, 1953), p. 207.

128 C 1921/4/18 of 16 March; DO 6882A/8, meetings of 13, 16, 19 March; C 2225/4/18 of 17 March; C 2124/4/18 of 19 March; and Carter, *Commonwealth,* p. 234.

129 C 1977/4/18 of 13 March; C 2738/4/18 of 13 March; C 2054/4/18 of 17 March; DDF, I, pp. 455-6, 606-7; C-V, pp. 100, 130-1; and the following press cuttings from FOL 6710: E506474, E506508, E506607, E506737-9, E507461-2, E507505, E508034-5, E508159-63, E509159-60, E509164-5 and E509218-22, all between 9 and 31 March.

130 'On all sides one hears sympathy for Germany', wrote Harold Nicolson on 10 March. 'The country will not stand for anything that makes for war.' (*Diaries,* pp. 248-9).

131 Eden, *Facing,* p. 338.

132 Lawford, *Bound,* pp. 276-7.

133 *Hansard,* vol. 309, cols. 2006-7 and vol. 310, cols. 1487-2488; Vansittart, *Mist,* pp. 523, 543; Amery, *Political Life,* III, pp. 198, 228; C 1831/4/18 of 12 March; and C 2239/4/18, minute by Wigram, 24 March.

134 C 2802/4/18, minute by Vansittart, 17 March; and Colvin, *Vansittart,* pp. 98, 101-2.

135 *Hansard,* vol. 310, col. 2488. See also W. S. Churchill, *Step by Step, 1936-1939* (London, 1959), pp. 13-15, 19-20; Lloyd George papers, G/4/5/21, letter from Churchill, 9 Sept 1937; and Medlicott, *Contemporary England,* p. 350n.

136 *Hansard,* vol. 310, col. 1498; and RIIA, *Rhineland,* p. 11. See also Boothby, *I Fight,* p. 136; and C 2214/4/18 of 14 March.

137 C 1619/4/18 of 10 March. See also C 1817/4/18 of 13 March; C 1986/4/18 of 17 March; and USFR, 1936, I, pp. 203, 215, 236, 249-50.

138 See, for example, Amery, *Political Life,* III, p. 189; Nicolson,

Diaries, p. 252; *Hansard,* vol. 311, col. 1823; *Survey,* 1936, p. 276n; and A. Chamberlain papers, 41/3/27, letter to Gilbert Murray, 16 March 1936.

139 This paragraph is based on CP 73(36) of 8 March; Eden, *Facing,* pp. 340, 341, 343, 346-7, 360; Colvin, *Vansittart,* pp. 97-8, 101; J. E. Wrench, *Geoffrey Dawson and Our Times* (London, 1955), p. 331; Medlicott, *Search,* pp. 24-5; CAB 18(36)1 of 11 March; CAB 20(36)3 of 16 March; Feiling, *Chamberlain,* p. 279; and DO 6882A/8, meetings of 9, 11, 13, 16 and 19 March.

140 In addition to the preceding citations, see C 2802/4/18, minute by Vansittart, 17 March; Percy, *Memories,* pp. 184-5; Halifax, *Fulness,* p. 197; and Strang, *Home and Abroad,* p. 122.

141 The government was still confronted by a public opinion which largely believed that Germany had not been treated as an equal since her defeat. For a sample, see *Hansard,* vol. 309, cols. 1863-4, 1877, 1926, 2036; vol. 310, cols. 1491-2, 1511-12; *Hansard,* Lords, vol. 99, col. 968; vol. 100, cols. 26, 193, 253, 553; and C 2802/4/18, minute by Wigram, 13 March 1936.

142 Amery, *Political Life,* III, pp. 188-9; C 1533/4/18 of 9 March; CAB 18(36)1 of 11 March; DO 6882A/8, meeting of 11 March; Feiling, *Chamberlain,* p. 279; Cecil, *All the Way,* p. 209; Birkenhead, *Halifax,* p. 350; and Iain Macleod, *Neville Chamberlain* (London, 1961), p. 190.

143 C 1905/4/18 of 8 March; C 1592/4/18 and C 1595/4/18, both of 9 March; C 1716/4/18 of 10 March; C 2470/4/18 of 28 March; J 2709/1000/1, minute by Cranborne, 7 April; C 3266/4/18 of 22 April, and C 3231/4/18 of 28 April.

144 CAB 18(36)1 of 11 March; CAB 23(36)1 of 19 March; and CAB 50(35)2 of 2 Dec 1935. See also Young, *Baldwin,* pp. 184, 223; and Jones, *Diary,* p. 231.

145 In addition to the citations in note 117, see Nicolson, *Diaries,* pp. 249-50, 269; Coote, *Editorial,* p. 195; and Jones, *Diary,* pp. 172-3, 211.

146 N 479/20/38, minute by Eden, 10 Jan 1936. See also C 7730/55/18, memorandum by Eden, 20 Nov 1935; and N 6030/17/38, minute by Eden, 21 Nov 1935.

147 C 5685/55/18 of 23 July 1935; minutes by Cranborne, Stanhope and Sargent on N 479/20/38, N 6642/76/38, N 307/307/38, all January 1936; C 1533/4/18 of 9 March; R 1983/1162/12 of 3 April; C 2737/4/18 of 6 April 1936; C 5356/4/18 of 3 July 1936; and C 8998/8998/18 of 31 Dec 1936.

148 CAB 18(36)1 of 11 March.

149 Ibid., and *Hansard,* vol. 309, col. 1841.

150 CAB 18(36)1 of 11 March.

151 Macleod, *Chamberlain,* pp. 189-90.

152 Dalton diaries, entry for 11 March 1936. See also Coote, *Com-*

panion, p. 157; Colvin, *Vansittart*, p. 101; and USFR, 1936, I, p. 243.

153 CAB 18(36)1 of 11 March.

154 CAB 18(36)1 of 11 March; C 1672/4/18 of 10 March; and DDB, IV, pp. 141-3.

155 Ibid.

156 CAB 18(36)1 of 11 March. See also CAB 19(36)1 of 12 March.

157 Ibid. See also Eden, *Facing*, p. 354.

158 Ibid.

159 C-V, p. 111; C 1671/4/18 of 11 March; FOL 7882H/E570829-32 of 11 March; C 1710/4/18 of 11 March; C 1723/4/18 of 11 March; and G. Ward Price, *I Know These Dictators* (London, 1937), p. 128.

160 The following is based on C 1671/4/18 and CAB 18(36)1, both of 11 March; C-V, pp. 110-11; and Eden, *Facing*, pp. 354-5.

161 Prevailing British estimates of troop strength in the Rhineland, including Landespolizei, ranged from 40,000 to 75,000, with the average around 45,000. (C 1940/4/18 of 12 March; and C 1775/-4/18, C 1795/4/18, C 1838/4/18, C 1847/4/18 and C 1848/4/18, all of 13 March 1936).

6 German crisis management

1 The following two paragraphs are based on C 1703/4/18 of 11 March; C 1983/4/18 of 16 March; C 2607/86/18 of 31 March; DDF, I, pp. 416, 537; Poncet, *Fateful*, p. 192 and *Survenus*, III, p. 767; Dodd, *Diary*, pp. 319-21; USFR, 1936, I, p. 215; *The Times* and *Le Temps*, 9, 10 March; William L. Shirer, *Berlin Diary* (New York, 1941), pp. 52-4, 58; Max Domarus, *Hitler, Reden und Proklamationen, 1932-1935*, I (Neustadt, 1962), p. 603; Dobler, *Survenus*, II, p. 481; IMT, XII, p. 158; and Bolen, 'Rhineland', pp. 254-7.

2 C 414/86/18 of 18 Jan 1936. See also C 1792/4/18 of 13 March.

3 C 1703/4/18 of 11 March.

4 In addition to the citations in note 1, see *Survey*, 1936, p. 261; Shirer, *Rise and Fall*, p. 294n; Walther Hofer, *Die Diktatur Hitlers* (Konstanz, 1960), p. 52; and Braubach, *Einmarsch*, p. 5.

5 C 2607/4/18 of 31 March. See also C 1661/4/18 of 11 March; and USFR, 1936, I, p. 261.

6 For German press reactions during the first five days after the coup see C 1497/4/18, C 1528/4/18, C 1594/4/18, C 1661/4/18, C 1702/4/18, C 1701/4/18, and C 1746/4/18 of 8-12 March; DDF, I, pp. 471-2, 508-12; and Ernest K. Bramsted, *Goebbels and National Socialist Propaganda* (East Lansing, Mich., 1965), pp. 138-9.

7 C 1528/4/18 of 9 March.

8 C 1661/4/18 of 11 March; Bramsted, *Goebbels*, pp. 138-9; and C 1684/4/18 of 10 March.

9 See, for example, C-V, pp. 47-8, 105-6, 114-15, 127n, 134n, 149,

150; C 1511/4/18 of 9 March; C 1723/4/18 of 11 March; C 1746/
4/18 of 12 March; Shirer, *Diary*, pp. 54-6; Hossbach, *Zwischen*,
p. 98; Krosigk, *Es Geschah*, p. 310; and FOL 6710/E506232-5 of
7 March.

10 Schmidt, *Statist*, p. 320; Hossbach, *Zwischen*, p. 23; Speer, *Inside*, p.
72; Frank, *Angesicht*, pp. 211-12; Kordt, *Akten*, p. 134; Dietrich,
Zwölf Jahre, pp. 44-5; Schuschnigg, *Requiem*, p. 17; Domarus,
Hitler, p. 601; and DDF, I, p. 600.

11 Kordt, *Akten*, p. 134; Manstein, *Soldatenleben*, p. 237; Erfurth,
Generalstab, p. 200; Carl H. Hermann, *Deutsche Militärgeschichte*
(Frankfurt am Main, 1966), pp. 430-1; and Hegner, *Reichskanzlei*,
p. 200.

12 IMT, XV, p. 352; Keitel, *Keitel*, p. 90; Manstein, *Soldatenleben*, p.
237; Speer, *Inside*, p. 72; Schmidt, *Statist*, p. 320; Frank, *Angesicht*,
p. 211; Kordt, *Akten*, p. 134; and Benoist-Méchin, *Armée*, II, p.
645.

13 The evidence suggests only that he was by no means as self-
assured as he later claimed. (Kordt, *Akten*, p. 134; Hans B. Gisevius, *Bis zum bitteren Ende* (Hamburg, 1960), p. 302; Meissner,
Staatssekretär, pp. 411-12; Domarus, *Hitler*, pp. 601-2; Manstein,
Soldatenleben, p. 237; Erfurth, *Generalstab*, p. 200; Braubach,
Einmarsch, p. 22; Schmidt, *Statist*, p. 320; Frank, *Angesicht*, pp.
211-12; and C 7997/3/18 of 12 Nov 1937).

14 C-V, pp. 29-31, 34-5, 41-3, 47-9, 55-9, 61, 79-80, 86, 92-5, 100-3, 106,
149, 150. See also C 1479/4/18 of 8 March, C 1511/4/18 of 9 March;
Meissner, *Staatssekretär*, p. 412; and DDF, I, p. 600.

15 C-V, pp. 29-115; FOL 63/43673-815; and FOL 6710/E506342-
E507086.

16 See, for example, C-V, pp. 33, 34, 40-1, 42, 54, 55-6, 57-8, 59, 62, 64,
66-7, 78, 81, 85, 88-9, 92-4, 97, 106, 112; *Survey*, 1936, p. 277; DDF,
I, pp. 414-15, 419; and USFR, 1936, pp. 210-11, 214.

17 This paragraph is based on C-V, pp. 36-8, 71; and Robertson,
Vierteljahreshefte, p. 205. See also C-V, pp. 51, 78, 104, 123, 206.

18 C-V, pp. 49, 65.

19 C-V, pp. 48-9, 65. See also C-V, p. 37.

20 C-V, pp. 37, 51, 71, 554.

21 C-V, p. 71.

22 C-IV, pp. 532, 822, 869, 974, 1005-6, 1173-6; and C-V, pp. 15, 37-8,
51, 66, 71, 123, 206.

23 See for example, DDF, I, pp. 26, 163, 318-19, 336-7, 396-7; C-V, p.
8; J 2061/571/1 of 28 Feb 1936; and J 1944/1000/1 of 29 Feb 1936.

24 C-V, pp. 37, 66, 71, 78, 104, 123, 206; and Robertson, *Vierteljahreshefte*, p. 205.

25 C-V, pp. 84, 104, 130, 151-2, 195, 206-7; DDF, I, pp. 467-9, 475-6,
497, 582-3; DDB, IV, p. 124; USFR, 1936, I, pp. 215, 231; and *The
Times*, 14 March.

26 C-IV, pp. 974, 1005-6, 1173-5, 1203; and C-V, pp. 21, 71, 206.
27 C-IV, pp. 1173-5.
28 C-IV, pp. 1005-6, 1016; C-V, pp. 151, 206; and Robertson, *Vierteljahreshefte*, p. 205.
29 Robertson, *Vierteljahreshefte*, p. 205.
30 C-V, pp. 38, 71-2, 104, 123, 207; and Robertson, *Vierteljahreshefte*, p. 205.
31 See, for example, C-IV, pp. 1143-4, 1165, 1174-5, 1213-14; C-V, pp. 48-9, 65.
32 C-V, p. 130. See also C-V, pp. 48-9, 82, 151-2, 155, 195, 206-8.
33 C-V, pp. 15, 48, 82.
34 C-V, p. 48.
35 C-V, pp. 15, 29, 37, 48, 130.
36 C-V, pp. 65-6, 82. See also C-V, pp. 124, 152.
37 C-V, p. 65; and FOL 6710/E506423 of 9 March.
38 C-V, p. 66. See also C-V, pp. 151-2.
39 C-V, p. 66.
40 C-V, pp. 50-2, 65-6, 80-2, 104, 123-4, 130, 151-2, 155-6.
41 C-V, pp. 66, 155-6, 193; C 1673/4/18 of 10 March; C 1815/4/18 of 12 March; Flandin, *Survenus*, I, p. 153; and Aloisi, *Journal*, pp. 356-8.
42 C-V, pp. 15-19; and Baynes, *Hitler's Speeches*, II, pp. 1271-1302.
43 C-V, pp. 78-80, 98, 109; *Hansard*, vol. 309, col. 1813; DDF, I, p. 452; and C 1671/4/18 and FOL 6710/E506675-6, both of 11 March.
44 *Daily Mail*, 11 March; DDF, I, pp. 514-15; and C-V, pp. 78-9, 98.
45 C-V, pp. 83 and 83n. See also C-V, pp. 70, 99, 118-19, 157-8, 439-47.
46 For a sample, see C-V, pp. 14-15, 55-8, 92-3, 106; C 1486/4/18, C 1487/4/18 and C 1488/4/18, all of 7 March; C 1533/4/18 and C 1643/4/18, both of 9 March; and *Hansard*, vol. 309, cols. 1862-4, 1926, 2035-7.
47 C 1480/4/18 of 7 March; C-V, p. 42; and *Hansard*, vol. 309, cols. 1809-13.
48 C-V, pp. 41-3, 59; and C 1480/4/18 of 7 March. See also C-V, pp. 55-8, 67-9, 79-80, 92-5; Eden, *Facing*, pp. 338-40; and DDB, IV, p. 97.
49 *Hansard*, vol. 309, cols. 1809-14, 1840-1; and C-V, pp. 43, 235.
50 C-V, pp. 79-80, 92-3, 102-3, 234-5, 237, 239; FOL 6710/E506552 of 10 March; and FOL 6710/E506702 of 11 March.
51 C-V, pp. 58, 69, 94-5, 237, 240; FOL 6710/E506964-6 of 12 March; and FOL 5730H/E415601-2, E415610 and E415682, of 13, 14 and 15 March.
52 C-V, p. 106. See also C-V, pp. 193-4, 239.
53 C-V, p. 57.
54 C-V, pp. 75-7.
55 *Hansard*, vol. 309, col. 1813 and vol. 310, cols. 1484-7; *The Times*,

12, 13, 16, 17, 18 and 20 March; and C-V, pp. 119, 127, 236, 238.

56 C-V, pp. 79-80, 93-4.

57 C-V, pp. 50, 84-5; FOL 6710/E506967-75 of 12 March; and FOL 6710/E507214-20 of 14 March.

58 C-V, pp. 50, 84-5, 107-8; FOL 63/43736-7 of 9 March; FOL 6710/ E506604 of 10 March; and FOL 6710/E507214-20 of 14 March.

59 FOL 63/43724-5 and C 1742/4/18, both of 11 March; Wullus-Rudiger, *Origines*, pp. 337-40; and Miller, *Belgian*, p. 222.

60 C-V, pp. 121-2, 149, 150, 297, 373-6; and the following FOL: 6710/E506344-6, 769/270863-4, 63/270877, 63/270881-2 and 63/270866-7 of 8, 8, 10, 11 and 12 March.

61 C-V, pp. 61, 101; DDF, I, p. 600; and Meissner, *Staatssekretär*, p. 411.

62 In addition to note 60, see Kordt, *Akten*, p. 135; and C-V, pp. 101, 131.

63 C-V, p. 101.

64 C-V, p. 45; Kordt, *Akten*, p. 135; and *Survey*, 1936, p. 268. See also C-V, p. 86; and Shirer, *Diary*, pp. 50, 55-8.

65 C-V, pp. 47-8; and Poncet, *Fateful*, p. 197.

66 *The Times*, 10 March. See also Poncet, *Fateful*, p. 197; Speer, *Inside*, p. 72; DDF, I, p. 600; and Dietrich, *Zwölf Jahre*, pp. 44-5.

67 *Der Hochsverratsprozess gegen Dr. Guido Schmidt* (Vienna, 1947), p. 43.

68 Ibid.; Hossbach, *Zwischen*, p. 23; Frank, *Angesicht*, p. 211; Schmidt, *Statist*, p. 320; Dietrich, *Zwölf Jahre*, p. 30; Schuschnigg, *Requiem*, p. 17; Trevor-Roper, *Table Talk*, p. 259; Hildegard Boeninger, 'Hitler and the German Generals, 1934-1938,' *Journal of Central European Affairs*, XIV, April 1954, p. 32; and Lossberg, *Wehrmachtführungsstab*, p. 11.

69 There is no evidence to suggest that any major decision was taken without consulting Neurath. Even Ribbentrop and his Büro worked with, rather than independently of, the foreign ministry.

70 Trevor-Roper, *Table Talk*, p. 259.

71 IMT, X, pp. 218-19, XVI, p. 625; and XVII, pp. 41-2.

72 C-V, pp. 47-8.

73 C-V, pp. 33, 34, 39, 40-1, 53-4, 56, 58, 60-1, 62, 64, 66-7, 81-2, 84, 86-9, 96-7, 99, 100, 108-9, 112-13, 114, 130-1, 133, 135-6, 149-50, 153, 154, 156.

74 C-V, pp. 33, 56, 83, 99, 118-19, 157-8, 194-5, 282, 298; and the following from FOL 6710: E506379-80 of 8 March; E506613 of 10 March; E506837 of 12 March; E507250-2 of 13 March; and E507233 of 14 March.

75 C-V, pp. 99, 118-19, 158, 182-3, 298.

76 C-V, pp. 298-9. That deal, which had been agreed save for a few minor points, was subsequently signed on 29 April.

77 C-V, pp. 52-3, 149, 150, 261-4, 297; and FOL 6710/E507098-100 of
    12 March.

78 C-V, pp. 261-2; C 1659/4/18 of 10 March; and FOL 6710/
    E507098-100 of 12 March.

79 C-V, pp. 52-3, 262; and DDF, I, p. 439.

80 C-V, pp. 52-3, 261-4, 298-9; and USFR, 1936, I, pp. 212-13.

81 C-V, pp. 298-9. See also C-V, pp. 261-2.

82 C-V, pp. 63, 82, 129-30, 150, 175; and FOL 6710/E507226-7 of 13
    March.

83 C-V, pp. 175, 184-5; and FOL 6710/E507226-7 of 13 March. See
    also C-V, p. 98; FOL 6710/E506959-62 of 10 March; and DDF, I,
    pp. 435-6.

84 C-V, p. 298; FOL 6710/E506709-10 of 11 March; and FOL 6710/
    E507226-7 and C 1832/4/18, both of 13 March; DDF, I, pp. 420-1;
    and USFR, 1936, I, p. 228.

85 C-V, pp. 39, 89, 95, 112; FOL 6710/E506318 of 7 March; and
    Szembek, *Journal,* p. 167.

86 C-V, pp. 39, 88-9, 144.

87 C-V, pp. 89, 95, 182; FOL 6710/E506392 of 8 March; Szembek,
    Journal, p. 169; C 1625/4/18 of 9 March; C 1748/4/18 of 11 March;
    DDF, I, pp. 533-5; and Richard Breyer, *Das deutsche Reich und
    Polen* (Würzburg, 1955), pp. 160-1, 163.

88 C-V, pp. 95, 144; FOL 6710/E506318 of 7 March; DDB, IV, p. 131;
    and Friedrich Berber (ed.), *Europäische Politik 1933-1938 im Spiegel
    der Prager Akten* (Essen, 1942), pp. 57-8.

89 C-V, pp. 89, 144-5; and DDF, I, pp. 487-8.

90 C-V, pp. 96, 144-5; and C-IV, pp. 72, 84-6. See also C-V, pp. 89,
    299; and Berber, *Spiegel,* pp. 57-8.

91 C-V, pp. 89, 96.

92 C-V, p. 89. See also C 1900/4/18 of 15 March; and Szembek,
    Journal, pp. 169-70.

93 C-V, p. 89. See also Noël, *Agression,* p. 136; DDF, I, pp. 434-5, 526,
    528; and DDB, IV, p. 149.

94 C-V, pp. 96, 144-5, 299. See also DDB, IV, p. 149.

95 C-V, pp. 112, 159-60, 166, 366. See also C-V, pp. 88-9; DDF, I, pp.
    570-1, 639-41; Berber, *Spiegel,* pp. 59-60; Szembek, *Journal,* pp.
    173; Beck, *Final Report,* pp. 111-14; and Noël, *Agression,* p. 137.

96 C-V, pp. 112, 166.

97 C-V, pp. 105-6, 121, 134n, 149, 150, 299. See also C-V, pp. 49, 136-
    40, 157; and Keitel, *Keitel,* p. 91.

98 C-V, pp. 57-9, 61, 79-80, 92-5, 101-3, 106.

99 C-V, p. 156; and FOL 6710/E506783-4 of 12 March. See also C-V,
    p. 126.

100 See, for example, C-V, pp. 103, 128-9, 140-1, 161-2.

101 C-V, pp. 105-6, 136-40; C 1657/4/18 of 11 March; C 1792/4/18 of
    13 March; C 1884/4/18 of 15 March; and C 2071/4/18 of 16 March.

102 C-V, pp. 106, 115; RIIA, *Documents,* 1936, pp. 57-61; C 1792/4/18 of 13 March; C 1884/4/18 of 15 March; and C 1975/4/18 of 17 March.

103 In addition to the citations in note 102, see Robertson, *Vierteljahreshefte,* pp. 203-4; USFR, 1936, I, pp. 223, 226; and DDF, I, p. 708.

104 Robertson, *Vierteljahreshefte,* pp. 203-5.

105 C 1792/4/18, C 1884/4/18, C 1975/4/18, C 2071/4/18, C 2175/4/18, C 2186/4/18, C 2208/4/18, C 2219/4/18, C 2276/4/18, C 2346/4/18, C 2604/86/18; and *The Times* all between 13 and 31 March; and Abetz, *Problem,* pp. 79-80.

106 C-V, pp. 114-17; C 1723/4/18 of 11 March; C 1737/4/18 of 12 March; C 1804/4/18 of 13 March; C 1933/4/18 of 14 March; and the first five citations from note 105.

107 C-V, pp. 115-16; C 1723/4/18 of 11 March; C 1737/4/18 of 12 March; C 1792/4/18 and C 1804/4/18, both of 13 March; C 1933/-4/18 of 14 March; and C 1884/4/18 of 15 March. See also USFR, 1936, I, p. 237.

108 C 1933/4/18, minutes by Vansittart and Eden, both 14 March; C 1879/4/18 of 14 March; C-V, pp. 163-4; and LP(L) 1st and 2nd meetings, both of 13 March.

109 This paragraph is based on C-V, pp. 116-17; and C 1813/4/18 of 12 March. See also C-V, pp. 126-7; and Eden, *Facing,* p. 355.

110 C 1737/4/18 of 12 March. See also C-V, pp. 115, 117-18n.

111 C-V, pp. 119-22, 126-9, 131-2, 134, 140-1.

112 C-V, pp. 120-2.

113 C-V, pp. 128-9, 131-2.

114 C-V, pp. 131-2. See also C-V, pp. 128-9, 424; *The Times,* 13 March; and *Le Temps,* 14 March.

115 C-V, pp. 119, 126, 236-7; and *The Times,* 13 March. See also *The Times,* 17 March; and LP(L) 1st meeting, 13 March.

116 C-V, pp. 119-20; and Geyr, *Critical Years,* pp. 57-9, 61-3.

117 This paragraph is based on C-V, pp. 126-7, 161-2. See also C-V, pp. 92-4, 102-3, 233-40.

118 C-V, pp. 126-7.

119 C-V, p. 134. See also Geyr, *Critical Years,* pp. 57-9, 61-3; FOL 5576H/E400417-20 of 16 March; USFR, 1936, I, p. 243; and C 1828/4/18 of 14 March.

120 This paragraph is based on Hossbach, *Zwischen,* pp. 84-5. See also Manstein, *Verlorene Siege,* p. 74; IMT, XX, p. 603; Geyr, *Critical Years,* p. 63; and Görlitz, *General Staff,* p. 306.

121 Hossbach, *Zwischen,* p. 98; C-V, p. 134; and Hegner, *Reichskanzlei,* p. 201.

122 C-V, p. 134n; and FOL 6710/E506873 of 13 March. See also C-V, pp. 105-6, 149, 150; and FOL 6710/E506777-78 of 12 March.

123 Keitel, *Keitel,* p. 91; IMT, XIII, p. 57; Manstein, *Verlorene Siege,*

p. 74; and Kordt, *Akten,* p. 134. See also C-V, p. 134n; Ernst von Weizsäcker, *Erinnerungen* (Munich, 1950), p. 134; and C 7997/3/18 of 12 Nov 1937.

124 C-V, pp. 134n, 149, 150; Erfurth, *Geschichte,* p. 200; Boeninger, 'Hitler,' p. 31; Manstein, *Verlorene Siege,* p. 74; and DDF, I, pp. 517, 554. Generals Jodl and Wilhelm Keitel, the chief of the Wehrmachtsamt, both favoured making some concession. (Hossbach, *Zwischen,* pp. 84-5; IMT, XV, p. 352; and Keitel, *Keitel,* p. 91).

125 C 1933/4/18 of 14 March.

126 C-V, pp. 149, 150; and USFR, 1936, I, pp. 245-6.

127 Bramsted, *Goebbels,* pp. 95n, 161; C 1894/4/18 of 15 March; and C 2015/4/18 and *The Times,* both of 17 March.

128 C-V, pp. 142-3, 151. Hitherto, only the number of battalions and batteries had been given. (C-V, pp. 44-5, 92).

129 Ibid.; FOL 9944H/E695972 of 11 March; FOL 6710/E507020-1 of 14 March; *The Times,* 12, 13 and 16 March; and *Le Temps,* 11 March.

130 See, for example C-V, pp. 149, 150, 152; USFR, 1936, I, pp. 244-5; DDF, I, p. 554; and FOL 6710/E507029-30, C 1878/4/18, C 1879/4/18 and C 1880/4/18, all of 14 March.

131 C 1884/4/18 of 15 March.

132 C-V, pp. 149, 297-301.

133 C-V, pp. 47-8; and C-IV, pp. 1142, 1164.

134 C-V, p. 113; C 1806/4/18 and C 1815/4/18, both of 12 March; C 1965/4/18 and *The Times,* both of 13 March; and C 1918/4/18 of 14 March.

135 C-V, p. 162. See also C-V, pp. 160, 237-8.

136 C-V, pp. 121-2, 149, 150, 297, 373-6; and the following from FOL 769: 270863-4, 270877-80, 270881-2, 270866-7, 270868-70, 270883-4, all between 8 and 15 March.

137 C-V, p. 150; and the preceding note.

138 C-V, pp. 121-2, 128-9, 131-2, 147-8, 149, 161-2, 163, 239.

139 C-V, p. 161; C 1938/4/18 of 12 March; *The Times,* and *Le Temps* (press extracts) both of 14 March; Nicolson, *Diaries,* p. 254; *Survey,* 1936, p. 279; and *New Statesman,* 21 March, p. 444.

140 C-V, p. 237.

141 Ibid.

142 C-V, pp. 162, 163. See also C 1933/4/18 of 14 March.

143 C-V, pp. 54, 58, 60-1, 62, 64, 66-7, 78-9, 81-2, 84, 87-9, 97, 99, 114, 130-1, 133, 135-6, 149-50, 153, 154, 156, 159-61, 165-7, 168.

144 In addition to citations in note 143, see also C-V, pp. 183, 243, 289, 302; C 1893/4/18 of 13, 14 March; CP 85(36) of 19 March; DDB, IV, pp. 152-3; DDF, I, p. 486; and USFR, 1936, I, pp. 230-2.

145 C-V pp. 154, 165-6 See also C-V, p. 219.

146 C 1819/4/18 of 13 March; For Norwegian reactions, see C

2249/4/18 of 14 March; C 2983/4/18 of 16 March; and the following FOL 6710: E506405-6, E506851-3, E507167-8, E507531-2, E507948, E508104 and E508355-8 of 9, 11, 14, 17, 21, 21 and 27 March.

147 C-V, p. 154; C 1811/4/18 of 12 March; C 1790/4/18 and C 1821/4/18, both of 13 March; and FOL 6710/E507091-7 of 14 March, For additional Swedish reactions, see the following FOL 6710; E506426-7, E506763-7, E507238-9, E507248, E507091-7, E507839 and E508492-3 of 9, 11, 12, 12, 14, 18 and 28 March.

148 C-V, p. 62; FOL 6710/E506855-7 of 12 March; DO 6882A/8 and C 1592/4/18, both of 9 March; C 1967/4/18 of 12 March; C 1860/4/18 of 14 March; and N 5947/1045/15 of 26 Nov 1936. See also C-V, pp. 165-6; FOL M286/M011834-6 of 8 March; FOL 6710/E506855-7 of 12 March; and note 230.

149 For German views of Dutch reactions, see C-V, pp. 34, 114, 168, 256; and the following FOL 6710: E506348, E506373-4, E506740, E507073-8 and E508335-6 of 8, 8, 9, 14 and 26 March. For German views of Swiss reactions, see C-V, pp. 53-4, 81, 134, 154; and the following FOL 6710: E506462, E506435-41, E506506, E507669-70, E506894 and E507043 of 9, 9, 10, 11, 13, and 13 March.

150 For the Hungarian reaction, see C-V, pp. 60-1, 91, 171-2; DDF, I, pp. 612-14; and the following FOL 6710: E506340, E508848 and E508362-3 of 7, 11 and 27 March. For the Bulgarian reaction, see the following FOL 6710: E506327, E506495, E506955-7, E508286-7 of 8, 9, 10 and 24 March.

151 C-V, pp. 108-10, 125-6, 297, 300; and the following FOL 6710: E506372, E506675-6 and E506747-9 of 8, 11 and 11 March.

152 For Turkish reactions, see C-V, pp. 40-1, 96-7, 135-6, 297, 300; and the following FOL 6710: E506609, E506887, E508030, E508100 and E508369-70, of 10, 13, 21, 23, and 25 March.

153 For Germany's view of Greek reactions, see C-V, pp. 133, 149-50, 300; and FOL 6710/E507479-80 of 14 March.

154 For Germany's view of Yugoslav reactions, see C-V, pp. 78-9, 84, 153, 278, 302-3; and the following FOL 6710: E506675-6, E507098-100, E507353 and E507848 of 11, 13, 17 and 21 March.

155 C-V, p. 153.

156 W 3359/403/36 of 7 April; W 18124/4169/36 of 9 Dec 1936; W 711/2381/36 of 10 April 1936; and *Survey*, 1936, pp. 122-3. An indication of Lisbon's attitude was given on 7 April when Dr Monteiro, the minister of foreign affairs, warned that collaboration with Russia was tantamount to signing Europe's own death warrant. (W 3359/403/36).

157 C-V, p. 64n. For press and other unofficial Spanish reactions, none hostile to Berlin, see the following from FOL 6710: E506484, E506578, E506815-16, E506890, E507293-4 and E507859-60, between 9 and 21 March.

158 FOL 6710/E506755 of 11 March; FOL 6710/E507963-4 of 16
     March; and FOL 63/43754 of 18 March. See also C-V, pp. 64, 159,
     299; and DDF, I, pp. 472-3, 519-21.

159 C-V, pp. 297-301.

160 C-V, pp. 100, 130-1, 156, 167, 230-1, 295-6, 395-6.

161 C-V, p. 99. See also C-V, pp. 204, 278-9; and FOL 6710; E507115-
     16, E507129-30, F507131-4 and E507138-9, all between 8 and 11
     March.

162 DDF, I, p. 499.

163 C-V, pp. 183, 205, 243; and FOL 6710/E506485 of 9 March. See
     also DDF, I, p. 624; and C-V, pp. 159, 183.

164 C-V, p. 243. See also C 2245/4/18 of 23 March.

165 C-V, p. 205n.

166 C-V, pp. 58, 204; FOL 6710/ E507277-8 of 10 March; FOL 6710/
     E508107 of 16 March; USFR, 1936, I, p. 232; and LNOJ, April
     1936, p. 324.

167 C-V, pp. 159, 183; DDF, I, p. 516; and C 2250/4/18 of 17 March.
     Germany increased her exports to Chile in 1935 by 150 per cent.
     In 1936 she surpassed this by another 54 per cent, becoming
     Chile's number one supplier. At the same time, total trade
     between Chile and Germany increased by 28.2 per cent. (A
     5330/410/9 of 28 May 1936; and C 2181/664/18 of 15 March 1937.)

168 C-V, p. 299. See also C 1815/4/18 of 12 March.

169 C-V, pp. 112, 166, 299; C 1900/4/18 of 15 March; and DDF, I, p.
     571.

170 C-V, p. 299.

171 C-V, pp. 57-8, 79, 92-5, 102-3, 106, 193-4, 299.

172 This paragraph is based on LNOJ, April 1936, pp. 310-15; C
     1860/4/18, C 1876/4/18 and LP(L) 3rd meeting, all of 14 March;
     and C-V, pp. 159-60, 165-7, 297-9.

173 C-V, p. 160; and C 1860/4/18 of 14 March.

174 C 1615/4/18 of 10 March; CAB 18(36)1 of 11 March; LP(L) 1st and
     2nd meetings, both of 13 March; and LP(L) 3rd meeting, 14
     March.

175 On this question, Eden felt the French, by resisting, had 'missed
     a chance, as they so often did', (LP(L) 3rd meeting, 14 March).

176 C 1878/4/18, C 1879/4/18 and C 1880/4/18, all of 14 March; C-V,
     p. 163; Kordt, *Akten,* p. 136; and DDF, I, pp. 555, 600-2.

177 C-V, pp. 159-60, 165-6.

178 C 1888/4/18 and C 1889/4/18, both of 15 March. See also DDF, I,
     p. 602; Dodd, *Diary,* p. 322; and *The Times,* 16 March.

179 C-V, pp. 162-3; and C 1884/4/18 of 15 March.

180 C-V, pp. 162-3.

181 C 1948/1/17 and C 1950/4/18, both of 16 March.

182 *Le Temps,* 17 March. See also *The Times* and C 2442/4/18, both of
     16 March; and Flandin, *Survenus,* I, p. 153.

183 C 1948/1/17 and C 1950/4/18, both of 16 March; and C 1988/4/18 of 17 March. See also C-V, p. 199; C 1949/4/18 of 17 March; and *Survey*, 1936, pp. 297-8.

184 In addition to the citations in note 183, see C 2024/4/18 of 16 March; *The Times*, 16-18 March; *Le Temps*, 17 March; Kordt, *Akten*, p. 137; and USFR, 1936, I, pp. 252-3.

185 C-V, p. 157; C 1884/4/18, C 1888/4/18 and C 1889/4/18, all of 15 March; and C 2071/4/18 of 16 March.

186 C 1898/4/18 of 16 March; and LNOJ, April 1936, p. 316. See also C 2045/4/18 of 17 March; and Kordt, *Akten*, p. 136.

187 LNOJ, April 1936, pp. 317-18; C 2024/4/18 of 16 March; and C-V, pp. 178, 238. See also C-V, pp. 215-16.

188 In addition to the citations in note 187, see CAB 20(36)4 of 16 March.

189 C-V, p. 161. See also C 2047/4/18 of 17 March; C-V, pp. 179-80; DDF, I, pp. 602-3; *The Times*, 19 March, and USFR, 1936, I, pp. 218-19.

190 C-V, pp. 180-2, 185; C 1964/4/18, C 2020/4/18 and C 2108/4/18, all of 17 March; and *The Times*, 18 March.

191 C-V, pp. 179-80; and C 1888/4/18, C 1889/4/18 and C 1898/4/18, all of 15 March.

192 This is conjecture, but see C 1884/4/18, C 1888/4/18 and C 1889/4/18, all of 15 March; C 2071/4/18 of 16 March; C 2108/4/18 of 17 March; C 2039/4/18 of 18 March; LNOJ, April 1936, p. 318; C-V, pp. 162-4, 179-80; and *Survey*, 1936, p. 299.

193 DDF, I, pp. 569-70, 585-6; LNOJ, April 1936, pp. 318-22; C 2108/4/18 of 17 March; and FOL 6710/E507705-8 of 20 March.

194 The following is based on LNOJ, April 1936, pp. 333-41. See also C-V, pp. 203-4; Ribbentrop, *Ribbentrop*, pp. 52-6; Schmidt, *Interpreter*, pp. 41-4; Kordt, *Akten*, pp. 138-9; and *The Times*, 20 March.

195 Louis Fischer, *Men and Politics* (London, 1941), p. 302; Schmidt, *Interpreter*, p. 43; *The Times*, 20 March; C-V, pp. 205, 243; and C 2245/4/18 of 23 March.

196 LNOJ, April 1936, p. 340.

197 Ibid.; and C-V, pp. 200-1.

198 This paragraph is based on LNOJ, April 1936, pp. 334-8, C-V, pp. 156, 179-80, 200-1, 203-4; and Ribbentrop, *Ribbentrop*, pp. 53-4.

199 For a listing of these, see C 247/247/18 of 12 Jan 1937. For a general picture of Schacht's efforts and successes, see R 664/81/92 of 31 Jan 1936; G(36)6 of 27 Feb 1936; and C 2181/664/18 of 15 March 1937.

200 C-V, pp. 297-301; C 1893/4/18 of 14, 15 and 16 March; and CP 85(36) of 12 March.

201 C 2228/99/18 of 20 March 1936; and C 2181/664/18 of 15 March 1937.

202 C 2228/99/18 of 20 March. See also C 1643/4/18 of 9 March; CP 85(36) of 12 March; and C 1983/4/18 of 16 March.

203 C-V, pp. 297-301.

204 C 1710/4/18 of 11 March. See also DDF, I, pp. 463, 511-12.

205 CP 85(36) of 12 March; C 1595/4/18 of 9 March; and C. A. Macartney, *Independent Eastern Europe* (London, 1962), p. 315.

206 Macartney, *Eastern Europe*, p. 315. See also G(36)6 of 27 Feb 1936; C 1893/4/18 of 14 March; C-V, p. 300; and Antonin Basch, *The Danube Basin and the German Economic Sphere* (New York, 1944), pp. 187-8.

207 C 2181/664/18 of 15 March 1937; Macartney, *Eastern Europe,* p. 315; DDF, I, pp. 199-200, 670; R 1079/11/92 of 21 Feb 1936; and R 1311/125/67 of 28 Feb 1936.

208 C 1699/4/18 of 11 March; C 1854/4/18 of 13 March; C-V, pp. 84, 153, 300; G(36)6 of 27 Feb 1936; and Basch, *Danube,* pp. 192-3.

209 G(36)6 of 27 Feb 1936; and Macartney, *Eastern Europe*, p. 315.

210 C 2181/664/18 of 15 March 1937.

211 N 682/110/15 of 3 Feb 1936; and N 811/110/15 of 7 Feb 1936.

212 The breakdown was Poland, 107.4 million RM; Switzerland, 371.3 million RM; and the Netherlands, 600.3 million RM (C.2181/664/18 of 15 March 1937).

213 USFR, 1936, I, p. 230.

214 C 2228/99/18 of 20 March; C 357/357/18 of 12 Jan 1937; and C 2181/664/18 of 15 March 1937. In 1936, Schacht's agents negotiated 39 commercial treaties and 16 clearing agreements with 27 countries.

215 DDB, IV, p. 157; and DDF, I, pp. 244-5.

216 The breakdown in millions of RM and percentage of each country's total export trade to Germany in 1935 was Czechoslovakia, 50m (38%); Poland, 37.5m (78%); Rumania, 36m (56%); Greece, 32m (65%); Austria, 26m (24%); Yugoslavia, 26m (65%); Hungary, 20m (32%); and Bulgaria, 6m (15%). (C-V, pp. 90n, 158; R 1140/1001/19 and G(36)6, both of 27 Feb 1936; R 1609/1167/67 of 17 March; R 1699/1001/19 of 20 March; R 2163/81/92 of 13 April; R3116/1167/67 of 25 May; R 3777/39/19 of 25 June; *The Times,* 20 March, 16 and 22 June 1936; C 341/341/55 of 1 Jan 1937; and C 2181/664/18 of 15 March 1937).

217 Chile's credit surplus was 20.2 million RM—38.6 per cent of her total sales to Germany in 1935. Berlin's debt to Turkey was described as 'high', while the Dutch minister told Dodd that Germany owed the Netherlands 'a great deal of money'. By the end of 1936, Denmark was said to be in the same position. (A 3239/269/9 of 14 April 1936; E 823/823/44 of 28 Jan 1937; N 699/699/15 of 30 Jan 1937; and Dodd, *Diary*, p. 320.)

218 The following is based on CP 85(36) and C 1938/4/18, both of 12 March; C 1989/4/18, minute by F. Ashton-Gwatkin, 18 March;

and C 2228/99/18 of 20 March.

219 See, for example, G(36)2 of 28 Feb 1936; C 1651/4/18 of 4 March; C 2228/99/18 of 20 March; R 3777/39/19 of 25 June; and A 8992/269/9 of 9 Oct 1936.

220 C-V, p. 158.

221 C-V, p. 158; Basch, *Danube*, pp. 191-2; and R 1821/32/12 of 24 March 1936.

222 C 235/55/18 of 7 Jan 1935; C 3182/55/18 of 6 April 1935; C 1395/4/18 of 9 March 1936; USFR, 1936, I, p. 260; C 3010/86/18 of 14 April 1936; and R 2800/73/3 of 12 May 1936.

223 A 3239/269/9 of 14 April 1936; and A 8992/269/9 of 9 Oct 1936.

224 See, for example C 2250/4/18 of 17 March; A 3239/269/9 and A 3241/410/9, both of 14 April 1936; C 357/357/18 of 12 Jan 1937; and C-V, pp. 64, 205n.

225 CP 85(36) of 12 March, C-V, pp. 297-301; and C 1893/4/18 of 13, 14 and 16 March 1936.

226 C-IV, pp. 166, 408, 485-6, 571-2, 627-8, 1046, 1070-1, 1078, 1099 and C-V, pp. 153, 278, 302-3, 765-6, 769-70.

227 C-III, p. 926; C-IV, p. 1201; Szembek, *Journal*, pp. 117-18; and N 6375/136/38 of 18 Dec 1936.

228 C-IV, pp. 172, 632-3, 772-3; and C 8364/55/18 of 16 Dec 1935.

229 For Belgian anxieties, see C-IV, pp. 715-16, 776-7, 804-6, 931, 938-41, 988-94, 1017-21, 1080-3. For Denmark's general concern about her relations with Berlin, see C 8533/55/18 of 22 Nov 1935; J 684/70/1 of 13 Jan 1936; C 1168/4/18 of 18 Feb 1936; N 5947/1045/15 of 26 Nov 1936; and N 699/699/15 of 30 Jan 1937.

230 Citations on the Austrian and Czech questions are too numerous to list, but see the appropriate categories in C-III, IV and V. For a picture of the Rexist movement, see C 4025/202/4 of 3 June 1936; and C-V, pp. 896-7, 947-9, 1058-9, 1061, 1091, 1148-9.

231 P 1426/103/150 of 19 March 1936. See also A 1378/1378/9 of 1 Jan 1937.

232 C-IV, pp. 781-2, 1184; R 1983/1162/12 of 3 April 1936; R 4419/282/37 of 17 July 1936; R 6091/282/37 of 7 Oct 1936; R 1159/37 of 12 Feb 1937; Macartney, *Eastern Europe*, pp. 333-6 and 1159; *October Fifteenth, a history of Modern Hungary*, I (Edinburgh, 1961), p. 148; H. L. Roberts, *Rumania* (London, 1951), p. 190; and Pavel Pavel, *Why Rumania Failed* (London, 1943), pp. 139-40.

233 C 1600/4/18 of 9 March; R 1371/1162/12 of 8 March; C 1592/4/18 of 9 March; and C 1791/4/18 of 13 March. It was already widely believed by Danes that Göring and Hitler planned in war to convert Denmark into a German food preserve. (N 1333/110/15 of 4 March 1936; and C 1967/4/18 of 12 March).

234 C 414/86/18, memorandum by Wigram, 21 Jan 1936; C 2747/4/18 of 31 March; and C 8998/8998/18 of 31 Dec 1936.

235 Citation possibilities are too numerous to list here, since the

Bolshevik peril was at this time feared at least as much as, frequently more than, Nazism.

236 C-V, p. 159.

237 LNOJ, April 1936, pp. 319-22; and Taylor, *Origins*, p. 100.

238 C-V, pp. 297-301; CP 85(36) of 12 March; C 1893/4/18 of 13, 14, 16 March; USFR, 1936, I, p. 230; and DDB, IV, pp. 156-7.

239 C-V, pp. 57-8, 94-5, 102-3, 106, 233-40, 274-5.

240 C 1827/4/18 and C 1892/4/18, both of 13 March.

241 LP(L) 1st, 2nd and 3rd meetings, 13 and 14 March.

242 Ibid. See also C 1806/4/18 of 12 March; C 1965/4/18 of 13 March; and C 1918/4/18 of 14 March.

7 A solution nevertheless

1 C 1806/4/18 and C 1815/4/18, both of 12 March; LP(L) 1st and 2nd meetings and C 1965/4/18, all of 13 March; LP(L) 3rd meeting and C 1918/4/18, both of 14 March; CAB 20(36)1 of 16 March; DO 6882A/8, meetings of 13 and 16 March; DDF, I, pp. 541-2; and USFR, 1936, I, pp. 235-6, 238, 242-3.

2 C 1962/4/18 of 17 March; C 2068/4/18, C 2069/4/18 and CAB 21(36)6, all of 18 March; CAB 22(36)3, CAB 23(36)1 and DO 6882A/8, meeting, all of 19 March; C 2193/4/18 of 21 March; and Eden, *Facing*, pp. 359-60.

3 Flandin, *Politique Française*, pp. 207-9 and *Survenus*, I, pp. 153-5; and CAB 20(36)1 of 16 March.

4 Flandin, *Survenus*, I, p. 156 and *Politique Française*, p. 200; CAB 21(36)6 of 18 March; C-V, 234; USFR, 1936, I, pp. 236, 265, 272; Zuylen, *Mains libres*, p. 354; and Miller, *Belgian*, pp. 222-3.

5 C 1614/4/18 of 10 March; C 1835/4/18 of 13 March; C 1985/4/18 of 17 March; and DDF, I, pp. 414-15.

6 C 1806/4/18 of 12 March; C 1805/4/18 of 13 March; C 2028/4/18, C 2068/4/18, C 2069/4/18 and CAB 21 (36)5, all of 18 March; and DDB, IV, pp. 147-8

7 C 2026/4/18 of 17 March; and DO 6882A/8, meeting of 19 March.

8 CP 73(36) of 8 March; CAB 18(36)1 of 11 March; and DO 6882A/8, meeting of 13 March.

9 LP(L) 1st meeting and DO 6882A/8, meeting, both of 13 March.

10 C 1614/4/18 of 10 March; C 1806/4/18 of 12 March; C 1965/4/18 of 13 March; and C 2069/4/18 of 18 March.

11 CAB 19(36)1 and C 1806/4/18, both of 12 March; LP(L) 1st and 2nd meetings, and C 1965/4/18, both of 13 March; LP(L) 3rd meeting and C 1918/4/18, both of 14 March; DDF, I, pp. 541-2; and CAB 20(36)1 of 16 March.

12 C 1806/4/18 of 12 March; LP(L) 1st meeting and C 1965/4/18, both of 13 March; C 1918/4/18 and LP(L) 3rd meeting, both of 14

March; and C 1899/4/18 of 15 March.

13 C 1614/4/18, C 1672/4/18 and C 1673/4/18, all of 10 March; LP(L) 1st and 2nd meetings, both of 13 March; and DDB, IV, pp. 134-5, 138-43.

14 For Zeeland's position, see C 1806/4/18 of 12 March; C 1805/-4/18, C 1965/4/18 and LP(L) 2nd meeting, all of 13 March; DO 6882A/8, meeting of 16 March; DDF, 1, pp. 541-2; and USFR, 1936, I, pp. 243-4, 247-9, 264-5.

15 For Flandin's plan, see: C 1806/4/18 of 12 March; LP(L) 1st meeting, 13 March; DDF, I, p. 542; and Eden, *Facing*, pp. 355-6.

16 C 1806/4/18 of 12 March; C 1965/4/18 and LP(L) 1st and 2nd meetings, all of 13 March; C 1918/4/18 of 14 March; CP 79(36) of 15 March; and DO 6882A/8, meeting, and CAB 20(36)1, both of 16 March.

17 LP(L) 2nd meeting, 13 March.

18 The following is based on C 1806/4/18 of 12 March; and C 1965/-4/18 and LP(L) 2nd meeting, both of 13 March.

19 Eden also asked Flandin and Zeeland to outline their security requirements pending negotiations and in the event of their breakdown.

20 C 1805/4/18 and C 1965/4/18, both of 13 March; C 1918/4/18 of 14 March; and C 1962/4/18 of 17 March.

21 CAB 20(36)1 of 16 March; C 1962/4/18 of 17 March; and CAB 21(36)6 of 18 March.

22 C 1965/4/18 and LP(L) 2nd meeting, both of 13 March; and C 1918/4/18 of 14 March.

23 C 1965/4/18 and LP(L) 2nd meeting and DO 6882A/8, meeting, all of 13 March; and CAB 20(36)1 of 16 March. See also DDB, IV, pp. 147-8.

24 DDF, I, pp. 549-52; and LP(L) 2nd meeting, 13 March.

25 See, for example, DDB, IV, pp. 147-50; Flandin, *Politique Francaise*, pp. 206-9; and Eden, *Facing*, pp. 357-8.

26 C 1792/4/18 of 13 March; *The Times* and *Le Temps*, 13 and 14 March; C 1948/4/18 of 16 March; C-V, pp. 128-9, 131-2; and FOL 6710/E507020-1 of 14 March.

27 DDF, I, pp. 499-501, 561-2; and Dobler, *Survenus*, II, pp. 486-8.

28 DDF, I, pp. 511-12, 533-4, 538-41, 559-61. See also DDF, I, pp. 244-5, 463; *Le Temps*, 9 and 10 March; and C-V, pp. 128-9, 131-2.

29 DDB, IV, pp. 150-1; DDF, I, pp. 502-3; C 1883/99/18 of 13 March; and C 1906/4/18, minute by Ashton-Gwatkin, 16 March.

30 DDB, IV, p. 150; USFR, 1936, I, pp. 267-8; C 1965/4/18 of 13 March; C 1989/4/18 of 17 March; C 2069/4/18 of 18 March; and C-V, pp. 128-9.

31 DDF, I, pp. 493, 532-3, 541-2, 601; C 1678/4/18 of 11 March; *Le Temps*, 12 and 14 March; C 1818/4/18 of 13 March; *The Times*, 14 and 17 March; and DDB, IV, p. 148. See also USFR, 1936, I, p.

238; and C-V, pp. 102, 127, 152.

32 DDF, I, pp. 532-3.

33 C-V, p. 236; LP(L) 1st meeting, 13 March; *The Times*, 13 and 17 March; Katharine M. Murray (Duchess of Atholl), *Working Partnership* (London, 1958), p. 201; and Jones, *Diary*, p. 185.

34 *The Times*, 13 March.

35 *The Times*, 12 March. See also C 1744/4/18 of 12 March; and C-V, p. 236.

36 C 2564/4/18 of 28 March; DO 6882A/8, meeting of 16 March; and Eden, *Facing*, p. 361.

37 C 1858/4/18 of 14 March. See also DDF, II, p. 29; C 2442/4/18 of 16 March; C 2047/4/18 of 17 March; and CAB 23(36)1 of 19 March.

38 C 1743/4/18 of 12 March; C 2026/4/18 of 17 March; C 2048/4/18 of 18 March; C 2110/4/18 of 19 March; C 2564/4/18 of 28 March; and C-V, p. 141.

39 This paragraph is based on C 1918/4/18 and LP(L) 3rd meeting, both of 14 March; C 1899/4/18 of 15 March; DO 6882A/8, meeting of 16 March; and Eden, *Facing*, pp. 357-8.

40 See the citations in note 39.

41 LP(L) 3rd meeting, 14 March. See also CAB 20(36)1 of 16 March.

42 See, for example, C 1806/4/18 and C 1940/4/18, both of 12 March; C 1965/4/18 of 13 March; C 1858/4/18 and C 1918/4/18 both of 14 March; C 1899/4/18 of 15 March; and C 1962/4/18 of 17 March.

43 See the citations in note 42.

44 The following is based on Flandin, *Politique Française*, pp. 205, 207 and *Survenus*, I, pp. 153, 155; Sarraut, *Survenus*, III, p. 564; C 1818/4/18 of 13 March; and *Le Temps*, 14 March. See also C-V, p. 237; DDF I, pp. 549-52; USFR, 1936, I, p. 264; and Feiling, *Chamberlain*, p. 279.

45 In addition, see DO 6882A/8, meeting of 13 March; C 2026/4/18 of 17 March; DDB, IV, p. 148; and Geneviève R. Tabouis, *They Called Me Cassandra* (New York, 1942), p. 276.

46 *Survey*, 1936, p. 276n; Amery, *Political Life*, III, p. 189; Churchill, *Storm*, pp. 171-2; Macmillan, *Winds*, p. 428; Nicolson, *Diaries*, pp. 250-2; M. Epstein (ed.), *Annual Register, 1936* (London, 1937), p. 22; and *The Times*, 18 March.

47 Flandin, *Politique Française*, pp. 205, 207; C 1818/4/18 of 13 March; *Le Temps*, 14 March; LP(L) 1st meeting, 13 March; and *The Times*, 17 and 20 March.

48 Jones, *Diary*, pp. 185, 188; Nicolson, *Diaries*, p. 252; C-V, pp. 237-8; FOL 5576H/E400428-9 of 19 March; and *The Times*, 18 March.

49 The following is based on Flandin, *Politique Française*, pp. 207-8 and *Survenus*, I, pp. 153-5. Flandin's is the only account of this conversation.

50 DDF, I, pp. 444, 504-6, 522-3, 696-700.

51 They do not disprove it, either. But the absence of any reference in the Belgian, British, French or German documents during this period must be weighted accordingly.

52 DDF, I, pp. 123, 445; DDB, IV, pp. 106, 125, 178-9; and Lazareff, *Dernière édition*, p. 301.

53 Flandin, *Survenus*, I, pp. 158-9.

54 Flandin, *Politique Française*, pp. 208-9 and *Survenus*, I, pp. 155-6, 158-9.

55 See, for example, DDF, I, pp. 484-5, 525; C 1734/4/18 of 11 March; C 1832/4/18 and C 1833/4/18, both of 13 March; and C 1989/4/18 of 17 March.

56 The following is based on DDF, II, pp. 112-13; CP 26(36) appendix of 21 Nov 1935; C 8998/8998/18 of 31 Dec 1936; Flandin, *Politique Française*, pp. 207-8; and Eden, *Facing*, pp. 351, 353.

57 Flandin, *Politique Française*, p. 208. See also DO 6882A/8, meetings of 13 and 16 March; and C-V, pp. 161-2, 235-6.

58 In addition to the citations in note 57, see USFR, 1936, I, pp. 233-4, 255, 268; Birkenhead, *Halifax*, pp. 352-3; and Taylor, *English History*, p. 387.

59 Flandin, *Survenus*, I, p. 153 and *Politique Française*, pp. 205-6; LP(L) 3rd meeting, 14 March; Sarraut, *Survenus*, III, p. 564; Paul-Boncour, *Entre deux*, III, pp. 38-9; and Eden, *Facing*, pp. 348, 358-9, 367.

60 In addition to the citations in note 59, see DDF, I, pp. 441, 580; C-V, pp. 112-13, 159-61, 165-7, 183; USFR, 1936, I, pp. 230-2, 252-3, 256, 265; DDB, IV, pp. 152-3, 156-7; C 1811/4/18 of 11 March; and C 1592/4/18 and C 1860/4/18, both of 14 March.

61 DDF, I, pp. 481, 497, 547-8; C 1809/4/18 and R 1785/1162/12, both of 12 March; R 1646/1162/12 of 17 March; C-V, p. 262; and USFR, 1936, I, p. 247.

62 DDF, I, pp. 646-7; C-V, pp. 175, 184-5; C 1832/4/18 of 13 March; C 2024/4/18 of 16 March; and C 2187/4/18 of 21 March.

63 DDF, I, pp. 476, 512, 517, 561. See also DDF, I, pp. 514, 538-41, 548.

64 C 1838/4/18 of 13 March; and C 1912/4/18 of 15 March.

65 DDF, I, pp. 501-3, 522-4 and II, p. 48.

66 Flandin, *Politique Française*, p. 208 and *Survenus*, I, p. 153; and CAB 20(36)1 of 16 March.

67 C 1877/4/18 of 12 March; C 1949/4/18 of 16 March; C 1987/4/18 of 17 March; C 2564/4/18 of 28 March; Sarraut, *Survenus*, III, pp. 565-9; André Tardieu, *La Note de semaine, 1936* (Paris, 1937) p. 154; C-V, pp. 128-9; and *New Statesman*, 28 March, pp. 485-6.

68 *Le Temps*, 13 March (quoting other French newspapers); C-V, pp. 132, 147-8, 199; Berber, *Spiegel*, p. 57; Micaud, *French Right*, p. 101n; and C 2050/4/18 of 18 March.

69 C 1858/4/18 of 14 March; CAB 20(36)1 of 16 March; C 2026/4/18

of 17 March; C 2048/4/18 of 18 March; and C 2564/4/18 of 28 March.

70 See, for example, C 1734/4/18 of 11 March; C 1806/4/18 and C 1940/4/18, both of 12 March; C 1965/4/18 of 13 March; C 1858/4/18 of 14 March; and C 1899/4/18 of 15 March.

71 Flandin, *Politique Française,* p. 208 and *Survenus,* I, p. 155. See also Paul-Boncour, *Entre deux,* III, p. 39.

72 C 1833/4/18 of 13 March; and C 2239/4/18 of 23 March. See also CAB 20(36) 1 of 16 March; and Chambre des Députés, *Journal Officiel,* 26 Jan 1937, p. 170.

73 This paragraph is based on Flandin, *Politique Française,* pp. 208-9 and *Survenus,* I, pp. 155, 159. See also C-V, p. 160.

74 Arguments in favour of the view that Flandin's motives in London from the outset had been to exploit the Rhineland affair in order to extract a promise of future British support may be found in USFR, 1936, I, pp. 229, 233-4, 255, 268; Knapp, 'Rhineland,' p. 81; Birkenhead, *Halifax,* pp. 352-3; and Taylor, *English History,* p. 387.

75 C 1672/4/18 of 10 March; and DDB, IV, pp. 141-3.

76 This feature of British policy is summarized in C 3456/G/66 of 17 June 1936. See also C 6952/6562/62, minute by Sargent, 9 Oct 1935.

77 C 344/3279/4 of 15 May 1934; C 5223/3279/4 of 30 July 1934; C 3103/4/18, minute by Wigram, 29 April 1936; and C 3456/G/66 of 17 June 1936.

78 C 5178/55/18 of 4 July 1935; CAB 21(36)6 of 18 March; C 3456/G/66 of 17 June 1936; DDF, I, p. 649; C-V, pp. 293, 295; *Hansard,* vol. 310, cols. 1476-81; *Hansard,* Lords, vol. 100, cols. 548, 556; and Eden, *Facing,* p. 362.

79 LP(L) 2nd, 3rd and 4th meetings, 13, 14 and 16 March; CAB 20(36)1 of 16 March; and C 1827/4/18 and C 1892/4/18, both of 13 March.

80 A force composed of British, Italian, Dutch and Swedish troops had policed the Saar for two months prior to the plebiscite of 13 Jan 1935.

81 LP(L) 3rd meeting, 14 March; and LP(L) 4th meeting and CAB 20(36)1, both of 16 March.

82 C 1827/4/18, C 1892/4/18 and LP(L) 2nd meeting, all of 13 March; and Price, *Dictators,* pp. 128-9.

83 The only reservation was expressed by Montgomery-Massingberd, who warned that the 9-10,000 men required would strip Britain 'practically bare' of regular troops. (LP(L) 2nd and 4th meetings, 13 and 16 March).

84 LP(L) 3rd meeting, 14 March.

85 CAB 20(36)1 of 16 March. See also Flandin, *Politique Française,* p. 209 and *Survenus,* I, pp. 155-6, 158-9; and C 2069/4/18 of 18

March.
86 F. P. Walters, *A History of the League of Nations*, II (London, 1952), p. 697.
87 This paragraph is based on C 1806/4/18 of 12 March; CAB 20(36)1 of 16 March; C 1962/4/18 of 17 March; CAB 21(36)6 of 18 March; CAB 23 (36)1 and Cmd 5134, both of 19 March; and DO 6882A/8, meeting of 20 March.
88 CAB 21(36)6 of 18 March; and DO 6882A/8, meeting of 20 March.
89 Cmd 5134 of 19 March.
90 This discussion of the international force is based on CP 79(36) of 15 March; LP(L) 4th meeting and CAB 20(36)1, both of 16 March; C 1962/4/18 of 17 March; C 2068/4/18, C 2069/4/18 and CAB 21(36)6, all of 18 March; DO 6882A/8, meetings of 19 and 20 March; and Cmd 5134 of 19 March.
91 See also C 2192/4/18 of 21 March.
92 CP 79(36) of 15 March; and C 1962/4/18 of 17 March.
93 C 2068/4/18 and CAB 21(36)6, both of 18 March.
94 DO 6882A/8, meeting of 19 March.
95 See, for example, C 3456/G/66 of 17 June 1936; and ADM 167. 95, DPM 3 of 29 July 1936.
96 C 2069/4/18 of 18 March.
97 CAB 23(36)1 and DO 6882A/8, meeting, both of 20 March; and C 2266/4/18 of 24 March.
98 C 2192/4/18 of 21 March; and C 2266/4/18 of 24 March.
99 C 1962/4/18 of 17 March; and C 2028/4/18 of 18 March. See also C 1805/4/18 of 13 March; and C 1858/4/18 of 14 March.
100 In addition to the citations in note 99, see C 2068/4/18 and C 2069/4/18, both of 18 March.
101 C 2068/4/18, C 2069/4/18 and CAB 21(36)6, all of 18 March; and Cmd 5134 of 19 March. See also CAB 23(36)1 of 19 March.
102 DO 6882A/8, meetings of 19 and 20 March. See also C 2192/4/18 of 21 March.
103 CP 79(36) of 15 March; and LP(L) 4th meeting and CAB 20(36)1, both of 16 March. See also DO 6882A/8, meeting of 16 March.
104 C 1962/4/18 of 17 March.
105 Ibid. See also C 2068/4/18, C 2069/4/18 and CAB 21(36)6, all of 18 March; and DO 6882A/8, meeting of 19 March.
106 C 2068/4/18 of 18 March. See also DO 6882A/8, meeting of 19 March.
107 C 2069/4/18 of 18 March.
108 Ibid. See also CAB 21(36)6 of 18 March.
109 CAB 20(36)1 of 16 March; C 2069/4/18 of 18 March; and Eden, *Facing*, pp. 359-60.
110 In addition to the citations in note 109, see DDF, I, pp. 501-3; and C 1989/4/18 of 17 March.

111 C 1614/4/18 and C 1673/4/18, both of 10 March; C 1806/4/18 of 12 March; C 1965/4/18 of 13 March; C 1962/4/18 of 17 March; and C 2068/4/18 of 18 March.

112 CAB 21(36)6 of 18 March. See also CAB 18(36)1 of 11 March.

113 C 2802/4/18, minute by Vansittart, 17 March; C 2442/4/18, minutes by Sargent and Vansittart, 17 March; CAB 21(36)6 of 18 March; DO 6882A/8, meeting of 19 March; Eden, *Facing,* pp. 353-4; and Feiling, *Chamberlain,* p. 279.

114 C 2069/4/18 of 18 March; and DO 6882A/8, meeting of 19 March.

115 LP(L) 3rd meeting, 14 March; C 2047/4/18, C 2108/4/18 and *Le Temps,* all of 17 March; C 2069/4/18 of 18 March; DO 6882A/8, meeting of 19 March; and DDF, I, pp. 569-70.

116 C 1989/4/18 and C 2026/4/18, both of 17 March; C 2048/4/18 of 18 March; C 2110/4/18 and C 2150/1/17, both of 19 March; Dalton, diaries, entry of 18 March; Nicolson, *Diaries,* pp. 251-2; and Macmillan, *Wings,* p. 428.

117 C 1989/4/18 of 17 March; and C 2069/4/18 of 18 March.

118 C 2069/4/18 of 18 March. See also C 1989/4/18 and C 2026/4/18, both of 17 March; and C 2150/1/17 of 19 March. Sarraut told Clerk on 19 March that he could easily arouse a wave of delirious enthusiasm for himself and his government by saying publicly: 'Italy is our friend and with her we will talk directly with the Führer.' (C 2110/4/18 of 19 March).

119 C 2068/4/18 of 18 March. See also CAB 20(36)1 of 16 March; C 1962/4/18 of 17 March; DDF, I, p. 622; and DO 6882A/8, meeting of 20 March.

120 C 1806/4/18 of 12 March; C 1805/4/18 and C 1965/4/18, both of 13 March; CAB 20(36)1 and DO 6882A/8, both of 16 March; and C 2068/4/18 of 18 March.

121 C 2028/4/18 and C 2069/4/18, both of 18 March.

122 CAB 21(36)6 of 18 March.

123 Ibid. See also DO 6882A/8 of 19 March.

124 In addition to the citations in note 123, see CP 79(36) of 15 March.

125 These are summarized in C 3456/G/66 of 17 June 1936. See also Cmd 5134 of 19 March; DO 6882A/8, meeting of 20 March; and C-V, pp. 322-5.

126 C 1806/4/18 of 12 March; C 1805/4/18 of 13 March; CP 79(36) of 15 March; CAB 20(36)1 of 16 March; C 1962/4/18 of 17 March; and C 2028/4/18 of 18 March.

127 CAB 20(36)1 of 16 March; and CAB 21(36)6 of 18 March. See also CAB 19(36)1 of 12 March.

128 LP(L) 4th meeting, 16 March. See also CP 79(36) of 15 March.

129 Cmd 5134 of 19 March.

130 C 2028/4/18, C 2068/4/18, C 2069/4/18 and CAB 21(36)6, all of 18 March; and DO 6882A/8, meeting of 19 March.

131 C 2068/4/18 of 18 March.

132 Ibid. See also C 2192/4/18 of 21 March.

133 C 2068/4/18 of 18 March.

134 C 2069/4/18 of 18 March.

135 Ibid.; CAB 21(36)6 of 18 March; and DO 6882A/8, meeting of 19 March.

136 C 2028/4/18, C 2069/4/18 and CAB 21(36)6, all of 18 March; and DO 6882A/8, meeting of 19 March.

137 This paragraph is based on CAB 21(36)6 of 18 March; and DO 6882A/8, meeting of 19 March.

138 CAB 21(36)6 of 18 March.

139 DO 6882A/8, meeting of 19 March.

140 CAB 21(36)6 of 18 March. No one believed that Germany had any such intentions; hence, the suggestion could be safely entertained. (CAB 21(36)6 of 18 March; and DO 6882A/8, meeting of 19 March).

141 CAB 21(36)6 of 18 March; DO 6882A/8, meetings of 19 and 20 March; CAB 23(36)1 of 19 March; *Hansard*, vol. 310, cols. 1441-2, 1543-7, 2304-7; C 3437/4/18 of 22 April 1936; C-V, p. 323; and C 3456/G/66 of 17 June 1936.

142 CAB 21(36)6 of 18 March.

143 Eden, *Facing*, p. 360. See also LP(L) 5th meeting, 30 March.

144 CAB 21(36)6 of 18 March.

145 C 1734/4/18, C 1744/4/18, C 1832/4/18, C 1833/4/18, C 1858/4/18, C 1989/4/18, C 2026/4/18, C 2048/4/18, C 2110/4/18 and C 2150/4/18, all of 11-19 March; C-V, pp. 161-2, 235, 237; and USFR, 1936, I, p. 243.

146 CAB 21(36)6 of 18 March; and DO 6882A/8, meeting of 19 March. See also CAB 20(36)1 of 16 March; C 2026/4/18 of 17 March; C 2048/4/18 of 18 March; and C 2110/4/18 and C 2150/4/18, both of 19 March.

147 CAB 21(36)6 of 18 March.

148 See, for example, CAB 21(36)6 of 18 March; C 2564/4/18 of 28 March; Flandin, *Survenus*, I, p. 153 and *Politique Française*, pp. 208-9; USFR, 1936, I, p. 264; DO 6882A/8, meeting of 16 March; and C-V, pp. 237-8.

149 Flandin, *Survenus*, I, p. 155 and *Politique Française*, pp. 208-10; C 2026/4/18 of 17 March; C 2150/1/17 and C 2110/4/18, both of 19 March; C 2192/4/18 of 21 March; C 2239/4/18 of 23 March; and C 2564/4/18 of 28 March.

150 Cmd 5134 of 19 March.

151 Ibid.; and CAB 23(36)1 of 19 March.

152 The following is based on CAB 21(36)6 of 18 March; CAB 23(36)1 of 19 March; and *Hansard*, vol. 310, cols. 1546-7.

153 In addition to the citations in note 152, see *Hansard*, vol. 310, col. 1545; C-V, p. 323; and DO 6882A/8, meetings of 20 March and 2 April 1936.

154 DO 6882A/8, meetings of 20 March and 2 April; CAB 24(36)1 of

25 March; *Hansard*, vol. 310, col. 1445; and Wickham Steed's letter to *The Times*, 21 March 1936.

155 *Hansard*, vol. 310, cols. 1445, 1546. See also C 2567/4/18 of 31 March.

156 Cmd 5134 of 19 March; CAB 23(36)1 of 19 March; DO 6882A/8, meeting of 20 March; and C 2193/4/18 of 21 March. The foreign office record of this key meeting is only twenty-five words long. Neither the cabinet minutes nor the dominion high commissioners' meetings shed any light on the arguments or proceedings.

157 As a counterpart, Brussels and Paris undertook to send no reinforcements to their eastern frontier areas and to permit the international commission to operate on their soil.

158 Cmd 5134 of 19 March.

159 CAB 23(36)1 of 19 March.

160 DO 6882A/8, meeting of 20 March.

161 Cmd 5134 of 19 March; CAB 23(36)1 of 19 March; C 2200/4/18 and C 2114/4/18, both of 20 March; and C 2192/4/18 of 21 March.

162 The following is based on C 2258/4/18 and C 2207/4/18, both of 23 March; C 2266/4/18 and C 2381/4/18, both of 24 March; CAB 25(36)1 of 25 March; C-V, pp. 253, 318, 381; DDF, I, pp. 649, 678; DDB, IV, p. 158; *Hansard*, vol. 310, cols. 1449-68, 1477, 1491, 1507-10, 1512, 2543-4; *Hansard*, Lords, vol. 100, col. 1560; *The Times*, 21-30 March; Jones, *Diary*, pp. 183-4; and RIIA, *Rhineland*, p. 38.

163 *The Times*, 23 and 24 March; and T 10799/264/384 of 2 July 1936. For a sample of the outrage over Italy's proposed rôle, see *Hansard*, vol 310, cols. 1450-1, 1466, 1504, 1533-4; DDF, I, p. 649; *The Times*, 23, 28, 30 and 31 March; *Survey*, 1936, p. 289, 311-12; and Seton-Watson, *Dictators*, p. 255.

164 *Hansard*, vol. 310, cols. 1451-2, 1464-6, 1476-81, 1489, 1499-1500, 1503-4, 1512-13, 1534, 2543-4; *Hansard*, Lords, vol. 100, col. 204; DDF, I, p. 649; DDB, IV, pp. 155, 158; Eden, *Facing*, p. 361; C2207/4/18 of 23 March; and C2266/4/18 of 24 March.

165 CAB 21(36)6 of 18 March; and CAB 22(36)3, DO 6882A/8, meeting, and C 2048/4/18, minute by Vansittart, all of 19 March.

166 Colvin, *Vansittart*, pp. 101-2.

167 Cecil papers, 51087, letter from Cranborne, 23 March 1936 and letter to Raymond Beazley, 30 March; and *The Times*, 21 March.

168 CAB 23(36)1 of 19 March; and DO 6882A/8, meetings of 19 and 20 March.

169 Cecil papers, 51087, letter from Cranborne, 23 March 1936.

170 *Hansard*, vol. 309, cols. 845-6 and vol. 310, cols. 859, 1445-7, 1542, 1548; and *The Times*, 21 and 24 March.

171 C2239/4/18, minute by Eden, 28 March 1936.

172 Wrench, *Dawson*, p. 332.

173 This paragraph is based on C 2114/4/18 and C 2158/4/18, both of 20 March; C 2195/4/18 of 21 March; DDF, I, p. 649; DDB, IV, pp. 152, 155, 172; Flandin, *Survenus*, I, pp. 137, 157-8, 161 and *Politique Francaise*, pp. 208-10; C-V, p. 295; and *The Times*, 20 and 23 March.

174 Gamelin was also pleased over the failure of Berlin's wedge-driving tactics. (C 2203/4/18 of 21 March).

175 This contrast is illustrated by comparing ministerial statements of 9 and 26 March. (*Hansard*, vol. 309, cols. 1808-13, 1840-1; and vol. 310, cols. 1435-49, 1538-49).

176 Flandin, *Survenus*, I, pp. 159, 161; and C 2192/4/18 of 21 March.

177 Flandin, *Politique Française*, p. 210 and *Survenus*, I, pp. 159, 161; and C 2192/4/18 of 21 March.

178 DDF, I, p. 658 and II, pp. 29-30; and C 2192/4/18 of 21 March.

179 In addition to the citations listed in footnote 173, see Sarraut, *Survenus*, III, pp. 564-5; Paul-Boncour, *Survenus*, III, p. 800; and C 2149/4/18 of 20 March.

180 C 2192/4/18 of 21 March.

181 Maurin, *Survenus*, IV, p. 909.

182 See, for example, *The Times*, 2, 4 April; Sarraut, *Survenus*, III, pp. 566, 570-3, 603; C 3006/1/17 of 16 April; C 3238/4/18 of 21 April; C 7997/3/18 of 12 Nov 1937; *Survey*, 1936, p. 329n; DDB, IV, p. 173; and C-V, pp. 404-5.

183 C 2157/4/18, C 2158/4/18 and FOL 5669H/H016014-15, all of 20 March; C 2195/4/18 and C 2239/4/18, both of 21 March; C 2369/1/17 of 26 March; C 2564/4/18 of 28 March; Flandin, *Survenus*, I, p. 159; Sarraut, *Survenus*, III, p. 565; and DDB, IV, pp. 152, 154.

184 DDB, IV, pp. 152-4; C 2149/4/18, C 2158/4/18 and C 2176/4/18, all of 20 March; C 2195/4/18 of 21 March; C 2239/4/18 of 23 March; C 2564/4/18 of 28 March; Sarraut, *Survenus*, III, pp. 565-6; and Gamelin, *Servir*, II, p. 212.

185 This paragraph is based on C 2192/4/18 of 21 March; C 2239/4/18 and *The Times*, both of 23 March; C 2564/4/18 of 28 March; DDB, IV, pp. 153-5; Eden, *Facing*, p. 362; C-V, pp. 252-3; and DDF, I, p. 636.

186 DDB, IV, p. 154. See also C 2547/4/18 of 31 March.

187 C 2239/4/18 of 23 March

188 DDB, IV, p. 153.

189 C 2200/4/18 of 20 March; *The Times*, and *Manchester Guardian*, both of 21 March; C-V, pp. 219-20; C 2459/4/18 of 27 March; and Zuylen, *Mains libres*, pp. 358-9.

190 See, for example, Arthur H. Furnia, *The Diplomacy of Appeasement* (Washington, DC 1960), pp. 189, 196; Bury, *France*, p. 281; and C 2192/4/18 of 21 March.

191 Flandin, *Politique Française*, pp. 209-10 and *Survenus*, I, p. 157; and Reynaud, *Thick*, p. 134.

192 DDF, I, p. 658 and II, pp. 29-30.

8   The agreement flounders

1 DDF, I, pp. 620, 632-3; and C-V, pp. 215-16.
2 DDF, I, pp. 620, 632, 635, 658-9, 676; C 2173/4/18, C 2174/4/18 and C 2293/4/18, all of 21 March; C 2274/4/18 of 24 March; C 2567/4/18 of 31 March; USFR, 1936, I, pp. 252-3, 265; C-V, pp. 222-3; and *The Times,* 24 March.
3 C 1975/4/18 and C 2015/4/18, both of 17 March; and *The Times,* 17-19 March.
4 C 1943/4/18 of 16 March; C 1997/4/18 of 18 March, and *The Times,* 18-19 March.
5 C-V, pp. 126-7, 140, 160-2.
6 DDF, I, pp. 632-3, 658, 675-6; C 2129/4/18 of 20 March; C 2173/4/18 and C 2174/4/18, both of 21 March; and C 2229/4/18 and C 2230/4/18, both of 23 March.
7 C 2173/4/18 of 21 March; and C 2229/4/18 of 23 March.
8 DDF, I, pp. 632, 656, 675; C 2154/4/18 of 20 March; C 2173/4/18, C 2174/4/18, C 2175/4/18 and C 2293/4/18, all of 21 March; C 2229/4/18 of 23 March; C 2248/4/18 of 24 March; USFR, 1936, I, p. 262; and *The Times,* 21 and 23 March.
9 C 2248/4/18 of 24 March.
10 USFR, 1936, I, p. 262; and C-V, p. 238.
11 C 2175/4/18 of 21 March; and C 2208/4/18 of 23 March.
12 C-V, pp. 51, 65-6, 151-2, 155-6, 193, 222-3, 232-3.
13 C-V, pp. 212, 223, 232, 245.
14 C-V, pp. 209-10, 213-14, 231-3, 244-5.
15 C 2157/4/18 and FOL 63/43933-9, both of 20 March.
16 C-V, pp. 222-3.
17 C-V, pp. 216-17, 222-3, 223n, 229, 248, 250. All four signatures were *ad referendum.*
18 C-V, p. 250; and Aloisi, *Journal,* p. 362. See also C-V, pp. 229-30.
19 C-V, pp. 216-17, 223, 223n, 249-51; and Aloisi, *Journal,* p. 362.
20 C-V, p. 233.
21 This paragraph is based on C-IV, pp. 974-7; C-V, pp. 229, 249-51, 288, 299; R 1721/614/22 of 20 March; C 2246/4/18 of 21 March; FOL 6710/E508101 of 24 March; and Aloisi, *Journal,* pp. 360-2.
22 This paragraph is based on C-V, pp. 288, 306, 438-9; DDF, I, pp. 688-90; C 2470/4/18 of 28 March; and *The Times,* 26 March.
23 See, for example, C-V, pp. 19-20, 22-3, 47-8; DDB, IV, p. 157; G(36)2 of 28 Feb 1936; and C 357/357/18 of 12 Jan 1937.
24 The following discussion is based on LNOJ, April 1936, pp. 341-6; C 2187/4/18 of 21 March; and C-V, pp. 220-1. See also C-V, pp. 215-16, 327; *The Times,* 23 March; and DO 6882A/8, meeting of 20

March.

25 LNOJ, April 1936, p. 342. See also C-V, p. 241; C 2393/4/18 of
    25 March; *The Times,* 21 and 23 March; and Machray, *Poland,*
    p. 449.

26 LNOJ, April 1936, pp. 341-2, 344-5; and C-V, pp. 220-1.

27 LNOJ, April 1936, p. 344.

28 LNOJ, April 1936, p. 342.

29 LNOJ, April 1936, pp. 341-5; C-V, pp. 220-1, DDF, I, pp. 632-3;
    and C 2187/4/18 of 21 March.

30 LNOJ, April 1936, p. 343. Members were surprised that Grandi
    could co-initial a document without Rome's knowledge of its
    contents. (C-V, p. 221).

31 Ibid.; and C2187/4/18 of 21 March.

32 C-V, pp. 231-2, 241n; C 2129/4/18, C 2130/4/18, C 2143/4/18, C
    2154/4/18, all of 20 March; C 2173/4/18 and C 2174/4/18, both of
    21 March; *The Times,* 21, 23 March; and DDF, I, pp. 632-3.

33 C 2268/4/18 of 21 March. See also C 1819/4/18 of 13 March; C-V,
    pp. 241, 256-7; USFR, 1936, I, pp. 270-1. The seven states were
    Norway, Denmark, Sweden, Switzerland, Spain, Finland and
    Holland.

34 C 2268/4/18 of 21 March. See also C 2392/4/18 of 25 March; DDB,
    IV, p. 165; and DDF, I, p. 633.

35 C-V, p. 328; C 2268/4/18 of 21 March; DO 6882A/8, meetings of
    20 March and 7 April; DDB, IV, p. 165; DDF, I. p. 633; and *The
    Times,* 23 March.

36 LNOJ, April 1936, pp. 346-7; and C-V, pp. 260, 276-7, 329.

37 Berber, *Spiegel,* p. 59; and DDB, IV, p. 165.

38 C-V, pp. 222-3, 231-2, 244-6; C 2154/4/18 and C 2171/4/18, both of
    20 March; C 2226/4/18 and C 2230/4/18, both of 23 March; DDF,
    I, pp. 620, 634; *The Times,* 23 March; and USFR, 1936, I, p. 262.

39 C-V, pp. 231, 233, 244, 250-1; C 2226/4/18 of 23 March; and DDF,
    I, p. 620.

40 C-V, pp. 231, 244-6.

41 C-V, pp. 231, 255; C 2226/4/18 of 23 March; C 2248/4/18 of 24
    March; *The Times,* 25 March; and DDF, I, pp. 633, 679.

42 *The Times,* 23 March 1936.

43 C-V, pp. 219, 230-1, 241, 243, 251, 253, 256-7, 278, 289; FOL 6710/
    E508026 of 23 March; DDF, I, pp. 632-3, 635-6; C 2173/4/18, C
    2174/4/18 and C 2186/4/18, all of 21 March; C 2229/4/18 of 23
    March; and *The Times,* 21 and 23 March.

44 C-V, pp. 223, 229-30, 231-3, 244-8; C 2171/4/18 of 20 March; C
    2175/4/18, C 2186/4/18 and *The Times,* all of 21 March; and C
    2208/4/18 of 23 March.

45 C 2276/4/18 of 25 March.

46 C-V, pp. 233, 244-6, 247-8. See also DDF, I, pp. 676-8; and C
    2226/4/18 of 23 March.

47 C-V, pp. 232, 245-6, 259-60. See also DDF, I, pp. 633, 658; C

2229/4/18 and C 2230/4/18, both of 23 March; and *The Times*, 21 March.

48 C-V, pp. 84, 87-8, 140, 153, 157-8, 297-301; FOL 6710/E506675-6 of 11 March; FOL 6710/E506838-9 of 13 March; and FOL 6710/ E507167-8 of 14 March.

49 C-V, pp. 215, 223, 232, 245-6, 253, 294; and DDF, I, pp. 635, 675, 687, 702.

50 C-V, pp. 283-7.

51 C 2274/4/18 of 24 March; and DDF, I, p. 678.

52 C 2192/4/18 of 21 March; and C 2240/4/18 of 23 March. See also DDB, IV, p. 153; *The Times*, 24 March; and *Le Temps*, 23 March.

53 DDB, IV, pp. 160-3, 170-2; C 2200/4/18 of 20 March; C 2266/4/18 of 24 March; CAB 24(36)1 of 25 March; C-V, p. 219; DDF, I, p. 649; and Zuylen, *Mains libres*, pp. 355-6.

54 C 2266/4/18 of 24 March.

55 C 2171/4/18 of 20 March; and C 2191/4/18 of 21 March. See also C-V, p. 198; DDF, I, p. 633; C 2169/4/18 of 18 March; Ribbentrop, *Ribbentrop*, p. 56; and *The Times*, 21 March 1936.

56 C 2194/4/18 of 22 March.

57 DDF, I, pp. 658-9, 678; C 2197/4/18 of 22 March; and C-V, p. 251. See also DDF, I, p. 636; *The Times*, 24 March. Poncet described the forty-eight hours of 20-21 March as 'le fond de la crise' for Berlin (DDF, I, p. 677).

58 C 2192/4/18 of 21 March; DDF, I, pp. 633, 659, 678; and C-V, pp. 251, 275, 293-5.

59 *Hansard*, vol. 310, col. 859; *The Times*, 20, 21, 23, 24 March; C-V, pp. 253, 274-5, 293-5; C 2381/4/18 of 24 March; DDF, I, p. 649; and *Survey*, 1936, pp. 311-12.

60 DDB, IV, pp. 155, 158; CAB 24(36)1 of 25 March; *Hansard*, vol. 310, cols. 1464-6, 1476-7, 1503-4, 1512-13; *Hansard*, Lords, vol. 100, col. 204. See also Flandin, *Politique Française*, pp. 209-10, 212, and *Survenus*, I, pp. 158-9; and Jones, *Diary*, pp. 183-4.

61 C-V, pp. 239, 293-4. See also C 2207/4/18 of 23 March.

62 See, for example, DDF, I, pp. 620, 633, 658; *The Times*, 21, 23, 24 March; C 2175/4/18 and C 2186/4/18, both of 22 March.

63 DDF, I, p. 677. See also DDF, I, pp. 620, 622; C-V, pp. 259-60; C 2175/4/18 of 21 March; *The Times*, 23 March; and C 2274/4/18 of 24 March.

64 C-V, p. 253. See also DDF, I, p. 635; and *The Times*, 23, 24 March.

65 C-V, p. 240. See also C-V, pp. 274-5, 294, 369.

66 C-V, pp. 253, 274-5, 318. See also C-V, p. 381; DDF, I, pp. 635, 677; Nicolson, *Diaries*, p. 254; and *Hansard*, vol. 310, cols. 1462-3.

67 See, for example, C-V, pp. 252-3, 290, 295; DDF, I, pp. 633, 635, 678; DDB, IV, p. 158; C 2233/4/18 of 23 March; and *The Times*, 24, 25 March.

68 C-V, pp. 283-7; and C 2274/4/18 of 25 March.

69 C 2312/4/18, CP 89(36) and CAB 25(36)1, all of 25 March; and DO
    6882A/8, meeting of 2 April.
70 C-V, p. 294; and C 2274/4/18 of 24 March. See also DDF, I, pp.
    659-60; *The Times*, 24 March; DDB, IV, pp. 168, 171-2; and Cecil
    papers, 51172, letter from Lady Muir, 25 March 1936.
71 DDB, IV, pp. 160-1.
72 C 2311/4/18 of 25 March; C 2314/4/18 of 25 March; USFR, 1936,
    I, pp. 267-8; and DDB, IV, p. 167.
73 *The Times*, 26 March; C-V, p. 321; and C 2230/4/18 of 23 March.
74 FOL 6710/E508476 of 24 March; C-V, pp. 320-1; and C 2230/4/18
    of 23 March.
75 C 2314/4/18 of 25 March; C 2727/4/18 of 27 March; C-V, p. 290;
    and *The Times*, 25, 26 March. See also DDB, IV, pp. 152-3, 166-72.
76 C 2314/4/18 of 25 March.
77 C 2256/4/18 and FOL 6710/E508476, both of 24 March; *Le Temps*,
    C 2307/4/18 and C 2314/4/18, all of 25 March; C 2369/4/18 and
    The Times, both of 26 March; C 2727/4/18 of 27 March; and C
    2564/4/18 of 28 March.
78 C 2314/4/18 and *Le Temps*, both of 25 March.
79 *Hansard*, vol. 310, col. 859; DDF, I, p. 649; C-V, pp. 253, 274-5,
    293-5; and *The Times*, 24 March.
80 See, for example, *Hansard*, vol. 310, cols. 1450-1, 1466, 1491, 1504,
    1512, 1533; C-V, p. 293; DDF, I, pp. 633, 649; and C 2381/4/18 of
    24 March.
81 C-V, pp. 274-5, 293-5, 315, 345; *The Times*, 24 March; and C 2307/
    4/18 of 25 March.
82 C 2256/4/18, C 2271/4/18 and C 2266/4/18, all of 24 March; and
    The Times, 24, 25 March 1936.
83 C 2207/4/18 of 23 March; C 2266/4/18 of 24 March; and C-V, pp.
    293-4. See also C-V, p. 253; DDF, I, p. 649; and *Hansard*, vol. 310,
    col. 1507.
84 C 2314/4/18 of 25 March.
85 DDF, I, pp. 640, 649; C-V, p. 290; FOL 6710/E508476 of 24 March;
    C 2271/4/18 and C 2266/4/18, both of 24 March; *The Times*, 26
    March; and DDB, IV, p. 168.
86 CAB 24(36)1 of 25 March; *Hansard*, vol. 310, cols. 1439, 1442; C
    2303/4/18 and C 2266/4/18, both of 24 March; DDF, I, p. 649; and
    DDB, IV, p. 170.
87 DDF, I, p. 640; C 2314/4/18 and C 2366/4/18, both of 25 March; C
    2564/4/18 of 28 March; DDB, IV, p. 163; and *The Times*, 24, 25
    March.
88 C 2256/4/18 of 25 March; FOL 6710/E508476 of 24 March; DDB,
    IV, p. 168; and *Survey*, 1936, p. 315.
89 C 2256/4/18 of 24 March. See also C 2182/4/18 of 20 March; and
    The Times, 26 March.
90 *The Times*, 25 March; and FOL 6710/E508476 of 24 March.

91 *Le Temps*, 23 March; C 2233/4/18 of 23 March; and C 2271/4/18 of 24 March.

92 CAB 24(36)1 of 25 March; C 2311/4/18 of 25 March; DO 6882A/8, meeting of 2 April; and C-V, pp. 289-90, 294.

93 C 2311/4/18 and C 2307/4/18, both of 25 March; C 2352/4/18 of 25 and 26 March; C 2373/4/18 of 26 March; DDB, IV, pp. 161-2, 166-72; and USFR, 1936, I, pp. 267-8.

94 CAB 24(36)1 of 25 March; and DO 6882A/8 of 2 April.

95 In addition to the citations in note 94, see *Hansard*, vol. 310, cols. 1464-5, 1545.

96 *Hansard*, Lords, vol. 100, cols. 203-4. See also DO 6882A/8, meeting of 20 March; DDB, IV, p. 158; Namier, *Decay*, pp. 21-2; and Jones, *Diary*, pp. 183-4.

97 In addition to the citations in note 96, see CAB 24(36)1 of 25 March; C 2266/4/18 of 24 March; DDF, I, p. 649; C-V, p. 324; and *The Times*, 28 March.

98 CAB 24(36)1 of 25 March; CAB 26(36)3 of 1 April; LP(L) 5th meeting, 30 March; and C 2311/4/18, minutes of 26 March.

99 CAB 24(36)1 of 25 March.

100 C 2169/4/18 of 18 March; C 2170/4/18 of 19 March; C 2171/4/18 of 20 March; C 2191/4/18 of 21 March; C 2197/4/18 of 22 March; C 2274/4/18 of 24 March; C 2276/4/18, C 2312/4/18 and CAB 24(36)1, all of 25 March; C 2455/4/18 of 26 March; C-V, pp. 198, 214-15, 251, 287, 290-1, 293; and *Hansard*, vol. 310, cols. 1438, 1446, 1542.

101 C 2312/4/18 of 25 March. See also CAB 28(36)2 of 8 April.

102 C-V, pp. 231, 244-5, 287, 293n; C 2293/4/18 of 21 March; C 2274/4/18 of 24 March; C 2455/4/18 of 26 March; and DDF, I, pp. 620, 622.

103 C-V, pp. 287, 291.

104 CAB 24(36)1 of 25 March.

105 This paragraph is based on *Hansard*, vol. 310, cols. 1435-49, 1455-6, 1461, 1499, 1501, 1507-8, 1518, 1520, 1523; C 2825/4/18 of 30 March; C 2724/4/18 of 3 April; *The Times*, 28 March; C-V, pp. 315-17; DDF, I, p. 686; Eden, *Facing*, pp. 362, 366; Feiling, *Chamberlain*, p. 280; Jones, *Diary*, p. 185; and Nicolson, *Diaries*, pp. 254, 267.

106 *Hansard*, vol. 310, col. 1442.

107 *Hansard*, vol. 310, col. 1445.

108 *Hansard*, vol. 310, cols. 1542-3, 1545-6; and CAB 24(36)1 of 25 March. See also DO 6882A/8, meeting of 2 April.

109 *Hansard*, vol. 309, cols. 848, 1813, 1841-3, 2008; vol. 310, cols. 1461, 1470, 1484-7, 1507-9, 1520-38, 2008, 2487-8, 2543-4; vol. 311, col. 1823; Labour Party Annual Report, 1936, pp. 182-207; Taylor, *English History*, pp. 199, 369, 388, 414; Medlicott, *Contemporary England*, p. 350n; and *The Times*, 19, 21, 28 March.

110 *Hansard*, vol. 310, cols. 1461-8, 1520-3, 1531-8.

111 Eden, *Facing*, p. 361; *Hansard*, vol. 310, cols. 1449-1549; RIIA, *Rhineland*, pp. 14, 26, 39-40, 43; and *The Times*, 19 and 21 March. See also C 2214/4/18 of 14 March.

112 *Hansard*, vol. 310, cols. 1462, 1470-2, 1485-7, 1517-18, 1520; and C 2825/4/18 of 30 March.

113 *Hansard*, vol. 310, cols. 1440, 1446-9, 1455-6, 1463, 1466, 1491-3; DDF, I, pp. 704-5; Feiling, *Chamberlain*, p. 280; and A. Chamberlain papers, 41/3/27, letter to Count Vladimir d'Ormesson, 28 March 1936.

114 C 2825/4/18 of 30 March; C 2724/4/18 of 3 April; *Hansard*, vol. 310, cols. 1455-6, 1470, 1484-7, 1501-11, 1516-18; DDF, I, pp. 704-5; C-V, p. 317; and *The Times*, 28 March, 1 April 1936.

115 C 2394/4/18, C 2427/4/18, C 2430/4/18 and C 2459/4/18, all of 27 March; C 2564/4/18 of 28 March; C 2473/4/18 of 29 March; C 2538/4/18 of 31 March; and C 2575/4/18 of 1 April.

116 *Hansard*, vol. 310, col. 1493; C2394/4/18 and C2430/4/18, both of 27 March; and *The Times*, 28 March.

117 *Hansard*, vol. 310, cols. 1441-2, 1541-4.

118 C 2394/4/18 and C 2430/4/18, both of 27 March; C 2473/4/18 of 29 March; C 2538/4/18 of 31 March; *The Times*, 28 March; and DDF, I, p. 704.

119 *Hansard*, vol. 310, col. 1448; DDB, IV, p. 173; Poncet, *Fateful*, p. 198; C 2394/4/18 and C 2430/4/18, both of 27 March; and C 2538/4/18 of 31 March.

120 CAB 24(36)1 of 25 March; *The Times*, 28 March; DDF, I, pp. 722-3; C 2508/4/18 of 30 March; and C 2538/4/18 of 31 March.

121 DO 6882A/8, meetings of 19, 20 March and 2 April; LP(L) 4th meeting, 16 March; CAB 23(36)1 of 19 March; CAB 24(36)1 of 25 March; C 2314/4/18 of 25 March; C 2538/4/18 of 31 March; and *The Times*, 26 March and 3 April.

122 DO 6882A/8, meeting of 2 April; and C 2311/4/18, minutes by Wigram, Sargent and Vansittart, all 26 March.

123 CAB 24(36)1 of 25 March; LP(L) 5th meeting and C 2508/4/18, both of 30 March; C 2538/4/18 of 31 March; CAB 25(36)3 of 1 April; and DDF, I, pp. 722-3.

124 CAB 25(36)3 of 1 April; C-V, p. 368; DO 6882A/8 of 2 April; and *The Times*, 4 April 1936. See also DDF, I, pp. 704-5.

125 DDF, I, pp. 649, 722-3; C 2307/4/18, C 2311/4/18 and C 2366/4/18, all of 25 March; C 2463/4/18 of 27 March; and C 2508/4/18 of 30 March.

126 CAB 26(36)2 and 3 of 1 April; Cmd 5149 of 1 April; C 2614/4/18 of 2 April; and *Hansard*, vol. 310, cols. 2309-12.

127 C-V, pp. 368, 380; CAB 26(36)2 and 3 of 1 April; DO 6882A/8, meeting, and C 2654/4/18, both of 2 April.

128 C 2314/4/18 of 25 March; C 2430/4/18 of 27 March; C 2538/4/18 of

31 March; C 2661/4/18 of 3 April; C 2677/4/18 of 4 April; and *The Times,* 4 April.

129 C 2588/4/18, C 2611/4/18, C 2612/4/18, all of 2 April; C 2661/4/18 of 3 April; C 2677/4/18 of 4 April; C 2679/4/18 of 5 April; and C-V, pp. 368, 376.

130 DDB, IV, p. 155; C 2239/4/18 of 23 March; C 2589/4/18 of 31 March; *The Times,* 23 March; Maurin, *Survenus,* IV, p. 909; and C 2239/4/18 of 23 March.

131 C 2751/4/18 of 3 April.

132 C 2389/4/18 of 27 March; C 2467/4/18 of 29 March; C 2575/4/18 of 1 April; C 2611/4/18 and C 2614/4/18 both of 2 April; C 2660/4/18 and C 2661/4/18, both of 3 April; C 2645/4/18 of 3 and 4 April; C 2707/4/18 of 4 April; C 2790/4/18 of 6 April; DDB, IV, pp. 187-8; *The Times,* 27, 28 March; DO 6882A/8, meeting of 7 April; and *Hansard,* vol. 310, col. 2509.

133 C 2175/4/18 of 20 March; C 2208/4/18 of 23 March; C 2276/4/18 of 25 March; C 2346/4/18 of 26 March; C 2604/86/18 of 31 March; and *The Times,* 23, 25, 26, 27, 28, 30 March. See also DDF, I, pp. 687-8.

134 *The Times,* 28 March.

135 Of the 45,453,691 registered voters, 99 per cent voted and 98.8 per cent of these approved Hitler's action.

136 C 2604/4/18 of 31 March; C 357/357/18 of 12 Jan 1937; DDF, I, pp. 727-33; and *The Times,* 31 March.

137 C-V, pp. 199, 221-2, 252, 274, 320-1, 376, 403-8, 413-15, 421-6, 428-9.

138 C-V, pp. 233-40, 251, 253, 286-7, 289-95, 315-18, 333-4, 342-5, 364-5, 367-9, 377-82, 396-400, 410-11, 435-6, 494-9.

139 *The Times,* 28 March 1936.

140 In addition to the citations in note 138, see USFR, 1936, I, pp. 269, 282, 296-7; DDF, I, pp. 704-5; FOL 6710/E508872-4 of 4 April; *The Times,* 4 April; and Jones, *Diary,* p. 185.

141 C-V, pp. 289-95; FOL 6710/E508222 of 24 March; FOL 6710/ E508609-24 of 2 April; DDF, I, p. 649; *Hansard,* vol. 310, cols. 1220, 1398, 1451-2, 1476-80, 1489, 1503, 1513, 1533-4; *The Times,* 28 March; *Daily Mail,* 28 March; C 2436/4/18 of 25 March; and C 2825/4/18 of 30 March.

142 C 2312/4/18 of 25 March; C-V, pp. 290-1; and Eden, *Facing,* p. 361.

143 In addition to citations in the preceding two notes, see: Eden, *Facing,* pp. 360, 362. Baldwin himself was anxious about the political repercussions of staff talks. (*Facing,* p. 362). See also J 3894/ 84/1 of 4 May 1936.

144 C-V, pp. 254-5, 290, 293, 323, 343, 359, 378-9; C 2455/4/18 of 26 March; and C 2428/4/18 of 27 March; and CP 100(36) of 1 April 1936.

145 C-V, pp. 292n, 293, 330, 378-9; C 2428/4/18 of 27 March; DDF, I,

pp. 693-4; *The Times,* 27 March; Ribbentrop, *Ribbentrop,* p. 56; Eden,*Facing,* p. 361; and Schmidt, *Hitler's Interpreter,* pp. 45, 49.

146 C-V, pp. 379, 381; and C 2428/4/18 of 27 March.

147 C 2346/4/18 of 26 March.

148 *Hansard,* vol. 310, cols. 1220, 1398, 1410, 1476-81, 1489, 1512-13, 1533-4; *Hansard,* Lords, vol. 100, cols. 520-1, 548, 556-7, 561; FOL 6710/E508609-24 of 2 April; C 3437/4/18 of 22 April; C-V, pp. 293, 295, 568n; Eden, *Facing,* p. 362; Macmillan, *Wings,* p. 463; and Aloisi, *Journal,* p. 362.

149 C-V, pp. 232, 245, 323, 343-5, 359, 378-82; DDF, I, p. 693; C 2428/4/18 of 27 March; C 2455/4/18 of 26 March; C 2544/4/18 of 30 March; CP 100(36) of 1 April; C 2615/4/18 of 2 April; C 2657/4/18 of 3 April; Geyr, *Critical Years,* pp. 69-70; and *The Times,* 2 April.

150 C 2311/4/18 of 26 March; *The Times,* 26, 31 March; and C-V, p. 368.

151 C-V, pp. 344-5, 368, 378-9, 381, 392, 463-4, 494-9, 568-70; C 2428/4/18 of 27 March; CAB 25(36)3 of 1 April; C 3437/4/18 of 22 April; and *Hansard,* vol. 310, cols. 1441-2, 1543-7, 1625, 1814, 2122, 2304-6, 2589-90, 2768-9, 2948.

152 Assurances were given by Eden to Ribbentrop on 25, 27 March, 2 and 3 April, and to the Commons on 26 March and 3 April. Other British sources made similar statements on 6, 21 and 29 April.

153 *Hansard,* vol. 310, cols. 1441-2, 2304-7.

154 *Hansard,* vol. 310, cols. 1441, 2306; C-V, p. 379; C 2428/4/18 of 27 March; CP 100(36) of 1 April; and C 3437/4/18 of 22 April.

155 *Hansard,* vol. 310, col. 1544; CP 100(36) of 1 April; and C 2615/4/18 of 2 April.

156 *Hansard,* vol. 310, cols. 1477, 1508, 1534-6; FOL 6710/E508609-24 of 2 April; *The Times,* 27, 28, 31 March; DDF, II, pp. 17-18; *Daily Mail,* 28 March; C 2825/4/18 of 30 March; C 2724/4/18 of 3 April; C 3238/4/18 of 21 April; and Clynes, *Memoirs,* II, p. 233.

157 C 2465/4/18 of 28 March; C 2499/4/18 of 29 March; C 2586/4/18 of 2 April; C 2646/4/18 of 3 April; C 2680/4/18 and C 2682/4/18, both of 4 April; C-V, pp. 359, 365, 378, 381; and *The Times,* 2, 3, 4, 6 April.

158 C 2788/4/18 of 7 April; DDF, I, p. 632 and II, p. 94; C-V, p. 368; Kordt, *Akten,* pp. 141, 144; and Schmidt, *Interpreter,* pp. 45, 49.

159 C-V, pp. 291-2, 344, 378, 392, 463-4, 494-9; and C 2428/4/18 of 27 March.

160 DDF, II, pp. 59-60, 94-5, 133-4; and *The Times,* 6 April.

161 C 2702/4/18 of 31 March; CAB 25(36)3 of 1 April; CP 105(36) of 2 April; CID 276th meeting, 3 April; C 2748/4/18 and C 2834/4/18, both of 7 April; CAB 28(36)3 and C 2831/4/18, both of 8 April; C 1142/271/18, minute by Sargent, 8 Feb 1937; DDB, IV, p. 197; and C-V, pp. 568-70.

NOTES

162 C-V, pp. 463-4, 569. See also C-V, p. 392.
163 DDF, II, pp. 13-14, 150-1, 158-9, 322-9; and CP 100(36) of 20 April. See also C 3439/4/18 of 6 May for a contrary view.
164 DDF, II, pp. 12-14, 46-9, 156, 186-9; C 2498/4/18 of 30 March; C 3006/4/18 and C 3017/4/18, both of 16 April; Gamelin, *Servir*, II, pp. 212-13; and Maurin, *Survenus*, IV, pp. 914-15.
165 DDF, I, pp. 643-5 and II, pp. 12-14, 156-9, 184-5, 575-6; DDB, IV, p. 153; C 2737/4/18 of 6 April; C 2864/4/18 of 11 April; C 3422/4/18 and C 3745/4/18, both of 15-16 April; and C 3017/4/18 of 16 April.
166 C 3422/4/18, C 3712/4/18 and C 3745/4/18, all of 15-16 April; DDF, II, pp. 156-8; Maurin, *Survenus*, IV, p. 909; CAB 31(36)4 of 29 April; CP 110(36) of 20 April; and Overstraeten, *Albert*, pp. 218-19.
167 DPM 3 of 29 July 1936.
168 C-V, pp. 426, 435-6, 513-17, 547-9, 713-14, 728, 742, 753-4, 767-8, 793-4, 819, 825-8; DDF, II, p. 31; USFR, 1936, I, p. 309; C 5405/3504/18 of 7 April; C 2827/4/18 of 8 April; and C 5052/4/18 of 13 July 1936.
169 See, for example, DDF, I, p. 658; II, pp. 29-31; C 2157/4/18 of 20 March; *The Times*, 28 March; and DDB, IV, p. 155.
170 C 2761/4/18, C 2826/4/18, C 2827/4/18, all of 8 April; USFR, 1936, I, p. 309; Flandin, *Politique Française*, p. 210 and *Survenus*, I, pp. 159, 161; DDB, IV, pp. 188, 192; and C-V, pp. 428-9, 461-2.
171 Paul-Boncour, *Survenus*, III, p. 800; USFR, 1936, I, pp. 246, 309; DDF, II, pp. 133-4; Flandin, *Politique Française*, p. 212 and *Survenus*, I, pp. 157, 159; Eden, *Facing*, p. 353; Taylor, *Origins*, p. 113; Tabouis, *Blackmail*, p. 142; and C 6528/4/18 of 17 Sept 1936.
172 *Hansard*, vol. 310, cols. 1435-49; DO 6882A/8, meeting of 7 April; CAB 28(36)2 of 8 April; CAB 30(36)2 of 22 April; CAB 31(36)5 of 29 April; CAB 32(36)3 and W 3935/79/89, both of 30 April; J 3894/84/1 of 7 May; C 9055/4/18 of 18 Dec 1936; and Eden, *Facing*, p. 362.
173 C 2604/4/18 of 31 March; C 2868/4/18 of 3 April; USFR, 1936, II, pp. 145, 149-50; Abetz, *Problem*, pp. 79-80; Frank, *Angesicht*, p. 210; Shirer, *Diary*, p. 210; Dodd, *Diary*, pp. 325, 327; Ivone Kirkpatrick, *Inner Circle* (London, 1959), p. 81; and Herbert von Dirksen, *Moscow, Tokyo, London* (London, 1951), pp. 180-1.
174 Frank, *Angesicht*, pp. 211-12.
175 DDF, I, pp. 620, 632, 635, 658-9, 676-8; C-V, pp. 230, 251-3, 293-5; USFR, 1936, I, pp. 262, 265; and C 2274/4/18 of 24 March.
176 See, for example, Schmidt, *Interpreter*, pp. 45, 49; Kordt, *Akten*, p. 144; DDF, I, p. 702; C-V, p. 359; and C 2521/4/18 of 31 March.
177 Schmidt, *Interpreter*, p. 46.
178 C 2788/4/18 of 7 April; and C-V, p. 323.
179 C 2788/4/18 of 7 April; and C 2844/4/18 of 9 April.

180 C-V, p. 570. See also C-V, pp. 232, 245, 323; and FOL 6710/
     E508782-3 of 11 April.

181 C-V, p. 47.

182 C-V, pp. 368-9, 378-9, 382n, 392, 463-4, 496-7, 568-70; and DDF, II,
     pp. 150-1.

183 C-V, pp. 209, 211, 231-2, 244-6, 322-5; and FOL 3242/D712503 of
     25 March.

184 See the citations in note 183.

185 C-V, pp. 18, 210, 325; CAB 23(36)1 and C 2170/4/18, both of 19
     March.

186 *Hansard,* vol. 310, cols. 1538-48.

187 C-V, pp. 161-2, 233-40, 293-5, 368-9; and CP 73(36) of 8 March.

188 C-V, pp. 213-14, 324-5; and DDF, II, pp. 29-31.

189 C-V, pp. 324-5. See also C 2567/4/18 of 31 March; C 2844/4/18 of 9
     April; and *Hansard,* vol. 310, col. 1546.

190 C-V, pp. 320-1, 331-2, 337-40; USFR, 1936, II, p. 141; FOL 3242/
     D712503 of 25 March; Geyr, *Critical Years,* p. 54; and C 2504/4/18
     of 30 March.

191 C-V, pp. 221-2, 247-8, 252-3, 274, 286-7, 289-93, 320-1, 340; and
     FOL 3242/D712503 of 25 March.

192 USFR, 1936, I, p. 300.

193 C-V, pp. 251, 253, 286-7, 289-93, 368. It was predicted at the end of
     March that Britain would erupt in a blaze of anti-French feeling
     if Paris broke off the negotiations (DDF, I, pp. 704-5; and C
     2724/4/18 of 3 April 1936).

9 Fait accompli

1 C-V, pp. 355-63. For some background on the preparation of the
   proposals, see C-V, pp. 331-2, 336-8, 339-40; FOL 3242/D712503
   of 25 March; Kordt, *Akten,* p. 143; and Schmidt, *Interpreter,* pp.
   47-9.

2 C-V, p. 360.

3 C-V, p. 353. For other restrictions on Rhineland troop activity,
   see C-V, pp. 115, 205-6, 314-15.

4 C-V, p. 365.

5 See for example C-V, pp. 364-5, 376; CAB 26(36)4, CP 100(36) and
   C 2532/4/18, all of 1 April; C 2588/4/18, C 2611/4/18, C 2612/4/18
   and *The Times,* all of 2 April; *The Times,* 6 April; C 2732/4/18 of 7
   April and T 10799/264/384 of 2 July 1936.

6 C-V, p. 376; C 2588/4/18 and C 2612/4/18, both of 2 April; C
   2661/4/18 of 3 April; and C 2679/4/18 of 5 April.

7 For favourable British and French reactions, see C 2661/4/18 of 3
   April; *The Times,* 3, 6 April; *New Statesman,* 4 April, pp. 513-14;
   Economist, 4 April, p. 1; *Survey,* 1936, p. 326; Seton-Watson,

Britain, p. 258; C-V, pp. 368-9, 376; Schmidt, *Interpreter,* pp. 47-9; and DDF, II, pp. 17-18, 20.

8 C-V, pp. 368-9.

9 DDF, II, pp. 17-18; C 2612/4/18 of 2 April; C 2661/4/18 of 3 April; and *The Times,* 6 April.

10 C-V, p. 405.

11 DDF, I, pp. 704-5; and C 2724/4/18 of 3 April 1936.

12 DDF, II, pp. 17-18, 29; C-V, p. 376; C 2661/4/18 of 3 April; and C 2677/4/18 of 4 April.

13 DDF, II, pp. 69-80; and C 2785/4/18 of 8 April. See also C-V, pp. 402-3, 406, 414, 415-20.

14 C 2835/4/18 and *The Times,* both of 9 April; C 2915/4/18 of 10 April; and C 3267/4/18 of 14 April.

15 Wheeler-Bennett, *Munich,* p. 225; C-V, pp. 413-15, 468; C 2846/4/18 of 8 April; C 2835/4/18 and *The Times,* both of 9 April; FOL 6710/E509007-9 of 10 April; C 3136/4/18 of 20 April; C 3157/4/18, minute by Wigram, 27 April; Berber, *Spiegel,* p. 62; and USFR, 1936, I, pp. 286-7, 295-6.

16 CAB 26(36)1 and C 2532/4/18, both of 1 April; C 2588/4/18 and C 2613/4/18, both of 2 April; C 2679/4/18 of 5 April; and C 2732/4/18 of 7 April.

17 CP 100(36) of 1 April; C 2588/4/18, C 2615/4/18 and DO 6882A/8, meeting, all of 2 April; C 2657/4/18 of 3 April; C 2679/4/18 of 5 April; CAB 28(36)2 of 8 April; and C-V, pp. 376-82, 405-6, 428-9.

18 C-V, pp. 356-8, 365; and CP 100(36) of 1 April.

19 CP 100(36) of 1 April.

20 C-V, pp. 339-40, 365, 377-8, 410.

21 C-V, p. 369.

22 C-V, pp. 274, 367-9, 376, 378, 380, 387, 399, 428. See also C 2670/4/18 of 3 April; and *The Times,* 3 and 6 April.

23 *New Statesman,* 4 April 1936, pp. 513-14; *Economist,* 4 April 1936, pp. 1-2; *The Times,* 3 and 6 April; C 2724/4/18 of 3 April; DDF, II, pp. 17-18, 20; T 10799/264/384 of 2 July; C-V, pp. 368-9; and Seton-Watson, *Great Britain,* p. 258.

24 USFR, 1936, I, p. 278.

25 C 9284/4/18 of 9 Dec 1936. See also USFR, 1936, I, pp. 219-27.

26 This paragraph is based on DDF, I, p. 622 and II, pp. 46-7; C 2203/4/18 of 21 March; C 2307/4/18 and C 2338/4/18, both of 25 March; and C 2827/4/18 of 8 April 1936.

27 C 2826/4/18 of 8 April. See also C 2827/4/18 of 8 April.

28 See the citations in note 27.

29 LP(L) 5th meeting, 30 March; CAB 26(36)2 and 3 of 1 April; C 2614/4/18 and C 2645/4/18, both of 2 April; DDF, I, pp. 705, 722-3; and DO 6882A/8, meetings of 2 and 7 April 1936.

30 C 2827/4/18 of 8 April; C 3101/4/18 of 23 April; CP 123(36) of 28 April; and DDF, II, pp. 116-17.

31 This is based on C 2827/4/18, C 2833/4/18 and CAB 28(36)2, all of
    8 April; C 2826/4/18, minute by Sargent, 10 April; C 2864/4/18,
    minute by Vansittart, 20 April; C 849/92/62, minute by Vansit-
    tart, 25 April 1936; DDF, I, pp. 704-5, 723; and C-V, pp. 405, 414.
32 This paragraph is based on C 2825/4/18 and LP(L) 5th meeting,
    both of 30 March; C 2724/4/18 of 3 April; CAB 30(36)2 and 3 of 22
    April; CP 121(36) of 25 April; CAB 31(36)5 of 29 April; and DDF,
    I, pp. 704-5 and II, pp. 17-18, 20.
33 C 2827/4/18 of 8 April.
34 Ibid.
35 LP(L) 6th meeting, 8 May; CAB 50(36)2 of 6 July; and CAB
    56(36)3 of 2 Sept. 1936.
36 CP 121(36) of 25 April; CAB 31(36)5 of 29 April; CAB 38(36)2 of
    20 May; and CAB 50(36)2 of 6 July 1936.
37 C 2827/4/18 of 8 April; C 2833/4/18 of 10 April; and CP 123(36) of
    28 April.
38 C 2841/4/18 and C 2850/4/18, both of 10 April; CP 123(36) of 28
    April; and C 902/1/18 of 30 Jan 1937.
39 DDF, II, pp. 171-3, 219-20, 232-3; C 3116/4/18 of 28 April; and C
    3395/4/18 of 2 May 1936.
40 C 3320/4/18 of 17 April; CP 123(36) of 28 April; CAB 31(36)3 of 29
    April; CAB 32(36)3 of 30 April; C 3395/4/18 of 2 May; CAB
    33(36)3 and J 3894/84/1, both of 4 May; C 3468/4/18 of 5 May;
    CAB 34(36)1 and 2, C 3421/4/18 and DO 6109A/22/9, all of 6
    May; C-V, pp. 505-6, 510-11, 513; and DDF, II, pp. 219-20, 232-3.
41 The following is based on C 2564/4/18 of 28 March; C 2547/4/18
    of 31 March; C 2679/4/18 of 5 April; C 3006/1/17 of 16 April; C
    3238/4/18 of 21 April; DDB, IV, pp. 173, 175; and Sarraut, *Sur-
    venus,* III, pp. 566, 570-3, 603.
42 Cmd, 5134 of 19 March; and C 2192/4/18 of 21 March. See also,
    DDF, II, p. 31.
43 G(36)4 of 2 March 1936; C 3456/G/66 of 17 June 1936; and C-IV,
    pp. 707-8, 1058-9.
44 C 3456/G/66 of 17 June 1936.
45 C-V, pp. 232, 245, 275, 284-5, 355-6; DDF, II, pp. 69-80; and C
    2785/4/18 of 8 April.
46 *Hansard,* vol. 313, col. 1209.
47 CAB 30(36)3 of 22 April; CP 121(36) of 25 April; and CAB 32(36)3
    of 30 April.
48 CAB 32(36)3 of 30 April.
49 CAB 30(36)3 of 22 April; CAB 31(36)5 of 28 April; CAB 32(36)3 of
    30 April; and CAB 38(36)2 of 20 May.
50 CAB 31(36)4 and 5 of 29 April; J 3894/84/1 of 7 May; C 3810/4/18
    of 21 May; C 3879/4/18, minute by Wigram, 27 May; CAB 48(36)6
    of 1 July; and C 8998/8998/18 of 31 Dec 1936.
51 CAB 31(36)4 of 29 April 1936.

52 CAB 31(36)5 of 29 April 1936.
53 CAB 31(36)5 of 29 April 1936.
54 C 4372/3511/17, minute of 17 June 1936.
55 C 3508/1/17 of 8 May; CAB 38(36)2 of 20 May; C 4465/1/17 of 18 June; CAB 48(36)6 of 1 July; C-V, p. 826; and Medlicott, *Search*, p. 27.
56 C 4467/1/17 of 19 June. See also C 4248/1/17 of 11 June 1936; and C 1903/1903/17 of 30 Jan 1937.
57 C-V, pp. 513-14; CAB 34(36)1, 2 and appendices I and II, and C 3421/4/18, all of 6 May.
58 C 3544/4/18 of 9 May; C 3575/4/18 of 11 May; C 3879/4/18 of 26 May; C-V, pp. 522-8; and DDF, II, pp. 289, 294-5, 308-12.
59 FOL 7629H/E545281-3 of 22 May; C 5313/4/18, minute by Vansittart, 19 July; *Economist*, 16 May 1936, p. 354; and *Hansard*, vol. 311, cols. 1744-5, 1833.
60 CAB 34(36)3 of 6 May; CAB 36(36)5 of 13 May; CAB 38(36)2 of 20 May; C 3505/4/18 of 8 May; C 3521/4/18 and C 3544/4/18, both of 9 May; and C-V, pp. 548-9.
61 DDF, II, pp. 289, 294-5, 311-12; C 3575/4/18 of 11 May; C 3676/4/18 of 13 May; and C-V, pp. 522-8, 537-8.
62 Seton-Watson, *Britain*, p. 261.
63 C 3677/4/18 of 15 May; CAB 38(36)2 of 20 May; C 4192/4/18 of 3 June; C 4198/4/18 of 10 June; C 4493/4/18, minute by Vansittart, 23 June; and Eden, *Facing*, p. 372.
64 C 3662/4/18 of 14 May; and C-V, pp. 548-9. See also CAB 33(36)4 of 4 May; C 3421/4/18 of 6 May; CAB 38(36)2 of 20 May; CAB 39(36)4 of 27 May; CAB 43(36)5 of 23 June; C 4825/4/18 of 2 July; and Colvin, *Vansittart*, p. 103.
65 C-V, pp. 537-8, 582-3, 630, 634-6, 713-15; *Hansard*, vol. 313, cols. 1207-10; vol. 315, cols. 1116-17; C 3878/4/18 of 26 May; C 3677/4/18 of 23 May; C 3904/4/18 of 27 May; C 4342/4/18 of 16 June; C 4782/4/18 of 1 July 1936.
66 C-V, p. 549; and C 3677/4/18 of 15 May. The questionnaire had not even mentioned fortifications.
67 C 1906/4/18 of 8 Feb 1937; and RIIA, *Documents*, 1937, p. 174.
68 CAB 38(36)2 of 20 May 1936.
69 C 4389/4/18, minute by Wigram, 17 June; C 5313/4/18, minutes by Wigram, 11 July and Vansittart, 19 July; CAB 30(36)2 of 22 April; and CAB 38(36)2 of 20 May 1936.
70 CAB 38(36)2 of 20 May; CAB 48(36)6 of 1 July; LP(B) 1st meeting 4 July; and CAB 50(36)2 of 6 July 1936.
71 C 3879/4/18, minute of 27 May 1936.
72 Ibid.; C 4593/4/18, minute by Vansittart, 4 July; and C 5491/4/18 of 20 July 1936.
73 C 3810/4/18 of 21 May 1936; and C 4342/4/18, minutes by Wigram and Vansittart, both of 17 June; C 4525/4/18, minute by

Wigram, 23 June; C 5313/4/18, minute by Vansittart, 19 July; and Zuylen, *Mains libres*, p. 358.

74 C 4925/4/18, minute by Sargent, 22 June; C 4721/4/18, minutes by Wigram and Sargent, 1 July; C 5052/4/18 of 3 July; C 5228/4/18, memorandum by O'Malley, 15 July; C 6528/4/18 of 17 Sept; C 7247/4/18 of 12 Oct; and C 8998/8998/18 of 31 December 1936.

75 C 4925/4/18, minute by Sargent, 22 June; CAB 48(36)6 and C 4721/4/18, both of 1 July; C 5052/4/18 of 3 July; C 5364/4/18 of 20 July; and C 6815/4/18, minute by Sargent, 2 Oct 1936.

76 C 4925/4/18, minute of 22 June 1936.

77 R 2736/341/22, minutes of 20 May; C 3905/4/18 of 27 May; C 4094/4/18, minute of 8 June; C 4925/4/18, minutes of 22-23 June; C 4687/4/18, minute of 1 July; C 4847/4/18, minute of 5 July; and C 8998/8998/18 of 31 Dec 1936.

78 C 3810/4/18, minute by Wigram, 21 May; C 3879/4/18, minute by Wigram, 27 May; and C 5315/4/18, minute by Vansittart, 19 July 1936.

79 C 3596/4/18 of 13 May 1936.

80 C 5449/4/18 and C 5450/4/18, both of 23 July; and DDF, III, pp. 38-47.

81 The following is based on C 5450/4/18 of 23 July; DDF, III, p. 45; and C-V, p. 360.

82 This paragraph is based on C 4846/4/18 of 4 July; CAB 50(36)2 of 6 July; FP(36) 2nd meeting, 15 July; CAB 54(36)3 of 22 July; C 5450/4/18 of 23 July; C 9055/4/18 of 18 Dec 1936; and DDF, III, p. 13.

83 CAB 50(36)2 of 6 July; CAB 53(36)1 of 16 July; C5491/4/18 of 20 July; and CAB 54(36)3 of 22 July.

84 *Hansard*, vol. 315, col. 1117; C 5469/4/18 of 23 July; CAB 54(36)3, annex of 22 July; and C-V, p. 819.

85 C-V, pp. 822, 840, 959, 973-4, 1150-1; C 3662/4/18 of 14 May; C 5384/4/18 of 17 July; C 5350/4/18 of 21 July; C 5451/4/18, C 5452/4/18, C 5453/4/18, C 5454/4/18 and C 5463/4/18, all of 24 July; C 5628/4/18 of 30 July; C 7251/4/18 and CAB 57(36)7, both of 14 Oct; and C 9055/4/18 of 18 Dec 1936.

86 C-V, pp. 852-3, 1075-9; and C 5703/4/18 of 1 Aug 1936.

87 C-V, pp. 1008-9.

88 Ibid.

89 In addition to the citations in note 85, this paragraph is based on C 4248/4/18, C 4279/4/18, C 4376/4/18, C 4986/4/18, C 5628/4/18, C 5750/4/18, C 5781/4/18, C 6832/4/18 and C 6896/4/18, all of June to October, 1936; and C 357/357/18 of 12 Jan 1937.

90 C-V, pp. 852-3, 956, 959, 1152; and C 6431/4/18 and C 6436/4/18, both of 11 Sept 1936.

91 C-V, p. 986; C 7470/4/18 of 20 Oct; and CAB 58(36)3 of 21 Oct

1936.

92 This paragraph is based on C-V, pp. 918, 921-2, 985-6, 988, 1010, 1076, 1078; C 3662/4/18 of 14 May; C 6896/4/18 of 2 Oct; C 7470/-4/18 of 20 Oct; and C 8701/4/18 of 28 Nov 1936.

93 This paragraph is based on: C-V, pp. 919-21, 957, 974, 987-8, 1009, 1076; C 6412/4/18 of 11 Sept; C 7470/4/18 of 20 Oct; C 8701/4/18 of 28 Nov; C 8792/4/18 of 8 Dec; and C 9055/4/18 of 18 Dec 1936.

94 C-V, pp. 1138-40; N 5715/187/38 of 16 Nov 1936; N 506/506/38 of 10 Jan 1937; C 357/357/18 of 12 Jan 1937; and Degras, *Soviet Documents*, III, pp. 219-20.

95 C 7278/270/4 of 15 Oct 1936; C-V, pp. 1084-95; and C 3530/1/18 of 6 May 1937. For a more general picture, see Miller, *Belgian*, pp. 226-41.

96 C 7470/4/18 of 20 Oct 1936; C 7571/4/18 of 23 Oct 1936; C 8323/4/18 of 20 Nov 1936; and C-V, p. 1158.

97 C 1311/270/4 of 13 March; C 7232/4/18 of 13 Oct 1936; C 7301/7284/4 of 15 Oct 1936; C 7309/7284/4, minutes by Wigram, 16 Oct 1936 and Sargent, 17 Oct 1936; C 493/493/4 of 19 Jan 1937; and C 3530/1/18 of 6 May 1937.

98 In addition to the citations in note 97, see Zuylen, *Mains libres*, pp. 366-7; and Miller, *Belgian*, pp. 220, 225.

99 C 6431/4/18, C 6436/4/18, C 7247/4/18, C 7284/7284/4, C 7301/7284/4, C 7338/7284/4 and C 7571/4/18, all between 11 Sept and 16 Oct 1936; CAB 57(36)7 of 14 Oct 1936; CAB 58(36)2 of 21 Oct 1936; and C-V, pp. 956, 973-4, 981-5, 1075-9, 1102.

100 C 7301/7284/4 of 15 Oct 1936; CAB 58(36)2 of 21 Oct 1936; and CAB 73(36)2 of 9 Dec 1936.

101 C-V, p. 1102; and William Phillips, *Ventures in Diplomacy* (London, 1955), p. 96.

102 CID 285th meeting, 10 Dec 1936. Of this, 60 miles were in Luxembourg and 65 miles in Belgium.

103 Phillips, *Ventures*, p. 96.

104 *Hansard*, vol. 310, cols. 2485-6; and *Survey*, 1936, p. 334n. See also C 357/357/18 of 15 Jan 1937; and DDF, II, pp. 217-18, 262-3, 286.

105 Keitel, *Keitel*, p. 25; C 2293/4/18 of 21 March 1936; C 3761/4/18 of 19 May 1936; C-V, pp. 314-15, 853-62, 1008-9; USFR, 1936, I, p. 301; and Lossberg, *Wehrmachtführungsstab*, p. 12.

106 Manstein, *Soldatenleben*, p. 234; Westphal, *German Army*, p. 43; IMT, XV, p. 349; and O'Neill, *German Army*, p. 176.

107 Manstein, *Soldatenleben*, pp. 234-5; TWC, X, pp. 529, 575; Westphal, *German Army*, p. 43; Baynes, *Hitler's Speeches*, II, pp. 1496, 1534, 1617; and Lossberg, *Wehrmachtführungsstab*, p. 12.

108 See, for example, C 1912/4/18 of 15 March; C 2203/4/18 of 21 March; DDF, II, pp. 46-7, 217-18; Narcisse Chauvineau, *Une invasion, est-elle encore possible?* (Paris, 1939), p. 210; and Gamelin, *Servir*, II, pp. 197, 213. At the Hossbach conference of 5 Nov 1937,

Blomberg and Fritsch stressed to Hitler the 'insignificant value of our present fortifications'. Even during the Czech crisis, the west wall was, according to Manstein, 'by no means ready for defence'. (*Soldatenleben*, p. 235; and D-I, p. 38).

109 This paragraph is based on C 1356/4/18 of 3 March 1936; C 2715/4/18 of 3 April; C 7840/172/17 of 3 Nov 1936; C 8060/172/17 of 10 Nov 1936; C 493/493/4 of 19 Jan 1937; Draper, *Six Weeks' War*, pp. 4-11, 21ff; Gamelin, *Servir*, II, p. 85; Reynaud, *Thick*, pp. 80-1, 91, 152; and Rowe, *Great Wall*, pp. 60-2, 86.

110 The cost of constructing some 87 miles of the Maginot line a few years earlier had been 7,000 million francs. According to March 1936 values, that would have been £93.3 million at a time when Britain's total expenditure on its navy and air force together was £92.3 million.

111 By autumn 1936, however, Vansittart, Sargent and Wigram had all written off any hope of negotiations bearing fruit. (C 6815/4/18 of 1-2 Oct 1936; C 8171/4/18 of 14 Nov 1936; and C 8265/4/18 of 2, 4 and 7 Dec 1936).

112 Eden, *Facing*, p. 518.

113 D-I, p. 151. See also D-I, pp. 13, 56, 70, 86, 90, 124, 127, 148.

114 Medlicott, *Search*, pp. 23, 27-8.

115 USFR, 1936, I, p. 300.

116 Ibid. See also C-V, pp. 853-62; and Medlicott, *Search*, p. 29.

117 C 3677/4/18 of 15 May 1936.

118 C-V, p. 862; and D-I, pp. 29-39.

119 C 357/357/18 of 12 Jan 1937; Frank, *Angesicht*, p. 210; Abetz, *Problem*, pp. 79-80; C 6149/99/18 of 17 Aug 1936; Nevile Henderson, *Failure of a Mission* (London, 1940), pp. 40-1; and Kirkpatrick, *Inner Circle*, p. 81.

120 USFR, 1936, II, pp. 149-50. See also Dodd, *Diary*, p. 327; and C 2868/4/18 of 3 April 1936.

121 C 3663/4/18 of 14 May 1936. 'Ja,' Hitler told Frank after the crisis had passed, 'dem Mutigen gehört die Welt. Ihm hilft Gott.' (Frank, *Angesicht*, p. 211).

122 See, for example, IMT, XX, p. 657; Boeninger, 'Hitler,' p. 32; Bor, *Halder*, p. 111; Shirer, *Rise and Fall*, p. 293; Erfurth, *Generalstab*, II, p. 201; Gordon A. Craig, 'The German Foreign Office', in *The Diplomats*, II (New York, 1963), p. 426; Hermann Foertsch, *Schuld und Verhängnis* (Stuttgart, 1951), p. 74; Wheeler-Bennett, *Nemesis*, pp. 353, 355; and Seton-Watson, *Britain*, p. 249.

123 Hossbach, *Zwischen*, pp. 96-7. See also *Zwischen*, pp. 45, 77; Ritter, *Resistance*, p. 74; C 2844/4/18 of 9 April 1936; O'Neill, *German Army*, p. 169; and USFR, 1936, II, p. 153.

124 D-I, pp. 29-38; and Hossbach, *Zwischen*, pp. 186-94.

125 Trevor-Roper, *Table Talk*, p. 259; and C 2841/164/18 of 14 April 1937. See also DDB, IV, p. 321; and Krosigk, *Es Geschah*, p. 311.

126 Doenitz, *Memoirs,* pp. 301-2; Keitel, *Keitel,* p. 91; Hossbach, *Zwischen,* pp. 81, 157; C 2844/4/18 of 9 April 1936; Dirksen, *Moscow, Tokyo, London,* pp. 180-1; Hilger and Meyer, *Incompatible,* pp. 272-3; Rahn,*Leben,* p. 123; and USFR, 1936, II, p. 153.

127 Ritter, *Resistance,* p. 74; USFR, 1936, II, p. 153; Hossbach, *Zwischen,* pp. 96-7; and C 2841/165/18 of 14 April 1937.

128 C-IV, p. 1165, DDF, I, p. 733; Beck,*Final Report,* p. 260; Kennedy, *Britain,* p. 142; Dirksen, *Moscow, Tokyo, London,* p. 181; and C 2947/3/18, minute by Sargent, 27 April 1937.

129 C 2775/86/18 of 6 April 1936; C 6149/99/18 of 17 Aug 1936; O'Neill, *German Army,* p. 184; Dietrich, *Zwölf Jahre,* pp. 30-1; Walter Görlitz, *Adolf Hitler* (Göttingen, 1960), p. 111; Meissner, *Staatssekretär,* p. 412; and Wheeler-Bennett, *Nemesis,* p. 225.

130 See, for example, C 1619/4/18 of 10 March 1936; C 2857/3/18 of 13 April 1937; C 2880/3/18 of 15 April 1937; C 2947/3/18, minutes by Eden, 15 April and Cadogan, 28 April 1937; and C 473/55/18 of 17 Jan 1935.

131 DBFP, I, 1938, p. 128; C 1986/4/18 of 17 March 1936; Meissner, *Staatssekretär,* p. 413; Forster, *Beck,* p. 57; DDF, I, p. 733; and Wheeler-Bennett, *Nemesis,* p. 353.

132 D-I, pp. 35, 36, 37, 38.

133 D-I, pp. 35, 38.

134 C 1905/4/18 of 8 March; C 1595/4/18 of 9 March; C 3266/4/18 of 22 April; C 3231/4/18 of 28 April 1936; and *Hansard,* vol. 309, col. 1863 and vol. 310, cols. 1454, 1466, 1504.

135 *The Times,* 9 March 1936. See also Amery, *Political Life,* III, pp. 188-9.

136 Meinck,*Aufrüstung,* pp. 155-6.

137 The state of Britain's armaments was not even mentioned in the report of the Hossbach conference.

138 IMT, XIX, p. 276; and C 357/357/18 of 12 Jan 1937.

139 Meinck,*Aufrüstung,* pp. 155-6.

140 C 7891/172/17 of 5 Nov 1936; Gamelin,*Servir,* II, p. 213; Flandin, *Politique Française,* p. 203; C 2475/4/18 of 29 March 1936; and USFR, 1936, I, pp. 260, 306.

141 C-V, pp. 856, 862. See also D-I, pp. 34-5.

142 Meinck, *Aufrüstung,* pp. 155-6; and Robertson, *Hitler's Plans,* p. 82.

143 CID 1219-B of 17 March 1936; and Gamelin, *Servir,* II, p. 213. See also C 5405/3504/18 of 7 April 1936.

144 Medlicott, *Contemporary England,* p. 366 and *Search,* p. 29; and NCA, VII, p. 464.

145 Medlicott, *Coming of War,* p. 13. See also DDF, I, pp. 177-8; and Geyr, *Critical Years,* p. 73.

146 C-V, pp. 853-62; Meinck, *Aufrüstung,* pp. 157-62; and Milward, *German Economy,* pp. 3, 15-27. See also C 357/357/18 of 12 Jan

1937; Robertson, *Hitler's Plans*, p. 82; and Rahn,*Leben*, p. 123.

147 C-IV, p. 1142.

148 C-IV, p. 1164. See also C-V, pp. 47-8.

149 C-V, pp. 223, 231-2, 1008-9.

150 See, for example, C 2827/4/18 of 8 April 1936; C 3662/4/18 of 14 May; C 9055/4/18 of 18 Dec 1936; C 2947/3/18, minutes by Sargent, 27 April 1937 and Eden, 15 April and 3 May 1937.

151 C-V, pp. 755-60, 1136-8. See the appropriate listings in C-IV and C-V for the background.

152 In addition to the other citations in this paragraph, see USFR, 1936, I, pp. 226, 272; Forster, *Beck*, p. 57; Geyr, *Critical Years*, p. 71; and Abshagen, *Canaris*, p. 107.

153 Robertson, *Vierteljahreshefte*, p. 205.

154 See, for example, C-V, pp. 67, 100, 121, 165, 175; and R 1647/444/7 of 13 March 1936.

155 C-V, pp. 121, 321, 406, 426; C 2203/4/18 of 21 March 1936; and Lazareff, *Dernière édition*, p. 305.

156 See, for example, C-V, pp. 62, 64, 114, 488-94, 964-6, 1068; and C 357/357/18 of 12 Jan 1937.

157 CP 73(36) of 8 March. See also Eden, *Facing*, pp. 60, 340-1.

158 See the citations in note 157.

159 C 2274/4/18 of 24 March; C 2312/4/18 of 25 March; CAB 24(36)1 of 25 March; C 2428/4/18 of 27 March; CP 100(36) of 1 April 1936; CAB 26(36)4 of 1 April; C 2615/4/18 of 2 April; C 2657/4/18 of 3 April; C 3904/4/18 of 27 May 1936; and DDF, I, p. 694.

160 Eden, *Facing*, pp. 430-1.

161 See, for example, CAB 31(36)5 of 29 April 1936; C 5313/4/18 of 8 July 1936; and Jones, *Diary*, p. 227.

162 Labour Party Annual Report, 1936, pp. 182-207.

163 Dalton, *Memoirs*, II, p. 97. See also Clynes, *Memoirs*, II, p. 233; and A. J. P. Taylor, *The Trouble Makers* (London, 1957), p. 187.

164 See, for example, C 5313/4/18 of 8 July 1936; Eden, *Facing*, p. 341; Medlicott, *Contemporary England*, p. 364; and Seton-Watson, *Britain*, pp. 189-90.

165 Amery, *Political Life*, III, p. 189.

166 *The Times*, 25 Aug 1936; C 357/357/18 of 12 Jan 1937; and Colvin, *Vansittart*, p. 134. See also DDB, IV, p. 178; and Challener, *Nation in Arms*, p. 229.

167 Colton, *Blum*, pp. 224-5; Gamelin, *Servir*, I, pp. 217-18, 220-1, 240-6 and II, p. 246; and C 1903/1903/17 of 30 Jan 1937.

168 See the citations in note 167. In February 1937, defence plans costing a further £190 million were laid before the French Chamber.

169 *The Times*, 5-7 March 1936.

170 *The Times*, 24 April, 1 May, 10 July, 2 Oct 1936.

171 CAB 30(36)3 of 22 April; CAB 31(36)5 of 29 April; CAB 55(36)13

of 29 July; CAB 57(36)6 of 14 Oct; and CAB 63(36)3 of 4 Nov 1936.

172 DDF, I, pp. 291, 300-2, 444, 696-700; II, pp. 185-6 and III, p. 66; C 7110/6562/62 of 7 Oct 1935; C 1912/4/18 of 15 March 1936; Dhers, 'Du 7 mars', p. 19; Chauvineau, *Une invasion,* pp. 205n, 210; and DDB, III, p. 449.

173 C 3156/1/17 of 24 April 1936; C 3228/1/17 of 28 April 1936; R 3302/341/22, minutes by O'Malley, 11 June and Vansittart, 16 June 1936; and C 5356/4/18 of 3 July 1936.

174 C 2656/55/18 of 28 March 1935; C 2819/55/18 of 2 April 1935; and C 62/1/17, minute by Wigram, 6 Jan 1936.

175 Taylor, *Origins,* pp. 100-1, 114. General Chauvineau wrote in 1938 that the demilitarized zone 'n'avait pour nous qu'un intérêt militaire insignifiant'. (*Une invasion,* p. 205n).

176 Brogan, *Modern France,* p. 701; and Taylor, *Origins,* pp. 59, 114.

177 Challener, *Nation in Arms,* pp. 269-70. See also Scott, *Alliance,* p. 266.

178 Alexis Léger, *Briand* (Aurora, N Y, 1943), p. 15; USFR, 1936, I, pp. 268, 308-9; Paul-Boncour, *Survenus,* III, p. 800; DDF, I, pp. 437-8, 493-4; C 1833/4/18 of 13 March; and C 2338/4/18 of 25 March 1936.

179 DDF, I, pp. 291, 300-2, 444, 696-700; II, pp. 185-6 and III, p. 66; C 5685/55/18 of 23 July 1935; C 7110/6562/62 of 7 Oct 1935; C 1912/4/18 of 15 March 1936; Dhers, 'Du 7 mars', p. 19; Chauvineau, *Une invasion,* pp. 205n, 210; DDB, III, p. 449 and IV, p. 165; and Taylor, *English History,* p. 387.

180 C 2547/4/18 of 31 March 1936; C 3156/1/17 of 24 April 1936; Kérillis,*Kérillis,* pp. 7-8, 12; Noël, *Agression,* p. 135 and *Survenus,* IV, p. 849; Blum, *Survenus,* I, pp. 126-8; and Beneš, *Memoirs,* pp. 34-5.

181 D-I, p. 35.

182 C 2239/4/18 of 23 March and minute by Eden, 28 March 1936. See also *Hansard,* vol. 310, col. 1446.

183 C2857/3/18 of 13 April 1937; C2947/3/18, minute by Sargent, 27 April 1937; C 3228/1/17 of 28 April 1936; and R 3302/341/22, minutes by O'Malley, 11 June and Vansittart, 16 June 1936.

184 D-I, pp. 35-6.

185 C 2239/4/18 of 23 March 1936; and C 2564/4/18 of 28 March 1936.

186 Maurin, *Survenus,* IV, p. 915; and Gamelin,*Servir,* II, p. 240.

187 Flandin, *Politique Française,* p. 212; Reynaud, *Thick,* p. 134; and Eden,*Facing,* pp. 353, 362.

188 DDF, II, pp. 13-14, 30-1, 134; Reynaud, *La France,* I, pp. 358-9; Flandin, *Politique Française,* p. 210 and *Survenus,* I, pp. 157-61; Sarraut, *Survenus,* III, pp. 564-5, and Paul-Boncour, *Survenus,* III, p. 800.

189 The following is based on CAB 18(36)1, CAB 31(36)5, CAB 38(36)2, CAB 50(36)2 and CAB 64(36)1 of 1936; CAB 1(37)2 of 13

Jan 1937; C 5356/4/18 of 3 July 1936; and Colvin, *Vansittart,* pp. 101-2.

190 C 8998/8998/18 of 31 Dec 1936.

191 Ibid. See also C 2802/4/18, minute by Vansittart, 17 March 1936; CAB 32(36)3 of 30 April 1936; CAB 50(36)2 of 6 July 1936; C 5313/4/18 of 9 July 1936; Colvin, *Vansittart,* pp. 92-3; Strang, *Home,* pp. 121-2; Hoare, *Nine Years,* p. 138; and Eden, *Facing,* pp. 241-2.

192 In addition to the citations in note 191, see Lawford, *Bound,* pp. 255-8, 273.

193 C 5313/4/18, minute of 19 July 1936.

194 CAB 18(36)1 of 11 March 1936; LP(L) 1st meeting, 13 March 1936; CAB 50(36)2 of 6 July 1936; Feiling, *Chamberlain,* pp. 279, 314, 319; Percy, *Memories,* pp. 184-5; and Eden, *Facing,* pp. 338, 353-4, 357.

195 C 1643/4/18 of 9 March 1936; Macmillan, *Winds,* pp. 467-8; *The Times,* IV, 2, p. 901; Medlicott, *Contemporary England,* p. 329; Butler, *Lothian,* p. 355; and Mowat, *Britain,* p. 564.

196 C 1493/4/18 of 7 March 1936. See also DDF, I, p. 303.

197 C 2802/4/18, minute by Wigram, 13 March 1936; C 1818/4/18, minute by Lawford, 14 March; C 1865/4/18, minute by R. M. A. Hankey, 17 March 1936; and USFR, 1936, I, p. 265.

198 C 1818/4/18, minute by Lawford, 14 March 1936; *Hansard,* vol. 309, cols. 1926-7, 2035; and vol. 310, cols. 1452, 1511-12; *Hansard,* Lords, vol. 99, col. 968; and vol. 100, cols. 547-8, 551-2; Medlicott, *Contemporary England,* p. 329; Jones, *Diary,* pp. 187-8; and Eden, *Facing,* p. 353.

199 C 1831/4/18 of 9 March 1936; C 2802/4/18 of 13 March; C 2015/4/18 of 17 March; CAB 63(36)3 of 4 Nov 1936; *Survey,* 1936, p. 279; *Hansard,* vol. 310, col. 2036; *Hansard,* Lords, vol. 100, cols. 253, 553; Eden, *Facing,* p. 341; Colvin, *Vansittart,* p. 104; and Seton-Watson, *Britain,* pp. 189-90.

200 C 1558/4/18, minute by Jebb, 16 March 1936. See also C 2213/99/18 of 14 March; and C 1558/4/18 of 23 March 1936.

201 C 1814/4/18 of 8 March 1936; C 1831/4/18 of 9 March; C 7834/226/18 of 12 Nov 1937; Jones, *Diary,* pp. 175, 181; D. W. Brogan, *Is Innocence Enough?* (London, 1941), p. 52; RIIA, 'Rhineland,' pp. 7, 18; Gibbs, *Ordeal,* p. 233; and Taylor, *English History,* p. 386.

202 CAB 31(36)5 of 29 April 1936; LP(B) 1st meeting, 4 July 1936; Colvin, *Vansittart,* pp. 99, 103; and *Hansard,* vol. 313, col. 1238.

203 CAB 32(36)3 of 30 April; and CAB 50(36)2 of 6 July 1936.

204 Lothian papers, 445, letter from Neville Chamberlain, 10 June 1936.

205 C 5313/4/18 of 9 July 1936; and LP(L) 6th meeting, 8 May 1936. See also USFR, 1936, I, pp. 282-3; Nicolson, *Diaries,* pp. 257, 269; and *New Statesman,* 4 April 1936, pp. 513-14.

206 C 2947/3/18, minute by Sargent, 27 April 1937; C 4757/3/18, minute by Strang, 2 July 1937; Strang, *Britain,* p. 323; Cecil papers, 51076, letter to General Smuts, 26 Nov 1936; Medlicott, *Contemporary England,* p. 364; and Wickham Steed, *Our War Aims* (London, 1939), pp. 68-9.

207 C 6528/4/18 of 17 Sept 1936; USFR, 1936, I, pp. 265, 282, 296; Eden, *Facing,* p. 337; Citrine, *Work,* p. 356; Norman Angell, *The Defence of the Empire* (London, 1937), p. 163; RIIA, *Rhineland,* p. 40; and Northedge, *Giant,* p. 426.

208 See, for example, C 2567/4/18 of 31 March 1936; USFR, 1936, I, p. 214, 272; Amery, *Political Life,* III, pp. 188-9; Dalton, *Memoirs,* II, p. 88; Grigg, *Faith,* p. 5; Nicolson, *Diaries,* p. 248; Stocks, *Rathbone,* pp. 234-5; and Eden, *Facing,* p. 353.

209 C 8998/8998/18 of 31 Dec 1936.

210 Ibid.; and CAB 50(36)2 of 16 July 1936. See also *Hansard,* vol. 310, col. 1498.

211 CAB 50(36)2 of 6 July 1936.

212 Eden even urged his foreign office colleagues to keep Ribbentrop fully informed and even entertained in order to 'raise his value' and encourage Hitler's sentiments toward Britain (C 2937/3/18, minute of 15 April 1937).

213 C 4757/3/18, minutes by Strang and Sargent, both of 2 July, and Eden, 8 July 1937.

214 Colvin, *Vansittart,* pp. 101-2.

215 Lawford, *Bound for Diplomacy,* pp. 265-6.

216 *Hansard,* vol. 311, col. 1736.

217 No apparatus existed for such an effort. The government had no minister of information until 1940. The foreign office news department in 1936 consisted of ten men, whose duties ranged from supplying information to the British and foreign press to cultural relations with foreign countries and supervision of the official wireless news service.

Bibliography

PRIMARY SOURCES (unpublished)

Official documents

GREAT BRITAIN

Most of the relevant unpublished British documents are available at the Public Records Office, Chancery Lane, London. The material may be divided as follows:
Diplomatic correspondence, 1933-7
Cabinet minutes and papers, 1933-7
Sub-committee minutes and papers, 1934-6
Dominion Office files, 1935-6

GERMANY

Photostat copies of all surviving documents from the Nazi period are available at the Foreign Office Library, Cornwall House, Stamford Street, London.

Private papers

GREAT BRITAIN

Lord Robert Cecil papers, British Library, London.
Sir Austen Chamberlain papers, University Library, Birmingham.
Hugh Dalton diaries and papers, British Library of Economics and Political Science, London.
David Lloyd George papers, Beaverbrook Library, London.
Philip Kerr (11th Marquis of Lothian) papers, Scottish Record Office, Registry House, Edinburgh.

PRIMARY SOURCES (published)

Official documents

AUSTRIA

Der Hochsverratsprozess gegen Dr Guido Schmidt vor dem Wiener Volksgericht, Vienna, 1947.

BELGIUM

Ministère des Affaires Etrangères: *Documents diplomatiques belges*, Third Series, vols. III and IV, Brussels, 1964.

FRANCE

Assemblée Nationale: *Rapport fait au nom de la commission chargée d'enquêter sur les évènements survenus en France de 1933 à 1945, par M. Charles Serre*, Témoignages et documents, vols. I-IX, Paris, 1947.

358 BIBLIOGRAPHY

Chambre des Députés: *Journal Officiel.*

Ministère des Affaires Étrangères: *Documents diplomatiques français 1932-1939,* Second Series, vols. I-III, Paris, 1963- .

GERMANY

Documents on German Foreign Policy 1918-1945, Series C, vols. I-V, London 1957- ; Series D, vols. I-IV, London 1946- .

Nuremberg documents

International Military Tribunal: *Trial of the major war criminals* Proceedings and documents, 42 vols., Nuremberg, 1947-9.

Nazi Conspiracy and Aggression Documentary evidence and guide materials prepared by the American and British prosecuting staffs, 10 vols., Washington, 1946-8.

Trials of War Criminals Case 11 (von Weizsäcker and twenty others) vols. XII and XIV, Nuremberg, 1946.

GREAT BRITAIN

Foreign Office *Documents on British Foreign Policy 1919-1939,* Second series (1930-8), London, 1946- .

Parliament Parliamentary Debates, House of Commons; Parliamentary Debates, House of Lords.

Parliamentary Papers Cmd 153 *Treaty of Peace between the Allied and Associated Powers and Germany, signed at Versailles, 28 June 1919.*

Cmd 221 *Treaty respecting assistance to France in the event of unprovoked aggression by Germany, 1919.*

Cmd 2169 *Papers respecting negotiations for an Anglo-French pact, 1924.*

Cmd 2525 *Final protocol of the Locarno conference, 16 October 1925.*

Cmd 4798 *Joint communiqué issued on behalf of His Majesty's Government in the United Kingdom and the Government of the French Republic as the result of the conversations between the French and British ministers in London, 1-3 February 1935.*

Cmd 4827 *Statement relating to defence issued in connexion with the House of Commons debate on 11 March 1935.*

Cmd 4880 *Joint resolution of the Stresa Conference including the Anglo-Italian declaration and the final declaration, Stresa, 14 April 1935.*

Cmd 5107 *Statement relating to defence, 3 March 1936.*

Cmd 5118 *Memorandum by the German Government respecting the Franco-Soviet treaty, the treaty of Locarno and the demilitarized zone, 7 March 1936.*

Cmd 5134 *Text of proposals drawn up by the representatives of Belgium, France, United Kingdom of Great Britain and Northern Ireland, London, 19 March 1936.*

Cmd 5143 *Correspondence showing the course of certain diplomatic discussions directed towards securing a European settlement, June 1934 to March 1936.*

Cmd 5149 *Correspondence with the Belgian and French ambassadors relating to 'Text of Proposals' contained in Cmd 5134, London, 1 April 1936.*

Cmd 5175 *Correspondence with the German government regarding the German proposals for a European settlement. 24 March— 6 May 1936.*

Cmd 5437 *International position of Belgium. Documents exchanged between His Majesty's Government in the United Kingdom and the French Government and the Belgian Government, Brussels, 24 April 1937.*

LEAGUE OF NATIONS

Official Journal, Minutes of the 91st (Extraordinary) Session of the Council, April 1936.

POLAND

Ministry for Foreign Affairs, *Official Documents concerning Polish-German and Polish-Soviet relations 1933-1939,* Polish White Book, London, no date.

UNITED STATES DEPARTMENT OF STATE

Foreign Relations of the United States. Diplomatic Papers, 1931-1937, Washington, 1946-1954.

Foreign Relations of the United States. The Soviet Union 1933-1939, Washington, 1952.

Peace and War. United States Foreign Policy, 1931-1941, Washington, 1943.

Private papers

Abetz, Otto, *Das offene Problem,* Cologne, 1951.

Allen, Reginald Clifford, *Peace in Our Time,* London, 1936.

Aloisi, Pompeo, *Journal,* Paris, 1957.

Amery, Leopold S., *My Political Life,* Vol. III, London, 1955.

Angell, Norman, *After All,* London, 1951.

Astor, Michael L., *Tribal Feeling,* London, 1963.

Attlee, Clement R., *As It Happened,* London, 1954.

Baldwin, Stanley, *Service of Our Lives,* London, 1937.

Baynes, Norman H. (ed.). *The Speeches of Adolf Hitler, April 1922-August 1939,* Vol. II, London, 1942.

Beck, Joseph, *Beiträge zur europäischen Politik,* Essen, 1939.

——*Final Report,* New York, 1957.

Beneš, Eduard, *Gedanke und Tat,* Vol. III, *Die Zusammenarbeit der Nationen,* Prague, 1937.

——*Memoirs of Dr Eduard Beneš, From Munich to New War and New Victory,* London, 1954.

Berber, Friedrich, *Locarno — A Collection of Documents,* London, 1936.

——(ed.), *Europäische Politik 1933-1938, im Spiegel der Prager Akten,* Essen, 1942.

Blücher, Wipert von, *Gesandter zwischen Diktatur und Demokratie,* Wiesbaden, 1951.

Blum, Léon, *Léon Blum before His Judges at the Supreme Court of Riom, 11-12 March 1942,* London, 1943.

Bonnet, Georges, *Défense de la paix,* Vol. I, Geneva, 1946.

—— *Quai d'Orsay,* Isle of Man, 1965.

Boothby, Robert J. G., *I Fight to Live,* London, 1947.

—— *My Yesterday, Your Tomorrow,* London, 1962.

Cecil, Robert, *Great Experiment: an autobiography,* London, 1941.

—— *All the Way,* London, 1949.

Cerruti, Elisabetta, *Ambassador's Wife,* London, 1952.

Chamberlain, Austen, *Down the Years,* London, 1935.

Chambrun, Charles P. de, *Traditions et souvenirs,* Paris, 1952.

Chatfield, Admiral A.E.M., *The Navy and Defence,* Vol. II, *It Might Happen Again,* London, 1947.

Churchill, Winston S., *Arms and the Covenant,* London, 1938.

——*Step by Step, 1936-1939,* London, 1959.

Ciano, Galeazzo, *Ciano's Diplomatic Papers,* London, 1948.

——*Diary, 1937-38,* London, 1952.

Citrine, Walter M., *Men and Work: an Autobiography,* London, 1964.

Clemenceau, Georges, *Grandeur and Misery of Victory,* London, 1930.

Clynes, John R., *Memoirs,* 2 vols., London, 1937.

Cockburn, Claud, *In Time of Trouble,* London, 1956.

Cooper, Alfred Duff, *Old Men Forget,* London, 1954.

Coote, Colin R., *Editorial — The Memoirs of Colin R. Coote,* London, 1965.

Coulondre, Robert, *De Staline à Hitler: Souvenirs de deux ambassades, 1936-1939,* Paris, 1950.

Dalton, Hugh, *The Fateful Years,* Vol. II, London, 1957.

Degras, Jane (ed.) *Soviet Documents on Foreign Policy, 1917-1941,* 3 vols., London, 1951-3.

Dietrich, Otto, *Zwölf Jahre mit Hitler,* Munich, 1955.

Dirksen, Herbert von, *Moscow, Tokyo, London,* London, 1951.

Dodd, Martha E., *My Years in Germany,* London, 1939.

Dodd, William E., Jr., and Martha, *Ambassador Dodd's Diary,* New York, 1941.

Doenitz, Admiral Karl, *Zehn Jahre und zwanzig Tage;* Bonn, 1958. (English edition: *Memoirs: Ten Years and Twenty Days,* London, 1959.)

Dollmann, Eugen, *The Interpreter: Memoirs of Doktor Eugen Dollmann*, London, 1967.
Dorlodot, R.M.G., *Souvenirs*, Vol. II, Brussels, 1964.

Eden, Anthony, *Facing the Dictators*, London, 1962.

Flandin, Pierre-Etienne, *Politique française, 1919-1940*, Paris, 1947.
Forster, Dirk, Letter to *Wiener Library Bulletin*, Vol. X, nos. 5-6, 1956.
Fotitch, Constantin, *The War We Lost*, New York, 1948.
François-Poncet, André, *Souvenirs d'une ambassade à Berlin*, Paris, 1946.
———*The Fateful Years*, London, 1949.
Frank, Hans, *Im Angesicht des Galgens*, Munich, 1953.

Gaertner, Margarete, *Botschafterin des guten Willens*, Bonn, 1955.
Gamelin, General Maurice, *Servir*. Vols. I and II, Paris, 1946.
Gedye, G.E.R., *Fallen Bastions: The Central European Tragedy*. London, 1939.
Geraud, André (Pertinax), *Les Fossoyeurs*, Paris, 1946.
Geyr von Schweppenburg, L. *The Critical Years*, London, 1952.
Guariglia, Raffaele, *La diplomatie difficile*, Paris, 1955.
Guderian, Heinz, *Panzer Leader*, New York, 1952.

Halifax, 1st Earl of, *Fulness of Days*, London, 1957.
Hart, Basil H. Liddell, *Memoirs*, 2 vols, London, 1965.
Henderson, Nevile, *Water under the Bridges, London, 1945*.
Herriot, Edouard, *Jadis*, Vol. II, Paris, 1952.
Hesse, Fritz, *Hitler and the English*, London, 1954.
Hilger, Gustav, and Alfred G. Meyer. *The Incompatible Allies: A Memoir-History of German-Soviet Relations, 1918-1941*. New York, 1953.
Hitler, Adolf, *Mein Kampf*, London, 1969.
Hoare, Samuel, *Nine Troubled Years*, London, 1954.
Hoffmann, Heinrich, *Hitler Was My Friend*, London, 1955.
Horthy, Admiral Nicholas, *Memoirs*, London, 1956.
Hossbach, Friedrich, *Zwischen Wehrmacht und Hitler, 1934-1938*, Göttingen, 1965.
Hull, Cordell, *The Memoirs of Cordell Hull*, Vol. I, New York, 1948.
Hymans, Paul, *Mémoires*, Vol. II, Brussels, 1958.

Ismay, Hastings Lionel, 1st Baron, *The Memoirs of General the Lord Ismay*, London, 1960.

Jones, Thomas, *A Diary with Letters, 1931-1950*, London, 1954.

Keitel, Wilhelm, *Generalfeldmarschall Keitel*, Göttingen, 1961.

Kesselring, Albert, *Kesselring — A Soldier's Record*, New York, 1954.
Kirkpatrick, Ivone, *Inner Circle*, London, 1959.
Kordt, Erich, *Nicht aus den Akten*, Stuttgart, 1950.
Krosigk, Lutz Schwerin von, *Es Geschah in Deutschland*, Tübingen, 1951.

Labour Party of Great Britain, *Report of the Thirty-Sixth Annual Conference of the Labour Party*, London, 1936.
Lagardelle, Hubert, *Mission à Rome-Mussolini*, Paris, 1955.
Laroche, Jules, *La Pologne de Pilsudski: Souvenirs d'une ambassade, 1926-1935*, Paris, 1953.
Laval, Pierre, *The Diary of Pierre Laval*, New York, 1948.
Lawford, Valentine, *Bound for Diplomacy*, London, 1963.
Lazareff, Pierre, *Dernière édition*, Montreal, 1942.
Lipski, Józef, *Diplomat in Berlin, 1933-1939*, Ed. Waclaw Jedrzejewicz, New York, 1968.
Litvinov, Maxim M., *Against Aggression*, London, 1939.
Londonderry, 7th (Marquess of), *Wings of Destiny*. London, 1943.
Lossberg, Bernhard von, *Im Wehrmachtführungsstab*. Hamburg, 1950.

Macmillan, Harold, *Winds of Change, 1914-1939*, London, 1966.
Manstein, Erich von, *Aus einem Soldatenleben*, Bonn, 1958.
Martin, Kingsley, *Editor*, Vol. II, London, 1968.
Massey, Vincent, *What's Past Is Prologue*, London, 1963.
Meissner, Otto, *Staatssekretär unter Ebert-Hindenburg-Hitler*, Hamburg, 1950.
Menzies, Robert, *Afternoon Light*, London, 1967.
Minney, R. J., *The Private Papers of Hore-Belisha*. London, 1960.
Morrison, Herbert, *Herbert Morrison — an Autobiography*, London, 1960.
Murray, Katharine M., (Duchess of Atholl), *Working Partnership*, London, 1958.
Mussolini, Rachele, *My Life with Mussolini*, London, 1959.

Nadolny, Rudolf, *Mein Beitrag*, Wiesbaden, 1955.
Nicolson, Nigel (ed.), *Harold Nicolson — Diaries and Letters, 1930-1939*, London, 1966.
Noël, Léon, *L'agression allemande contre la Pologne: Une ambassade à Varsovie 1935-1939*, Paris, 1946.

Overstraeten, General R. van, *Albert I — Leopold III: Vingt ans de politique militaire belge, 1920-1940*, Bruges, 1946.

Papen, Franz von, *Memoirs*, London, 1952.

Paul-Boncour, Joseph, *Entre deux guerres,* Vol. III, Paris, 1946.
Percy, Eustace, *Some Memories,* London, 1958.
Pertinax, *see* Geraud.
Peterson, Maurice, *Both Sides of the Curtain,* London, 1950.
Phillips, William, *Ventures in Diplomacy,* London, 1955.
Poncet, *see* François-Poncet.

Raeder, Erich, *Mein Leben,* Vol. II, Tübingen, 1957.
Rahn, Rudolf, *Ruheloses Leben — Aufzeichnungen und Erinnerungen,* Düsseldorf, 1950.
Reynaud, Paul, *In the Thick of the Fight,* London, 1955.
——— *Mémoires,* Vol. I, Paris, 1960.
Ribbentrop, Joachim von, *The Ribbentrop Memoirs,* London, 1954.
Rintelen, Enno von, *Mussolini als Bundesgenosse. Erinnerungen des deutschen Militärattachés im Rom, 1936-43,* Tübingen and Stuttgart, 1951.
Royal Institute of International Affairs, *Documents on International Affairs,* (annual), London, 1929-1937.

Samuel, Herbert Lewis, 1st Viscount, *Memoirs,* London, 1945.
Schacht, Hjalmar, *Account Settled,* London, 1949.
Schmidt, Paul, *Statist auf Diplomatischer Bühne, 1923-1945,* Bonn, 1949, (English edition: *Hitler's Interpreter,* London, 1951).
Schuschnigg, Kurt von, *Ein Requiem in Rot-Weiss-Rot.* Zürich, 1946, (English edition: *Austrian Requiem,* London, 1947).
——— *The Brutal Takeover.* London, 1969.
Selby, Walford, *Diplomatic Twilight, 1930-1940,* London, 1953.
Sforza, Carlo, *Europe and Europeans,* London, 1936.
Shirer, William L., *Berlin Diary: the Journal of a Foreign Correspondent, 1934-1941,* New York, 1941.
Simon, John, *Retrospect,* London, 1952.
Simoni, Leonardo, *Berlin, Ambassade d'Italie, 1939-43,* Paris, 1947.
Speer, Albert, *Inside the Third Reich,* London, 1971.
Starhemberg, Prince Ernst Rudiger, *Between Hitler and Mussolini,* New York, 1942.
Strang, William, *Home and Abroad,* London, 1956.
Stuart, James G., *Within the Fringe,* London, 1967.
Swinton, Viscount (Philip Cunliffe-Lister), *I Remember,* London, 1966.
Szembek, Jean, *Journal, 1933-1939,* Paris, 1952.

Tabouis, Geneviève, *Vingt ans de 'suspense' diplomatique,* Paris, 1958.
Tardieu, André, *The Truth about the Treaty,* London, 1921.
Templewood, Viscount, *see* Hoare, Samuel.
Thomas, J. H., *My Story,* London, 1938.

Thompson, Geoffrey, *Front-line Diplomat.* London, 1959.
Thyssen, Fritz, *I Paid Hitler,* London, 1941.
Trevor-Roper, Hugh R. (ed.), *Hitler's Table Talk, 1941-1944,* London, 1953.

Vansittart, Robert, *The Mist Procession,* London, 1958.

Weizsäcker, Ernst von, *Erinnerungen,* Munich, 1950. (English edition: *Memoirs,* Chicago, 1950.)
Welles, Sumner, *The Time for Decision,* London, 1944.
Wellesley, Victor, *Diplomacy in Fetters,* London, 1944.
Wheeler-Bennett, John W., and Stephen Heald (eds.), *Documents on International Affairs, 1935, 1936, 1937,* London, 1936, 1937, 1938.
Wilson, Arnold, *Walks and Talks Abroad,* London, 1936.
—— *Thoughts and Talks, 1935-1937,* London, 1938.

Zay, Jean, *Souvenirs et solitude,* Paris, 1945.
Zuylen, Pierre van, *Les mains libres; politique extérieure de la Belgique, 1914-1940,* Paris, 1950.

SECONDARY SOURCES

Contemporary studies

Angell, Norman, *The Defence of the Empire,* London, 1937.
—— *The Great Illusion,* London, 1938.
Attlee, Clement R., *Labour Party in Perspective,* London, 1937.

Benoist-Méchin, Jacques, *Histoire de l'armée allemande depuis l'armistice,* Vol. II, Paris, 1938.
Béraud, Henri, *Faut-il réduire l'Angleterre en esclavage?* Paris, 1935.
Beuve-Méry, H., *Vers la plus grande Allemagne,* Paris, 1939.

Cammaerts, Emile, *Albert of Belgium,* London, 1935.
Carr, Edward H., (ed.), *Ambassadors at Large,* 3 vols., London, 1939.
Carrias, Col. Eugène, *L'armée allemande,* Paris, 1938.
Central European Observer, The, Prague, 1936.
Chauvineau, General Narcisse A.G.L., *Une invasion, est-elle encore possible?* Paris, 1939.
Cripps, R. Stafford, *The Struggle for Peace,* London, 1936.

Dalton, Hugh, *Government's Air Muddle Exposed,* London, 1938.
Davis, Shelby C., *The French War Machine,* London, 1937.
Dean, Vera Micheles, 'Origins of the Locarno Crisis', *Foreign Policy Reports,* Vol. XII, 15 June 1936, pp. 78-92.
Dell, Robert E., *The Geneva Racket, 1920-39,* London, 1940.
Domville, Admiral Sir Barry, *Look to Your Moat,* London, 1937.

Economist, London, 1935-6.

Eden, Anthony, *Foreign Affairs*, New York, 1939.

Einzig, Paul, *Bloodless Invasion: German Economic Penetration into the Danubian States and the Balkans*, London, 1938.

Empire Review, London, January-June 1936.

Fanshawe, M., and C.A. Macartney, *What the League Has Done, 1920-1936*, London, 1936.

Fischer, Louis, *Men and Politics*, London, 1941.

Fortnightly, The, London, January-June, 1936.

Freund, Richard, *Zero Hour*, London, 1936.

Freytagh-Loringhoven, Axel von, *Deutschlands Aussenpolitik, 1933-1939*, Berlin, 1939.

Fuller, John F. G., *Towards Armageddon*, London, 1937.

Gibbs, Philip, *Ordeal in England*, London, 1937.

Gibson, Irving M., 'Maginot and Liddell Hart—The Doctrine of Defence', in *The Makers of Modern Strategy*, E.M. Earle (ed.), Princeton, NJ, 1943.

Graves, Robert, *Goodbye to All That*, London, 1929.

Griffin, R. Jonathan T., *Alternative to Rearmament*, London, 1936.

Grigg, Edward, *The Faith of an Englishman*, London, 1937.

——*Britain Looks at Germany*, London, 1938.

Groves, P.R.C., *Behind the Smoke Screen*, London, 1934.

—— *Our Future in the Air*, London, 1935.

Guillebaud, C. W., *The Economic Recovery of Germany, from 1933 to the Incorporation of Austria in March 1938*, London, 1939.

Gunther, John, *Inside Europe*, London, 1936.

Gwynn, Stephen, 'British Policy in the Crisis'. *The Fortnightly*, April, 1936. pp. 385-91.

Hadamovsky, Eugen, *Hitler kämpft um den Frieden Europas*, Munich, 1936.

Hancock, W. K., *Survey of British Commonwealth Affairs*. Vol. I, *Problems of Nationality, 1918-1936*, London, 1937.

Hart, Basil H. Liddell, *Europe in Arms*, London, 1937.

—— *The Defence of Britain*, London, 1939.

Henderson, Nevile, *Failure of a Mission, Berlin 1937-1939*, London, 1940.

Hillson, Norman, *I Speak of Germany*, London, 1937.

Hobhouse, Charles E., 'International Disorder'. *Contemporary Review*, May 1936, pp. 513-21.

Hodson, Henry V., *Slump and Recovery, 1929-1937*, London, 1938.

Howard, Harry N., 'The Little Entente and the Balkan Entente', ch. XX in *Czechoslovakia*, Robert J. Kerner (ed.), Berkeley, 1940.

Jones, S. Shepard, *The Scandinavian States and the League of Nations*, New York, 1939.

Kennedy, A. L., *Britain Faces Germany*, London, 1937.
Kérillis, Henri de, *Français, voici la guerre*. Paris, 1937.
———and Raymond Cartier, *Kérillis on the Causes of the War*, London, 1939.
Keynes, J. M., *Economic Consequences of the Peace*, London, 1919-20.
King-Hall, Stephen, *Our Own Times, 1915-1939*, London, 1941.
Krivitsky, W. G., *I Was Stalin's Agent*, London, 1939.
Krofta, Kamil, *Czechoslovakia and the International Tension*, Prague, 1937.

Lansbury, George, *My Quest for Peace*, London, 1938.
Laurie, Arthur P., *The Case for Germany*, Berlin, 1939.
Lichtenberger, Henri, *The Third Reich*, New York, 1937.
Londonderry, 7th Marquess of, *Ourselves and Germany*, London, 1938.

Macartney, C. A., *Hungary and Her Successors*, London, 1937.
——— *The Danubian Basin*, Oxford, 1939.
Macartney, Maxwell H. H., and Paul Cremona, *Italy's Foreign and Colonial Policy, 1914-1937*, New York, 1938.
McCallum, Ronald B., *Public Opinion and the Last Peace*, London, 1944.
Machray, Robert, *The Poland of Pilsudski*, London, 1936.
——— *The Struggle for the Danube and the Little Entente, 1929-1938*, London, 1938.
Mackenzie, Compton, *Dr Beneš*, London, 1946.
Mackiewicz, M. S., *Colonel Beck and His Policy*, London, 1944.
Maillaud, Pierre, *France*, London, 1942.
——— *The English Way*, London, 1945.
Maisky, Ivan, *Russian Foreign Policy*, London, 1936.
Margueritte, Victor, *The League Fiasco (1920-1936)*, London, 1936.
Marshall-Cornwall, J. H., *Geographic Disarmament*, London, 1935.
Medlicott, W. N., *British Foreign Policy Since Versailles, 1919-1939*, London, 1940.
Micaud, Charles A., *The French Right and Nazi Germany*, Durham, NC, 1943.
Mowat, C. L., *Britain Between the Wars, 1918-1940*, London, 1940.
Mowrer, Edgar A., *Germany Puts the Clock Back*, London, 1937.
Müller, Albert, *Hitlers Stossarmee*, Paris, 1936.
Murray, Arthur C., *Reflections on Some Aspects of British Foreign Policy Between the Wars*, London, 1946.

Nathan, Otto, *The Nazi Economic System: Germany's Mobilization for War*, Durham, NC, 1944.
National Review, London, January-June 1936.
New Leader, London, January-July 1936.
New Statesman and Nation, London, January-July 1936.

Olden, Rudolf, *Hitler the Pawn*, London, 1936.
d'Ormesson, Wladimir, *France*, London, 1939.

Pavel, Pavel, *Why Rumania Failed*, London, 1943.
Potiemkine, Vladimir (ed.), *Histoire de la Diplomatie*, Vol. III, Paris, 1947.
Price, Ward, *I Know These Dictators*, London, 1937.
—— *Years of Reckoning*, London, 1939.

Rathbone, Eleanor F., *War Can Be Averted*, London, 1938.
Reed, Douglas, *Insanity Fair*, London, 1938.
Reynaud, Paul, *Le problème militaire français*, Paris, 1937.
—— *La France a sauvé Europe*, Vol. I, Paris, 1947.
Roberts, Stephen H., *The House that Hitler Built*, London, 1937.
Royal Institute for International Affairs, *Germany and the Rhineland*. London, 1936.

Schmitt, Bernadotte E. (ed.), *Poland*, Berkeley, Calif., 1945.
Schuman, F.L., *Europe on the Eve*, London, 1939.
Schwarz, Paul, *This Man Ribbentrop*, New York, 1943.
Seton-Watson, R.W., *Britain and the Dictators*, Cambridge, 1938.
Slessor, John C., *Air Power and Armies*, London, 1936.
Slocombe, George Edward, *A Mirror to Geneva*, New York, 1938.
Spender, Robert A., *Great Britain and the Empire*, London, 1938.
Steed, Wickham, *Our War Aims*, London, 1939.
Sternberg, Fritz, *Germany and a Lightning War*, London, 1938.
Stewart, Charles S.H.V.T., *see* Londonderry

Tabouis, Geneviève R., *Blackmail or War*, London, 1938.
—— *Perfidious Albion — Entente Cordiale*, London, 1938.
—— *They Called Me Cassandra*, New York, 1942.
Tardieu, André, *La Note de semaine, 1936*, Paris, 1937.
Temperley, Major-General A.C., *The Whispering Gallery of Europe*, London, 1939.
Temperley, H.W.V. (ed.), *A History of the Peace Conference of Paris*, Vol. III, London, 1920.
Le Temps, Paris, January-April 1936.
Thorez, Maurice, *Son of the People*, London, 1938.
The Times, London, 1935-6.

Torres, Henry, *Pierre Laval*, London, 1941.
Toynbee, A.J., *Survey of International Affairs, 1935, 1936, 1937*, London, 1936, 1937, 1938.

Vansittart, Robert, *Black Record: Germans Past and Present*, London, 1941.
———— *Bones of Contention*, London, n.d.
———— *Lessons of My Life*, London, 1944.
Voigt, F.A. *Unto Caesar*, London, 1938.

Werth, Alexander, *The Destiny of France*, London, 1937.
———— *The Twilight of France, 1933-1940*, London, 1942.
Whittier, Richard, 'Belgium Emphasizes Security', *Contemporary Review*, Vol. 115, January 1937, pp. 31-7.
Wolfers, Arnold, *Britain and France Between Two Wars*, New York, 1940.

Zweig, Ferdynand, *Poland Between Two Wars: A Critical Study of Social and Economic Changes*, London, 1944.

Historical studies

Abrahamsen, Samuel, *Sweden's Foreign Policy*, Washington, DC, 1957.
Abshagen, K.H., *Canaris*, London, 1956.
Adam, C.F., *Life of Lord Lloyd*, London, 1948.
Adler, Selig, *The Uncertain Giant— 1921-1941*, New York, 1965.
Albord, Tony, 'Les relations de la politique et de la stratégie', *La Défense Nationale*, Université d'Aix-Marseille, Centre de sciences politiques de l'institut d'études juridiques de Nice, Paris, 1958.
Albrecht-Carrié, René, *see* Carrié
Anderson, Mosa, *Noel Buxton: A Life*, London, 1952.
Anfuso, Filippo, *Du Palais de Venise au Lac de Garde*, Paris, 1949.
Ashton-Gwatkin, F.T.A., *The British Foreign Service*, Syracuse, N.Y. 1950.
Assmann, Kurt, *Deutsche Schicksalsjahre*, Wiesbaden, 1950.
Aubert, Louis, *et al.*, *André Tardieu*, Paris, 1957.

Baldwin, A.W., *My Father: The True Story*, London, 1955.
Bankwitz, Philip C.F., *Maxime Weygand and Civil-Military Relations in Modern France*, Cambridge, Mass., 1967.
Basch, Antonín, *The Danube Basin and the German Economic Sphere*, New York, 1944.
Bassett, R., 'Telling the Truth to the People— The Myth of the Baldwin "Confession",' *Cambridge Journal*, November 1948, pp. 84-95.

Baumont, Maurice, *La faillite de la paix, 1918-1939*, Paris, 1960.

Beloff, Max, *The Foreign Policy of Soviet Russia, 1929-1941*, 2 vols, London, 1947-9.

—— 'The Sixth of February', *St Antony's Papers*, no. 5, James Joll (ed.), London, 1959.

Bilainkin, George, *Maisky, Ten Years Ambassador*, London, 1944.

Birkenhead, Frederick Winston Furneaux Smith, 2nd Earl, *Halifax*, London, 1965.

Bishop, Donald G., *The Administration of British Foreign Relations*, Syracuse, N.Y., 1961.

Blaxland, Gregory, *J.H. Thomas: A Life for Unity*, London, 1964.

Blücher,Wipert von, *Wege und Irrwege der Diplomatie*, Wiesbaden, 1953.

Boeninger, Hildegard, 'Hitler and the German Generals, 1934-1938', *Journal of Central European Affairs*, Vol. XIV, April 1954, pp. 19-37.

Bolen, C. Waldron, 'Hitler Remilitarizes the Rhineland', *Power, Public Opinion and Diplomacy*, Durham, NC, 1959.

Bor, Peter, *Gespräche mit Halder*, Wiesbaden, 1950.

Boyle, Andrew, *Montagu Norman*, London, 1967.

Bramsted, Ernest K., *Goebbels and National Socialist Propaganda, 1925-1945*, East Lansing, Mich., 1965.

Brand, Carl F., *The British Labour Party*, Stanford, Calif., 1965.

Braubach, Max, 'Der Einmarsch deutscher Truppen in die entmilitärisierte Zone am Rhein im März 1936', *Arbeitsgemeinschaft für Forschung des Landes Nordrhein-Westfalen*. Vol. 54, Köln, 1956.

Breyer, Richard, *Das deutsche Reich und Polen, 1932-1937*, Würzburg, 1955.

Brogan, D.W., *Is Innocence Enough?* London, 1941.

—— *The Development of Modern France, 1870-1939*, London, 1947.

—— *The French Nation*, London, 1957.

Budurowycz, Bohdan B., *Polish-Soviet relations, 1932-1939*, New York, 1963.

Buell, Raymond L., *Poland: Key to Europe*, London, 1939.

Bullock, Alan, *Hitler: A Study in Tyranny*, London, 1952.

—— *The Life and Times of Ernest Bevin*, Vol. I, London, 1960.

Burns, James M., *Roosevelt: the Lion and the Fox*, New York, 1956.

Bury, J.P.T., *France 1814-1940*, London, 1962.

Butler, J.R.M., *Lord Lothian, 1882-1940*, London, 1960.

Callender, Geoffrey A.R., and F.H. Hinsley, *The Naval Side of British History, 1485-1945*, London, 1952.

Cameron, Elizabeth R., *Prologue to Appeasement: a Study in French Foreign Policy*, Washington, DC, 1942.

Campbell-Johnson, Alan, *Sir Anthony Eden*, New York, 1955.

Carr, E.H. *The Twenty Years' Crisis*, London, 1946.
—— *International Relations Between the Two World Wars, 1919-1939*, London, 1947.
—— *German-Soviet Relations Between the Two World Wars, 1919-1939*, Baltimore, 1951.
Carrié, René Albrecht, *A Diplomatic History of Europe Since the Congress of Vienna*, London, 1958.
—— *France, Europe and the Two World Wars*. Paris, 1960.
—— *The Meaning of the First World War*, Englewood Cliffs, NJ, 1965.
Carter, G.M., *The British Commonwealth and International Security*, Toronto, 1947.
Castellan, Georges, *La réarmament clandestin du Reich, 1930-35*, Paris, 1954.
Challener, Richard D., *The French Theory of the Nation in Arms, 1866-1939*, New York, 1952.
Chambers, Frank P. *et al., This Age of Conflict*, New York, 1950.
Churchill, Winston S., *The Second World War*, Vol. I, *The Gathering Storm*, London, 1964.
Coates, William P. and Zelda, *A History of Anglo-Soviet Relations*, London, 1943.
Cobban, Alfred, *A History of Modern France*, Vol. III, London, 1965.
Cole, G.D.H., *A History of the Labour Party from 1914*, London, 1948.
Cole, Hubert, *Laval — a biography*, London, 1963.
Collis, Maurice S., *Nancy Astor*, London, 1960.
Colton, Joel G., *Léon Blum: Humanist in Politics*, New York, 1966.
Colvin, Ian, *Vansittart in Office*, London, 1965.
Compton, James V., *The Swastika and the Eagle*, Boston, 1967.
Cooke, Colin, *The Life of Richard Stafford Cripps*, London, 1957.
Coote, Colin R., *A Companion of Honour: The Story of Walter Elliot*, London, 1965.
Cot, Pierre, *Triumph of Treason*, Chicago, 1944.
Craig, Gordon A. and Felix Gilbert (eds.), *The Diplomats 1919-1939*, 2 vols, Princeton, NJ, 1953.
Craig, Gordon A., *The Politics of the Prussian Army 1640-1945*, Oxford, 1955.
Cross, Colin, *Philip Snowden*, London, 1966.

De la Gorce, Paul-Marie, *The French Army*, London, 1963.
Debicki, Roman, *Foreign Policy of Poland, 1919-1939*, London, 1963.
Demeter, Karl, *The German Officer-Corps in Society and State 1650-1945*, London, 1965.
Deutscher, I., *Stalin: a Political Biography*, London, 1949.
Dhers, Pierre, 'Du 7 mars 1936 à l'Ile d'Yeu', *Revue d'Histoire de la deuxième guerre mondiale*, January 1952, pp. 17-26.
Divine, Robert A., *The Illusion of Neutrality*, Chicago, 1962.

Domarus, Max, *Hitler, Reden und Proklamationen, 1932-45*, Vol. I, Neustadt, 1962.
Draper, Theodore, *The Six Weeks' War*, London, 1946.
Duroselle, J.B., *Histoire diplomatique de 1919 à nos jours*. Paris, 1953.
—— *Les relations Germano-Sovietiques de 1933 à 1939*, Paris, 1954.

Eayrs, James, "'A Low Dishonest Decade': Aspects of Canadian External Policy, 1931-1939", in Hugh L. Keenleyside (ed.), *The Growth of Canadian Policies in External Affairs*, London, 1960.
—— *In Defence of Canada*, Vol. II, Toronto, 1965.
Ebeling, Hans, *The Caste: the Political Role of the German General Staff Between 1918 and 1938*, London, 1945.
Erfurth, Waldemar, *Geschichte des Deutschen Generalstabs*, Vol. I, Göttingen, 1962.
Erickson, John, *The Soviet High Command*, London, 1962.
Estorick, Eric, *Stafford Cripps*, London, 1949.

Feiling, Keith, *The Life of Neville Chamberlain*, London, 1946.
Foerster, W., *Generaloberst Ludwig Beck — sein Kampf gegen Krieg*, Munich, 1953.
Foertsch, Hermann, *Schuld und Verhängnis*, Stuttgart, 1951.
Foot, Michael, *Aneurin Bevan*, Vol. I, London, 1963.
Frischauer, Willi, *Göring*, London, 1951.
Funke, Manfred, '7 März 1936: Studie zum aussenpolitischen Führungsstil Hitlers', *Aus Politik und Zeitgeschichte*, 3 October 1970, pp. 3-34.
Furnia, Arthur H., *The Diplomacy of Appeasement: Anglo-French Relations and the Prelude to World War II, 1931-1938*, Washington, DC, 1960.

Gehl, Jurgen, *Austria, Germany and Anschluss, 1931-38*, London, 1963.
George, Margaret, *The Warped Vision — British Foreign Policy, 1933-1939*, Pittsburgh, 1965.
Gilbert, Felix, and R.W. Gott, *The Appeasors*, London, 1963.
Gilbert, Martin, *Britain and Germany between the Wars*, London, 1964.
—— *Plow My Own Furrow: the Story of Lord Allen of Hurtwood*, London, 1965.
Gisevius, Hans B., *Bis zum bitteren Ende*, Hamburg, 1960.
Goguel, François, *La politique des partis sous la Troisième République*, Vol. II, Paris, 1958.
Gooch, G.P., *Under Six Reigns*, London, 1958.
Görlitz, Walter, *The German General Staff — its History and Structure 1657-1945*, London, 1953.

Görlitz, Walter, *Adolf Hitler,* Göttingen, 1960.

Greaves, Jean Corder, *Corder Catchpool,* London, 1953.

Hanč, Josef, *Eastern Europe,* London, 1943.

Hancock, W.K., and M.M. Gowing, *British War Economy,* London, 1949.

Hasluck, Paul, *Australia in the War of 1939-45,* Canberra, 1952.

Hegner, H.S., *Die Reichskanzlei, 1933-1945,* Frankfurt, 1959.

Heiden, Konrad, *Der Führer,* New York, 1944.

Hermann, Carl H., *Deutsche Militärgeschichte,* Frankfurt, 1966.

Hibbert, Christopher, *Benito Mussolini,* London, 1965.

Hinshaw, David, *Sweden: Champion of Peace,* New York, 1949.

Hofer, Walther, *War Premeditated,* London, 1959.

—— *Die Diktatur Hitlers — Bis zum Beginn des zweiten Weltkrieges,* Konstanz, 1960.

—— *Die Vorgeschichte des zweiten Weltkrieges,* Zürich, 1963.

Hossbach, Friedrich, *Die Entwicklung des Oberbefehls über das Heer in Brandenburg, Preussen und im deutschen Reich von 1655-1945,* Würzburg, 1957.

Hutchison, Bruce, *Mackenzie King — The Incredible Canadian,* London, 1953.

Jenkins, Roy, *Mr Attlee: an Interim Biography,* London, 1948.

Johnson, Alan C., *Viscount Halifax,* London, 1941.

Johnson, Franklyn A., *Defence by Committee: The British Committee of Imperial Defence, 1885-1959,* London, 1960.

Joll, James, 'The Making of the Popular Front', *St Antony's Papers,* no. 5, London, 1959.

Kavaler, Lucy, *The Astors,* London, 1966.

Keith, Arthur B., *The British Cabinet System,* London, 1952.

Kerner, R.J. (ed.), *Czechoslovakia,* Berkeley, Calif., 1940.

—— *Yugoslavia,* Berkeley, Calif., 1949.

Kertesz, Stephen D., *Diplomacy in a Whirlpool — Hungary between Nazi Germany and Soviet Russia,* Notre Dame, Ind., 1953.

Kilic, Altemur, *Turkey and the World,* Washington, DC, 1959.

Kirkpatrick, Ivone, *Mussolini,* London, 1964.

Klein, Burton, *Germany's Economic Preparedness for War,* Cambridge, Mass., 1959.

Knapp, W.F., 'The Rhineland Crisis of March 1936', *St Antony's Papers,* no. 5. London, 1959.

Kordt, Erich, *Wahn und Wirklichkeit,* Stuttgart, 1948.

Krug, Mark M., *Aneurin Bevan: Cautious Rebel,* New York, 1961.

Langer, William L., and S. Everett Gleason, *The Challenge to Isolation,* New York, 1952.

Larmour, Peter J., *The French Radical Party in the 1930s*, Stanford, Calif., 1964.

Lauret, René, *France and Germany*, London, 1965.

Lefranc, Georges, *Le Mouvement socialiste sous la IIIe République, 1875-1940*, Paris, 1963.

Léger, Alexis, *Briand*, Aurora, NY, 1943.

Macartney, C.A., *October Fifteenth: a history of modern Hungary*. Part 1, Edinburgh, 1961.

—— *Independent Eastern Europe*, London, 1962.

Macleod, Iain, *Neville Chamberlain*, London, 1961.

Magistrati, Massimo, 'La Germania e l'impresa italiana di Etiopia', *Rivista di Studi Politici Internazioni*. XVII, no. 4, 1950, pp. 563-606.

—— *L'Italia a Berlino, 1937-39*, Milan, 1956.

Maisky, Ivan, *Who Helped Hitler?* London, 1964.

Mansergh, Nicholas, *Survey of British Commonwealth Affairs*, Vol. III, London, 1952.

Manstein, Fritz E. von, *Lost Victories*, London, 1958. (German edition: *Verlorene Siege*, Bonn, 1955).

Marwick, Arthur, *Clifford Allen: Open Conspirator*, London, 1964.

Medlicott, W. N., *The Coming of War in 1939*, London, 1963.

—— *Contemporary England*, London, 1967.

—— *Britain and Germany: The Search for Agreement, 1930-1937*, London, 1969.

Meinck, Gerhard, *Hitler und die deutsche Aufrüstung, 1933-1937*, Wiesbaden, 1959.

Meissner, Hans-Otto, *The Man with Three Faces*, London, 1955.

Miller, Jane K., *Belgian Foreign Policy Between the Wars*, New York, 1951.

Milward, Alan S., *The German Economy at War*, London, 1965.

Mueller-Hillebrand, Burkhart, *Das Heer, 1933-1945*, Vol. I, Darmstadt, 1954.

Namier, L. B., *Diplomatic Prelude*, London, 1948.

—— *Europe in Decay: a Study in Disintegration 1936-1940*, London, 1950.

Nelson, Harold I., *Land and Power—British and Allied Policy on Germany's Frontiers, 1916-1919*, London, 1963.

Nevins, Allan, *The New Deal and World Affairs... 1933-1945*, New Haven, Conn., 1950.

Nicolson, Harold, *King George the Fifth, His Life and Reign*, London, 1952.

Nolte, Ernst, *Three Faces of Fascism*, New York, 1966.

Northedge, F. S., *The Troubled Giant: Britain among the Great Powers, 1916-1939*, London, 1966.

O'Neill, Robert J., *The German Army and the Nazi Party 1933-39*, London, 1968.
Örvik, Nils, *The Decline of Neutrality, 1914-1941*, Oslo, 1953.
Owen, Frank, *Tempestuous Journey: Lloyd George, His Life and Times*. London, 1954.

Parker, R.A.C., 'France and the Rhineland Crisis, 1936', *World Politics*. Vol. VIII, 1955-6.
Petrie, Charles, *The Life and Letters of Austen Chamberlain*, Vol. II, London, 1940.
Pirow, Oswald, *James Barry Munnik Hertzog*, London, 1958.
Postan, M. M., *British War Production*, London, 1952.
Postgate, Raymond, *The Life of George Lansbury*, London, 1951.
Powers, R. H., 'Winston Churchill's Parliamentary Commentary on British Foreign Policy, 1935-1938', *Journal of Modern History*, June 1954, pp. 179-82.
Prittie, Terence, *Germans Against Hitler*, London, 1964.

Renouvin, Pierre, *Histoire des Relations Internationales*, Vol. VIII, Paris, 1958.
Rhode, Gotthold, 'Aussenminister Josef Beck and Staatssekretär Graf Szembek' *Vierteljahreshefte für Zeitgeschichte*, January 1954, pp. 86-94.
Richards, Denis, *Royal Air Force, 1939-1945*, Vol. I, London, 1953.
Richmond, Herbert, *Statesmen and Seapower*, Oxford, 1946.
Ritter, Gerhard, *The German Resistance*, New York, 1958.
Roberts, H. L., *Rumania: Political Problems of an Agrarian State*, London, 1951.
Robertson, E. M., 'Zur Wiederbesetzung des Rheinlandes 1936', *Vierteljahreshefte für Zeitgeschichte*. April 1962, pp. 178-205.
———— *Hitler's Pre-War Policy and Military Plans*, London, 1963.
Robertson, J. H., *The Office: A Study of British Foreign Policy and Its Makers, 1919-1951*, London, 1958.
Roos, Hans, *Polen und Europa*, Tübingen, 1957.
Rowe, Vivian, *The Great Wall of France — The Triumph of the Maginot Line*, London, 1959.

Salvemini, Gaetano, *Prelude to World War II*, London, 1953.
Scott, William E., *Alliance against Hitler*, Durham, NC, 1962.
Seabury, Paul, *The Wilhelmstrasse*, Berkeley, Calif., 1954.
Seton-Watson, R. W., and Laffan, R. G. D, 'Yugoslavia between the Wars', ch. 10 in *A Short History of Yugoslavia*, Cambridge, 1966.
Sherwood, John, 'The Tiger's Club: the last years of Georges Mandel', *St Antony's Papers*, no. 5, London, 1959.

Shirer, William L., *The Rise and Fall of the Third Reich*, New York, 1960.

Slessor, John C., *The Central Blue*, London, 1956.

Soulié, Michel, *La vie politique d'Édouard Herriot*, Paris, 1962.

Stocks, M. D., *Eleanor Rathbone*, London, 1949.

Strang, William, *The Foreign Office*, London, 1955.

—— *Britain in World Affairs*, London, 1961.

Tannenbaum, Edward Ṛ., *The Action Française*, New York, 1962.

Taylor, A. J. P. *The Trouble Makers*, London, 1957.

—— *The Origins of the Second World War*, London, 1963.

—— *English History 1914-1945*, London, 1965.

Taylor, Telford, *Sword and Swastika*, London, 1953.

Tessin, Georg, *Formationsgeschichte der Wehrmacht 1933-39 — Stäbe und Truppenteile des Heeres und der Luftwaffe*, Boppard am Rhein, 1959.

The Times, *The History of 'The Times'*, Vol. IV, Part 2, London, 1952.

Tingsten, Herbert, *The Debate on the Foreign Policy of Sweden, 1918-1939*, London, 1949.

Tint, Herbert, *The Decline of French Patriotism 1870-1940*, London, 1964.

Toscano, Mario, *Pagine de Storia Diplomatica Contemporanea*, Vol. II, Milan, 1963.

Toynbee, Arnold and Veronica M., (eds.), *The Eve of War*, London, 1958.

Treue, Wilhelm, 'Hitler Denkschrift zum Vierjahresplan 1936', *Vierteljahreshefte für Zeitgeschichte*, April 1955, pp. 184-205.

Vandenbosch, Amry, *Dutch Foreign Policy since 1815*, The Hague, 1959.

Wagenführ, Rolf, *Die deutsche Industrie im Kriege, 1939-1945*, Berlin, 1965.

Walters, F. P., *A History of the League of Nations*, Vol. II, London, 1952.

Wandycz, Poitr S., *France and Her Eastern Allies, 1919-1925*, Minneapolis, 1962.

Watt, D. C., 'The Anglo-German Naval Agreement of 1935: An Interim Judgment', *Journal of Modern History*, June 1952, pp. 155-75.

—— 'The Reoccupation of the Rhineland, 1936', *History Today*, 1956.

—— 'The Rome-Berlin Axis, 1936-1940', *Review of Politics*, October 1960, pp. 519-43.

Watt, D. C., *Personalities and Policies*, London, 1965.
—— 'German Plans for the Reoccupation of the Rhineland: A Note', *Journal of Contemporary History*, October 1966, pp. 193-9.
—— South African Attempts to Mediate between Britain and Germany, 1935-1938', *Studies in International History*, ed. Kenneth Bourne and D. C. Watt, London, 1967.
Webster, Charles, and Noble Frankland, *The Strategic Air Offensive against Germany, 1939-1945*, Vols. I and IV. London, 1961.
—— *et al.*, *United Kingdom Policy, Foreign, Strategic and Economic*, London, 1950.
Westphal, General Siegfried, *The German Army in the West*, London, 1951.
Wheeler-Bennett, John W., *Munich: Prologue to Tragedy*, New York, 1948.
—— *The Nemesis of Power: The German Army in Politics*, London, 1954.
—— *John Anderson, Viscount Waverly*, London, 1962.
Wiener Library. 'The Rhineland Occupation in 1936 — How the West was Bluffed', *Wiener Library Bulletin*, Vol. X, nos. 1-2, 1956, pp. 4, 6, and nos. 5-6, 1956, p. 48.
Williams, Francis, *Fifty Years' March: The Rise of the Labour Party*, London, 1949.
Wiskemann, Elizabeth, *The Rome-Berlin Axis*, London, 1949.
—— *Europe of the Dictators, 1919-1945*, London, 1966.
Wrench, John Evelyn, *Geoffrey Dawson and Our Times*, London, 1955.
Wullus-Rudiger, J., *Les origines internationales du drame belge de 1940*, Brussels, 1950.

Young, G. M., *Stanley Baldwin*, London, 1952.
Young, Kenneth, *Churchill and Beaverbrook*, London, 1966.

Zagoroff, S. D., J. Vegh and A. D. Bilimovich, *The Agricultural Economy of the Danubian Countries, 1933-1945*, Stanford, Calif., 1955.
Zeman, Z. A. B., *Nazi Propaganda*, London, 1964.

Reference works

Annual Register 1936, edited by M. Epstein, London, 1937.

Chester, D. N. (ed.). *The Organization of British Central Government, 1914-1956*, London, 1957.

Foreign Office List, 1936, London, 1936.
Freuendienst, Werner (ed.), *Weltgeschichte der Gegenwart in Dokumenten, 1935-1936*, Vol. III, Essen, 1937.

Gantenbein, James W. (ed.), *Documentary Background of World War II, 1931 to 1941,* New York, 1948.

Gebhardt, Bruno (ed.), *Handbuch der Deutschen Geschichte,* Part 4, *Die Zeit der Weltkriege* by Karl Dietrich Erdmann, Stuttgart, 1959.

Holldack, Heinz, *Was wirklich geschah: die diplomatische Hintergründe der deutschen Kriegspolitik, Darstellung und Dokumente,* Munich, 1949.

Thurauf, Ulrich (ed.), *Schulthess' Europäischer Geschichtskalender,* Part 77, *1936, Munich, 1937.*

Whitaker's Almanac. 1920, 1933-1940, London, 1921, 1934-1941.

Index